Mathematics for Digital Science 3

SCIENCES

Computer Science, Field Directors –
Jean-Charles Pomerol

Operational Research and Decision,
Subject Head – Patrick Siarry

Mathematics for Digital Science 3

Data Analysis and Optimization

Gérard-Michel Cochard
Mhand Hifi

iSTE

WILEY

First published 2025 in Great Britain and the United States by ISTE Ltd and John Wiley & Sons, Inc.

ISTE Ltd
27-37 St George's Road
London SW19 4EU
UK

www.iste.co.uk

John Wiley & Sons, Inc.
111 River Street
Hoboken, NJ 07030
USA

www.wiley.com

Library of Congress Control Number: 2025935043

British Library Cataloguing-in-Publication Data
A CIP record for this book is available from the British Library
ISBN 978-1-78945-196-2

ERC code:
PE1 Mathematics
PE1_17 Mathematical aspects of computer science
PE1_20 Control theory, optimisation and operational research

Contents

Preface

The term “*digital*” relates to information and communication sciences and technologies, including computing, digital electronics and telecommunications. Over the past 50 years, advancements in these fields, through discoveries, developments and applications, have grown at an exponential rate. Such progress has profoundly transformed human activities, making the transition to an “all digital” world a significant economic and political issue. At the same time, professions related to digital technology are continuously evolving. It is noteworthy that these technological advancements are grounded in a substantial mathematical foundation. Consequently, any engineer or researcher aiming to drive innovation must possess extensive knowledge of mathematics.

Many students opt for computer science-related courses early on without first acquiring the essential mathematical foundations they might need in the future. While they may excel as technicians, they might not be as well-prepared to become effective engineers or researchers.

It should be recognized that computer science cannot be fully understood without a solid mathematical foundation. Advances in digital technologies have been closely linked to mathematical support. The pioneers of computing were primarily mathematicians: Alan Turing, Claude Shannon, John von Neumann and Charles Babbage, often referred to as the “grandfather of computing”. They could never have designed computers without their mathematical expertise. Other historical figures such as Euclid, who formulated the first algorithm, George Boole, the father of binary algebra, Ada Lovelace, a pioneer in the creation of the first computer programs, Grace Hopper, who developed the first language compiler, and Margaret Hamilton, a key figure in software engineering, were also mathematicians. Today, areas such as artificial intelligence, managing large datasets and information security are central to computer science research. Once again, it is evident that without a robust mathematical foundation, innovation in these areas would be challenging.

The digital mathematics courses offered are designed to provide the fundamental mathematical knowledge essential for mastering and advancing digital technologies. While the book primarily targets university and engineering students, it also serves as a resource for IT professionals looking to enhance their mathematical skills as part of their ongoing professional development in the field.

The three-volume series compiles lessons taught to multiple generations of students in the first two university cycles, specifically within bachelor's and master's programs in Computer Science or in Computer Methods Applied to Business Management. The first volume covers the essential mathematical foundations necessary for understanding digital technologies. The second volume focuses on digital information. The third – and current – volume is dedicated to data analysis and optimization, as detailed below.

For data analysis, Chapter 1 revisits the fundamentals of descriptive statistics, linear regression and linear correlation, as covered in Volume 1.

In Chapter 2, these concepts are extended to multi-dimensional arrays, which are graphically represented as point clouds in n-dimensional space. Analyzing these point clouds forms the basis for principal component analysis and factor analysis.

Chapter 3 focuses on automatic classification through partitioning methods, highlighting the k-means algorithm, as well as hierarchical classification using aggregation strategies such as Ward's method.

Chapter 4 provides a detailed examination of linear programming techniques, which aim to identify an optimal solution among numerous variable combinations that must satisfy a set of linear constraints.

Chapter 5 introduces graph theory in its basic form, covering fundamental definitions and properties, before progressing to more advanced concepts such as connectedness and extremal spanning trees.

Chapter 6 focuses on the classic problem of finding a path with minimum or maximum length in a graph, using various algorithms.

Chapter 7 presents several graph-based traffic problems that involve optimizing a function, including the maximum flow problem, the minimum cost transportation problem and the assignment problem.

Finally, Chapter 8 examines scheduling problems related to project planning and shop floor scheduling, using the flow-shop and job-shop as examples.

To achieve the goal of mastering the application of mathematical results, proofs are presented whenever they are accessible to the reader, who is assumed to have a basic knowledge of the subject. In some cases, the validity of the results is accepted without detailed proofs, with references to more advanced works where such demonstrations can be found.

Each chapter includes numerous examples illustrating the concepts presented. These examples are generally elaborated in detail to enhance the reader's understanding.

Finally, each topic is presented in detail, starting with the foundational definitions and hypotheses. While many readers may already be familiar with these basic concepts, this thorough approach is designed to help those with potential knowledge gaps, minimizing the need to consult additional sources.

May 2025

1

Linear Modeling for Two-Dimensional Data

CONCEPTS COVERED IN THIS CHAPTER.–

This brief chapter serves as a reminder of the concepts presented in detail in Volume 1. It primarily provides an overview of basic statistical analysis tools, particularly linear regression and correlation for two-dimensional data.

References: [SAP 11].

1.1. Basic statistics

Consider a population of n elements. Each element i is characterized by the value of a variable $x = x_i$. The n values x_i constitute a one-dimensional statistical series, whose characteristics are:

– The *average* $\bar{x}$ is defined by:

$$\bar{x} = \frac{1}{n}\sum_{i=1}^{n} x_i$$

In this definition, it is assumed that all elements have the same statistical weight ($p_i = \frac{1}{n}$). If the weights are not equal, the following expression is used:

$$\bar{\bar{x}} = \sum_{i=1}^{n} p_i x_i \text{ with } \sum_{i=1}^{n} p_i = 1$$

where p_i represents the statistical weight of individual i.

– *Variance* $v(x)$ is defined as the average of the squares of the deviations from the average:

$$v(x) = \frac{1}{n}\sum_{i=1}^{n} (x_i - \bar{x})^2 \quad \text{or} \quad v(x) = \sum_{i=1}^{n} p_i \,(x_i - \bar{x})^2$$

Huygens' theorem provides another method for calculating variance:

$$v(x) = \overline{x^2} - \bar{x}^2, \text{ where } \overline{x^2} = \frac{1}{n}\sum_{i=1}^{n} x_i^2 \text{ or } \overline{x^2} = \sum_{i=1}^{n} p_i \, x_i^2$$

This relationship is often summarized as "the average of squares minus the square of the mean".

– *Standard deviation* $\sigma(x)$ is defined as the square root of the variance:

$$\sigma(x) = \sqrt{v(x)}$$

EXAMPLE 1.1.– Consider the statistical series shown in Figure 1.1, which represents the number of rainy days over 10 consecutive years at a given location.

x
50
120
70
90
150
80
100
30
110
40

Figure 1.1. *Statistical series*

The average $\bar{x} = 84$ can be easily calculated by assigning equal statistical weight to each measurement. The average of the squares $\overline{x^2} = 8340$, the variance $v(x) = 1284$ and the standard deviation $\sigma(x) = 35{,}83$ are also determined.

Figure 1.2 shows the graphical representation of the statistical series in the form of a histogram. This histogram illustrates the distribution of data regarding the number of rainy days over the 10 years.

The average is a measure of the position of the statistical series along the number of days axis, while the standard deviation serves as a dispersion parameter, providing an indicator of the spread of the statistical series.

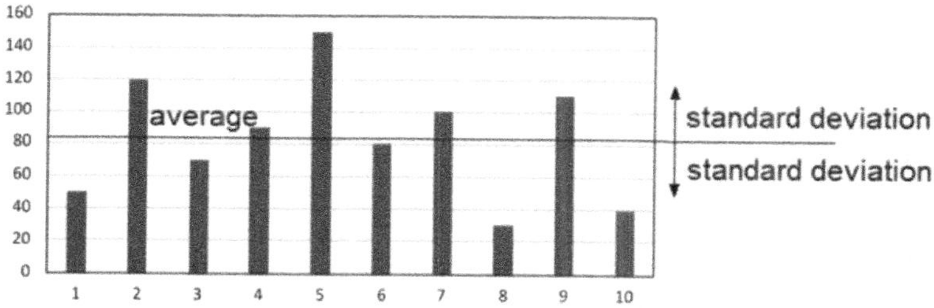

Figure 1.2. *Graphical representation of the statistical series*

1.2. Linear adjustment

Now, consider a two-dimensional statistical series, where each element is characterized by the values of two variables, x and y. For each variable, various statistical measures can be calculated, such as the average, variance and standard deviation.

To graphically represent this two-dimensional series, a two-dimensional Cartesian coordinate system is used. The x-axis represents the variable x, and the y-axis represents the variable y. Each element i of the series is represented as a point (x_i, y_i) in this coordinate system, where the coordinate x_i corresponds to the value of the variable x, and the coordinate y_i corresponds to the value of the variable y. Figure 1.3 shows examples of graphical representations of two two-dimensional series.

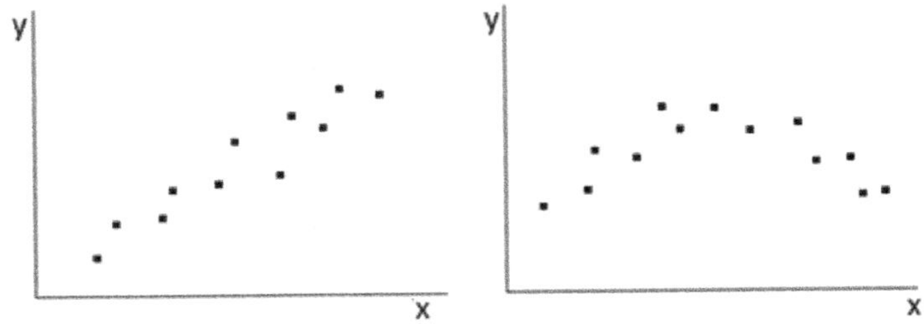

Figure 1.3. *Example of two two-dimensional series*

When observing a two-dimensional series and detecting a certain structure in the set of representative points, we may be inclined to model this structure using a curve. This involves finding a mathematical function that best describes the relationships between the variables x and y. In the examples shown in Figure 1.3, a straight line can be proposed for modeling the first example, and a parabola for the second example, as shown in Figure 1.4. These models are *adjustments* that simplify the representation of trends or relationships observed in the data.

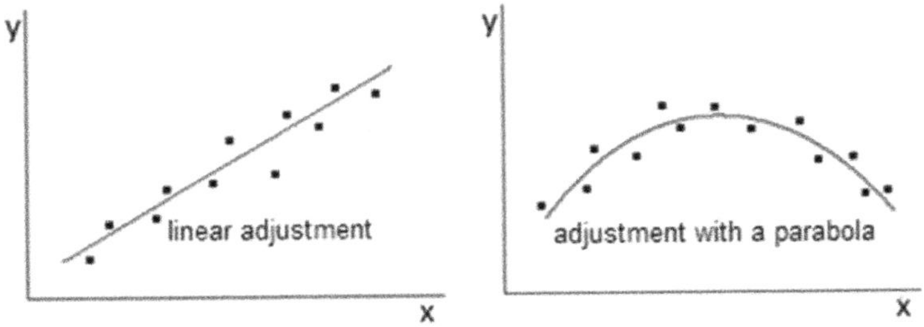

Figure 1.4. *Examples of adjustments*

The linear adjustment is the simplest of all analytical adjustments. It involves obtaining the equation of the straight line that "best fit" the set of representative points of the series.

A classic method for obtaining the equation of the line in linear adjustment is the least squares method. This method involves minimizing the sum of the squares of the deviations between the observed values and the values predicted by the line. For the variables x and y, the respective means, denoted by $\bar{x}$ and $\bar{y}$, are calculated assuming equal statistical weight for each value of i:

$$\bar{x} = \frac{1}{n}\sum_{i=1}^{n} x_i \text{ and } \bar{y} = \frac{1}{n}\sum_{i=1}^{n} y_i$$

Next, the deviations from these averages for each point in the series are calculated (convenient to work with "centered" coordinates):

$$X_i = (x_i - \bar{x}) \text{ and } Y_i = (y_i - \bar{y}).$$

It is easy to verify that:

$$\sum_{i=1}^{n} X_i = \sum_{i=1}^{n} Y_i = 0.$$

The squares of these deviations are obtained by squaring these values:

$$(x_i - \bar{x})^2 \quad \text{and} \quad (y_i - \bar{y})^2.$$

The least squares method involves finding the coefficients a and b of the equation of the line $y = ax + b$. Alternatively, using the centered coordinates, the equation becomes $Y' = AX + B$, where for each of the representative points, $Y_i' = AX_i + B$. The relationship between (A, B) and (a, b) is:

$$a = A \quad \text{and} \quad b = B - a\bar{x} + \bar{y}$$

The goal is to optimize the sum of squared deviations to a minimum. Mathematically, this involves minimizing the following objective function:

$$F(a,b) = \sum_{i=1}^{n} \left[\left(y_i - (ax_i + b) \right)^2 \right]$$

In other words, the aim is to minimize the following quantity:

$$M = \sum_{i=1}^{n} (Y_i - Y'_i)^2$$
$$= \sum_{i=1}^{n} (Y_i - AX_i - B)^2 = \sum_{i=1}^{n} Y_i^2 - 2A\sum_{i=1}^{n} X_i Y_i + A\sum_{i=1}^{n} X_i^2 + nB^2 = f(A,B)$$

The minimum of M corresponds to the cancellation of the first derivatives with respect to A and B, the only unknowns in M. Taking the partial derivatives:

$$\frac{\partial M}{\partial A} = -2\sum_{i=1}^{n} X_i Y_i + 2A\sum_{i=1}^{n} X_i^2 = 0 \quad \Leftrightarrow \quad \frac{\partial M}{\partial B} = 2nB = 0$$

which leads to:

$$A = \frac{\sum_{i=1}^{n} X_i Y_i}{\sum_{i=1}^{n} X_i^2} \text{ and } B = 0$$

These conditions lead to the following equations:

$$a = \frac{\sum_{i=1}^{n} X_i Y_i}{\sum_{i=1}^{n} X_i^2} = \frac{\sum_{i=1}^{n} x_i y_i - n\bar{x}\bar{y}}{\sum_{i=1}^{n} x_i^2 - n\bar{x}^2} \text{ and } b = \bar{y} - a\bar{x}$$

EXAMPLE 1.2. Let us consider the statistical series showing the number of rainy days (x) and umbrella sales in local currency (y) (see Figure 1.5).

x	y
50	65000
120	180000
70	90000
90	140000
150	200000
80	125000
100	130000
30	50000
110	145000
40	65000

Figure 1.5. *Statistical series (x, y)*

	x	y
	50	65000
	120	180000
	70	90000
	90	140000
	150	200000
	80	125000
	100	130000
	30	50000
	110	145000
	40	65000
averages	84	119000

	X	Y	X²	XY
	-34	-54000	1156	1836000
	36	61000	1296	2196000
	-14	-29000	196	406000
	6	21000	36	126000
	66	81000	4356	5346000
	-4	6000	16	-24000
	16	11000	256	176000
	-54	-69000	2916	3726000
	26	26000	676	676000
	-44	-54000	1936	2376000
		sums	12840	16840000

Figure 1.6. *Detailed adjustment calculations*

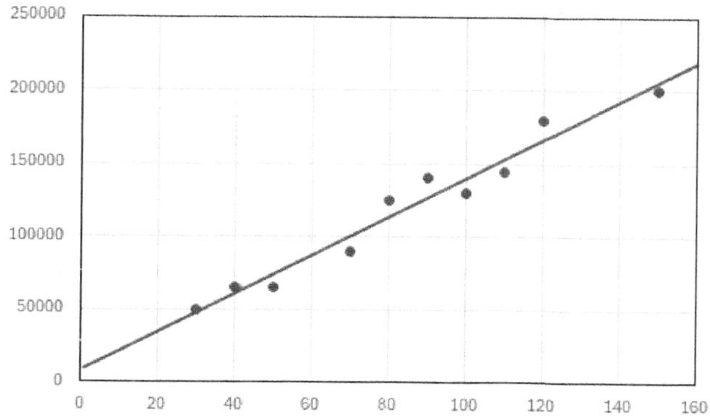

Figure 1.7. *Adjustment line. For a color version of this figure, see www.iste.co.uk/cochard/mathematics3.zip*

Figure 1.6 summarizes the calculations required to determine the best-fit adjustment line, with the values of $a = 1311.53$ and $b = 8831.78$. Figure 1.7 displays the best-fit adjustment line.

1.3. Linear correlation

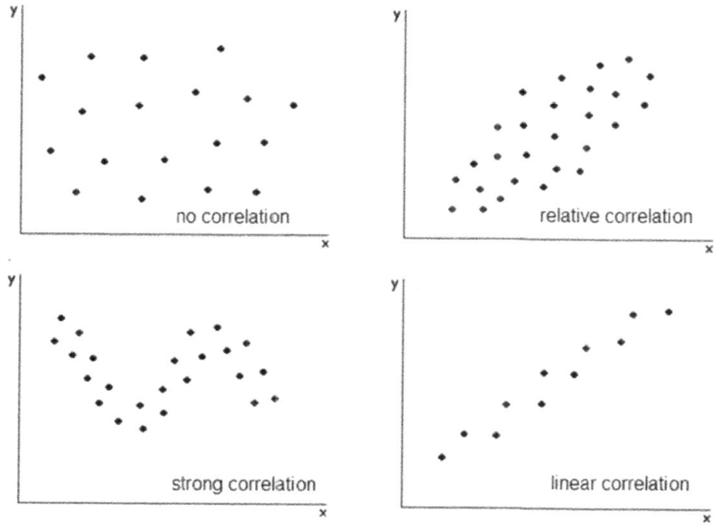

Figure 1.8. *Different correlation situations*

In the case of adjustment, the goal is to express y as a function of x. This choice is arbitrary, as x could be expressed as a function of y. In this case, two adjustment lines would be obtained, both intersecting at the point $(\bar{x}, \bar{y})$:

$$y = ax + b \quad \text{and} \quad x = a'y + b'$$

By treating the variables x and y symmetrically, the concept of *correlation* between these variables can be introduced. Correlation measures the relationship between two variables and quantifies the possible influence of one on the other. Figure 1.8 presents various examples of scatter plots to illustrate different correlation situations.

In particular, in the case of linear correlation, it is interesting to note that when the two best-fit adjustment lines, $y = f(x)$ and $x = f'(y)$, coincide, this indicates maximum linear correlation between the variables x and y.

EXAMPLE 1.3.– For the series in Example 1.2, the following two best-fit adjustment lines are obtained:

$$y = 1311.53x + 8831.78 \text{ and } x = 0.0007\,y - 3.17.$$

Figure 1.9 shows that the two straight lines are very close to each other, indicating a strong correlation between the variables.

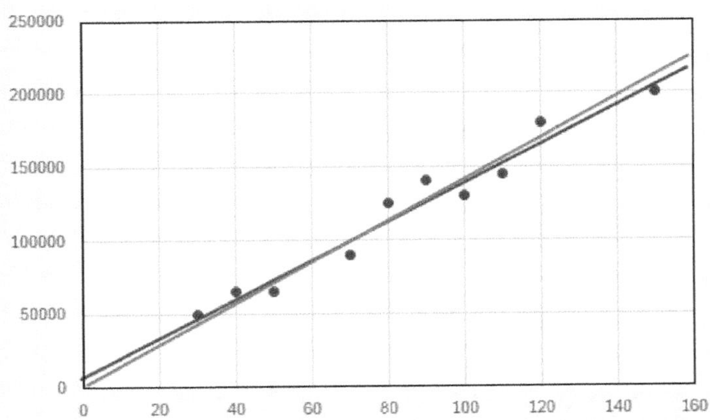

Figure 1.9. *Adjustment lines. For a color version of this figure, see www.iste.co.uk/cochard/mathematics3.zip*

The two best-fit adjustment lines have direction coefficients a and a'. If the lines coincide, then $a = \frac{1}{a'}$ or equivalently, $a \times a' = 1$. Now,

$$a = \frac{\sum_{i=1}^{n} X_i Y_i}{\sum_{i=1}^{n} X_i^2}, a' = \frac{\sum_{i=1}^{n} X_i Y_i}{\sum_{i=1}^{n} Y_i^2}, \text{so } a \times a' = \frac{(\sum_{i=1}^{n} X_i Y_i)^2}{(\sum_{i=1}^{n} X_i^2)(\sum_{i=1}^{n} Y_i^2)}.$$

The maximum correlation corresponds to the following equality (known as the Cauchy–Schwarz equality):

$$\left(\sum_{i=1}^{n} X_i Y_i\right)^2 = \left(\sum_{i=1}^{n} X_i^2\right)\left(\sum_{i=1}^{n} Y_i^2\right).$$

The analytical definition of the linear correlation is:

$$r = \frac{\sum_{i=1}^{n} X_i Y_i}{\sqrt{\sum_{i=1}^{n} X_i^2}\sqrt{\sum_{i=1}^{n} Y_i^2}}$$

which is simply $\sqrt{a \times a'}$.

EXAMPLE 1.3 (CONTINUED).– Let us return to Example 1.3. The equations of the adjustment lines are:

$$y = 1311.53x + 8831.78 \quad \text{and} \quad x = 0.0007\,y - 3.17$$

The linear correlation coefficient is close to 1, i.e. $r = 0.98 \approx 1$. This indicates an almost maximal linear correlation between the variables x and y. In this case, a strong relationship exists between x and y.

The linear correlation coefficient r is often written in another form, using the standard deviations $\sigma(x)$ and $\sigma(y)$:

$$\sigma(x) = \sqrt{v(x)} = \sqrt{\frac{\sum_{i=1}^{n} X_i^2}{n}} \quad \text{and} \quad \sigma(y) = \sqrt{v(y)} = \sqrt{\frac{\sum_{i=1}^{n} Y_i^2}{n}}$$

Furthermore, the covariance $\mathrm{cov}(x, y)$ is defined by:

$$\mathrm{cov}(x, y) = \frac{\sum_{i=1}^{n} X_i Y_i}{n}$$

It follows that:

$$r = \frac{\text{cov}(x, y)}{\sigma(x)\sigma(y)}$$

In the case of linear fitting, the expression for M is:

$$M = \sum_{i=1}^{n} Y_i^2 - 2A\sum_{i=1}^{n} X_i Y_i + A\sum_{i=1}^{n} X_i^2 + nB^2$$

The minimum is found by replacing A and B with the values obtained:

$$M_{min} = \sum_{i=1}^{n} Y_i^2 - \frac{\left(\sum_{i=1}^{n} X_i Y_i\right)^2}{\sum_{i=1}^{n} X_i^2} = \frac{\left(\sum_{i=1}^{n} X_i^2\right)\left(\sum_{i=1}^{n} Y_i^2\right) - \left(\sum_{i=1}^{n} X_i Y_i\right)^2}{\sum_{i=1}^{n} X_i^2}$$

By definition, M and therefore M_{min} are positive or zero quantities. This leads to the Cauchy–Schwarz inequality:

$$\left(\sum_{i=1}^{n} X_i^2\right)\left(\sum_{i=1}^{n} Y_i^2\right) \geq \sum_{i=1}^{n} (X_i Y_i)^2$$

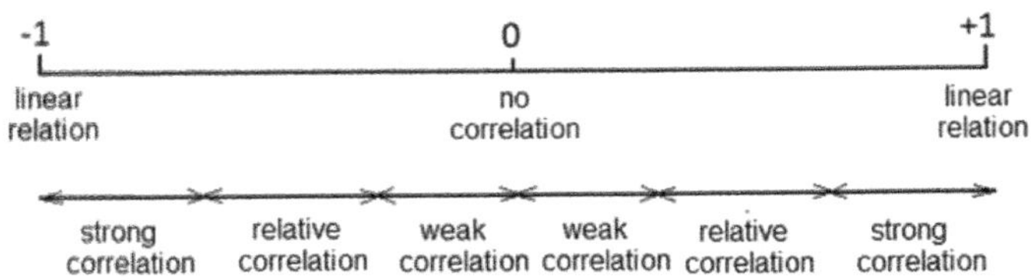

Figure 1.10. *Variations in the linear correlation coefficient*

This inequality implies that the linear correlation coefficient lies in the range $-1 \leq r \leq 1$. This means that the linear correlation coefficient can take values between -1 and 1, inclusive. Figure 1.10 shows such a correlation scale, where different ranges of r values are associated with specific degrees of correlation.

Note that there can be "accidental" correlations, as the following example shows. It is important to distinguish between correlation and causation.

EXAMPLE 1.4.– A statistical study of the French town of Perpette-les-Oisettes (Marne-et-Garonne) has determined the values of the following two variables over 10 successive years (see Figure 1.11): the annual number of personal computers purchased (x) and the annual number of recorded mental illnesses (y).

year	x	y
2013	124	25
2014	132	30
2015	144	35
2016	155	40
2017	166	45
2018	170	50
2019	180	55
2020	185	60
2021	195	65
2022	200	70

Figure 1.11. *The statistical series*

The calculations described in Figure 1.12 allow for the determination of the correlation coefficient r. The result is $r = 0.98$, indicating a strong correlation. The conclusion is left to the reader!

year	x	y	X	Y	X²	Y²	XY
2013	124	25	-41,10	-22,50	1689,21	506,25	924,75
2014	132	30	-33,10	-17,50	1095,61	306,25	579,25
2015	144	35	-21,10	-12,50	445,21	156,25	263,75
2016	155	40	-10,10	-7,50	102,01	56,25	75,75
2017	166	45	0,90	-2,50	0,81	6,25	-2,25
2018	170	50	4,90	2,50	24,01	6,25	12,25
2019	180	55	14,90	7,50	222,01	56,25	111,75
2020	185	60	19,90	12,50	396,01	156,25	248,75
2021	195	65	29,90	17,50	894,01	306,25	523,25
2022	200	70	34,90	22,50	1218,01	506,25	785,25
averages	165,10	47,50		sums	6086,90	2062,50	3522,50

Figure 1.12. *Calculation details*

2

Multidimensional Data Analysis

CONCEPTS COVERED IN THIS CHAPTER.–

The accumulation of digital data results in vast amounts of information (Big Data), from which it is often necessary or advantageous to extract additional information using statistical methods.

After introducing multidimensional tables, which represent a point cloud in an n-dimensional space, an approach for analyzing this cloud in both the individual space and the variable space is presented.

This study naturally leads to principal component analysis, illustrated with an example. In practice, calculations are performed not "by hand", but with the aid of specialized software. Two such programs, Tanagra and R, are introduced.

References: [CIB 84, COR 18, FOU 85, HUS 16, RAK 10, SAP 11, TAN 00].

Just a decade ago, the Data Scientist profession was relatively unknown. Today, it has become a highly sought-after role and a rapidly growing field. A data scientist's primary responsibility is to explore and analyze data using advanced IT tools to identify specific characteristics of sub-populations and group together individuals with similar traits.

Chapters 2 and 3 introduce the essential tools of data mining. These tools allow data scientists to uncover trends, patterns and hidden information within datasets. By applying these techniques, data scientists can extract valuable information and support informed decision-making across fields, including business, research, healthcare and more.

2.1. Multidimensional tables

Up to this point, one- and two-dimensional statistical series have been examined. This concept is now extended to multidimensional statistical series. These series are typically represented as multidimensional tables, with variables organized in columns and individuals in rows (see Figure 2.1).

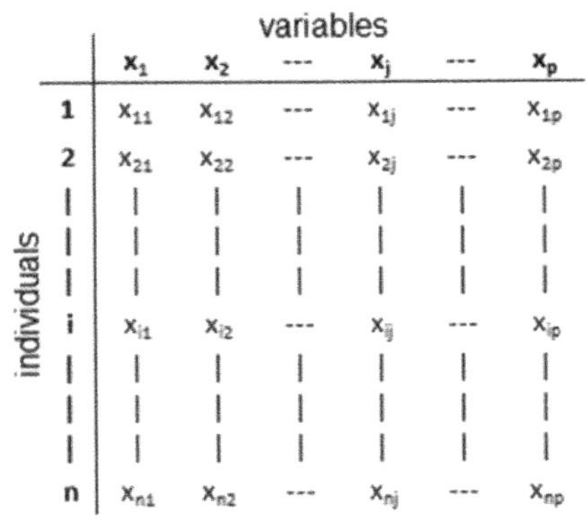

Figure 2.1. *Multidimensional table*

The table consists of n rows, representing the number of individuals, and p columns, corresponding to the number of independent variables a priori. Each value in the table, x_{ij}, represents the value of variable x_j for the individual i. Mathematically, such a table is represented as a matrix of dimensions $n \times p$, often denoted by $\boldsymbol{X}$, which can be expressed as:

$$\boldsymbol{X} = \begin{bmatrix} x_{11} & \cdots & x_{1p} \\ \vdots & \ddots & \vdots \\ x_{n1} & \cdots & x_{np} \end{bmatrix}$$

This table, or the corresponding matrix, can also be depicted graphically through a geometric representation in a multidimensional space (though this requires some imagination!). For ease of interpretation, a three-dimensional diagram is provided below. In practice, two complementary spaces are considered for analysis:

– Space $\mathbb{R}^p$ or ***individual space*** (see Figure 2.2): In this space, an individual i is represented as a point with coordinates x_{ij} $(j = 1, \dots, p)$.

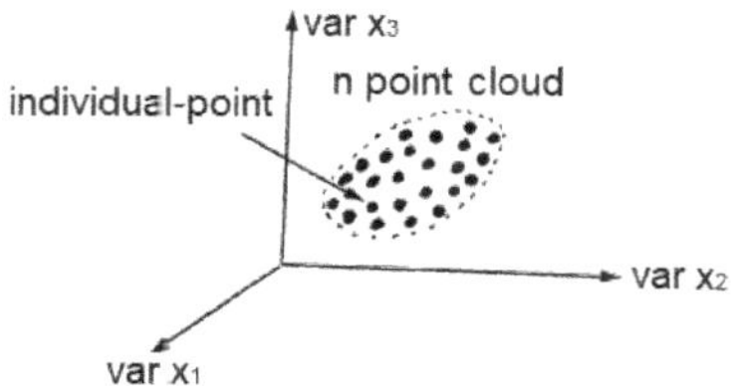

Figure 2.2. *Individual space*

– Space $\mathbb{R}^n$ or ***variable space*** (see Figure 2.3.): in this space, a variable x_j is represented by a point with coordinates x_{ij} $(i = 1, \dots, n)$.

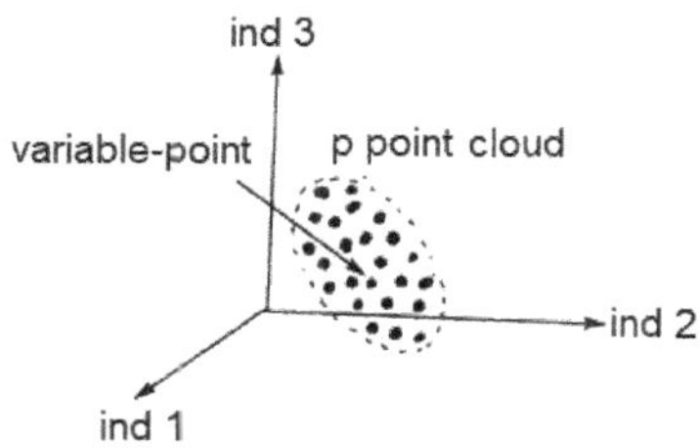

Figure 2.3. *Variable space*

In the individual space, a statistical weight p_i can be assigned to each individual, with the condition:

$$\sum_{i=1}^{n} p_i = 1$$

If the set of individuals is *homogeneous*, then $p_i = \frac{1}{n}$.

For each variable x_j, the following is defined:

– The average: $\overline{x_j} = \sum_{i=1}^{n} p_i x_{ij}$

– The variance: $v(x_j) = \sum_{i=1}^{n} p_i (x_{ij} - \bar{x}_j)^2$

– The standard deviation: $\sigma(x_j) = \sqrt{v(x_j)}$

"Reduced-centered" coordinates X_{ij} are useful to calculations and are defined as:

$$X_{ij} = \frac{x_{ij} - \bar{x}_j}{\sigma(x_j)}$$

The "*covariance*" between two variables x_j and x_k is defined as:

$$cov(x_j, x_k) = \sum_{i=1}^{n} p_i (x_{ij} - \bar{x}_j)(x_{ik} - \bar{x}_k) = \sigma(x_j)\sigma(x_k) \sum_{i=1}^{n} p_i X_{ij} X_{ik}$$

and the "*correlation*" between variables x_j and x_k is defined as:

$$\text{cor}(x_j, x_k) = \frac{\text{cov}(x_j, x_k)}{\sigma(x_j)\sigma(x_k)} = \frac{\sum_{i=1}^{n} p_i X_{ij} X_{ik}}{\sigma(x_j)\sigma(x_k)}$$

For $j = k$, it follows that: $\text{cor}(x_j, x_j) = 1$ and $V_j = \text{cov}(x_j, x_j) = v(x_i)$.

Covariances and correlations can be arranged in matrices. For example, for three variables, the covariance matrix $\boldsymbol{C}$ is:

$$\boldsymbol{C} = \begin{bmatrix} V_1 & \text{cov}(x_1, x_2) & \text{cov}(x_1, x_3) \\ \text{cov}(x_2, x_1) & V_2 & \text{cov}(x_2, x_3) \\ \text{cov}(x_3, x_1) & \text{cov}(x_3, x_2) & V_3 \end{bmatrix}$$

And the correlation matrix $\boldsymbol{c}$ is:

$$\boldsymbol{c} = \begin{bmatrix} 1 & \text{cor}(x_1, x_2) & \text{cor}(x_1, x_3) \\ \text{cor}(x_2, x_1) & 1 & \text{cor}(x_2, x_3) \\ \text{cor}(x_3, x_1) & \text{cor}(x_3, x_2) & 1 \end{bmatrix}$$

These two matrices are symmetrical, since $\text{cov}(x_j, x_k) = \text{cov}(x_k, x_j)$ and $\text{cor}(x_j, x_k) = \text{cor}(x_k, x_j)$. The correlation coefficient $\text{cor}(x_j, x_k)$ has the special property of being between -1 and $+1$. This property follows from Cauchy–Schwarz's inequality, a well-established mathematical result. Cauchy–Schwarz's inequality guarantees (for any pair of variables x_j and x_k) that:

$$\left(\sum_{i=1}^{n} R_i^2\right)\left(\sum_{i=1}^{n} S_i^2\right) \geq \sum_{i=1}^{n} (R_i S_i)^2$$

where R_i and S_i are the two sequences of n real numbers. Taking:

$$R_i = \sigma(x_j)\sqrt{p_i}X_{ij} \text{ and } S_i = \sigma(x_k)\sqrt{p_i}X_{ik}$$

the inequality becomes:

$$(\sigma(x_j)^2 \sum_{i=1}^{n} p_i X_{ij}^2)(\sigma(x_k)^2 \sum_{i=1}^{n} p_i X_{ik}^2) \geq \sigma(x_j)^2 \sigma(x_k)^2 \left(\sum_{i=1}^{n} p_i X_{ij} X_{ik}\right)^2$$

After reduction:

$$\sum_{i=1}^{n} p_i X_{ij}^2 \sum_{i=1}^{n} p_i X_{ik}^2 \geq \left(\sum_{i=1}^{n} p_i X_{ij} X_{ik}\right)^2$$

Yet,

$$\sum_{i=1}^{n} p_i X_{ij}^2 = \sum_{i=1}^{n} p_i \frac{(x_{ij} - \bar{x}_j)^2}{\sigma(x_j)^2} = \frac{1}{\sigma(x_j)^2} v(x_j) = 1 \text{ and similarly } \sum_{i=1}^{n} p_i X_{ik}^2 = 1$$

which means that $c_{jk}{}^2 = \left[cor(x_j, x_k)\right]^2 \leq 1$

It is concluded that the correlation coefficient lies between -1 and $+1$.

Covariance matrices $\boldsymbol{C}$ and correlation matrices $\boldsymbol{c}$ have some remarkable properties:

1) Matrices $\boldsymbol{C}$ and $\boldsymbol{c}$ are symmetrical. This means that the elements at position (j, k) are equal to the elements at position (k, j).

2) Elements $\boldsymbol{c}_{jk}$ are between -1 and $+1$, and elements $\boldsymbol{C}_{jk}$ are between $-\sigma(x_j)\sigma(x_k)$ and $\sigma(x_j)\sigma(x_k)$. This property follows from the definition of correlation and covariance. Correlation coefficients are normalized and lie in the range -1 to $+1$, reflecting the direction of the linear relationship between variables

3) The matrix $\boldsymbol{c}$ has p positive or zero eigenvalues, usually numbered in descending order. Eigenvalues of the correlation matrix $\boldsymbol{c}$ represent the variances explained by each principal component. They are often ordered, which makes it possible to determine which dimensions are most important in explaining data variability.

4) Matrices $\boldsymbol{C}$ and $\boldsymbol{c}$ have orthogonal eigenvectors. The eigenvectors of these matrices are linear combinations of the original variables. They are orthogonal to each other, meaning that they intersect at right angles.

The eigenvectors $\boldsymbol{u}_\alpha$, of the matrix $\boldsymbol{c}$ form an orthogonal matrix $\boldsymbol{U}$ (the vectors $\boldsymbol{u}_\alpha$ are the columns of $\boldsymbol{U}$):

$$\boldsymbol{U} = \begin{bmatrix} u_{11} & u_{21} & \cdots & u_{p1} \\ u_{12} & u_{22} & \cdots & u_{p2} \\ \vdots & \vdots & \ddots & \vdots \\ u_{1p} & u_{2p} & \cdots & u_{pP} \end{bmatrix}, \quad \text{with the properties} \sum_{i=1}^{p} u_{\alpha i}^2$$

$$= 1, \quad \sum_{i=1}^{p} u_{\alpha i} u_{\beta i} = 0 \text{ for } \alpha \neq \beta$$

The transposed matrix $\boldsymbol{U}^t$ is orthogonal and is the inverse of $\boldsymbol{U}$:

$$\boldsymbol{U}^t = \begin{bmatrix} u_{11} & u_{12} & \cdots & u_{1p} \\ u_{21} & u_{22} & \cdots & u_{2p} \\ \vdots & \vdots & \ddots & \vdots \\ u_{p1} & u_{p2} & \cdots & u_{pp} \end{bmatrix}, \quad \sum_{\alpha=1}^{p} u_{i\alpha}^2 = 1, \quad \sum_{\alpha=1}^{p} u_{i\alpha} u_{j\alpha} = 0 \text{ for } i \neq j$$

In particular, the matrix product $\boldsymbol{u}_\alpha \boldsymbol{u}_\alpha^t$ gives:

$$\boldsymbol{u}_\alpha \boldsymbol{u}_\alpha^t = \begin{bmatrix} u_{\alpha 1} \\ u_{\alpha 2} \\ \vdots \\ u_{\alpha p} \end{bmatrix} [u_{\alpha 1} \quad u_{\alpha 2} \quad \cdots \quad u_{\alpha p}] = \begin{bmatrix} u_{\alpha 1}^2 & u_{\alpha 1} u_{\alpha 2} & \cdots & u_{\alpha 1} u_{\alpha p} \\ u_{\alpha 2} u_{\alpha 1} & u_{\alpha 2}^2 & \cdots & u_{\alpha 2} u_{\alpha p} \\ \vdots & \vdots & \ddots & \vdots \\ u_{\alpha p} u_{\alpha 1} & u_{\alpha p} u_{\alpha 2} & \cdots & u_{\alpha p}^2 \end{bmatrix}$$

The column vectors of $\boldsymbol{U}$ and $\boldsymbol{U}^t$, denoted by $\boldsymbol{u}_\alpha$ and $\boldsymbol{w}_k$ (with $w_{k\alpha} = u_{\alpha k}$), satisfy:

$$\sum_{\alpha=1}^{p} \boldsymbol{u}_\alpha \boldsymbol{u}_\alpha^t = \begin{bmatrix} \sum_{\alpha=1}^{p} u_{\alpha 1}^2 & \sum_{\alpha=1}^{p} u_{\alpha 1} u_{\alpha 2} & \cdots & \sum_{\alpha=1}^{p} u_{\alpha 1} u_{\alpha p} \\ \sum_{\alpha=1}^{p} u_{\alpha 2} u_{\alpha 1} & \sum_{\alpha=1}^{p} u_{\alpha 2}^2 & \cdots & \sum_{\alpha=1}^{p} u_{\alpha 2} u_{\alpha p} \\ \vdots & \vdots & \ddots & \vdots \\ \sum_{\alpha=1}^{p} u_{\alpha p} u_{\alpha 1} & \sum_{\alpha=1}^{p} u_{\alpha p} u_{\alpha 2} & \cdots & \sum_{\alpha=1}^{p} u_{\alpha p}^2 \end{bmatrix}$$

$$= \begin{bmatrix} \sum_{\alpha=1}^{p} w_{1\alpha}^2 & \sum_{\alpha=1}^{p} w_{1\alpha}w_{2\alpha} & \cdots & \sum_{\alpha=1}^{p} w_{1\alpha}w_{p\alpha} \\ \sum_{\alpha=1}^{p} w_{2\alpha}w_{1\alpha} & \sum_{\alpha=1}^{p} w_{2\alpha}^2 & \cdots & \sum_{\alpha=1}^{p} w_{2\alpha}w_{p\alpha} \\ \vdots & \vdots & \ddots & \vdots \\ \sum_{\alpha=1}^{p} w_{p\alpha}w_{1\alpha} & \sum_{\alpha=1}^{p} w_{p\alpha}w_{2\alpha} & \cdots & \sum_{\alpha=1}^{p} w_{p\alpha}^2 \end{bmatrix} = \begin{bmatrix} 1 & 0 & \cdots & 0 \\ 0 & 1 & \cdots & 0 \\ \vdots & \vdots & \ddots & \vdots \\ 0 & 0 & \cdots & 1 \end{bmatrix} = \mathbf{1}$$

EXAMPLE 2.1.– Consider a study of 20 students in a class, where their marks (out of 20) in five subjects are examined: French (x_1), Math (x_2), Physics (x_3), History (x_4) and Geography (x_5). These grades are shown in Figure 2.4, where the first column of the table represents the student number (ranging from 1 to 20).

students	French	Math	Physics	History	Geography
1	12	6	7	14	12
2	15	8	9	13	17
3	9	12	14	8	15
4	6	18	16	5	12
5	4	17	15	5	10
6	12	10	11	13	11
7	13	9	10	14	8
8	17	5	7	16	9
9	8	8	7	7	13
10	5	14	15	6	15
11	2	16	15	3	12
12	14	18	16	15	10
13	12	11	10	10	9
14	10	13	12	10	15
15	10	7	8	11	12
16	18	9	9	16	10
17	8	10	8	7	6
18	5	15	16	6	8
19	9	17	19	10	16
20	15	8	9	13	14

Figure 2.4. *Student results*

From the data in this table, the averages are calculated: $\overline{x_1} = 10.2$, $\overline{x_2} = 11.55$, $\overline{x_3} = 11.65$, $\overline{x_4} = 10.1$ *and* $\overline{x_5} = 11.7$. Similarly, the squares of the variable values (see Figure 2.5) and their averages are calculated. Variances are computed using the relation $v(x_i) = \overline{x_i^2} - \overline{x_i}^2$. Standard deviations are then determined (see Figure 2.6).

The centered and reduced coordinates are then derived, leading to the matrix $\boldsymbol{X}$ (see Figure 2.7). From $\boldsymbol{X}$, the covariance matrix $\boldsymbol{C}$ and the correlation matrix $\boldsymbol{c}$ are obtained:

$$\boldsymbol{C} = \begin{bmatrix} 18.760 & -10.910 & -8.880 & 16.280 & -0.440 \\ -10.910 & 16.648 & 14.043 & -9.255 & 0.815 \\ -8.880 & 14.053 & 13.428 & -7.065 & 2.245 \\ 16.280 & -9.255 & -7.065 & 15.490 & -0.720 \\ -0.440 & 0.815 & 2.245 & -0.720 & 8.510 \end{bmatrix}$$

$$\boldsymbol{c} = \begin{bmatrix} 1 & -0.617 & -0.559 & 0.955 & -0.035 \\ -0.617 & 1 & 0.939 & -0.576 & 0.068 \\ -0.559 & 0.939 & 1 & -0.490 & 0.210 \\ 0.955 & -0.576 & -0.490 & 1 & -0.063 \\ -0.035 & 0.068 & 0.210 & -0.063 & 1 \end{bmatrix}$$

	x_1^2	x_2^2	x_3^2	x_4^2	x_5^2
	144	36	49	196	144
	225	64	81	169	289
	81	144	196	64	225
	36	324	256	25	144
	16	289	225	25	100
	144	100	121	169	121
	169	81	100	196	64
	289	25	49	256	81
	64	64	49	49	169
	25	196	225	36	225
	4	256	225	9	144
	196	324	256	225	100
	144	121	100	100	81
	100	169	144	100	225
	100	49	64	121	144
	324	81	81	256	100
	64	100	64	49	36
	25	225	256	36	64
	81	289	361	100	256
	225	64	81	169	196
averages	122.8	150.05	149.15	117.5	145.4

Figure 2.5. *Table of squared variables*

variable	x_1	x_2	x_3	x_4	x_5
variance	18.76	16.6475	13.4275	15.49	8.51
standard deviation	4.33128	4.080135	3.66436	3.93573	2.91719

Figure 2.6. *Variance and standard deviation*

There is a significant correlation between French and History (0.955), as well as between Math and Physics (0.939), while the correlations between French and Geography (−0.035), Math and Geography (0.068), and History and Geography (−0.063) are practically non-existent.

Using software such as MATLAB or Scilab (especially with Scilab, where [vecp, valp]=spec(c) is used), the eigenvalues and eigenvectors of the matrix c can be determined (see Figure 2.8).

X =

X_1	X_2	X_3	X_4	X_5
0.416	-1.360	-1.269	0.991	0.103
1.108	-0.870	-0.723	0.737	1.817
-0.277	0.110	0.641	-0.534	1.131
-0.970	1.581	1.187	-1.296	0.103
-1.431	1.336	0.914	-1.296	-0.583
0.416	-0.380	-0.177	0.737	-0.240
0.646	-0.625	-0.450	0.991	-1.268
1.570	-1.605	-1.269	1.499	-0.926
-0.508	-0.870	-1.269	-0.788	0.446
-1.201	0.600	0.914	-1.042	1.131
-1.893	1.091	0.914	-1.804	0.103
0.877	1.581	1.187	1.245	-0.583
0.416	-0.135	-0.450	-0.025	-0.926
-0.046	0.355	0.096	-0.025	1.131
-0.046	-1.115	-0.996	0.229	0.103
1.801	-0.625	-0.723	1.499	-0.583
-0.508	-0.380	-0.996	-0.788	-1.954
-1.201	0.846	1.187	-1.042	-1.268
-0.277	1.336	2.006	-0.025	1.474
1.108	-0.870	-0.723	0.737	0.788

Figure 2.7. *Reduced centered coordinates*

	λ_1	λ_2	λ_3	λ_4	λ_5
eigenvalues	3.086	1.038	0.788	0.059	0.029

eigenvectors

	u_1	u_2	u_3	u_4	u_5
	-0.507	0.248	-0.393	-0.499	-0.527
	0.508	0.083	-0.468	-0.569	0.439
u =	0.488	0.250	-0.476	0.501	-0.471
	-0.489	0.243	-0.479	0.416	0.547
	0.089	0.900	0.413	-0.061	0.088

Figure 2.8. *Eigenvalues and eigenvectors*

It can be verified (with rounding errors) that:

$$\sum_{i=1}^{5} u_{\alpha i}^2 = 1 \quad \text{and} \quad \sum_{\alpha=1}^{5} u_{i\alpha}^2 = 1 \quad \text{for} \quad \alpha = 1 \text{ to } 5$$

$$\sum_{i=1}^{5} u_{\alpha i} u_{\beta i} = 0 \quad \text{and} \quad \sum_{i=1}^{5} u_{i\alpha} u_{i\beta} = 0 \quad \text{for} \quad \alpha, \beta = 1 \text{ to } 5 \ (\alpha \neq \beta)$$

$$\sum_{\alpha=1}^{5} \mathbf{u}_\alpha \mathbf{u}_\alpha^t = 1 \quad \text{for} \quad \alpha = 1 \text{ to } 5$$

To conclude this section, some useful expressions are provided for the matrix $\boldsymbol{X}$ of data in reduced centered coordinates.

The matrix $\boldsymbol{X}$ is of size $n \times p$. Its transpose, denoted by $\boldsymbol{X^t}$, is a matrix of size $p \times n$.

The matrix product $\boldsymbol{X^t}.\boldsymbol{X}$ is therefore a matrix of size $p \times p$, while the matrix product $\boldsymbol{X}.\boldsymbol{X^t}$ is a matrix of size $n \times n$. More precisely, the representation of the matrix $\boldsymbol{X^t}.\boldsymbol{X}$ is given by:

$$\boldsymbol{X^t}.\boldsymbol{X} = \begin{bmatrix} \sum_{i=1}^{n} X_{i1}^2 & \sum_{i=1}^{n} X_{i1}X_{i2} & \cdots & \sum_{i=1}^{n} X_{i1}X_{ip} \\ \sum_{i=1}^{n} X_{i2}X_{i1} & \sum_{i=1}^{n} X_{i2}^2 & \cdots & \sum_{i=1}^{n} X_{i2}X_{ip} \\ \vdots & \vdots & \ddots & \vdots \\ \sum_{i=1}^{n} X_{ip}X_{i1} & \sum_{i=1}^{n} X_{ip}X_{i2} & \cdots & \sum_{i=1}^{n} X_{ip}^2 \end{bmatrix}$$

and that of the matrix $\boldsymbol{X}.\boldsymbol{X^t}$ is given by:

$$\boldsymbol{XX^t} = \begin{bmatrix} \sum_{j=1}^{p} X_{1j}^2 & \sum_{j=1}^{p} X_{1j}X_{2j} & \cdots & \sum_{j=1}^{p} X_{1j}X_{nj} \\ \sum_{j=1}^{p} X_{2j}X_{1j} & \sum_{j=1}^{p} X_{2j}^2 & \cdots & \sum_{j=1}^{p} X_{2j}X_{nj} \\ \vdots & \vdots & \ddots & \vdots \\ \sum_{j=1}^{p} X_{nj}X_{1j} & \sum_{j=1}^{p} X_{nj}X_{2j} & \cdots & \sum_{j=1}^{p} X_{nj}^2 \end{bmatrix}$$

Note that these two matrices are symmetrical. As they are real, they are diagonalizable.

In particular, if the population is homogeneous, i.e. if $p_i = \frac{1}{n}$, then:

$$\sum_{i=1}^{n} X_{ij} X_{ik} = n \times \operatorname{cor}(x_j, x_k)$$

and

$$\sum_{i=1}^{n} X_{ij}^2 = \sum_{i=1}^{n} \left(\frac{x_{ij} - \bar{x}_j}{\sigma(x_j)} \right)^2 = \sum_{i=1}^{n} \frac{v(x_j)}{v(x_j)} = n$$

so that $\boldsymbol{X^t.X} = n\boldsymbol{c}$

EXAMPLE 2.2.– Calculate the matrices $\boldsymbol{X^t.X}$ and $\boldsymbol{X.X^t}$ (see Figure 2.9 for details) for Example 2.1.

$x^t x =$

20.00	-12.35	-11.19	19.10	-0.70
-12.35	20.00	18.78	-11.53	1.37
-11.19	18.78	20.00	-9.80	4.20
19.10	-11.53	-9.80	20.00	-1.25
-0.70	1.37	4.20	-1.25	20.00

$xx^t =$

7.90	3.97	-1.23	-0.28	-3.37	0.54	-4.85	-1.71	3.04	-1.23	0.57	1.08	-0.92	0,46	4.13	-2.17	-1.55	-3.43	-4.56	3.59
3.97	3.07	-0.86	-1.00	-1.42	0.13	-3.44	0.60	0.17	-0.80	1.70	1.97	0.26	0,01	0.90	-0.99	-1.86	-2.09	-1.85	1.52
-1.23	-0.86	1.44	0.12	1.16	-1.05	0.64	-1.08	-0.43	3.05	-1.31	-1.55	1.25	0,38	0.09	2.03	-1.67	0.32	0.30	-1.59
-0.28	-1.00	0.12	0.70	-0.17	0.20	1.01	-1.00	1.00	-0.09	-1.06	-1.07	-0.67	0,12	0.74	-0.18	1.14	0.44	-0.16	0.22
-3.37	-1.42	1.16	-0.17	1.92	-0.85	1.61	0.50	-1.79	2.14	-0.42	-0.72	1.32	-0,02	-1.78	1.96	-0.89	1.19	1.87	-2.25
0.54	0.13	-1.05	0.20	-0.85	0.88	0.08	0.54	0.61	-2.41	0.60	0.76	-1.21	-0,27	0.05	-1.59	1.84	0.06	-0.11	1.20
-4.85	-3.44	0.64	1.01	1.61	0.08	4.01	-0.02	-0.52	0.13	-1.42	-1.70	-0.47	-0,19	-1.57	0.75	2.58	2.53	2.47	-1.62
-1.71	0.60	-1.08	-1.00	0.50	0.54	-0.02	3.23	-2.27	-2.40	2.57	2.61	0.10	-0,74	-2.90	-0.85	0.71	0.51	1.85	-0.24
3.04	0.17	-0.43	1.00	-1.79	0.61	-0.52	-2.27	2.94	-0.87	-1.36	-1.15	-1.56	0,36	2.97	-1.35	1.26	-0.80	-2.24	1.99
-1.23	-0.80	3.05	-0.09	2.14	-2.41	0.13	-2.40	-0.87	6.89	-2.46	-2.91	3.01	0,91	0.66	4.37	-4.67	-0.11	-0.10	-3.10
0.57	1.70	-1.31	-1.06	-0.42	0.60	-1.42	2.57	-1.36	-2.46	2.59	2.76	-0.07	-0,55	-1.60	-1.31	0.09	-0.50	0.48	0.71
1.08	1.97	-1.55	-1.07	-0.72	0.76	-1.70	2.61	-1.15	-2.91	2.76	2.98	-0.28	-0,58	-1.41	-1.68	0.26	-0.69	0.24	1.08
-0.92	0.26	1.25	-0.67	1.32	-1.21	-0.47	0.10	-1.56	3.01	-0.07	-0.28	1.94	0,22	-0.78	2.15	-2.84	-0.16	0.50	-1.78
0.46	0.01	0.38	0.12	-0.02	-0.27	-0.19	-0.74	0.36	0.91	-0.55	-0.58	0.22	0,20	0.64	0.43	-0.59	-0.23	-0.46	-0.10
4.13	0.90	0.09	0.74	-1.78	0.05	-1.57	-2.90	2.97	0.66	-1.60	-1.41	-0.78	0,64	3.63	-0.58	-0.46	-1.51	-2.99	1.77
-2.17	-0.99	2.03	-0.18	1.96	-1.59	0.75	-0.85	-1.35	4.37	-1.31	-1.68	2.15	0,43	-0.58	3.08	-2.78	0.48	0.85	-2.59
-1.55	-1.86	-1.67	1.14	-0.89	1.84	2.58	0.71	1.26	-4.67	0.09	0.26	-2.84	-0,59	-0.46	-2.78	5.30	1.58	1.01	1.57
-3.43	-2.09	0.32	0.44	1.19	0.06	2.53	0.51	-0.80	-0.11	-0.50	-0.69	-0.16	-0,23	-1.51	0.48	1.58	1.69	1.91	-1.19
-4.56	-1.85	0.30	-0.16	1.87	-0.11	2.47	1.85	-2.24	-0.10	0.48	0.24	0.50	-0,46	-2.99	0.85	1.01	1.91	2.89	-1.91
3.59	1.52	-1.59	0.22	-2.25	1.20	-1.62	-0.24	1.99	-3.10	0.71	1.08	-1.78	-0,10	1.77	-2.59	1.57	-1.19	-1.91	2.72

Figure 2.9. *The matrices* $\boldsymbol{XX^t}$ *and* $\boldsymbol{X^t}X$

It can be confirmed that $\boldsymbol{X^t.X} = n\boldsymbol{c}$, which is in line with expectations. However, the matrix $\boldsymbol{X.X^t}$ calculated here will be used later in Section 2.2.2.

2.2. Analysis of a point cloud

The graphical representation of a multidimensional series (n individuals, p variables) is a point cloud in the space $\mathbb{R}^p$ of individuals and in the space $\mathbb{R}^n$ of variables. In the following, it will be assumed that these spaces are related to orthonormal reference frames. It will also be assumed that $n > p$, in order to describe highly populated populations a priori.

2.2.1. *Spatial analysis of individuals*

To begin with, consider the individual space and work with centered and reduced coordinates. For simplicity's sake, assume that each individual has the *same statistical weight*, i.e. that $p_i = \frac{1}{n}$. In this scenario, the point cloud's center of gravity lies at the origin of the axes.

Similar to the practice of linear fitting for a one-dimensional series, it is relevant to look for the axis that aligns optimally with the scatterplot (see Figure 2.10). This axis is known as the *first factorial axis* or *principal axis 1*.

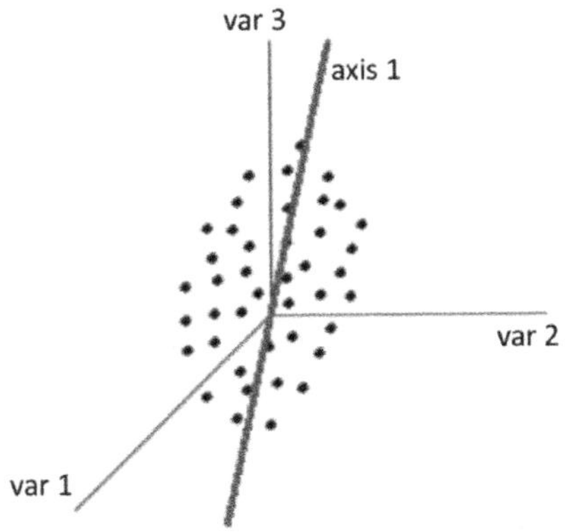

Figure 2.10. *First factorial axis 1. For a color version of this figure, see www.iste.co.uk/cochard/mathematics3.zip*

The main axis 1 is characterized by a unit vector $\boldsymbol{u_1}$ (of length 1). Let us clarify the meaning of the expression "at best": it means that the sum of the squares of the distances of the points from axis 1 is minimal.

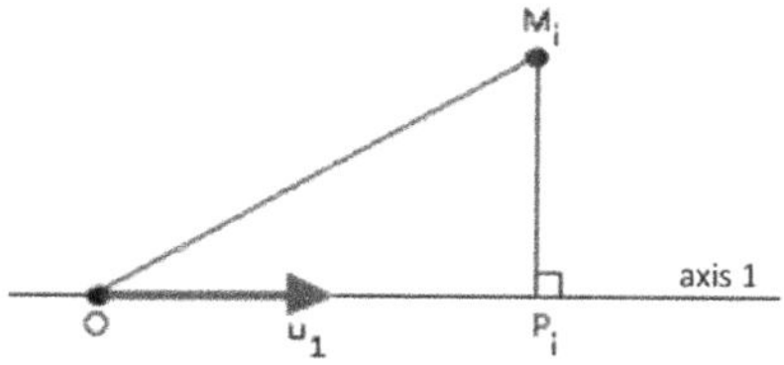

Figure 2.11. *The right-angled triangle OM_iP_i. For a color version of this figure, see www.iste.co.uk/cochard/mathematics3.zip*

Since the points M_i are fixed, the projection of M_i onto the principal axis 1 satisfies Pythagoras' theorem (see Figure 2.11): $OM_i^2 = OP_i^2 + M_iP_i^2$.

Minimizing length M_iP_i, means maximizing OP_i. Therefore, "at best" means maximizing the sum of the squares of the projections of the vectors $\mathbf{OM_i}$ onto the principal axis 1.

As the principal axis 1 is defined by a unit vector $\boldsymbol{u_1}$,

$$OP_i = \mathbf{OM_i} \cdot \mathbf{u_1} = \sum_{j=1}^{p} X_{ij}u_{1j} = X_i^t\,\mathrm{u}_1$$

To maximize the quantity M, which is the sum of the squared projections of each data point onto the principal axis 1:

$$M = \sum_{i=1}^{n}\left(\sum_{j=1}^{p} X_{ij}u_{1j}\right)^2$$

This can be expressed as:

$$\mathbf{X}.\mathbf{u_1} = \begin{bmatrix} \sum_{j=1}^{p} X_{1j}u_{1j} \\ \sum_{j=1}^{p} X_{2j}u_{1j} \\ \vdots \\ \sum_{j=1}^{p} X_{nj}u_{1j} \end{bmatrix} \quad (\mathbf{Xu_1})^t = \begin{bmatrix} \sum_{j=1}^{p} X_{1j}u_{1j} & \sum_{j=1}^{p} X_{2j}u_{1j} & \cdots & \sum_{j=1}^{p} X_{nj}u_{1j} \end{bmatrix}$$

$$(\boldsymbol{X}\boldsymbol{u}_1)^t(\boldsymbol{X}\boldsymbol{u}_1) = \sum_{i=1}^{n}\left(\sum_{j=1}^{p} x_{ij}u_{1j}\right)^2$$

So, $M = (\boldsymbol{X}\boldsymbol{u}_1)^t(\boldsymbol{X}\boldsymbol{u}_1) = \boldsymbol{u}_1^t\boldsymbol{X}^t\boldsymbol{X}\boldsymbol{u}_1$ and using a result from the previous section, namely $\boldsymbol{X}^t.\boldsymbol{X} = n\boldsymbol{c}$, we have $M = n\boldsymbol{u}_1^t\boldsymbol{c}\boldsymbol{u}_1$.

The matrix $\boldsymbol{c}$, which has positive or zero eigenvalues, is diagonalizable in an orthonormal basis. The basis change formula is:

$$\boldsymbol{c} = \boldsymbol{P}^t\boldsymbol{d}\boldsymbol{P}$$

where $\boldsymbol{P}$ is the basis change matrix and $\boldsymbol{d}$ is the diagonal matrix composed of the eigenvalues of $\boldsymbol{c}$:

$$\boldsymbol{d} = \begin{bmatrix} \lambda_1 & 0 & \cdots & 0 \\ 0 & \lambda_2 & \cdots & 0 \\ \vdots & \vdots & \ddots & \vdots \\ 0 & 0 & \cdots & \lambda_3 \end{bmatrix}$$

The eigenvalues are numbered in descending order, so λ_1 is the largest (and obviously positive). With the basis change formula, the expression becomes:

$$M = n\boldsymbol{u}_1^t\boldsymbol{c}\boldsymbol{u}_1 = n\boldsymbol{u}_1^t\boldsymbol{P}^t\boldsymbol{d}\boldsymbol{P}\boldsymbol{u}_1 = n(\boldsymbol{P}\boldsymbol{u}_1)^t\boldsymbol{d}(\boldsymbol{P}\boldsymbol{u}_1) = n\boldsymbol{w}\boldsymbol{d}\boldsymbol{w}$$

where $\boldsymbol{w} = \boldsymbol{P}\boldsymbol{u}_1$. Since $\|\boldsymbol{u}_1\| = 1$, then $\boldsymbol{w}^2 = (\boldsymbol{P}\boldsymbol{u}_1)^t(\boldsymbol{P}\boldsymbol{u}_1) = \boldsymbol{u}_1{}^t\boldsymbol{P}^t\boldsymbol{P}\boldsymbol{u}_1 = \boldsymbol{u}_1^t\boldsymbol{u}_1 = 1$. Therefore:

$$\sum_{j=1}^{p} w_j^2 = 1$$

On the other hand,

$$M = n\begin{bmatrix} w_1 & w_2 & \cdots & w_p \end{bmatrix}\begin{bmatrix} \lambda_1 & 0 & \cdots & 0 \\ 0 & \lambda_2 & \cdots & 0 \\ \vdots & \vdots & \ddots & \vdots \\ 0 & 0 & \cdots & \lambda_p \end{bmatrix}\begin{bmatrix} w_1 \\ w_2 \\ \vdots \\ w_p \end{bmatrix} = n\sum_{j=1}^{p} \lambda_j w_j^2$$

Since λ_1 is the largest eigenvalue of $\boldsymbol{c}$, the following holds:

$$w_1^2 = 1 - w_2^2 - w_3^2 - \cdots - w_p^2$$

and:

$$M = n\left[\lambda_1 - (\lambda_1 - \lambda_2)w_1^2 - (\lambda_1 - \lambda_3)w_2^2 - \cdots - (\lambda_1 - \lambda_p)w_p^2\right] \leq n\,\lambda_1$$

The maximum value of M is reached when it is equal to $n\,\lambda_1$. This value corresponds to the value M when $\boldsymbol{u_1}$ is the eigenvector associated with λ_1. In this case,

$$M = n\boldsymbol{u_1^t c u_1} = n\lambda_1 \boldsymbol{u_1^t u_1} = n\lambda_1.$$

Thus, this eigenvector $\boldsymbol{u_1}$ defines the principal axis 1.

EXAMPLE 2.3.– Take Example 2.2. again. The eigenvector $\boldsymbol{u_1}$ (shown below), which was obtained from Example 2.1, corresponds to the largest eigenvalue $\lambda_1 = 3.086$. This eigenvector is used to define the principal axis 1 in the space $\mathbb{R}^5$:

$$\boldsymbol{u_1} = \begin{bmatrix} -0.507 \\ 0.508 \\ 0.488 \\ -0.489 \\ 0.089 \end{bmatrix}$$

Axis 1 has been defined. Now, the other $p-1$ axes that best fit the point cloud need to be defined. The p factor axes form an orthonormal reference frame. The unit vectors defining them satisfy the following relationships:

$$\|\boldsymbol{u_j}\|^2 = \boldsymbol{u_j^2} = 1 \qquad \forall\, j = 1, \dots, p$$

$$\boldsymbol{u_j u_k} = 0 \qquad \forall j, k = 1, \dots, p \text{ with } j \neq k$$

To find the vectors $\boldsymbol{u_j}$ ($j > 1$), the same method used for $\boldsymbol{u_1}$ is applied. Consequently, the eigenvectors $\boldsymbol{u_2}, \boldsymbol{u_3}, \dots, \boldsymbol{u_p}$ of the matrix $\boldsymbol{c}$ are the vectors of interest. Furthermore, since the system $\boldsymbol{u_1}, \boldsymbol{u_2}, \dots, \boldsymbol{u_p}$ is orthonormal, the above relationships hold.

Thus, the search for factorial axes $1, 2, \dots, p$ is equivalent to calculating the values and eigenvectors of the correlation matrix $\boldsymbol{c}$. The importance of a factorial axis k is quantified by the ratio I_k as follows:

$$I_k = \frac{\lambda_k}{\sum_{j=1}^{p} \lambda_j} = \frac{\lambda_k}{p}$$

This ratio represents the inertia of the point cloud with respect to the axis k, often expressed as a percentage.

The next step is to determine the coordinates of the individual points on the factorial axes. These coordinates are given by the matrix $\boldsymbol{X}.\boldsymbol{u}$, where $\boldsymbol{u}$ is the matrix formed by juxtaposing the eigenvectors of matrix c:

$$\boldsymbol{Xu} = \begin{bmatrix} X_{11} & X_{12} & \cdots & X_{1p} \\ X_{21} & X_{22} & \cdots & X_{2p} \\ \vdots & \vdots & \ddots & \vdots \\ \vdots & \vdots & \ddots & \vdots \\ X_{n1} & X_{n2} & \cdots & X_{np} \end{bmatrix} \begin{bmatrix} u_{11} & u_{21} & \cdots & u_{p1} \\ u_{12} & u_{22} & \cdots & u_{p2} \\ \vdots & \vdots & \ddots & \vdots \\ u_{1p} & u_{2p} & \cdots & u_{pp} \end{bmatrix}$$

$$= \begin{bmatrix} \sum_{j=1}^{p} X_{1j}u_{1j} & \sum_{j=1}^{p} X_{1j}u_{2j} & \cdots & \sum_{j=1}^{p} X_{1j}u_{pj} \\ \sum_{j=1}^{p} X_{2j}u_{1j} & \sum_{j=1}^{p} X_{2j}u_{2j} & \cdots & \sum_{j=1}^{p} X_{2j}u_{pj} \\ \vdots & \vdots & \ddots & \vdots \\ \sum_{j=1}^{p} X_{nj}u_{1j} & \sum_{j=1}^{p} X_{nj}u_{2j} & \cdots & \sum_{j=1}^{p} X_{nj}u_{pj} \end{bmatrix}$$

The columns of the matrix $\boldsymbol{u}$ are the components of the eigenvectors $\boldsymbol{u_k}$. The rows of the resulting product matrix are the coordinates of the individuals on the factorial axes.

EXAMPLE 2.4.– Return to Example 2.3 and visualize the individual points in the $(1,2)$, $(1,3)$ and $(2,3)$ planes of the factorial axes. The coordinates are calculated as shown in Figure 2.12 (formed by tables). Calculating the inertia of the scatter plot in relation to each axis (see Figure 2.13.), it becomes apparent that restricting the analysis to the first three axes, as there is a satisfaction, as there is a significant decrease in the value of λ_4 compared with λ_3. The first three axes explain over 98% of the cumulative inertia. Consequently, only the projections of the point cloud onto the $(1,2)$, $(1,3)$ and $(2,3)$ planes (see Figure 2.14(a)–(c)).

Xu =

X_1	X_2	X_3	X_4	X_5
0,42	-1,36	-1,27	0,99	0,10
1,11	-0,87	-0,72	0,74	1,82
-0,28	0,11	0,64	-0,53	1,13
-0,97	1,58	1,19	-1,30	0,10
-1,43	1,34	0,91	-1,30	-0,58
0,42	-0,38	-0,18	0,74	-0,24
0,65	-0,62	-0,45	0,99	-1,27
1,57	-1,61	-1,27	1,50	-0,93
-0,51	-0,87	-1,27	-0,79	0,45
-1,20	0,60	0,91	-1,04	1,13
-1,89	1,09	0,91	-1,80	0,10
0,88	1,58	1,19	1,25	-0,58
0,42	-0,13	-0,45	-0,03	-0,93
-0,05	0,36	0,10	-0,03	1,13
-0,05	-1,12	-1,00	0,23	0,10
1,80	-0,62	-0,72	1,50	-0,58
-0,51	-0,38	-1,00	-0,79	-1,95
-1,20	0,85	1,19	-1,04	-1,27
-0,28	1,34	2,01	-0,03	1,47
1,11	-0,87	-0,72	0,74	0,79

×

u_1	u_2	u_3	u_4	u_5
-0,51	0,25	-0,39	-0,50	-0,53
0,51	0,08	-0,47	-0,57	0,44
0,49	0,25	-0,48	0,50	-0,47
-0,49	0,24	-0,48	0,42	0,55
0,09	0,90	0,41	-0,06	0,09

=

axis 1	2	3	4	5
-2,00	0,01	0,65	0,34	0,33
-1,56	1,84	0,71	-0,23	-0,06
0,87	0,99	0,48	0,11	-0,30
2,52	-0,03	-0,26	-0,36	-0,05
2,43	-0,85	-0,12	-0,09	0,15
-0,87	-0,01	-0,35	0,24	0,08
-1,46	-0,90	-0,75	0,30	0,03
-3,05	-0,53	-0,36	0,17	-0,20
-0,38	-0,31	1,77	-0,24	0,09
1,97	0,75	0,72	0,21	[illegible]
2,85	-0,50	0,70	0,03	0,07
0,28	0,43	-2,49	-0,19	0,30
-0,57	-0,86	-0,26	-0,31	-0,16
0,36	1,05	0,29	-0,21	0,22
-1,13	-0,21	0,95	0,25	0,14
-2,37	0,05	-1,03	-0,25	-0,11
-0,21	-2,36	0,42	-0,24	-0,03
2,01	-1,32	-0,52	0,36	-0,24
1,94	1,87	-0,85	0,28	-0,10
-1,65	0,91	0,29	-0,16	-0,15

Figure 2.12. *Coordinates in the factorial axes*

eigenvalues	3.086	1.038	0.788	0.059	0.029
inertia (%)	61.719	20.761	15.751	1.184	0.584
cumulative inertia (%)	61.719	82.481	98.232	99.416	100.000

Figure 2.13. *Eigenvalues and inertia*

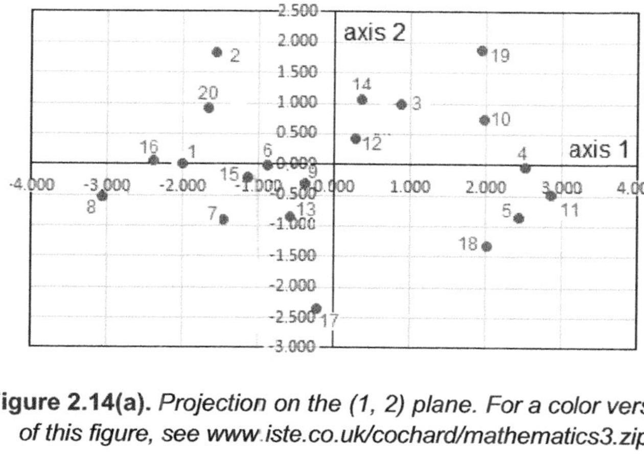

Figure 2.14(a). *Projection on the (1, 2) plane. For a color version of this figure, see www.iste.co.uk/cochard/mathematics3.zip*

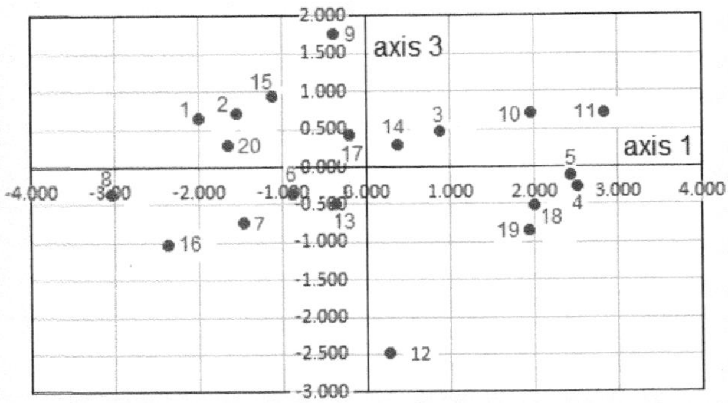

Figure 2.14(b). *Projection on the (1, 3) plane (continued). For a color version of this figure, see www.iste.co.uk/cochard/mathematics3.zip*

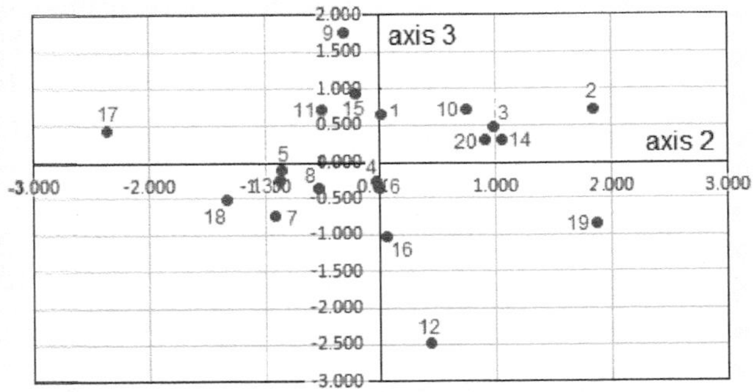

Figure 2.14(c). *Projection on the (2, 3) plane (continued and end). For a color version of this figure, see www.iste.co.uk/cochard/mathematics3.zip*

2.2.2. *Analysis in variable space*

Moving on to variable space, denoted by $\mathbb{R}^n$, which is associated with an orthonormal reference frame, factorial axes represented by the orthonormal vectors $\boldsymbol{v}_i$ can also be defined.

Following a similar approach as for space $\mathbb{R}^p$, the objective is to minimize the following quantity:

$$M' = \sum_{j=1}^{p} \left(\sum_{i=1}^{n} X_{ij} v_{\alpha i} \right)^2 ,$$

where $\boldsymbol{v}_\alpha$ is a vector defining a principal axis α.

Noting that:

$$\boldsymbol{X}^t \boldsymbol{v}_\alpha = \begin{bmatrix} \sum_{i=1}^{n} X_{i1} v_{\alpha i} \\ \sum_{i=1}^{n} X_{i2} v_{\alpha i} \\ \vdots \\ \sum_{i=1}^{n} X_{ip} v_{\alpha i} \end{bmatrix}, \quad (\boldsymbol{X}^t \boldsymbol{v}_\alpha)^t = \left[\sum_{i=1}^{n} X_{i1} v_{\alpha i} \quad \sum_{i=1}^{n} X_{i2} v_{\alpha i} \quad \cdots \quad \sum_{i=1}^{n} X_{ip} v_{\alpha i} \right]$$

and:

$$(\boldsymbol{X}^{t\boldsymbol{v}_\alpha})^t (\boldsymbol{X}^{t\boldsymbol{v}_\alpha}) = \sum_{j=1}^{p} \left(\sum_{i=1}^{n} X_{ij} \, v_{\alpha i} \right)^2$$

it follows that:

$$M' = (\boldsymbol{X}^t \boldsymbol{v}_\alpha)^t (\boldsymbol{X}^t \boldsymbol{v}_\alpha) = \boldsymbol{v}_\alpha^t \boldsymbol{X} \boldsymbol{X}^t \boldsymbol{v}_\alpha .$$

As in the individual space, the maximum of M' is achieved when $\boldsymbol{v}_\alpha$ is the eigenvector corresponding to the eigenvalue μ_α of the matrix $\boldsymbol{X}.\boldsymbol{X}^t$ (with eigenvalues μ_α numbered in descending order).

The vectors $\boldsymbol{v}_1, \boldsymbol{v}_2, \ldots, \boldsymbol{v}_n$, which are orthonormal, define the main axes in the variable space $\mathbb{R}^n$.

EXAMPLE 2.5.– Returning to the previous example, consider the variable space $\mathbb{R}^n$ (here, $n = 20$).

The matrix $\boldsymbol{X}.\boldsymbol{X}^t$ is previously calculated (see Figure 2.9).

Using software such as MATLAB or Scilab, it is possible to compute the eigenvalues and eigenvectors of $\boldsymbol{X}.\boldsymbol{X}^t$.

Given the 20 variables, in this case, the matrix yields 20 eigenvalues and 20 corresponding eigenvectors (see Figure 2.15).

Similar to the space $\mathbb{R}^5$, the first three eigenvalues in $\mathbb{R}^{20}$ stand out as being significantly larger. This observation highlights that the first three principal axes hold the most relevance for data analysis within variable space.

eigenvalues

μ_1	μ_2	μ_3	μ_4	μ_5	μ_6	μ_7	μ_8	μ_9	μ_{10}	μ_{11}	μ_{12}	μ_{13}	μ_{14}	μ_{15}	μ_{16}	μ_{17}	μ_{18}	μ_{19}	μ_{20}
61.73	20.77	15.74	1.19	0.58	0.00	0.00	0.00	0.00	0.00	0.00	0.00	0.00	0.00	0.00	0.00	0.00	0.00	0.00	0.00

eigenvectors

$\mathbf{v}_1$	$\mathbf{v}_2$	$\mathbf{v}_3$	$\mathbf{v}_4$	$\mathbf{v}_5$	$\mathbf{v}_6$	$\mathbf{v}_7$	$\mathbf{v}_8$	$\mathbf{v}_9$	$\mathbf{v}_{10}$	$\mathbf{v}_{11}$	$\mathbf{v}_{12}$	$\mathbf{v}_{13}$	$\mathbf{v}_{14}$	$\mathbf{v}_{15}$	$\mathbf{v}_{16}$	$\mathbf{v}_{17}$	$\mathbf{v}_{18}$	$\mathbf{v}_{19}$	$\mathbf{v}_{20}$
0.25	0.00	0.16	0.31	-0.44	0.22	0.38	-0.06	0.04	-0.03	-0.26	0.00	-0.05	-0.30	-0.05	0.29	-0.27	-0.12	0.19	-0.24
0.20	0.40	0.18	-0.21	0.08	-0.06	-0.05	0.23	0.06	-0.26	-0.09	-0.31	0.13	0.32	-0.01	0.40	-0.09	0.24	-0.24	-0.29
-0.11	0.22	0.12	0.10	0.40	0.27	0.25	0.37	-0.06	0.14	0.01	0.34	-0.29	-0.03	-0.05	0.01	-0.11	0.43	0.24	0.08
-0.32	-0.01	-0.07	-0.34	0.07	0.26	0.06	-0.03	0.11	-0.24	-0.20	0.21	0.26	-0.36	0.52	-0.02	-0.15	0.03	-0.22	-0.10
-0.31	-0.19	-0.03	-0.08	-0.20	-0.19	0.27	-0.08	0.19	-0.06	0.14	0.06	-0.32	-0.05	-0.39	-0.07	-0.14	0.27	-0.52	-0.17
0.11	0.00	-0.09	0.22	-0.10	-0.14	-0.37	0.39	0.40	-0.16	0.23	0.06	-0.09	-0.03	0.16	-0.31	-0.44	-0.06	0.11	-0.18
0.19	-0.20	-0.19	0.27	-0.04	-0.07	0.13	0.04	-0.35	-0.68	0.00	0.08	0.20	0.02	-0.03	-0.17	0.11	0.34	0.03	0.11
0.39	-0.12	-0.09	0.16	0.26	0.37	0.04	0.10	0.28	0.09	-0.32	0.06	0.13	0.11	-0.21	-0.21	0.01	-0.16	-0.47	0.16
0.05	-0.07	0.45	-0.22	-0.12	0.18	-0.24	-0.30	0.43	-0.21	-0.15	0.04	-0.01	0.01	-0.19	-0.20	0.19	0.30	0.31	0.07
-0.25	0.16	0.18	0.20	0.01	0.46	-0.10	-0.26	-0.34	-0.07	0.18	-0.04	0.04	0.31	-0.08	-0.32	-0.18	-0.15	-0.07	-0.36
-0.36	-0.11	0.18	0.03	-0.09	-0.04	0.24	0.30	0.17	-0.33	-0.17	0.13	-0.13	0.44	0.05	0.08	0.16	-0.46	0.09	0.14
-0.04	0.09	-0.63	-0.17	-0.40	0.21	0.00	-0.05	0.07	0.16	-0.22	0.07	-0.04	0.43	0.04	-0.02	-0.07	0.23	0.18	0.01
0.07	-0.19	-0.06	-0.29	0.21	-0.18	0.29	0.07	0.06	0.10	0.06	0.21	0.48	0.08	-0.30	-0.12	-0.05	-0.11	0.29	-0.45
-0.05	0.23	0.07	-0.19	-0.29	0.20	0.19	0.20	0.02	-0.01	0.42	-0.14	0.38	-0.10	-0.22	-0.07	-0.19	-0.06	-0.01	0.51
0.14	-0.05	0.24	0.23	-0.18	-0.06	0.31	-0.05	0.19	0.28	0.29	0.12	0.19	0.26	0.50	-0.10	0.26	0.24	-0.16	-0.07
0.30	0.01	-0.26	-0.23	0.15	0.30	0.18	-0.13	0.18	-0.27	0.50	-0.03	-0.36	-0.05	0.08	0.12	0.24	-0.20	0.07	-0.13
0.03	-0.52	0.11	-0.22	0.04	0.16	0.16	0.24	-0.14	0.10	-0.07	-0.62	-0.15	0.05	0.18	-0.21	-0.14	0.12	0.10	-0.02
-0.26	-0.29	-0.13	0.33	0.31	0.10	-0.03	-0.28	0.30	-0.03	0.16	-0.17	0.23	0.14	-0.02	0.45	-0.27	0.12	0.12	0.14
-0.25	0.41	-0.21	0.26	0.13	-0.10	0.27	-0.03	0.28	-0.04	-0.15	-0.46	0.06	-0.20	-0.03	-0.32	0.28	0.01	0.12	-0.10
0.21	0.20	0.07	-0.15	0.20	-0.31	0.30	-0.42	0.00	-0.09	-0.11	0.02	-0.17	0.19	0.16	-0.23	-0.49	-0.09	0.04	0.26

Figure 2.15. *Eigenvalues, eigenvectors*

2.2.3. *Link between the two spaces*

The relationship between the two spaces, $\mathbb{R}^p$ and $\mathbb{R}^n$ (the individual space and the variable space), is not immediately apparent since they are distinct. However, when $n > p$, a connection between eigenvectors $\boldsymbol{v}_\alpha$ and $\boldsymbol{u}_\alpha$ can be established for $a \leq p$.

Starting from the eigenvalue equation for the eigenvectors defining the principal axes of $\mathbb{R}^n$,

$$\boldsymbol{X}\boldsymbol{X}^t\boldsymbol{v}_\alpha = \mu_\alpha \boldsymbol{v}_\alpha$$

and multiplying on the left by $\boldsymbol{X}^t$, results in:

$$\boldsymbol{X}^t\boldsymbol{X}\boldsymbol{X}^t\boldsymbol{v}_\alpha = \mu_\alpha \boldsymbol{X}^t\boldsymbol{v}_\alpha \quad \text{or} \quad (\boldsymbol{X}^t\boldsymbol{X})\boldsymbol{X}^t\boldsymbol{v}_\alpha = \mu_\alpha \boldsymbol{X}^t\boldsymbol{v}_\alpha \quad \text{or} \quad \boldsymbol{c}\,\boldsymbol{X}^t\boldsymbol{v}_\alpha = \frac{\mu_\alpha}{n}\boldsymbol{X}^t\boldsymbol{v}_\alpha$$

This is the eigenvalue equation for the matrix $\boldsymbol{c}$ when $\alpha = 1, \dots, p$. From this, the following relationships are deduced:

$$\lambda_\alpha = \frac{\mu_\alpha}{n}, \qquad \alpha = 1, \dots, p$$

and a proportional relationship exists between the eigenvectors $\boldsymbol{X}^t\boldsymbol{v}_\alpha$ and $\boldsymbol{u}_\alpha$ (for $\alpha = 1, \dots, p$), i.e. $\boldsymbol{u}_\alpha = k_\alpha \boldsymbol{X}^t\boldsymbol{v}_\alpha$, $\alpha = 1, \dots, p$.

Furthermore, the eigenvectors $\boldsymbol{u}_\alpha$ and $\boldsymbol{v}_\alpha$ belong to orthonormal systems $\boldsymbol{u}_\alpha^t\boldsymbol{u}_\alpha = 1$ and $\boldsymbol{v}_\alpha^t\boldsymbol{v}_\alpha = 1$, the constant k_α satisfies:

$$1 = k_\alpha^2(\boldsymbol{X}^t\boldsymbol{v}_\alpha)^t(\boldsymbol{X}^t\boldsymbol{v}_\alpha) = k_\alpha^2\boldsymbol{v}_\alpha^t\boldsymbol{X}\boldsymbol{X}^t\boldsymbol{v}_\alpha = k_\alpha^2\mu_\alpha\boldsymbol{v}_\alpha^t\boldsymbol{v}_\alpha = k_\alpha^2\mu_\alpha = nk_\alpha^2\lambda_\alpha$$

This implies:

$$k_\alpha = \frac{1}{\sqrt{n\lambda_\alpha}}.$$

Thus, the relationship between the vectors $\boldsymbol{u}_\alpha$ and $\boldsymbol{v}_\alpha$ is expressed as:

$$\boldsymbol{u}_\alpha = \frac{1}{\sqrt{n\lambda_\alpha}}\boldsymbol{X}^t\boldsymbol{v}_\alpha = \frac{1}{\sqrt{\mu_\alpha}}\boldsymbol{X}^t\boldsymbol{v}_\alpha \quad \text{or} \quad \boldsymbol{v}_\alpha = \frac{1}{\sqrt{\mu_\alpha}}\boldsymbol{X}\boldsymbol{u}_\alpha = \frac{1}{\sqrt{n\lambda_\alpha}}\boldsymbol{X}\boldsymbol{u}_\alpha, \quad \alpha = 1, \dots, p$$

EXAMPLE 2.6.– Let us revisit the results of the previous examples.

individuals space

	λ_1	λ_2	λ_3
eigenvalues	3.086	1.038	0.788

	u_1	u_2	u_3
eigenvectors	-0.507	0.248	-0.393
	0.508	0.083	-0.468
	0.488	0.250	-0.476

variables space

	μ_1	μ_2	μ_3
eigenvalues	61.733	20.766	15.738

	v_1	v_2	v_3
eigenvectors	0.254	0.001	0.163
	0.198	0.403	0.181
	-0.111	0.217	0.120

Figure 2.16. *Limitation to q = 3*

Xu_1	Xu_2	Xu_3
-2.00	0.01	0.65
-1.56	1.84	0.71
0.87	0.99	0.48
2.52	-0.03	-0.26
2.43	-0.85	-0.12
-0.87	-0.01	-0.35
-1.46	-0.90	-0.75
-3.05	-0.53	-0.36
-0.38	-0.31	1.77
1.97	0.75	0.72
2.85	-0.50	0.70
0.28	0.43	-2.49
-0.57	-0.86	-0.26
0.36	1.05	0.29
-1.13	-0.21	0.95
-2.37	0.05	-1.03
-0.21	-2.36	0.42
2.01	-1.32	-0.52
1.94	1.87	-0.85
-1.65	0.91	0.29

$$\mathbf{v}_1 = \frac{1}{\sqrt{n\lambda_1}}\mathbf{Xu}_1 = \begin{bmatrix} -0.25 \\ -0.20 \\ 0.11 \end{bmatrix}$$

$$\mathbf{v}_2 = \frac{1}{\sqrt{n\lambda_2}}\mathbf{Xu}_2 = \begin{bmatrix} 0.00 \\ 0.40 \\ 0.22 \end{bmatrix}$$

$$\mathbf{v}_3 = \frac{1}{\sqrt{n\lambda_3}}\mathbf{Xu}_3 = \begin{bmatrix} 0.16 \\ 0.18 \\ 0.12 \end{bmatrix}$$

Figure 2.17. *Variable space (q = 3)*

It is evident that limiting the analysis to one dimension is sufficient, with $q = 3$. In both the individual and variable spaces, the first three principal axes account for a substantial proportion of the point cloud's inertia. These results are shown in Figure 2.16.

Based on the relationships established earlier, the following results are derived (with minor deviations due to rounding errors), as shown in Figure 2.17:

$$\mu_1 = 20, \quad \lambda_1 = 61.728, \quad \mu_2 = 20, \quad \lambda_2 = 20.76,$$
$$\mu_3 = 20, \quad \lambda_3 = 15.76$$

The results align perfectly with those presented in Example 2.4, apart from the sign, which is inherently arbitrary.

2.3. Principal component factor analysis

2.3.1. *Principles*

Principal component (factorial) analysis (PCA) is a statistical method designed to model a scatter plot. Statistics outputs often take the form of multidimensional data tables with numerous observations, making it challenging to derive meaningful conclusions. The objective of PCA is to identify patterns in the data by "reducing" its dimensionality, thus facilitating interpretation.

The fundamental problem arises as follows: the *matrix* $\boldsymbol{X}$, representing the data table, contains $n \times p$ elements. Extracting relevant information from such a dataset is often complex.

Therefore, the goal is to **construct** a lower-dimensional representation that approximates the original matrix $\boldsymbol{X}$ as **closely** as possible.

Assume it is possible to find two vectors U and V such that:

$$X = UV^t.$$

In this case, a substantial amount of data can be constructed using a smaller set of elements: with only $n + p$ elements, $n \times p$ elements can be generated. For example:

$$\boldsymbol{U} = \begin{bmatrix} U_1 \\ U_2 \\ \vdots \\ \vdots \\ U_n \end{bmatrix} \quad \boldsymbol{V} = \begin{bmatrix} V_1 \\ V_2 \\ \vdots \\ V_p \end{bmatrix} \quad \boldsymbol{UV^t} = \begin{bmatrix} U_1V_1 & U_1V_2 & \cdots & U_1V_p \\ U_2V_1 & U_2V_2 & \cdots & U_2V_p \\ \vdots & \vdots & \ddots & \vdots \\ \vdots & \vdots & \ddots & \vdots \\ U_nV_1 & U_nV_2 & \cdots & U_nV_p \end{bmatrix}$$

The inverse problem is to determine U and V from $n \times p$ elements that approximate the original matrix. Generally, it is not possible to find vectors U and V such that $X = UV^t$. However, it is possible to identify vectors $\boldsymbol{U_1}, \boldsymbol{U_2}, \ldots, \boldsymbol{U_q}$ and $\boldsymbol{V_1}, \boldsymbol{V_2}, \ldots, \boldsymbol{V_q}$ (where U_i and V_i share the same dimension) such that:

$$\boldsymbol{X} \approx \boldsymbol{U_1} \times \boldsymbol{V_1^t} + \boldsymbol{U_2} \times \boldsymbol{V_2^t} + \cdots + \boldsymbol{U_q} \times \boldsymbol{V_q^t} + \boldsymbol{E},$$

where $\boldsymbol{E}$ is an error matrix assumed to be negligible.

This implies that the matrix X can be approximated using a linear combination of q pairs of vectors U and V. The value of q depends on the proportion of data deemed important to retain. Thus, the matrix X is nearly reconstructed using $q \times (n + p)$ elements.

Subsequent sections will detail the methods for determining the vectors $\boldsymbol{U_1}, \boldsymbol{U_2}, \dots, \boldsymbol{U_q}$ and $\boldsymbol{V_1}, \boldsymbol{V_2}, \dots, \boldsymbol{V_q}$..

EXAMPLE 2.7.– Consider a population of $n = 1000$ individuals studied using $p = 100$ variables. The data matrix $\boldsymbol{X}$ therefore contains $n \times p = 100{,}000$ elements. By approximating the date with $q = 10$, the number of elements is reduced to:

$$q(n + p) = 10(1000 + 100) = 11{,}000.$$

This reduction is substantial, representing approximately 10 times fewer elements to analyze. This simplification allows a more straightforward interpretation of the data while retaining the essential aspects of the information contained in the matrix $\boldsymbol{X}$.

PCA builds upon the results obtained from scatterplots by reducing the spaces $\mathbb{R}^p$ and $\mathbb{R}^n$ to $\mathbb{R}^q$. The choice of dimension q is primordial for achieving a meaningful representation of the data within the model.

In practice, from the p factorial axes in the individuals' space, the analysis focuses on the q axes that capture a significant portion of the inertia. Therefore, $q \leq p$, and typically, since there are often more individuals than variables ($p \leq n$), it follows that $q \leq n$. This reduction allows for a smaller number of dimensions to be analyzed while retaining the most relevant information.

Once q has been determined, it is necessary to verify whether the $q(n + p)$ elements can adequately approximate the original $n \times p$ elements with a negligible error $\boldsymbol{E}$. In other words, the goal is to ensure that the reduced representation retains the essential information without significant loss.

This verification can be performed by comparing the original data with the data reconstructed from the q factorial axes. If the error $\boldsymbol{E}$ between the two datasets is negligible, the reduced representation is considered sufficiently accurate and faithful to the original data.

EXAMPLE 2.8.– In Example 2.1, the results for both the individual space and the variable space are presented.

Subsequently, in Examples 2.3 and 2.4 (within the individual space), the eigenvalues and eigenvectors corresponding to the three primary axes of major significance were determined.

Similarly, for the variable space (Example 2.5), the coordinates of the "variable" points in the (1,2), (1,3) and (2,3) planes were computed using the matrix $\boldsymbol{X}^t\boldsymbol{v}$, where $\boldsymbol{v}$ is the matrix whose columns are the vectors $\boldsymbol{v}_i$.

Figure 2.18(a)–(c) provides a graphical representation of these coordinates.

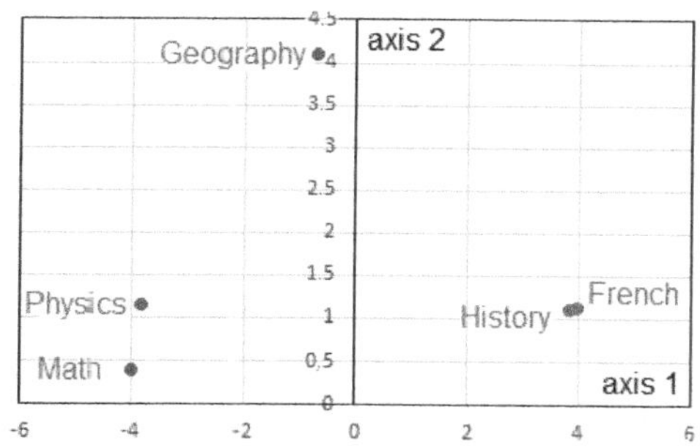

Figure 2.18(a). *Coordinates of variables in the (1, 2) plane. For a color version of this figure, see www.iste.co.uk/cochard/mathematics3.zip*

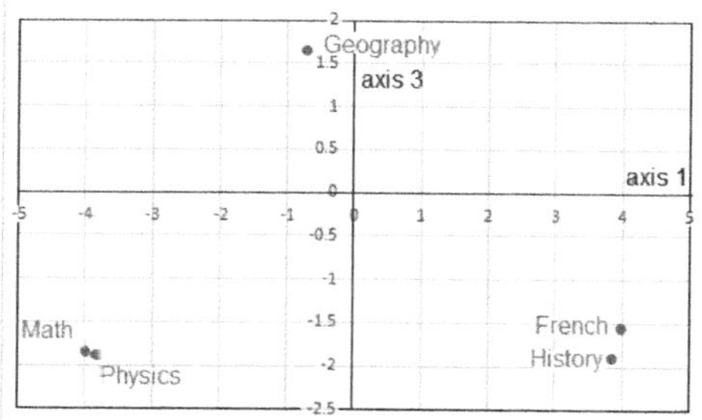

Figure 2.18(b). *Coordinates of variables in the (1, 3) plane. For a color version of this figure, see www.iste.co.uk/cochard/mathematics3.zip*

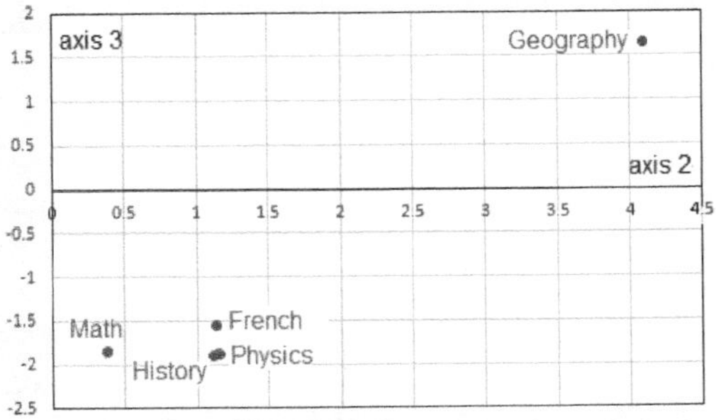

Figure 2.18(c). *Coordinates of variables in the (2, 3) plane. For a color version of this figure, see www.iste.co.uk/cochard/mathematics3.zip*

To justify the reduction of $\boldsymbol{X}$ (i.e. the data table) to just $q(n+p)$ elements for its reconstitution, consider the equation expressing the eigenvalues:

$$\boldsymbol{X}^t\boldsymbol{X}\boldsymbol{u}_\alpha = n\lambda_\alpha\boldsymbol{u}_\alpha \qquad [1]$$

For $\alpha = 1, \ldots, p$, a link can be established between the spaces $\mathbb{R}^p$ and $\mathbb{R}^n$. The relationship between the eigenvectors $\boldsymbol{u}_\alpha$ of the individual space and $\boldsymbol{v}_\alpha$ of the variable space is given as:

$$\boldsymbol{u}_\alpha = \frac{1}{\sqrt{n\lambda_\alpha}}\boldsymbol{X}^t\boldsymbol{v}_\alpha \qquad \boldsymbol{v}_\alpha = \frac{1}{\sqrt{n\lambda_\alpha}}\boldsymbol{X}\boldsymbol{u}_\alpha, \quad \alpha = 1, \ldots, p$$

This implies:

$$\boldsymbol{X}\boldsymbol{u}_\alpha = \sqrt{n\lambda_\alpha}\boldsymbol{v}_\alpha$$

By multiplying on the left by $\boldsymbol{u}_\alpha^t$ and summing over $\alpha = 1, \ldots, p$, it follows:

$$\boldsymbol{X}\sum_{\alpha=1}^{p}\boldsymbol{u}_\alpha\boldsymbol{u}_\alpha^t = \boldsymbol{X} = \sum_{\alpha=1}^{p}\sqrt{n\lambda_\alpha}v_\alpha u_\alpha^t = \sum_{\alpha=1}^{p}\boldsymbol{X}\boldsymbol{u}_\alpha\boldsymbol{u}_\alpha^t$$

If $q \leq p$ is chosen in a reasonable way (e.g. to achieve a significant cumulative inertia), the approximation is given by:

$$\boldsymbol{X} \cong \sum_{\alpha=1}^{q}\boldsymbol{X}\boldsymbol{u}_\alpha\boldsymbol{u}_\alpha^t$$

Thus, $\boldsymbol{Xu_\alpha}$ and $\boldsymbol{u_\alpha}$ play the roles of vectors $\boldsymbol{U_\alpha}$ and $\boldsymbol{V_\alpha}$ introduced at the beginning of this section.

EXAMPLE 2.9.– Let the table $\boldsymbol{X}$ be reconstructed with the approximation $q = 3$. The results are shown in Figure 2.19. It can be observed that most of the values in the table $\boldsymbol{X}$ are well approximated. However, there are also a few values that differ slightly from those in the original table. These differences may be due to the approximation made by using only the first three principal axes to reconstruct the table $\boldsymbol{X}$.

$\mathbf{Xu_1u_1^t + Xu_2u_2^t + Xu_3u_3^t} =$

0.759	-1.315	-1.280	0.669	0.094
0.962	-0.971	-0.640	0.866	1.808
-0.383	0.302	0.447	-0.413	1.164
-1.180	1.397	1.344	-1.115	0.085
-1.397	1.219	1.030	-1.341	-0.601
0.578	-0.278	-0.260	0.593	-0.232
0.809	-0.469	-0.586	0.852	-1.253
1.553	-1.421	-1.448	1.534	-0.898
-0.580	-1.048	-1.105	-0.737	0.423
-1.096	0.724	0.805	-1.128	1.145
-1.843	1.076	0.933	-1.853	0.099
0.942	1.341	1.424	1.158	-0.621
0.176	-0.240	-0.371	0.192	-0.930
-0.035	0.138	0.305	-0.058	1.099
0.150	-1.035	-1.055	0.050	0.106
1.617	-0.715	-0.653	1.664	-0.588
-0.643	-0.500	-0.893	-0.672	-1.966
-1.146	1.153	0.896	-1.062	-1.226
-0.187	1.539	1.819	-0.090	1.500
0.946	-0.896	-0.714	0.889	0.792

Figure 2.19. *Reconstructing table **X***

In the variable space, an alternative to the Euclidean distance can be useful for defining the distance between two points. The columns of the matrix $\boldsymbol{X}$ represent variable points $\boldsymbol{X_j}$ with coordinates $X_{1j}, X_{2j}, \ldots, X_{nj}$ in $\mathbb{R}^n$.

Using the Euclidean norm, which is commonly applied to measure the distance between two points in the variable space, yields:

$$\|\boldsymbol{X}_j\|^2 = \sum_{i=1}^{n} X_{ij}^2 = \sum_{i=1}^{n}\left(\frac{(x_{ij} - \bar{x}_j)}{\sigma(x_j)}\right)^2 = \frac{nv(x_j)}{v(x_j)} = n \quad \text{such that} \quad \|\boldsymbol{X}_j\| = \sqrt{n}$$

To simplify the analysis, it is convenient to divide the variable coordinates by the square root of n (i.e. $\sqrt{n}$), thereby placing all variable points *on a hypersphere of radius* 1 in the variable space.

When these variable points are projected onto a plane defined by two factorial axes, the projections lie within *a circle of radius* 1, known as the *correlation circle.*

If the following is defined:

$$Y_{ij} = \frac{X_{ij}}{\sqrt{n}}$$

then the correlation between two variables x_j and x_k is expressed as:

$$\begin{aligned}\operatorname{cor}(x_j, x_k) &= \frac{\operatorname{cov}(x_j, x_k)}{\sigma(x_j)\sigma(x_k)} = \frac{1}{n}\sum_{i=1}^{n} \frac{x_{ij} - \overline{x_j}}{\sigma(x_j)} \cdot \frac{x_{ik} - \overline{x_k}}{\sigma(x_k)} \\ &= \frac{1}{n}\sum_{i=1}^{n} X_{ij}X_{ik} = \sum_{i=1}^{n} Y_{ij}Y_{ik} = \boldsymbol{Y}_j . \boldsymbol{Y}_k\end{aligned}$$

Thus, the correlation between two variables x_j and x_k can be calculated by taking the scalar product of the vectors $\boldsymbol{Y}_j$ and $\boldsymbol{Y}_k$ where the components of these vectors are the coordinates of the variable points representing the two variables.

More precisely, the projection of a vector $\boldsymbol{Y}_j$ on a principal axis defined by a vector $\boldsymbol{v}_\alpha$ represents the correlation of the corresponding variable with this axis. If the vector $\boldsymbol{Y}_j$ is close to the principal axis and its length is close to 1, this indicates a strong correlation between the variable and the axis.

Similarly, if the scalar product $\boldsymbol{Y}_j.\boldsymbol{Y}_k$ is close to 1 or – 1, this suggests a strong correlation between the variables j and k.

Conversely, if the scalar product $\boldsymbol{Y}_j.\boldsymbol{Y}_k$ is close to 0, this indicates little to no correlation between the two variables j and k.

EXAMPLE 2.10.– The graphical representations from Example 2.8 are scaled by dividing the point coordinates by $\sqrt{n} = \sqrt{20}$ (see Figure 2.20).

In the (1,2) plane, a strong correlation appears between French and History, on the one hand, and Math and Physics, on the other.

The Geography vector is nearly perpendicular to the others, indicating a negligible correlation.

In the other planes, (1,3) and (2,3), the proximity between Math and Physics, as well as French and History, confirms that their relationship in the (1,2) plane is not coincidental.

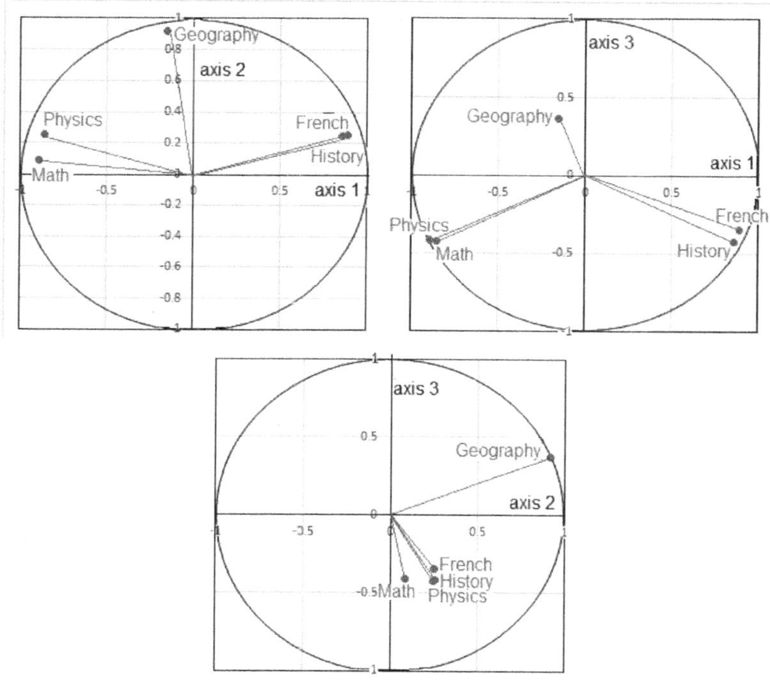

Figure 2.20. *Correlation circles in various factorial designs. For a color version of this figure, see www.iste.co.uk/cochard/mathematics3.zip*

2.3.2. *Principal component factor analysis in practice*

PCA aims not only to model data with a reduced number of parameters but also to explain the distribution of the data along the factor axes and analyze the correlation between variables.

The calculations involved can be automated using various software tools dedicated to PCA, such as R and Tanagra. A brief overview of these programs is provided in the appendix. Once results are obtained, interpreting them becomes important. As with many statistical methods, interpreting PCA results can be challenging.

A common question that arises in the interpretation of axes 1, 2, and others in the individual space. Understanding their meaning and implication is essential for effective data analysis.

EXAMPLE 2.11.– In the previous examples, the main axes for the student scatterplot were identified. Comparing the students' coordinates on principal axis 1 with the marks in various subjects allows for a graphical representation to be constructed (see Figure 2.21).

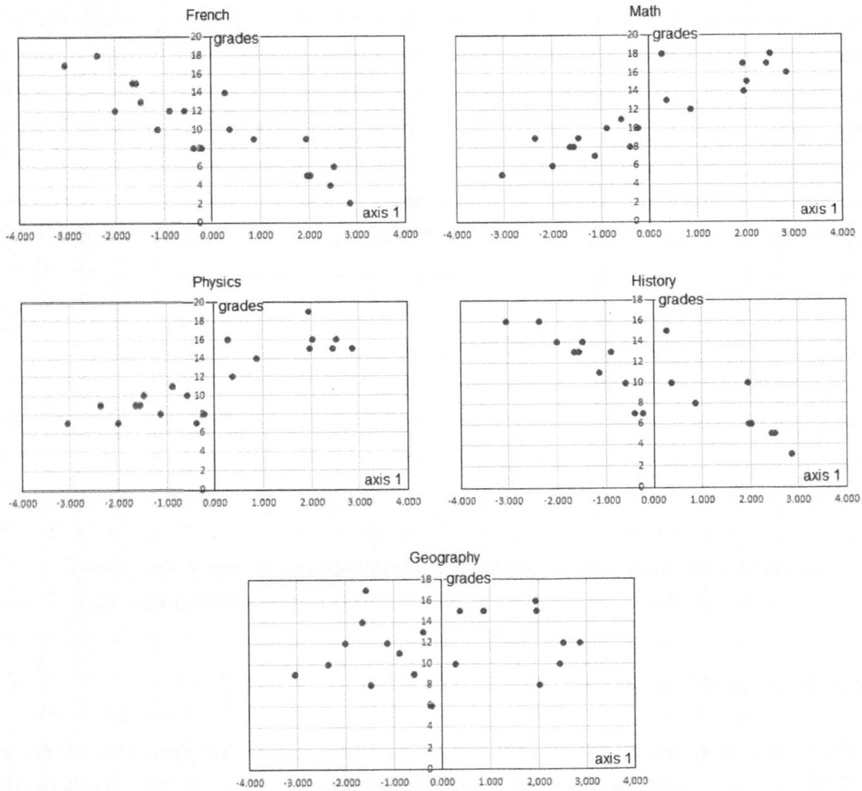

Figure 2.21. *Individual coordinate axis 1 – grades. For a color version of this figure, see www.iste.co.uk/cochard/mathematics3.zip*

Figure 2.21 shows an interpretation of principal axis 1. Grades in Math and Physics increase along this axis, while grades in French and History decrease. Consequently, principal axis 1 can be understood as distinguishing students oriented towards "scientific" disciplines on its positive side and those inclined towards "literary" disciplines on its negative side.

For Geography, the distribution along axis 1 appears relatively "neutral", showing no particular trend. This observation aligns with Figure 2.22, which indicates no significant variation in Geography grades along axis 1. Geography may be considered a subject that bridges both "scientific" and "literary" aspects.

However, examining axis 2 reveals that Geography grades increase along this axis. Figure 2.22 shows that students with higher Geography grades are positioned on the positive side of axis 2, while those with lower grades are on the negative side. This distinction helps characterize students based on their geographical skills.

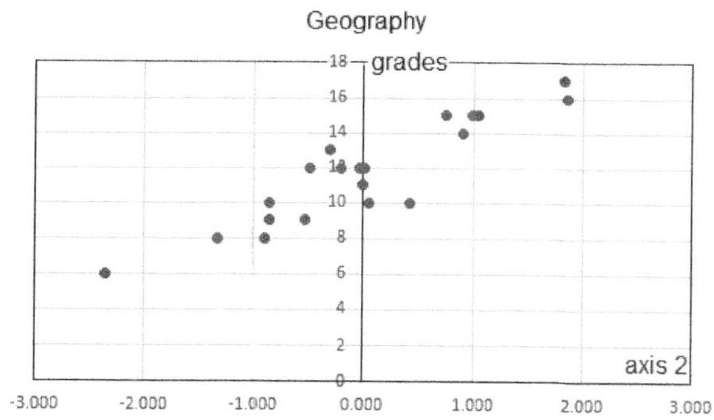

Figure 2.22. *Axis 2 individual coordinates – Geography grades. For a color version of this figure, see www.iste.co.uk/cochard/mathematics3.zip*

With these observations, the interpretation shown in Figure 2.23 can be proposed for the individual space.

On axis 1, students are distinguished based on their orientation towards "scientific" subjects (Math and Physics) versus "literary" subjects (French and History). Math and Physics grades increase along axis 1, whereas French and History grades decrease.

Axis 2 reflects variations in Geography grades. Students positioned on the positive side of axis 2 achieve higher marks in Geography, while those on the negative side show lower performance in this subject.

Additionally, the graphical representation in Example 2.9 confirms the strong correlations between French and History, as well as between Math and Physics, as indicated by the correlation matrix $\boldsymbol{c}$. This observation highlights the close connections between these pairs of variables, aligning with the results of previous analyses.

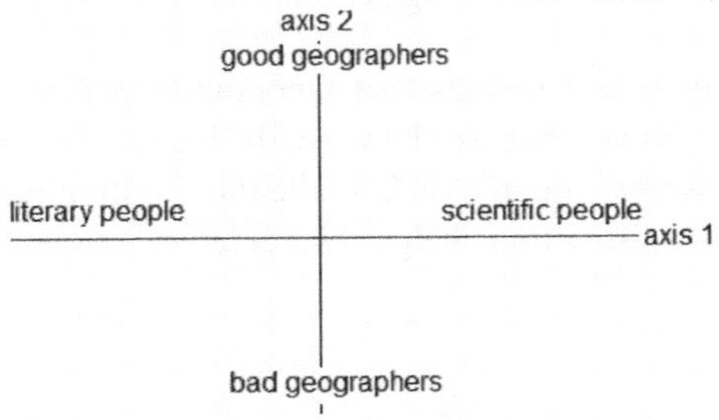

Figure 2.23. *Interpretation of factorial axes*

Interpretation aids are provided by specific PCA parameters. These parameters include eigenvalues, percentages of explained inertia, contributions of individuals and variables, squared cosines of variables, variable-individual correlations, etc. They provide additional information on the significance of axes, the dispersion of individuals, the contribution of variables, relationships between variables, etc.:

1) The "cosine squared" parameters measure the quality of the representation of an individual in the individual space. For a plane defined by two factorial axes, α and β, an individual point i is projected onto $P(i)$, with coordinates $(\boldsymbol{Xu}_\alpha)_i$ and $(\boldsymbol{Xu}_\beta)_i$, as determined previously.

The proximity of individual i to the plane (α, β) is quantified by using the square of the cosine of the angle formed by the vector $\boldsymbol{\Omega}_i$ and its projection $\boldsymbol{\Omega P(i)}$ onto the plane (see Figure 2.24). The closer point i is to the plane (α, β), the closer the squared cosine value is to 1, indicating a better representation of the individual in the space defined by axes α and β:

$$\cos^2(\theta) = \frac{\|\boldsymbol{\Omega P}(i)\|^2}{\|\boldsymbol{\Omega i}\|^2} = \frac{(Xu_\alpha)_i^2 + (Xu_\beta)_i^2}{\sum_{j=1}^{p} X_{ij}^2}$$

Since:

$$\cos^2(\theta_\alpha) = \frac{(Xu_\alpha)^2}{\sum_{j=1}^{p} X_{ij}^2} \quad \text{and} \quad \cos^2(\theta_\beta) = \frac{(Xu_\beta)^2}{\sum_{j=1}^{p} X_{ij}^2}$$

It follows that:

$$\cos^2(\theta) = \cos^2(\theta_\alpha) + \cos^2(\theta_\beta).$$

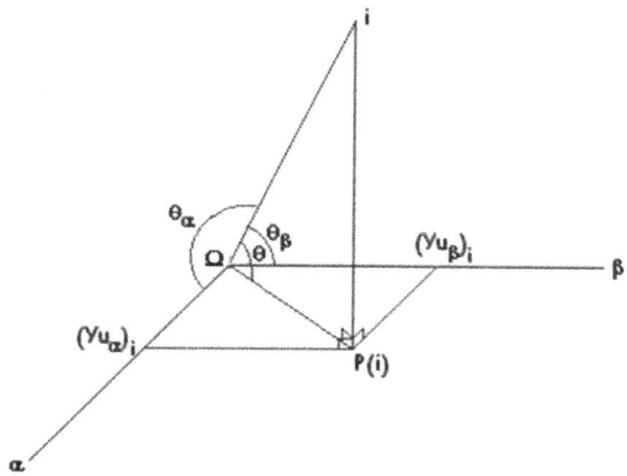

Figure 2.24. *Proximity of individual i to the plane $\alpha\beta$*

EXAMPLE 2.12.– For the example studied so far, the "cosine squared" parameters are used to access the quality of the representation of individuals in the individual space.

	$\cos^2(\alpha)$					plane(1,2)
students	axis 1	axis 2	axis 3	axis 4	axis 5	$\cos^2(\theta)$
1	0.862	0.000	0.090	0.024	0.024	0.862
2	0.381	0.530	0.080	0.008	0.001	0.911
3	0.368	0.474	0.109	0.005	0.044	0.842
4	0.969	0.000	0.010	0.020	0.000	0.969
5	0.884	0.109	0.002	0.001	0.003	0.993
6	0.801	0.000	0.131	0.061	0.007	0.801
7	0.594	0.227	0.154	0.024	0.000	0.821
8	0.951	0.029	0.013	0.003	0.004	0.980
9	0.042	0.027	0.912	0.017	0.002	0.069
10	0.776	0.111	0.104	0.009	0.000	0.887
11	0.916	0.028	0.056	0.000	0.001	0.944
12	0.012	0.028	0.941	0.005	0.014	0.039
13	0.259	0.591	0.053	0.077	0.021	0.850
14	0.093	0.783	0.058	0.031	0.034	0.876
15	0.557	0.018	0.390	0.026	0.008	0.575
16	0.832	0.000	0.157	0.009	0.002	0.832
17	0.008	0.952	0.030	0.010	0.000	0.960
18	0.648	0.280	0.042	0.021	0.009	0.928
19	0.468	0.432	0.090	0.010	0.001	0.899
20	0.738	0.225	0.023	0.007	0.006	0.963

Figure 2.25. *$\cos^2(\alpha)$ values*

Figure 2.25 shows the cosine squared values for each individual projected onto the $(1, 2)$ plane. It is evident that some individuals are closer to the plane, with cosine squares closer to 1, while others are farther away, with cosine squares closer to 0. This variation reflects the quality of the representation of individuals in this space. Specifically, students 9 and 12 are positioned further from the $(1, 2)$ plane, as indicated by the gray boxes in the last column of the figure.

This observation aligns with what is seen in Figures 2.20 and 2.21, where the projections of students 9 and 12 onto the $(1, 2)$ plane are more spread out compared to the projections of the other students. In contrast, most other students are relatively close to the $(1, 2)$ plane, suggesting that their projections are more tightly clustered together.

2) The RTC (Rank Totalized Contributions) parameters measure an individual's contribution to the inertia of a principal axis. They are defined as:

$$CTR(i,\alpha) = \frac{(\boldsymbol{X}\boldsymbol{u}_\alpha)_i^2}{\sum_{i=1}^{n}(\boldsymbol{X}\boldsymbol{u}_\alpha)_i^2}$$

Note that this definition implies that:

$$\sum_{i=1}^{n} CTR(i,\alpha) = 1$$

In practice, RTCs are typically presented as a percentage of inertia.

Following the mechanical definition of inertia $I = md^2$, where $m = \frac{1}{n}$ represents the "mass" of a point and d is the point's distance from the axis, the greatest contributions to inertia come from the points that are farthest from the axis. In other words, points that are farther from the main axis contribute more to the total inertia of the set of points.

EXAMPLE 2.13.– From the vectors $\boldsymbol{Xu}_\alpha$, the RTC parameters shown in Figure 2.26 are obtained.

It can be observed that student 8 contributes the most to axis 1, student 17 contributes the most to axis 2, student 12 contributes the most to axis 3, student 4 contributes the most to axis 4 and student 1 contributes the most to axis 5.

	RTC(i,α)				
students	axis 1	axis 2	axis 3	axis 4	axis 5
1	6.456	0.000	2.651	9.499	19.190
2	3.917	16.217	3.247	4.321	0.695
3	1.229	4.712	1.435	0.940	15.638
4	10.258	0.006	0.435	11.214	0.504
5	9.579	3.513	0.090	0.673	3.925
6	1.231	0.000	0.791	4.878	1.104
7	3.464	3.942	3.533	7.421	0.135
8	15.026	1.356	0.829	2.521	6.641
9	0.232	0.454	19.949	4.937	1.458
10	6.285	2.678	3.310	3.846	0.004
11	13.166	1.184	3.147	0.063	0.812
12	0.124	0.871	39.288	3.012	15.832
13	0.524	3.561	0.418	8.106	4.509
14	0.214	5.348	0.520	3.760	8.434
15	2.075	0.204	5.703	5.136	3.310
16	9.083	0.014	6.729	5.159	2.262
17	0.072	26.751	1.122	4.716	0.177
18	6.570	8.449	1.686	10.828	9.655
19	6.104	16.754	4.583	6.725	1.632
20	4.392	3.986	0.533	2.246	4.082

Figure 2.26. *RTC (i, α) values*

Although the parameters COS^2 and RTC are typically used for individuals, they can also be defined in variable space.

2.4. Appendix: useful software

Numerous software packages are available for data analysis. This section highlights two widely used free programs in the academic world:

1) *Tanagra* software: Tanagra is a software package developed by Ricco Rakotomalala at Lyon 2 University. It offers a user-friendly graphical interface for manipulating objects and filling in data tables. It can be used alongside the Excel spreadsheet program to facilitate statistical analysis and data exploration.

2) *R* software (or *R* language): *R* is a programming language specifically designed for statistical analysis and data visualization. It provides a broad range of packages and functions for flexible data manipulation and analysis. *R* is highly popular in the field of statistics and research, offering many advanced features for data analysis.

The information provided here is not intended to serve as a complete guide to all software features.

For more detailed instructions, users are encouraged to refer to the specific documentation for each software.

2.5. Tanagra software

Tanagra[1] is a free, open-source software package developed by Ricco Rakotomalala. It has been chosen as the analysis tool due to its ease of use. Although many other software packages are available, Tanagra is preferred for its user-friendliness and accessibility.

Tanagra software consists of three main windows. The left-hand window is used to define the desired treatment, while the right-hand window displays the results of the analysis. The bottom window contains a menu with various functions available (see Figure 2.27).

1 See: https://tanagra.software.informer.com/2.0/.

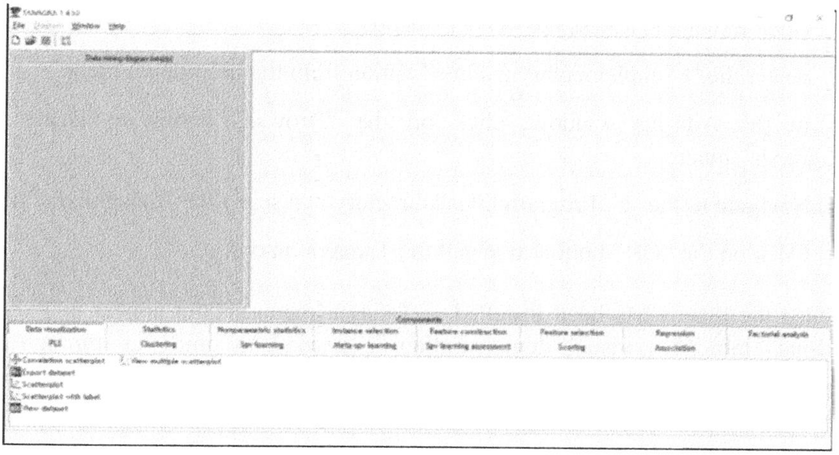

Figure 2.27. *Tanagra windows. For a color version of this figure, see www.iste.co.uk/cochard/mathematics3.zip*

Tanagra can work in conjunction with the Excel spreadsheet program, which is particularly practical since the initial data is often available in a spreadsheet. To use Tanagra, it must first be installed, a process that can be done easily and routinely by following the steps outlined below (for a PC version):

1) Download the Tanagra software by clicking on the appropriate download button on the official website.

2) Once the download is complete, locate the "setup_tanagra.exe" file on our computer and move it to an appropriate directory, for example, "C:\Tanagra".

3) Run "setup_tanagra.exe" to start the installation process. Follow the on-screen instructions to install Tanagra.

4) During installation, it is recommended to choose the default options, which will create a Tanagra directory in "C:\Program Files".

5) Be sure to check that the installation directory contains the "tanagra.xla" macro, which is required for Tanagra to function correctly.

Once installation is complete, Tanagra can be opened using the corresponding icon on our desktop or by accessing the installation directory and running the Tanagra application.

Next, in Excel, the "tanagra.xla" macro needs to be installed by following these steps:

1) Open Excel and access the "Tools" menu.

2) Select the "Complementary macros" option from the drop-down menu.

3) In the Add-ins window, click on the "Browse" button to locate the "tanagra.xla" macro.

4) Navigate to the "C:\Program Files" directory and select the "tanagra.xla" file.

5) Click on the "OK" button to install the Tanagra macro.

Once the macro has been installed, a Tanagra menu should appear in Excel's "Add-ins" tab. If a visual demonstration is needed to guide us through the Tanagra macro installation process, we can visit the following link: https://www.youtube.com/watch?v=LIedD4lPdG0.

Note that the steps may vary slightly depending on the version of Excel we are using. Be sure to consult the documentation specific to our version of Excel for detailed instructions.

a) Importing data into Tanagra

To use Tanagra, follow these steps:

1) Select the data table in Excel.

2) Go to the "Add-ins" tab in the Excel menu bar.

3) Click on the "Tanagra" option in the supplements drop-down menu.

4) Select "Run Tanagra" from the submenu.

5) A dialog box will appear to confirm the selected data range.

6) Click "OK" to confirm the chosen area.

Once this has been done, Tanagra will open, and we will be able to see the data imported into the software (as shown in Figure 2.28).

To view the table loaded in Tanagra, follow these steps:

1) In Tanagra's **Data visualization** section, select the *View dataset* component.

2) Once selected, a window will open, displaying the loaded table.

3) We will be able to see all the data in the table, including the variables and their values.

Figure 2.29 gives an idea of the appearance of the table visualization in Tanagra.

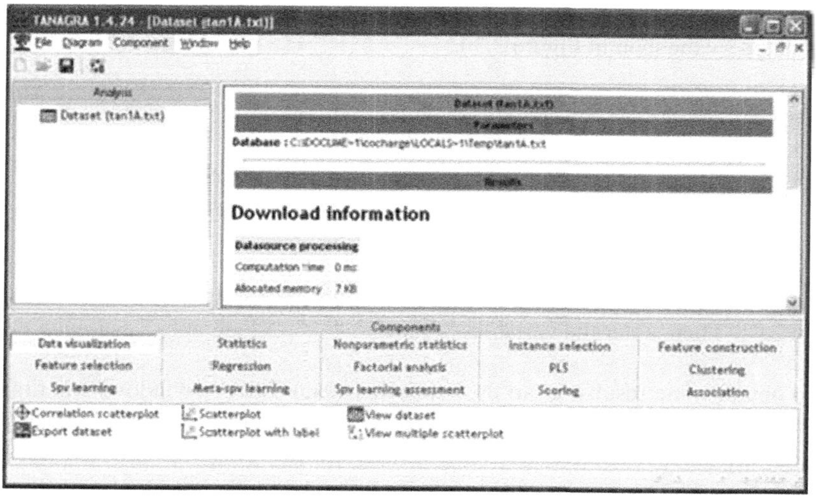

Figure 2.28. *Importing data. For a color version of this figure, see www.iste.co.uk/cochard/mathematics3.zip*

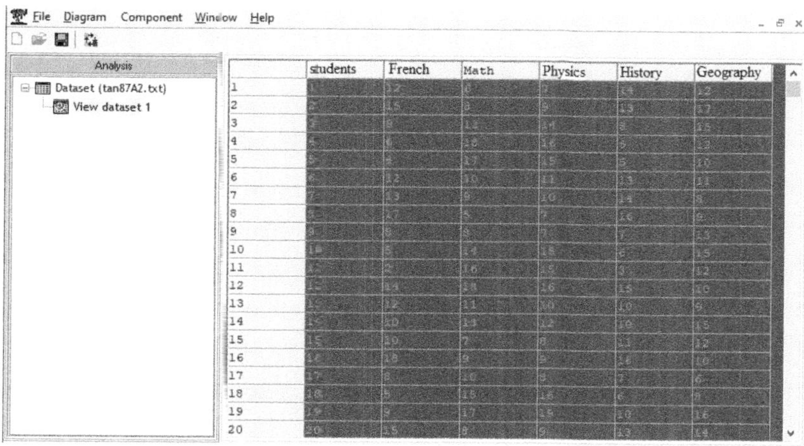

Figure 2.29. *Imported data. For a color version of this figure, see www.iste.co.uk/cochard/mathematics3.zip*

b) Basic statistics with Tanagra

To obtain statistical results in Tanagra, use the **Define status** component, represented by the icon in Figure 2.30.

Figure 2.30. *Define status component. For a color version of this figure, see www.iste.co.uk/cochard/mathematics3.zip*

In the submenu of this icon, select the **Define parameters** option, as shown in Figure 2.31. Then, enter the variables "French", "...", "Geography" as *inputs*.

To obtain some results, go to the **Statistics** menu (bottom window) and drag the **Univariate continuous stat** icon (note that the variables, although appearing as integers, are in fact continuous) onto **Define status**. This will provide, for each variable, the minimum and maximum values, the mean, the standard deviation and the ratio of standard deviation to mean, as shown in Figure 2.32.

For more detailed results, the **More univariate cont stat** icon can be used. This will provide access to additional statistics for each variable.

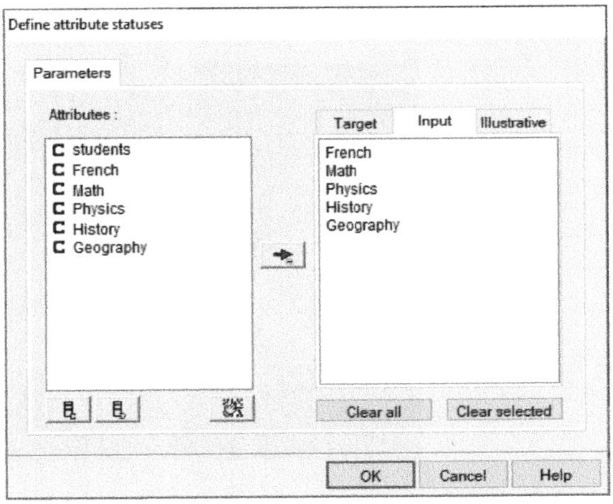

Figure 2.31. *Attribute status definition. For a color version of this figure, see www.iste.co.uk/cochard/mathematics3.zip*

c) PCA with Tanagra

Moving on to PCA:

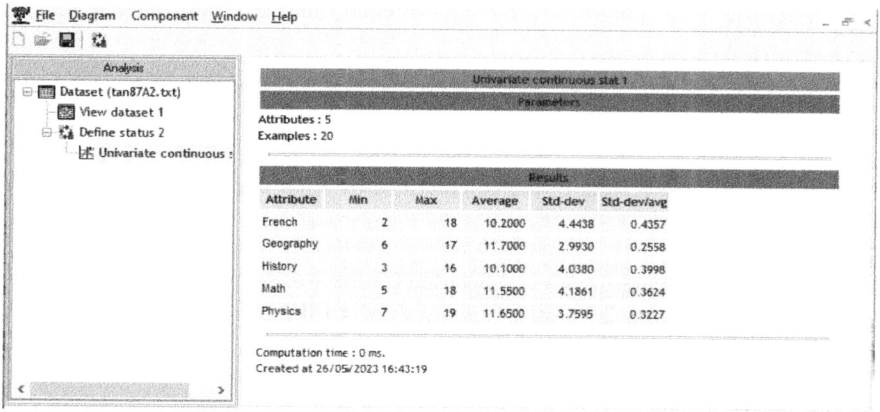

Figure 2.32. *Statistical parameters. For a color version of this figure, see www.iste.co.uk/cochard/mathematics3.zip*

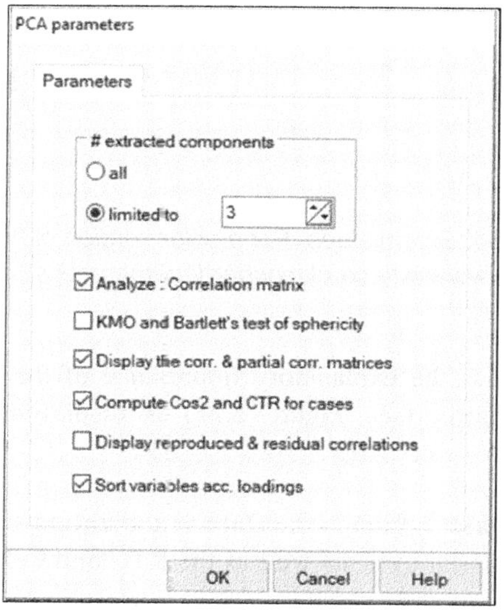

Figure 2.33. *Options*

1) Select the **Factorial analysis** menu in the lower window.

2) Then, drag the Principal component analysis icon onto Define status.

3) Define the PCA parameters by right-clicking and selecting the **Parameters** menu.

4) Choose to use three axes and calculate the values of **$\mathbf{COS}^2$** and RTC values (see Figure 2.33).

Next, visualize the results of the calculations by right-clicking and selecting the **View** menu.

In the right-hand window, several detailed results are obtained in tabular form. In the first table (see Figure 2.34), the "*eigenvalues*" of the correlation matrix and the relative inertia of each factorial axis can be seen.

Eigen values

Matrix trace	5.000000
Average	1.000000

Axis	Eigen value	Difference	Proportion (%)	Histogram	Cumulative (%)
1	3.086637	2.048349	61.73 %		61.73 %
2	1.038288	0.251390	20.77 %		82.50 %
3	0.786899	0.727575	15.74 %		98.24 %
4	0.059323	0.030472	1.19 %		99.42 %
5	0.028852	-	0.58 %		100.00 %
Tot.	5.000000	-	-	-	-

Figure 2.34. *Eigenvalues. For a color version of this figure, see www.iste.co.uk/cochard/mathematics3.zip*

The histogram shows the explanatory importance of the axes. A little further on, the correlation matrix (see Figure 2.35) is displayed, highlighting strong correlations.

Using the **View dataset** option in the **Data visualization** section, the coordinates of the points in the factorial axes, as well as the RTC and COS^2 parameters, can be obtained.

Note that all this data can be exported to a spreadsheet program using the **Component/Copy results** menu. This command copies the results from the right-hand window into memory. Then, simply paste them into a spreadsheet.

Matrices

Correlations

	Math	French	History	Physics	Geography
Math	1.00000	-0.61735	-0.57634	0.93923	0.06847
French	-0.61735	1.00000	0.95502	-0.55950	-0.03482
History	-0.57634	0.95502	1.00000	-0.48988	-0.06271
Physics	0.93923	-0.55950	-0.48988	1.00000	0.21002
Geography	0.06847	-0.03482	-0.06271	0.21002	1.00000

Figure 2.35. *Correlation matrix. For a color version of this figure, see www.iste.co.uk/cochard/mathematics3.zip*

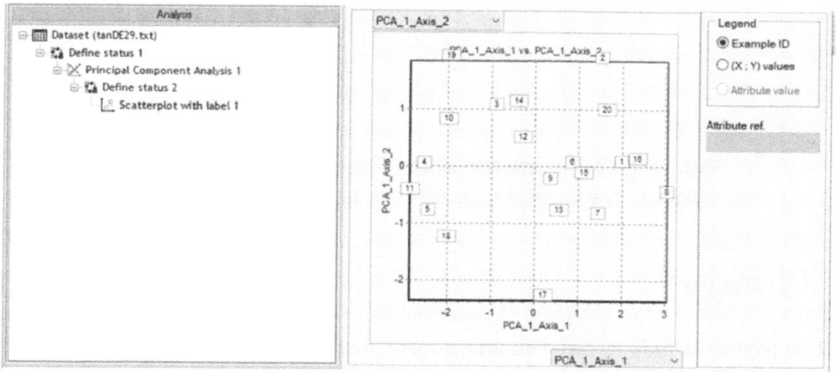

Figure 2.36. *Projection on the (1,2) plane. For a color version of this figure, see www.iste.co.uk/cochard/mathematics3.zip*

Move on to the graphical representations. First, represent the individuals in the first three factorial axes, taken in pairs. To begin with, position a **Define status** to include the variables "French" to "Geography" as Input, axes 1, 2 and 3 as Target and the students (their numbers) as Illustrative.

Next, drag the **Scatterplot with label** icon onto **Define status**. This will give the projections of the scatterplot onto the planes defined by the factorial axes 1, 2 and 3. Figure 2.36 shows the projection onto the (1, 2) plane.

Now, in the variable space, redefine the parameters using **Define status**. To obtain the correlation circle in the (1,2) plane, include the variables "French" to "Geography" as **Input**, axes 1 and 2 as **Target** and students as **Illustrative**. Then, in the **Data visualization** menu, select the **Correlation scatterplot** icon to visualize the correlation circle (refer to Figure 2.37 for an overview of this graph).

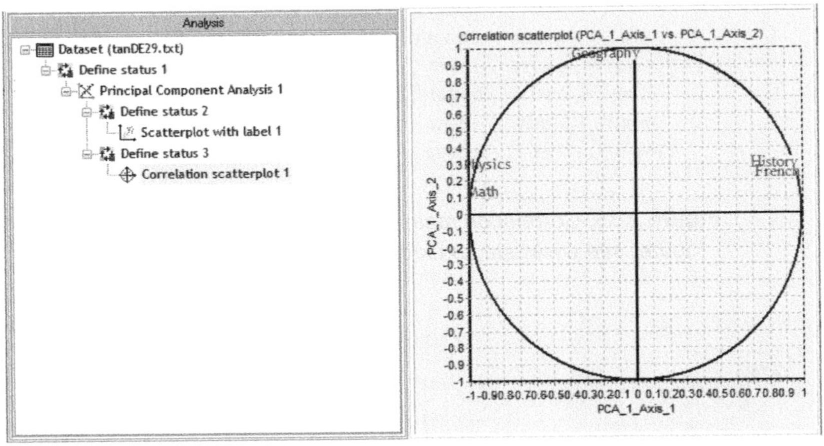

Figure 2.37. *Correlation circle. For a color version of this figure, see www.iste.co.uk/cochard/mathematics3.zip*

2.6. R software

Released in 1997, R has become a very popular software package. It offers a wide range of statistical applications, including PCA.

The basic R distribution is R-Project from CRAN (Comprehensive R Archive Network), which is a platform for installing the software. Other distributions are also available, such as Microsoft R Open. In this example, the R-Project distribution will be used. R's interface is minimalist, which is why R-Studio was developed to offer a more user-friendly interface.

For details of the installation procedure, consult:

https://larmarange.github.io/analyse-R/installation-de-R-et-RStudio.html.

To install R from http://cran.r-project.org, simply download the software and follow the instructions provided. We can then download R-Studio from https://www.rstudio.com. The installer should run smoothly.

Once R-Studio is open (see Figure 2.38), we will see a main window with four sub-windows (script window, console window, environment and history window, file window).

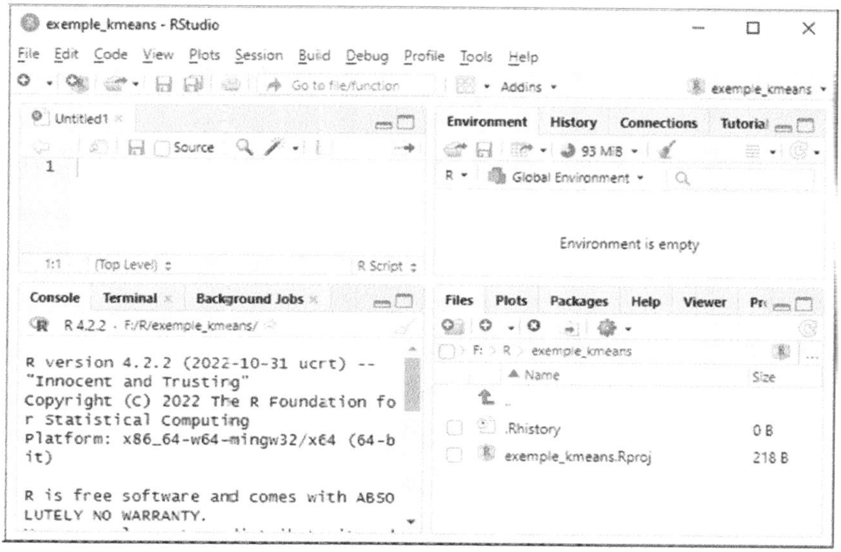

Figure 2.38. *R-Studio's four subwindows. For a color version of this figure, see www.iste.co.uk/cochard/mathematics3.zip*

The top-left window is the script window, where we can write and execute our code. The bottom-left window is the console, where we will see the “>” command prompt to enter our R commands. The top-right window is the environment window, where we can see the objects and variables created in our R session. The bottom-right window is a resource window, where we can access files, graphics and other resources.

To create a project in R-Studio, we can use the **File** tab. It is recommended to create a folder with the project name to organize our files.

Then, depending on the processing we want to perform, we will need to load the necessary libraries. R has a large number of libraries containing additional functions and tools.

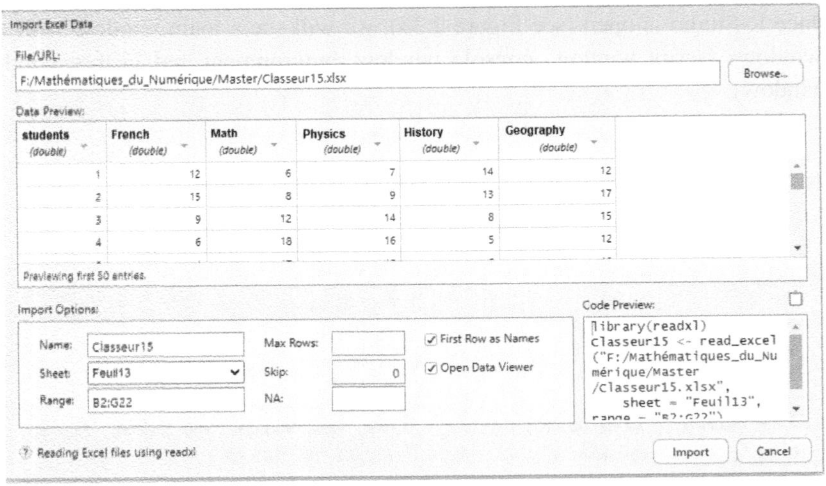

Figure 2.39. *Importing data. For a color version of this figure, see www.iste.co.uk/cochard/mathematics3.zip*

a) Importing data with R software

R allows data import from various sources, such as text files (.txt or .csv), Excel files and statistical software files such as SPSS or SAS. This example focuses on importing data from an Excel file using data from Example 2.1.

To import data:

1) Click on the **Import dataset** tab in the top right-hand window of R-Studio.

2) Select the **Excel** option and confirm.

3) A new window will open to specify the location of the Excel file, the sheet containing the data and the data range (see Figure 2.39).

4) After selecting the options, click **Import**.

The **Console** window will show the corresponding code for this action. The "*readxl*" library will load automatically, and the "*read_excel*" function will create a data table, typically named "Workbook15". The **view()** function displays the imported data in the top left-hand window:

```
> library(readxl)

> Classeur15 <-
read_excel("F:/Mathématiques_du_Numérique/Master/Classeur15.xlsx",

+ sheet = "Feuil13", range = "B2:G22")

> View(Classeur15)
```

b) Basic statistics with R software

The **summary()** function in R can be used to obtain basic statistical information for each column in a dataset, such as "Workbook15". This function provides the following statistics for each variable: the minimum value, the first quartile (25th percentile), the median (50th percentile), the mean, the third quartile (75th percentile) and the maximum value:

```
> summary(Classeur15)

    students          French           Math

 Min.   : 1.00   Min.   : 2.00   Min.   : 5.00

 1st Qu.: 5.75   1st Qu.: 7.50   1st Qu.: 8.00

 Median :10.50   Median :10.00   Median :10.50

 Mean   :10.50   Mean   :10.20   Mean   :11.55

 3rd Qu. :15.25   3rd Qu. :13.25   3rd Qu. :15.25

 Max.   :20.00   Max.   :18.00   Max.   :18.00

    Physics         History         Geography

 Min.   : 7.00   Min.   : 3.00   Min.   : 6.00

 1st Qu.: 8.75   1st Qu.: 6.75   1st Qu.: 9.75

 Median :10.50   Median :10.00   Median :12.00

 Mean   :11.65   Mean   :10.10   Mean   :11.70

 3rd Qu. :15.00   3rd Qu. :13.25   3rd Qu. :14.25

 Max.   :19.00   Max.   :16.00   Max.   :17.00
```

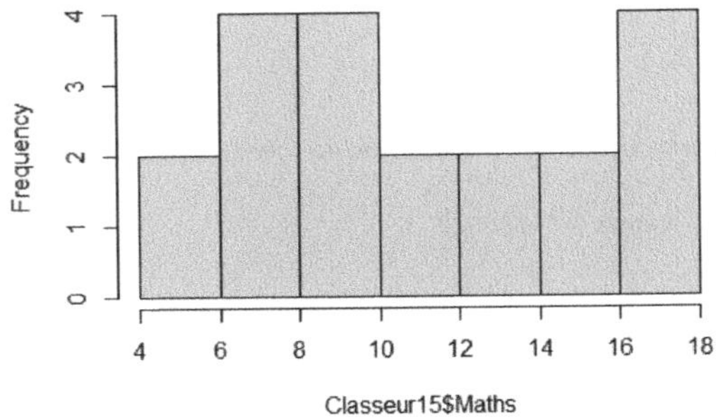

Figure 2.40. *Histogram of the Math variable*

The histogram of a variable, such as "Math", can be obtained using the **hist()** function in R (see Figure 2.40). It is important to note that the "$" symbol is used to access a specific component of an object. In this example, "Classeur15$Math" refers to the "Math" column of the "Classeur15" object:

```
> hist(Classeur15$Math)
```

The mean can be calculated using the **mean()** function, and the standard deviation using the **sd()** function. For example, to obtain the mean of the "Math" variable in the "Workbook15" object, the following code can be used:

```
> mean(Classeur15$Math)

[1] 11.55
```

and for the standard deviation:

```
> sd(Classeur15$Math)

[1] 4.18613
```

c) PCA with R software

To perform PCA on the data table, first select only the columns corresponding to the variables of interest. In the example, retain only the variable columns and exclude any categorical variables, such as student identifiers:

```
> tab <- Classeur15[,2:6]
```

In Classeur 15, only columns 2–6 are kept, while all the rows are retained. Note the "<-" assignment sign.

To perform PCA, the **PCA()** function in the **FactoMineR** library will be used. Additionally, the **factoextra** library is required to visualize the PCA results. Here is how to load these libraries and run the PCA:

```
> library(FactoMineR)

> library(factoextra)

> res.PCA <- PCA(tab)
```

res.PCA contains the results of the factorial analysis. Note that the correlation circle is displayed automatically (see Figure 2.41).

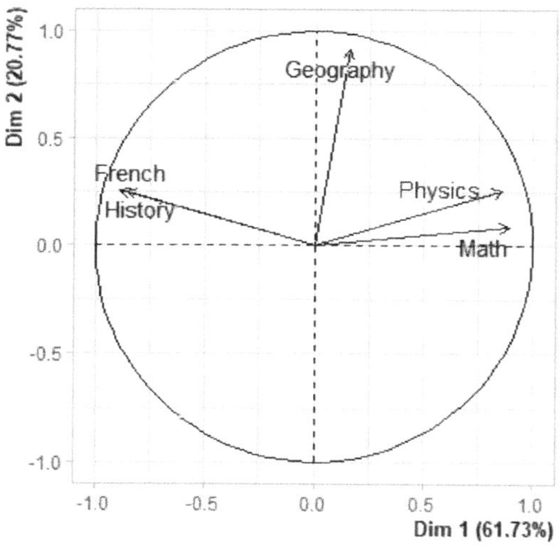

Figure 2.41. *Correlation circle*

The **summary()** function displays details of the **res.PCA** result, including eigenvalues, variance explained, variable coordinates on factorial axes and other information. Here is how to use the **summary()** function:

```
> summary(res.PCA)

> summary(res.PCA)

Call:
```

```
PCA(X = tab)

Eigenvalues

                      Dim.1   Dim.2   Dim.3   Dim.4   Dim.5

Variance              3.087   1.038   0.787   0.059   0.029

% of var.            61.733  20.766  15.738   1.186   0.577

Cumulative % of var. 61.733  82.499  98.236  99.423 100.000

Individuals (the 10 first)

      Dist    Dim.1    ctr   cos2    Dim.2    ctr   cos2    Dim.3    ctr   cos2

1  |  2.151 | -1.996  6.456  0.862 |  0.005  0.000  0.000 | -0.646  2.648  0.090|

2  |  2.520 | -1.555  3.917  0.381 |  1.835 16.208  0.530 | -0.716  3.259  0.081|

3  |  1.437 |  0.871  1.229  0.368 |  0.989  4.707  0.473 | -0.476  1.440  0.110|

4  |  2.557 |  2.516 10.258  0.969 | -0.034  0.005  0.000 |  0.261  0.434  0.010|

5  |  2.586 |  2.432  9.579  0.884 | -0.854  3.512  0.109 |  0.120  0.091  0.002|

6  |  0.974 | -0.872  1.231  0.801 | -0.009  0.000  0.000 |  0.353  0.791  0.131|

7  |  1.898 | -1.462  3.464  0.594 | -0.904  3.938  0.227 |  0.747  3.541  0.155|

8  |  3.123 | -3.046 15.026  0.951 | -0.530  1.355  0.029 |  0.362  0.832  0.013|

9  |  1.856 | -0.379  0.232  0.042 | -0.308  0.458  0.028 | -1.772 19.946  0.911|

10 |  2.237 |  1.970  6.284  0.776 |  0.745  2.674  0.111 | -0.722  3.316  0.104|

Variables

             Dim.1    ctr   cos2    Dim.2    ctr   cos2    Dim.3    ctr   cos2

French   |  -0.890 25.659  0.792 |  0.253  6.154  0.064 |  0.348 15.405  0.121 |

Math     |   0.892 25.774  0.796 |  0.086  0.706  0.007 |  0.415 21.913  0.172 |

Physics  |   0.858 23.831  0.736 |  0.255  6.277  0.065 |  0.422 22.623  0.178 |

History  |  -0.860 23.945  0.739 |  0.248  5.946  0.062 |  0.425 22.903  0.180 |

Geography|   0.156  0.791  0.024 |  0.917 80.916  0.840 | -0.367 17.156  0.135 |
```

To obtain the eigenvalues directly and display their histogram, we can use the *get_eigenvalue()* function on the *res.PCA* object, followed by the *barplot()* function to plot the histogram:

```
> get_eigenvalue(res.PCA)
      eigenvalue variance.percent cumulative.variance.percent
Dim.1 3.08663727        61.7327454                    61.73275
Dim.2 1.03828848        20.7657696                    82.49852
Dim.3 0.78689880        15.7379759                    98.23649
Dim.4 0.05932348         1.1864697                    99.42296
Dim.5 0.02885197         0.5770393                   100.00000
> fviz_eig(res.PCA)
```

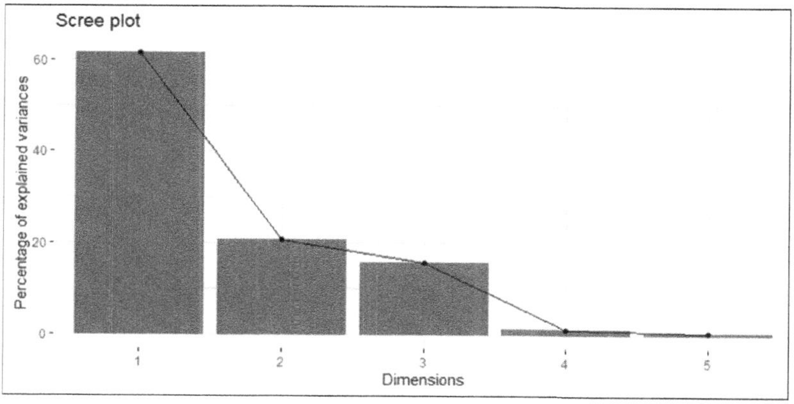

Figure 2.42. *Histogram of eigenvalues. For a color version of this figure, see www.iste.co.uk/cochard/mathematics3.zip*

To obtain the projection of the individual space onto the first two factorial axes, use the **fviz_pca_ind()** function with the **res.PCA** object as the argument. Similarly, to project the variable space, use the **fviz_pca_var()** function, also with the **res.PCA** object as the argument (see Figure 2.43):

```
> fviz_pca_ind(res.PCA)
> fviz_pca_var(res.PCA)
```

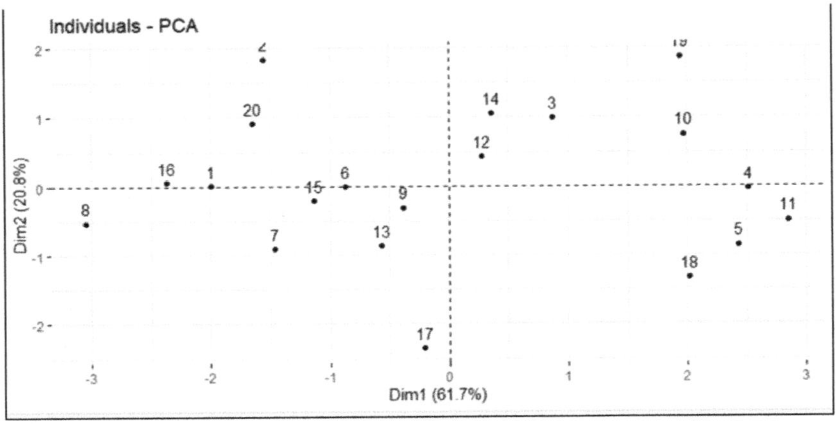

Figure 2.43. *Individual projections on the (1, 2) plane*

For more details on PCA with R, visit the STHDA website[2].

This practical guide provides detailed explanations of the key concepts of PCA, along with sample R code for each stage of the analysis. It covers various aspects of PCA, including data import, pre-processing, interpretation of results and graph visualization.

Feel free to consult this guide to deepen our knowledge of PCA with R and discover practical tips for data analysis and visualization.

2 See: www.sthda.com/french/articles/38-methodes-des-composantes-principales-dans-r-guide-pratique/73-acp-analyse-en-composantes-principales-avec-r-l-essentiel/.

3

Introduction to Automatic Classification

CONCEPTS COVERED IN THIS CHAPTER.–

This chapter serves as a natural extension of Chapter 2, focusing on data analysis within a specific framework: the automated categorization of a population, commonly referred to as automatic classification.

It begins by introducing the foundational concepts of similarity, dissimilarity and distance. Using principles from information theory and the notion of entropy, an example illustrates how classification can be performed based on defined criteria.

Two key classification approaches are then explored:

– partitioning classification through the moving center method (*k-means*), and

– hierarchical classification using aggregation strategies, including Ward's strategy.

The appendix provides practical application to Tanagra and R for automatic classification, building on the methodologies discussed in the preceding chapter.

References: [KEL 20, SAP 11, TUF 12, COR 18, HUS 16, TAN 00].

Mathematics for Digital Science 3,
by Gérard-Michel COCHARD and Mhand HIFI.

The aim of classification, also referred to as clustering, is to group a statistical set of individuals into homogeneous categories. When the structure of the population of individuals is unknown and the number of individuals is large, as is often the case in statistical studies, mechanical procedures become essential. These procedures rely on algorithms, which are implemented using computer. Such an approach is termed "automatic" cluster analysis, in contrast to manual classification.

3.1. Similarity and distance

3.1.1. *Similarity, dissimilarity*

Several algorithms are essential for defining classes and assigning individuals to them. To belong to the same class, individuals must share similar characteristics, whereas those in different classes should display different characteristics. These requirements necessitate a precise definition of the fundamental concepts of similarity and dissimilarity.

Similarity is a function, denoted by f, that assigns a real number $f(i,j)$ to any pair of individuals (i,j), where individuals are numbered by integers. The function satisfies the following properties:

– Symmetry: $f(i,j) = f(j,i)$ for any pair (i,j) of individuals.

– Non-negativity: $f(i,j) \geq 0$ for any pair (i,j) of individuals.

– Increase: $f(i,i) \geq f(i,j)$ for any pair (i,j) of distinct individuals $(i \neq j)$.

These properties ensure that similarity is a symmetrical, non-negative measure reflecting the degree of similarity (resemblance) between individuals.

Dissimilarity is a function, denoted by g, that assigns a real number $g(i,j)$ to any pair of individuals (i,j). The function satisfies the following properties:

– Symmetry: $g(i,j) = g(j,i)$ for any pair (i,j) of individuals.

– Non-negativity: $g(i,j) \geq 0$ for any pair (i,j) of individuals.

– Reflexivity: $g(i,i) = 0$ for any individual i.

These properties guarantee that dissimilarity is a symmetrical, non-negative measure, with the dissimilarity between an individual and itself being zero.

3.1.2. *Distance*

The definition of dissimilarity is closely related to that of distance, which is more commonly used in statistics.

A *distance* is a function, denoted by d, that assigns a real number $d(i,j)$ to any pair of individuals (i,j). The function satisfies the following properties:

– Symmetry: $d(i,j) = d(j,i)$ for any pair (i,j) of individuals.

– Non-negativity: $d(i,j) \geq 0$ for any pair (i,j) of individuals.

– Reflexivity: $d(i,i) = 0$ for any individual i.

– Identity: $d(i,j) = 0$ if and only if $i = j$ (the distance between two individuals is zero if and only if they are identical).

– Triangular inequality: $d(i,j) \leq d(i,k) + d(k,j)$ for any triplet of individuals (i,j,k).

Note that "distance" possesses all the properties of dissimilarity, but the reverse is not always true. This distinction allows distance to be used as a measure of dissimilarity. However, there are various ways to define a distance, which will be explored in more detail later.

When the characteristics of individuals are expressed as numbers, these characteristics represent quantitative variables, allowing for the definition of distance measures based on these numbers.

For simplicity, assume that individuals are characterized by a set of p quantitative variables: $x_1, x_2, \dots, x_p$. For each individual i, a set of values is available: $x_1(i), x_2(i), \dots, x_p(i)$. In practice, all values for all individuals can be organized in a matrix of individuals by variables, as seen in factorial analysis. For an individual i, the vector $\boldsymbol{x}(i)$ can be considered, where the components are $x_1(i), x_2(i), \dots, x_p(i)$.

The most common definition of a distance (squared) is given by the following matrix expression:

$$d^2(i,j) = d^2(\boldsymbol{x}(i), \boldsymbol{x}(j)) = [\boldsymbol{x}(i) - \boldsymbol{x}(j)]^t \, \boldsymbol{M} \, [\boldsymbol{x}(i) - \boldsymbol{x}(j)],$$

where $\boldsymbol{M}$ is a square matrix of size $p \times p$, and the symbol $[.]^t$ represents the transpose of a vector or matrix.

When the matrix $\boldsymbol{M}$ is the identity matrix, the expression simplifies to:

$$d^2(i,j) = \sum_{k=1}^{p} [x_k(i) - x_k(j)]^2$$

This corresponds to the *Euclidean distance*, which is widely used in classical geometry.

If the matrix $\boldsymbol{M}$ is a diagonal matrix with the values $1/\sigma_k^2$ on the diagonal, where σ_k^2 is the variance of the variable x_k, the following squared distance is obtained:

$$d^2(i,j) = \sum_{k=1}^{p} \frac{[x_k(i) - x_k(j)]^2}{\sigma_k^2} = \sum_{k=1}^{p} \left[\frac{x_k(i)}{\sigma_k} - \frac{x_k(j)}{\sigma_k}\right]^2$$

This relationship expresses normalization by standard deviation.

Another distance definition uses the matrix $\boldsymbol{M} = \boldsymbol{V}^{-1}$, where $\boldsymbol{V}$ is the covariance matrix of the variables (i.e. each element of $\boldsymbol{V}$ represents the covariance between the variables x_k and x_l: $cov(x_k, x_l)$). This distance is known as the *Mahalanobis distance*.

The Mahalanobis distance between individuals i and j is defined as follows:

$$d(i,j) = \sqrt{\left(x(i) - x(j)\right)^t \times \mathbf{V}^{(-1)} \times \left(x(i) - x(j)\right)}$$

This allows correlations between variables to be considered, and the similarity between individuals can be quantified while accounting for the statistical structure of the data.

In addition to the distance measures discussed above, other commonly used distance measures include the "*Manhattan distance*" and the "*Chebyshev distance*".

The *Manhattan distance*, also known as the L_1-distance, is defined as follows:

$$d(i,j) = \sum_{k=1}^{p} |x_k(i) - x_k(j)|$$

This distance represents the total distance covered by moving exclusively along the axes (horizontally and vertically) in a *Cartesian plane*, which is why it is called the *Manhattan distance*, after the neighborhood where the streets are perpendicular.

As for the *Chebychev distance,* also called infinite distance or distance $L_\infty - distance$, is defined as:

$$d(i,j) = \max_k |x_k(i) - x_k(j)|$$

This distance measures the maximum difference along all axes, considering the greatest difference between the coordinates.

Another commonly used distance measure is the *Minkowski distance,* which generalizes both the Manhattan and Euclidean distances. The Minkowski distance is defined as follows, for a parameter q greater than zero:

$$d(i,j) = \left[\sum_{k=1}^{p} |x_k(i) - x_k(j)|^q\right]^{\frac{1}{q}}$$

Such a distance includes both the Manhattan distance (for $q = 1$) and the Euclidean distance (for $q = 2$).

As illustrated (and this is just a sample), there are many different definitions of distance. Consequently, it is essential to specify the distance definition used each time it is referred. However, in most cases, the Euclidean distance is commonly used, the distance normalized by standard deviations, which ensures all variables are given equal weight.

It is also worth noting that the Euclidean distance is often preferred due to its simplicity and interpretability. It measures the geometric distance between two points in a multidimensional space, defined as the square root of the sum of the squares of the differences between the values of the variables. However, it is important to note that the Euclidean distance is not always the best option, as it can be sensitive to the scale of the variables.

3.2. Basics of information theory

The foundations of information theory were primarily established by Claude Shannon, who introduced the concept of information entropy (the term *entropy* has already been used as a measure of state in thermodynamics).

To start with simple concepts, consider a text composed of n symbols, from which one symbol, denoted by i, is randomly selected. The probability of the symbol i occurring is given by $p(i)$, and the amount of information conveyed by the symbol i is defined as:

$$Q(i) = -\log_s\big(p(i)\big).$$

In this expression, s represents the base of the logarithm, which is initially arbitrary. The negative sign ("–") is used to ensure positive values. Typically, $s = 2$ is chosen, allowing the quantity of information to be measured in bits. Recall that:

$$\log_s(x) = \frac{\ln(x)}{\ln(s)}$$

where "ln" represents the natural logarithm.

Using the quantity $Q(i)$, Claude Shannon defined the entropy S of the set of symbols by the following expression:

$$S = \sum_{i=1}^{n} p(i)Q(i) = -\sum_{i=1}^{n} p(i)\log_2\big(p(i)\big)$$

This formula calculates the entropy of a set of symbols, taking into account the probabilities $p(i)$ associated with each symbol and the amount of information they contain, $Q(i)$.

EXAMPLE 3.1.– Let us apply this definition of entropy to an example to better understand its meaning. Consider a deck of 52 distinct cards. The probability of drawing any card i from this deck is $p(i) = \frac{1}{52} = 0.0192$, and the entropy of the deck is:

$$S = -52 \times \frac{1}{52}\log_2\left(\frac{1}{52}\right) = 5.7 \text{ bits}$$

Now, consider drawing a card from a given suit (diamonds, or clubs, or hearts, or spades). The corresponding probability is $p(color) = \frac{13}{52}$, and the entropy of the game, where cards are distinguished by suit only, is:

$$S = -4 \times \frac{13}{52}\log_2\left(\frac{13}{52}\right) = 2 \text{ bits}$$

Since $-\log_2(x)$ decreases as x increases, it is therefore normal to find a smaller result for $S(color)$ than for $S(card)$.

Let us go a step further and consider a four-card deck. Here are various cases:

1) All cards identical $p(i) = 1$:

$$S = -1 \times \log_2(1) = 0 \text{ bit}$$

2) Three identical cards of one kind and one card of another kind:

With $p(i) = \frac{3}{4}$ and $p(j) = \frac{1}{4}$,

$$S = -\frac{3}{4} \times \log_2\left(\frac{3}{4}\right) - \frac{1}{4} \times \log_2\left(\frac{1}{4}\right) = 0.811 \text{ bits}$$

The reader can calculate the entropy for the other situations in Figure 3.1, and verify the results.

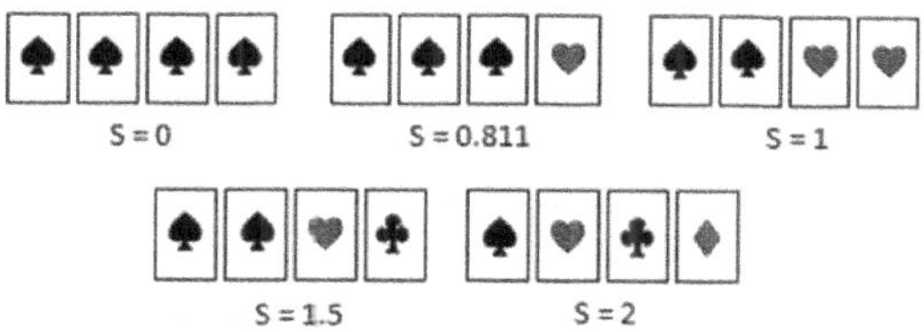

Figure 3.1. *Entropy for various situations. For a color version of this figure, see www.iste.co.uk/cochard/mathematics3.zip*

An intuitive understanding of entropy can be derived from the previous example: it measures the heterogeneity of a set. When the set is homogeneous, meaning all symbols have the same probability of occurrence, entropy is minimal and equal to zero. On the other hand, when the set is heterogeneous, with different probabilities for each symbol, entropy increases.

This interpretation is consistent with common sense: low entropy indicates that the system is predictable and contains little information, while high entropy suggests a greater level of unpredictability and more information.

So, what is the connection between entropy and classification?

EXAMPLE 3.2.– For better clarity, consider the following example, which involves determining whether or not to play tennis based on three criteria: the sky, wind and temperature. The possible values for each criterion are:

– *Sky*: sunny (*S*), cloudy (*C*), risk of rain (*R*).

– *Wind*: strong (*s*), light (*l*).

– *Temperature*: high (*h*), medium (*m*), cool (*c*).

The objective is to decide whether or not tennis can be played according to these criteria. A set of observations is available to help with this decision.

By referring to the table in Figure 3.2, which lists the observations, a classification can be made using the three criteria of sky, wind and temperature. Figure 3.3 shows this classification.

observation	sky	wind	temperature	play
1	S	s	h	no
2	C	l	m	yes
3	S	s	c	no
4	R	l	h	yes
5	C	s	m	no
6	R	l	c	no
7	S	s	h	no
8	C	l	m	yes
9	S	l	c	yes
10	R	s	h	no
11	S	l	m	yes
12	C	l	c	yes

Figure 3.2. *Table of observations*

sky					
S		C		R	
1	yes	2	yes	1	yes
3	no	5	no	6	no
7	no	8	yes	10	no
9	yes	12	yes		
11	yes				

wind			
s		l	
1	no	2	yes
3	no	4	yes
5	no	6	no
7	no	8	yes
10	no	9	yes
		11	yes
		12	yes

temperature					
h		m		c	
1	no	2	yes	3	no
4	yes	5	no	6	no
7	no	8	yes	9	yes
10	no	11	yes	12	yes

Figure 3.3. *Classification according to the three criteria*

In the table in Figure 3.2, there are six observations where tennis is not played (no) and six observations where tennis is played (yes). To calculate the total entropy, the entropy formula given earlier is used:

$$S = -p(no) \times \log_2(p(no)) - p(\text{yes}) \times \log_2(p(\text{yes}))$$

where $p(\text{no})$ is the probability of obtaining the no class (in this case, 6/12) and $p(\text{yes})$ is the probability of obtaining the "yes" class (also $6/12$).

The total entropy is calculated as:

$$S = -\left(\frac{6}{12}\right)\log_2\left(\frac{6}{12}\right) - \left(\frac{6}{12}\right)\log_2\left(\frac{6}{12}\right) = 1 \text{ bit}$$

Thus, the total entropy in this example is 1 bit.

In the tables of Figure 3.3, different datasets are provided, allowing for entropy calculations as follows:

$$S(sky, S) = -\frac{3}{5}\log_2\left(\frac{3}{5}\right) - \frac{2}{5}\log_2\left(\frac{2}{5}\right) = 0.971 \text{ bit}$$

$$S(sky, C) = -\frac{3}{4}\log_2\left(\frac{3}{4}\right) - \frac{1}{4}\log_2\left(\frac{1}{4}\right) = 0.811 \text{ bit}$$

$$S(sky, R) = -\frac{1}{3}\log_2\left(\frac{1}{3}\right) - \frac{2}{3}\log_2\left(\frac{2}{3}\right) = 0.918 \text{ bit}$$

Thus, $S(sky) = \frac{5}{12}S(sky, S) + \frac{4}{12}S(sky, C) + \frac{3}{12}S(sky, R) = 0.904$ bit.

Similarly,

$$S(wind, s) = -\frac{5}{5}\log_2\left(\frac{5}{5}\right) = 0 \text{ bit}$$

$$S(wind, l) = -\frac{6}{7}\log_2\left(\frac{6}{7}\right) - \frac{1}{7}\log_2\left(\frac{1}{7}\right) = 0.592 \text{ bit}$$

Thus,

$$S(wind) = \frac{5}{12}S(wind, s) + \frac{7}{12}S(wind, l) = 0.345 \text{ bit}$$

and,

$$S(temperature, h) = -\frac{1}{4}\log_2\left(\frac{1}{4}\right) - \frac{3}{4}\log_2\left(\frac{3}{4}\right) = 0.811 \text{ bit}$$

$$S(temperature, m) = -\frac{3}{4}\log_2\left(\frac{3}{4}\right) - \frac{1}{4}\log_2\left(\frac{1}{4}\right) = 0.811 \text{ bit}$$

$$S(temperature, c) = -\frac{2}{4}\log_2\left(\frac{2}{4}\right) - \frac{2}{4}\log_2\left(\frac{2}{4}\right) = 1 \text{ bit}$$

Thus,

$$S(temperature) = \frac{4}{12}S(temperature, h) + \frac{4}{12}S(temperature, m) + \frac{4}{12}S(temperature, c) = 0.874 \text{ bit}$$

In this case, the "bulk" system corresponds to unclassified data, and the "classified" system refers to data classified according to the criteria.

The information gain is defined as the difference between the entropy of the "bulk" system and the entropy of the "classified" system. The information gain G is calculated as follows:

$$G(total > sky) = S(total) - S(sky) = 1 - 0.904 = 0.096 \text{ bit}$$

$$G(total > wind) = S(total) - S(wind) = 1 - 0.345 = 0.655 \text{ bit}$$

$$G(total > temperature) = S(total) - S(temperature) = 1 - 0.874 = 0.126 \text{ bit}$$

The highest gain among the three classifications is that of $G(\text{total} > \text{wind})$, indicating that the wind criterion is the most discriminating in the decision-making process. This can be illustrated as the start of a decision tree, as shown in Figure 3.4.

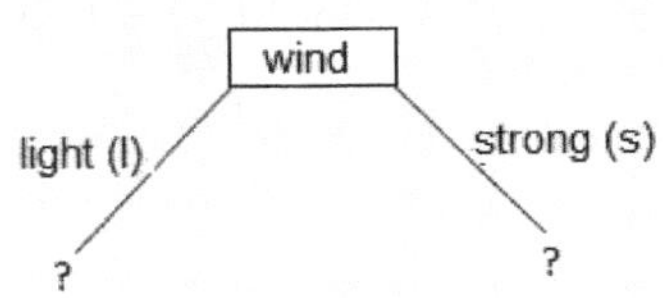

Figure 3.4. *Beginning of a decision tree*

To continue tracing the decision tree from the light and strong wind situations, the next criterion to consider is either sky or temperature for each case. The complete decision tree is shown in Figure 3.5. It displays the different combinations of the wind, sky and temperature criteria, along with the "yes" or "no" results associated with each combination.

strong wind > sky					
S		C		R	
1	no	5	no	10	no
3	no				
7	no				

strong wind > temperature					
h		m		c	
1	no	5	no	3	no
7	no				
10	no				

light wind > sky					
S		C		R	
9	yes	2	yes	4	yes
11	yes	8	yes	6	no
		12	yes		

light wind > temperature					
h		m		c	
4	yes	2	yes	6	no
		8	yes	9	yes
		11	yes	12	yes

Figure 3.5. *Complete situation for the decision tree*

The following can be deduced from these tables:

$$S(wind\ l > sky\ S) = -\frac{2}{2}\log_2\left(\frac{2}{2}\right) = 0 \text{ bit}$$

$$S(wind\ l > sky\ C) = -\frac{3}{3}\log_2\left(\frac{3}{3}\right) = 0 \text{ bit}$$

$$S(wind\ l > sky\ R) = -\frac{1}{2}\log_2\left(\frac{1}{2}\right) - \frac{1}{2}\log_2\left(\frac{1}{2}\right) = 1 \text{ bit}$$

$$S(wind\ l > sky) = \frac{2}{7} \times 0 + \frac{3}{7} \times 0 + \frac{2}{7} \times 1 = 0.286 \text{ bit}$$

$$S(wind\ l > temperature\ h) = -\frac{1}{1}\log_2\left(\frac{1}{1}\right) = 0 \text{ bit}$$

$$S(wind\ l > temperature\ m) = -\frac{3}{3}\log_2\left(\frac{3}{3}\right) = 0 \text{ bit}$$

$$S(wind\ l > temperature\ c) = -\frac{2}{3}\log_2\left(\frac{2}{3}\right) - \frac{1}{3}\log_2\left(\frac{1}{3}\right) = 0.918 \text{ bit}$$

$$S(wind\ l > temperature) = \frac{1}{7} \times 0 + \frac{3}{7} \times 0 + \frac{3}{7} \times 0.918 = 0.393 \text{ bit}$$

Hence, for the gains:

G(wind l > sky) = *S(wind l)* - *S(wind l > sky)* = 0.592 - 0.286 = 0.306 bit

G(wind l > temperature) = *S(wind l)* - *S(wind l > temperature)* = 0.592 - 0.393 = 0.199 bit

The highest gain is obtained for the *light wind > sky* classification. This means that the sky criterion is the most informative for predicting the outcome when the wind is light. In other words, the decision tree branch continues with the sky criterion.

On the other hand:

$$S(wind\ s > sky\ S) = -\frac{3}{3}\log_2\left(\frac{3}{3}\right) = 0 \text{ bit}$$

$$S(wind\ s > sky\ C) = -\frac{1}{1}\log_2\left(\frac{1}{1}\right) = 0 \text{ bit}$$

$$S(wind\ s > sly\ R) = -\frac{1}{1}\log_2\left(\frac{1}{1}\right) = 0 \text{ bit}$$

$$S(wind\ s > sky) = 0 \text{ bit}$$

$$S(wind\ s > temperature\ h) = -\frac{3}{3}\log_2\left(\frac{3}{3}\right) = 0 \text{ bit}$$

$$S(wind\ s > temperature\ m) = -\frac{1}{1}\log_2\left(\frac{1}{1}\right) = 0 \text{ bit}$$

$$S(wind\ s > temperature\ c) = -\frac{1}{1}\log_2\left(\frac{1}{1}\right) = 0 \text{ bit}$$

$$S(wind\ s > temperature) = 0$$

An analysis of the data shows that the information gain for the *strong wind > sky* and *strong wind > temperature* classifications is equal to 0 bits. This means that both criteria provide the same amount of information for predicting the result when the wind is strong.

Consequently, either the *sky* or the *temperature* criterion can be chosen to continue the branch corresponding to strong wind in the decision tree.

In this example, the *sky* criterion is selected to continue building the tree. After completing the decision tree (see Figure 3.6) based on the *wind* and *sky* criteria, the following correspondences for each branch can be observed:

– The *light wind* > *sky S* branch corresponds only to "yes" answers.

– The *light wind* > *sky C* branch corresponds only to "yes" answers.

– The *strong wind* > *sky S* branch corresponds solely to "no" answers.

– The *strong wind* > *sky C* branch corresponds only to "no" answers.

– The *strong wind* > *sky R* branch corresponds solely to "no" answers.

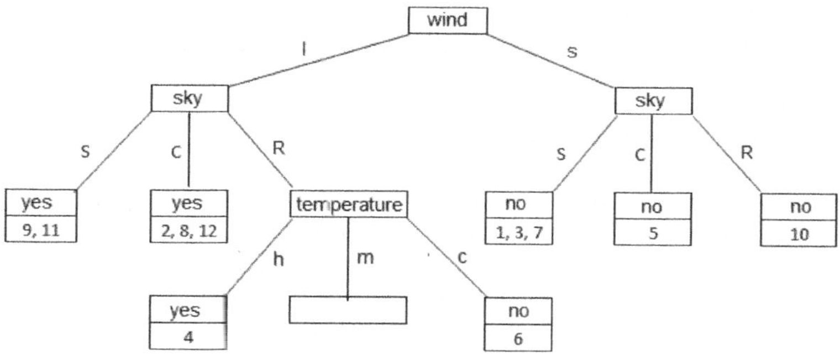

Figure 3.6. *The decision tree*

These correspondences indicate the resulting predictions of the decision tree for each combination of criteria. For example, if the wind is strong and the sky is sunny (*S*), then the prediction would be "no".

This leaves the *light wind* > *sky R* branch, where the remaining criterion, temperature, must be considered. However, there are only two possibilities for temperature in the observation set: *high* (*h*) and *cool (c)*. Thus, the branch *light wind* > *sky R* > *temperature m* remains empty, meaning that the observation set does not provide data for this specific combination.

Indeed, if it is considered that there are two possibilities for wind (light and strong), three possibilities for sky (sunny, overcast, risk of rain) and three possibilities for temperature (high, medium, cool), this results in a total of 18 possible combinations, assuming the criteria are independent. However, the observation set covers only 10 of these combinations, leaving some cases unobserved and limiting the ability to draw complete conclusions from the available data.

Note that in the decision tree, all observations are considered and classified appropriately. Each branch of the tree represents a combination of criteria that leads to a final decision, which corresponds to the classification of the observations.

3.3. Classification methods

Various classification methods can generally be grouped into two main categories:

– Partitioning methods: these involve dividing the dataset into a number of partitions or clusters, so that each element of the dataset belongs to a single cluster.

– Hierarchical methods: these construct a tree structure or *dendrogram* to represent the relationships between data.

Recall that, in set theory, a "partition" of a set E is a set of K parts Ω_k (or subsets) of E which satisfy the following conditions:

– None of the parts are empty: $\Omega_k \neq \emptyset$ for all $k = 1, \dots, K$.

– The union of all parts is the whole $E = \Omega_1 \cup \Omega_2 \cup \dots \cup \Omega_K$.

– The parts Ω_k are disjoint two by two: $\Omega_k \cap \Omega_{k'} = \emptyset$ for $k \neq k'$.

EXAMPLE 3.3.– Consider the set $E = \{a, b, c, d, e, f\}$.

This set can be partitioned into three parts as follows:

$$\Omega_1 = \{a, c, d\},\ \Omega_2 = \{b, f\},\ \Omega_3 = \{e\}.$$

Note that there are many other ways of partitioning this set into three parts, and this example represents just one of many possibilities. The way in which the set is partitioned often depends on the specific criteria and objectives of the classification.

In classification, partitioning methods aim to obtain a partition of the set of individuals, where each partition groups together individuals with similar characteristics. In this case, the term "cluster" is generally used to designate an element of the partition. A class, therefore, is a subset of individuals who share common properties and display a certain homogeneity.

A hierarchy H is defined as follows: it is a set of non-empty clusters Ω_k, also known as tiers, which satisfy the following properties:

– The *hierarchy* H contains all singletons: for all $i \in \Omega_k, i \in H$.

– Two clusters Ω_k and $\Omega_{k'}$ are:

- either disjoint ($\Omega_k \cap \Omega_{k'} = \emptyset$);

- or one is contained in the other ($\Omega_k \subset \Omega_{k'}$ or $\Omega_{k'} \subset \Omega_k$).

EXAMPLE 3.4.– Let E be the set defined in Example 3.3. A hierarchy $H = \{E, \{a, c, d\}, \{b, e, f\}, \{a, c\}, \{d\}, \{b, e\}, \{f\}, \{b\}, \{e\}\}$ is an example of a hierarchy. This hierarchy can be represented as a tree, where the "leaves" of the tree correspond to the singletons. In this tree-like representation, each node represents a cluster in the hierarchy, with the root node representing the entire set E. The branches illustrate the relationships between the clusters, and the leaves represent the individual elements. The resulting tree structure visualizes the relationships between the various classes in the hierarchy, showing how different elements are grouped at different levels (see Figure 3.7).

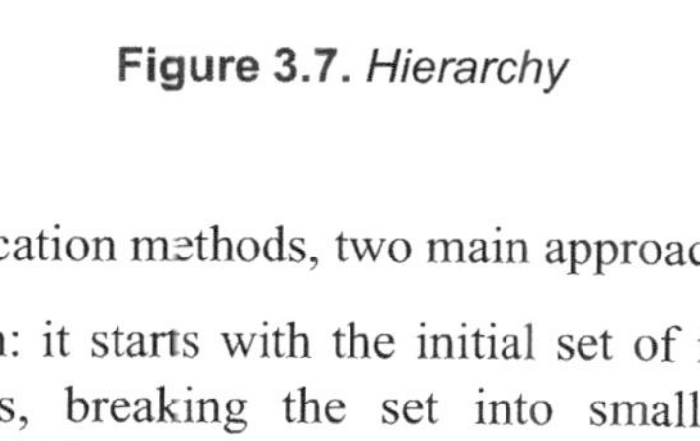

Figure 3.7. *Hierarchy*

In hierarchical classification methods, two main approaches can be adopted:

1) Top-down approach: it starts with the initial set of individuals and performs successive fragmentations, breaking the set into smaller and smaller groups, ultimately resulting in individual groups or "singletons". This method progressively divides the data into smaller clusters.

2) Bottom-up approach: each individual starts as its own group. Successive regroupings are then made, merging smaller group into larger ones, until a single group represents the entire set of individuals. This method progressively combines data into larger clusters.

Both approaches lead to the formation of group hierarchies, which can be represented visually as "classification trees".

3.4. Classification by partitioning

3.4.1. *Partitioning principle*

Given a set E composed of n individuals, the objective is to find an optimal partition of this set. The term "optimal" refers to a criterion W which generally measures the homogeneity of the classes forming the partition. Such a criterion is optimized among all candidate partitions. In this case, a fixed number K of partitions is generally defined.

In a "good" partition, elements of the same class are as similar as possible, while elements of different classes are as dissimilar as possible. Thus, the problem involves finding, among all possible partitions with K classes, the one for which the criterion W is "optimal".

A simple solution is to list all possible partitions with K classes and calculate the value of the criterion W for each of them. The partition that minimizes the value of W is then selected (typically, the optimization consists of minimizing). However, this method becomes difficult to apply when the number of individuals n increases. In fact, the number of possible partitions with K classes is of the order of magnitude of $\left(\frac{K^n}{K!}\right)$. For example, if $n = 100$ individuals are involved and partitions made up of three classes are sought, the number of such partitions would be of the order of $\left(\frac{3^{100}}{6}\right)$.

To solve this problem in a more practical way, an iterative approach is used. Initially, a partition P_0 of the set E with K classes is found, and the value of the criterion W_0 is calculated. Next, efforts are made to improve the initial partition P_0 to obtain a new partition P_1 with a criterion value W_1 less than or equal to W_0 (because optimization typically involves minimization). This improvement process is repeated on P_1 to obtain P_2, then P_3, etc.

To apply this resolution method, it is necessary to define several elements:

– The homogeneity criterion: this is generally intra-class inertia (to be discussed further).

– The iterative algorithm: this could be an algorithm such as *k-means* (which will be examined later).

3.4.2. *Inertia*

The notion of inertia is well known in mechanics and is also used as an optimality criterion W for partitioning.

Consider a set E composed of n individuals, each characterized by the values of p variables X_j. Let us assume that each individual has a weight ω_i and a distance $d(i,i')$ is defined. The inertia I_A with respect to a point A in the space $\mathbb{R}^p$ of individuals is expressed by:

$$I_A = \sum_{i=1}^{n} \omega_i d^2\,(i, A)$$

Thus, inertia will be lower, the closer the individuals are to A.

The center of gravity (or barycenter or centroid) g of the set of n individuals is defined by its coordinates:

$$g_j = \frac{\sum_{i=1}^{n} \omega_i x_j(i)}{\sum_{i=1}^{n} \omega_i}$$

where $x_j(i)$ designates the coordinate j of the point i.

This relationship is fully equivalent to the following relationship, which can also be taken as a definition of the center of gravity:

$$\sum_{i=1}^{n} \omega_i \left(x_j(i) - g_j\right) = 0$$

Total inertia I_g is defined as the inertia of the cloud of individuals with respect to the center of gravity g:

$$I_g = \sum_{i=1}^{n} \omega_i d^2(i, g)$$

Suppose a partition P of K classes is found. For each class C_k, calculate the coordinates of the center of gravity g_k of the class:

$$g_{jk} = \frac{\sum_{i \in C_k} \omega_i x_j(i)}{\sum_{i \in C_k} \omega_i}$$

as well as the inertia of a class C_k in relation to its center of gravity:

$$I_k = \sum_{i \in C_k} \omega_i d^2(i, g_k)$$

where, for simplicity, denote I_k for $I(C_k)$.

The *intra-class inertia* is defined as the sum of the inertia of each class:

$$W = \sum_{k=1}^{K} I_k$$

Similarly, *inter-class inertia* can be defined as the inertia of the cloud of class centers of gravity in relation to the total center of gravity:

$$Q = \sum_{k=1}^{K} \left(\sum_{i \in C_k} \omega_i \right) d^2(g, g_k)$$

There is a simple relationship between total inertia, intra-class inertia and inter-class inertia: total inertia is equal to the sum of intra-class inertia and inter-class inertia, i.e.:

$$I_g = W + Q$$

This result is a special application of the Huygens–König theorem, which is demonstrated in Appendix 1.

3.4.3. *Mobile center algorithm*

This algorithm, also known as *k-means* or Forgy's algorithm, is based on a simple principle. It proceeds in the following iterative steps:

1) Start by searching for a partition into K classes, where K is a fixed number.

2) Select K individuals, represented by points in space $\mathbb{R}^p$ with p descriptive variables, for example, at random.

3) Calculate the distances between each individual and the selected K individuals.

4) Compare the distances between an individual i and the K selected individuals. Retain the minimum distance, which defines an initial partition around the K selected individuals.

5) For each class in this partition, calculate the center of gravity (sometimes called the barycenter or centroid). The K centers of gravity replace the K individuals from step 2.

6) With these new K individuals, repeat from step 3.

Steps 3–6 are repeated until the partitioning no longer changes (convergence). Obviously, the result largely depends on the choice of K points (step 2) of the algorithm. Different choices may lead to different results. Running the algorithm with several initial choices yields a collection of results, and the best choice is the one that minimizes intra-class inertia.

EXAMPLE 3.5.– The table in Figure 3.8 presents the scores (out of 20) in French and Mathematics (Math) for 20 students.

	x	y
students	French	Math
1	12	6
2	15	8
3	9	12
4	6	18
5	4	17
6	12	10
7	13	9
8	17	5
9	8	8
10	5	14

	x	y
students	French	Math
11	2	16
12	14	18
13	12	11
14	10	13
15	10	7
16	18	9
17	8	10
18	5	15
19	9	17
20	15	8

Figure 3.8. *Student grades*

A three-class classification is chosen, a priori.

Three starting points – such as 1, 10 and 20 – are selected, and the squared distances from these points to all others are calculated.

For each point, the shortest distance is selected. This defines three classes (see Figure 3.9).

	x	y	distance²		
students	French	Maths	1	10	20
1	12	6	0.00	113.00	13.00
2	15	8	13.00	136.00	0.00
3	9	12	45.00	20.00	52.00
4	6	18	180.00	17.00	181.00
5	4	17	185.00	10.00	202.00
6	12	10	16.00	65.00	13.00
7	13	9	10.00	89.00	5.00
8	17	5	26.00	225.00	13.00
9	8	8	20.00	45.00	49.00
10	5	14	113.00	0.00	136.00
11	2	16	200.00	13.00	233.00
12	14	18	148.00	97.00	101.00
13	12	11	25.00	58.00	18.00
14	10	13	53.00	26.00	50.00
15	10	7	5.00	74.00	26.00
16	18	9	45.00	194.00	10.00
17	8	10	32.00	25.00	53.00
18	5	15	130.00	1.00	149.00
19	9	17	130.00	25.00	117.00
20	15	8	13.00	136.00	0.00

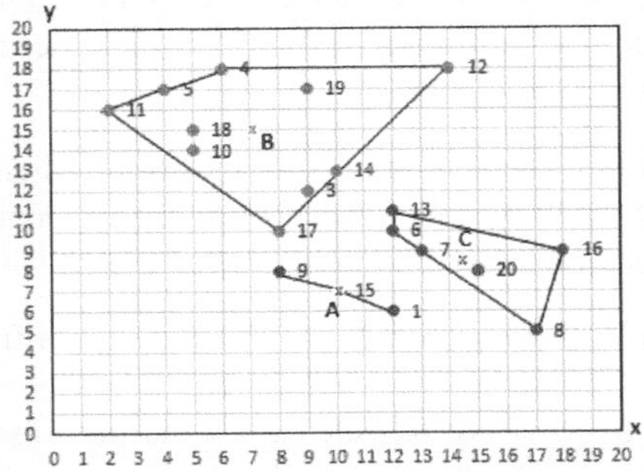

centroids

	x	y
A	10.00	7.00
B	7.20	15.00
C	14.57	8.57

Figure 3.9. *First partition. For a color version of this figure, see www.iste.co.uk/cochard/mathematics3.zip*

	x	y	distance²					
students	French	Math	1	10	20	A	B	C
1	12	6	0	113	13	5.00	104.04	13.22
2	15	8	13	136	0	26.00	109.84	0.51
3	9	12	45	20	52	26.00	12.24	42.80
4	6	18	180	17	181	137.00	10.44	162.37
5	4	17	185	10	202	136.00	14.24	182.80
6	12	10	16	65	13	13.00	48.04	8.65
7	13	9	10	89	5	13.00	69.64	2.65
8	17	5	26	225	13	53.00	196.04	18.65
9	8	8	20	45	49	5.00	49.64	43.51
10	5	14	113	0	136	74.00	5.84	121.08
11	2	16	200	13	233	145.00	28.04	213.22
12	14	18	148	97	101	137.00	55.24	89.22
13	12	11	25	58	18	20.00	39.04	12.51
14	10	13	53	26	50	36.00	11.84	40.51
15	10	7	5	74	26	0.00	71.84	23.37
16	18	9	45	194	10	68.00	152.64	11.94
17	8	10	32	25	53	13.00	25.64	45.22
18	5	15	130	1	149	89.00	4.84	132.94
19	9	17	130	25	117	101.00	7.24	102.08
20	15	8	13	136	0	26.00	109.84	0.51

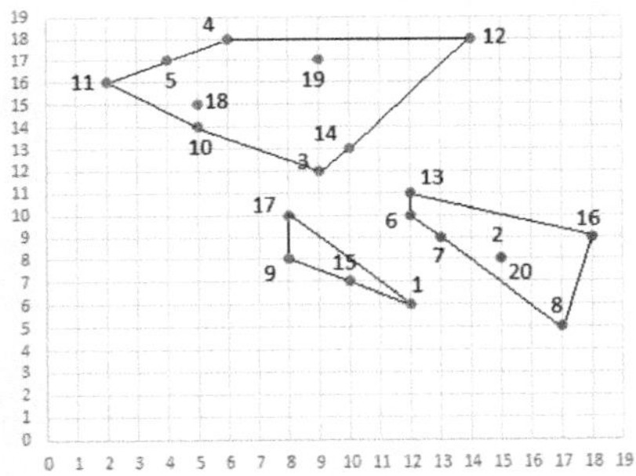

centroids

	x	y
D	9.5	7.75
E	7.11	15.6
F	14.6	8.57

Figure 3.10. *Second partition. For a color version of this figure, see www.iste.co.uk/cochard/mathematics3.zip*

The centers of gravity (centroids) of these classes are calculated, and the squared distances of these centroids from all other points are calculated (see Figure 3.10). New classes are obtained, with only one point changing class in this case, along with new centroids. The same operations are repeated (returning to step 2), as shown in Figure 3.11.

	x	y	distance²									
students	French	Math	1	10	20	A	B	C	D	E	F
1	12	6	0	113	13	5.00	104.04	13.22	9.31	115.21	13.22
2	15	8	13	136	0	26.00	109.84	0.51	30.31	119.32	0.51
3	9	12	45	20	52	26.00	12.24	42.80	18.31	16.21	42.80
4	6	18	180	17	181	137.00	10.44	162.37	117.31	7.21	162.37
5	4	17	185	10	202	136.00	14.24	182.80	115.81	11.77	182.80
6	12	10	16	65	13	13.00	48.04	8.65	11.31	54.77	8.65
7	13	9	10	89	5	13.00	69.64	2.65	13.81	77.65	2.65
8	17	5	26	225	13	53.00	196.04	18.65	63.81	209.21	18.65
9	8	8	20	45	49	5.00	49.64	43.51	2.31	57.88	43.51
10	5	14	113	0	136	74.00	5.84	121.08	59.31	6.88	121.08
11	2	16	200	13	233	145.00	28.04	213.22	124.31	26.32	213.22
12	14	18	148	97	101	137.00	55.24	89.22	125.31	53.43	89.22
13	12	11	25	58	18	20.00	39.04	12.51	16.81	44.65	12.51
14	10	13	53	26	50	36.00	11.84	40.51	27.81	14.88	40.51
15	10	7	5	74	26	0.00	71.84	23.37	0.81	81.54	23.37
16	18	9	45	194	10	68.00	152.64	11.94	73.81	161.54	11.94
17	8	10	32	25	53	13.00	25.64	45.22	7.31	31.65	45.22
18	5	15	130	1	149	89.00	4.84	132.94	72.81	4.77	132.94
19	9	17	130	25	117	101.00	7.24	102.08	85.81	5.65	102.08
20	15	8	13	136	0	26.00	109.84	0.51	30.31	119.32	0.51

Figure 3.11. *Third partition*

The new iteration has not modified either the classes or the centroids, indicating that algorithm convergence has been reached.

Using the previous table and assuming that all students have the same statistical weight, the value of the intra-class inertia is calculated as $W = 211.15$.

Example 3.5 shows the basic algorithm. Can the result be considered satisfactory? Of course not. Try again with a new choice of the three initial points.

EXAMPLE 3.6.– Using the same data as in Example 3.5, selecting indices 4, 14 and 18 as initial points results in a different class configuration, as shown in Figure 3.12. For this new partition, the intra-class inertia is $W = 204.56$. This value is lower (a minimization problem) than that of the previous partition (i.e. $W = 211.15$), indicating better class homogeneity.

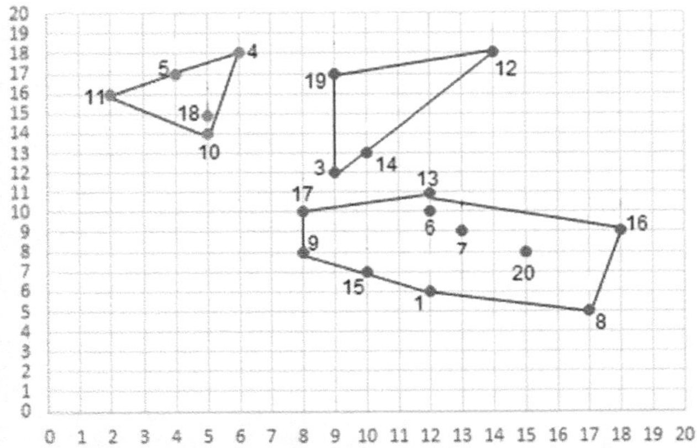

Figure 3.12. *New partition. For a color version of this figure, see www.iste.co.uk/cochard/mathematics3.zip*

However, the question of whether this partition is "optimal" remains to be examined and will be addressed later.

Of course, to determine whether there is another, even better partition, it is necessary to explore all possible initial configurations. In the case of choosing three points from among n points, the number of potential choices is:

$$\frac{n!}{(n-3)!\,3!} = \frac{n(n-1)(n-2)}{6} = 1140$$

Hence, for a set of 20 individuals, as in Example 3.5, this provides 1,140 possible configurations.

However, this example is primarily used for teaching purposes. In the real world, problems often involve much larger datasets, with much larger values of n. For example, for $n = 100$ individuals, the number of possible choices of three points would be 161,700. As a result, the computation times required to determine the "optimal" partition (i.e. the best among all possible configurations) may become considerably longer.

When using specialized software (as presented in appendix 3.6.2), it is rarely necessary to explore all possible combinations of initial points. Instead, it is common to set a predefined number of trials or iterations.

EXAMPLE 3.7.– Using dedicated partitioning software, a partition for the data from Example 3.5 is obtained, as shown in Figure 3.13, with a value of $W = 189.92$.

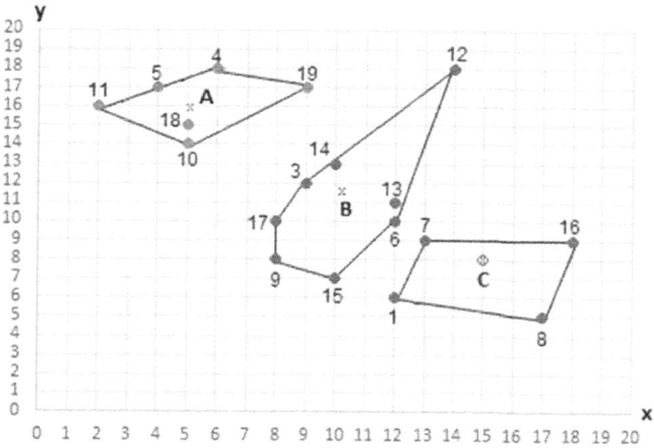

Figure 3.13. *New partition. For a color version of this figure, see www.iste.co.uk/cochard/mathematics3.zip*

Efficient initialization: a variant of the moving center method, known as *k-means++*, often provides a more efficient approach to the initial selection of reference points. Instead of selecting several initial points at random, a single point, M_1, is chosen initially. Then, the point M_2 that is furthest from M_1 is selected. Following this, the point M_3 , which is furthest from M_2, is chosen. This process continues until the required number of reference points, say $K = 3$ for three classes, is reached. The standard algorithm is then applied. This method significantly reduces the number of choices to be explored, as it requires only n choices for n points, making it a more efficient way to explore initial selection possibilities.

In the moving center method, the choice of the number of classes K is often set in advance. However, determining the optimal value of K can be challenging, as there are generally no clear indications in the data that suggest the best value.

One of the most common ways to identify a "better" value for K used in approaches is through the elbow method. This involves testing different values of K and plotting the curve $W_{min} = f(K)$, which represents the evolution of minimum intra-class inertia as a function of K. This curve typically shows a decreasing trend.

EXAMPLE 3.8.– In Example 3.5, it is possible to plot the curve representing the minimum intra-class inertia (W_{min}) as a function of the number K of classes. This graph is shown in Figure 3.14.

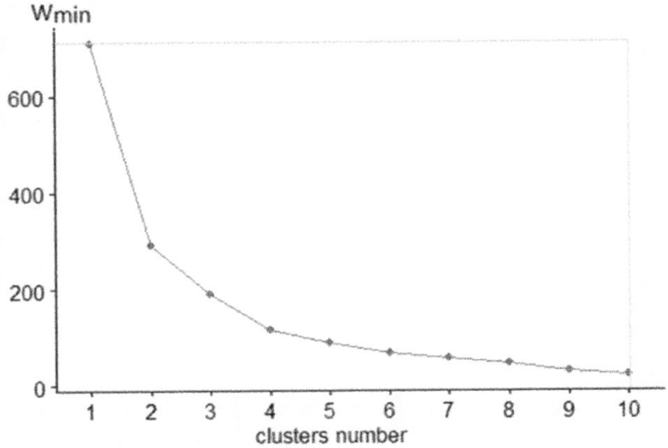

Figure 3.14. *Minimal intra-class inertia versus K*

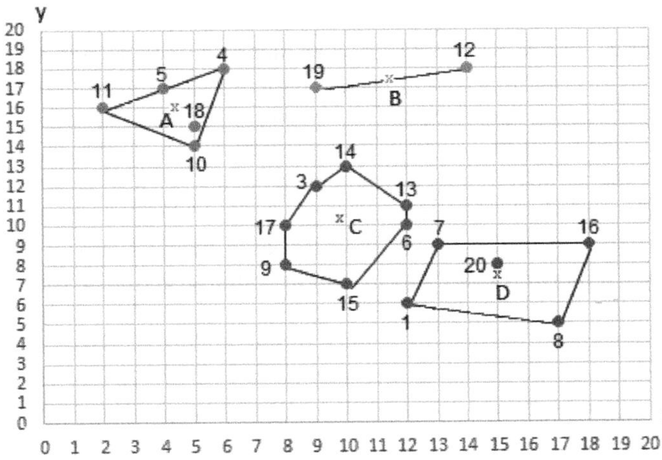

Figure 3.15. *Partition for K = 4. For a color version of this figure, see www.iste.co.uk/cochard/mathematics3.zip*

It is observed that a plateau begins between $K = 4$ and $K = 5$. Consequently, it would be wiser to choose $K = 4$ rather than $K = 3$.

This leads to the class distribution shown in Figure 3.15, with an intra-class inertia of $W = 115.41$.

3.5. Hierarchical classification

3.5.1. *Principle*

As mentioned above, it is possible to adopt either a bottom-up or top-down approach. However, the bottom-up method, known as hierarchical ascending classification (HAC), is the most commonly used. In this section, the focus is on this method.

The HAC classification principle is relatively simple and is based on the following aggregation strategy:

1) Start with singletons as an initial base: as many classes as there are singletons.

2) Calculate the distances between classes.

3) Merge the two closest classes, i.e. those separated by the smallest aggregation measure, into a single class.

4) Repeat steps 2 and 3, continuing the iteration until only one class remains.

The aggregation measure is a criterion for grouping classes. The sequence of classes can be represented by a tree, generally called a *dendrogram*. An example of a dendrogram is shown in Figure 3.16.

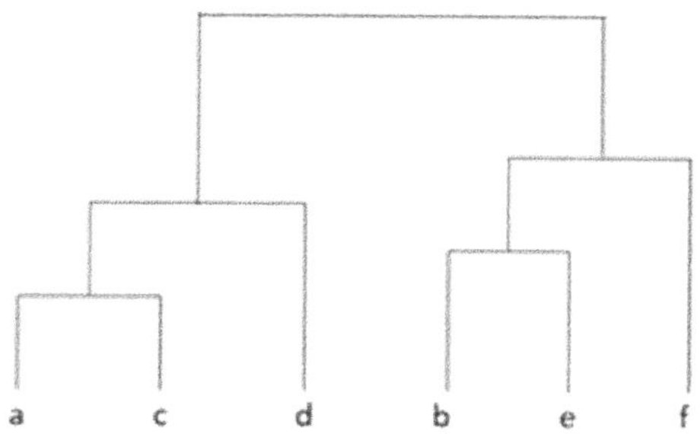

Figure 3.16. *Dendrogram*

Each horizontal line in the dendrogram in Figure 3.16 corresponds to a class, and each vertical line has a defined height. The height of a class (and therefore of a bearing) is determined as follows:

– For singletons (located at the bottom of the dendrogram), the height is 0.

– For two different classes A and B, with A being a subset of B, the height of A is less than that of $A \subset B$, $h(A) < h(B)$.

In practice, the height is chosen as the value of the aggregation measure $D(A, B)$ (or a proportional number) of classes A and B when they are grouped together. The aggregation measure is defined in the aggregation strategies.

3.5.2. *Aggregation strategies*

Classic strategies rely on simple aggregation measures to group two classes. The following measures are distinguished:

– single linkage algorithm;

– complete linkage algorithm;

– average linkage algorithm.

These three measures correspond to simple definitions, as shown in Figures 3.17 and 3.18.

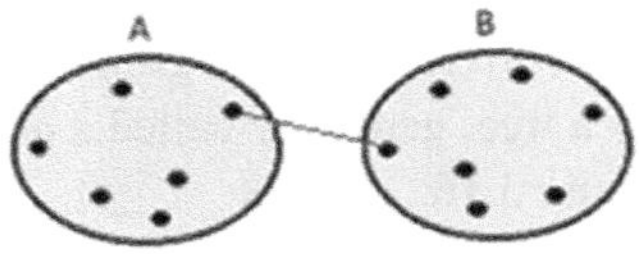

Figure 3.17. *Single linkage. For a color version of this figure, see www.iste.co.uk/cochard/mathematics3.zip*

Single linkage: the aggregation measure $D(A, B)$ is the distance between the closest individuals in the two classes:

$$D'A, B) = \min_{i \in A, i' \in B} d(i, i')$$

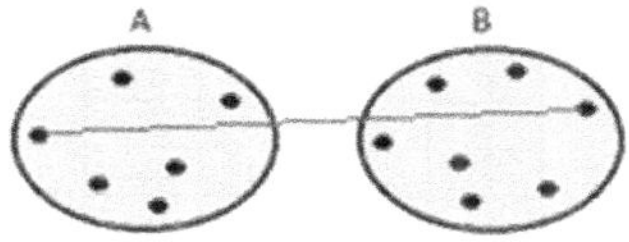

Figure 3.18. *Complete linkage. For a color version of this figure, see www.iste.co.uk/cochard/mathematics3.zip*

Complete linkage: the aggregation measure *D(A, B)* is the distance between the most distant individuals in the two classes:

$$D(A,B) = \max_{i \in A, i' \in B} d(i,i')$$

The "*average linkage*" aggregation measure consists of calculating the average of the minimum and maximum link aggregation measures. This also provides a more balanced measure of minimum and maximum proximities between classes.

To be more precise, consider the Euclidean distance as a measure of distance between individuals. Using the minimum link algorithm to aggregate the classes, an aggregation measure matrix is constructed using the distances between singletons, and the smallest measure is selected to merge two classes. Such a process is repeated until a single class containing all the individuals remains.

EXAMPLE 3.9.– French metropolitan regions are ranked according to three criteria: unemployment rate, number of students and number of movie theaters (see Figure 3.19).

Region	unemployment rate (%)	student rate (%)	nb of movie theaters per inhabitant
HdF - Hauts de France	8.70	4.27	1.21
N - Normandie	6.70	3.50	1.30
B - Bretagne	5.80	4.36	1.46
GE - Grand Est	7.00	4.05	1.20
IdF - Ile de France	6.90	6.41	1.99
PdL - Pays de la Loire	5.80	4.01	1.46
CVL - Centre Val de Loire	6.70	2.81	1.19
BFC - Bourgogne Franche Comté	6.30	3.11	1.19
NA - Nouvelle Aquitaine	6.40	3.74	1.40
ARA - Auvergne Rhône Alpes	6.10	4.67	1.42
O - Occitanie	8.60	4.53	1.31
PACA - Provence Alpes Côte d'Azu	8.00	3.72	1.53
C - Corse	6.00	1.75	0.96

Figure 3.19. *Statistical table*

Region	X	Y	Z
HdF	1.94	0.34	-0.62
N	-0.15	-0.40	-0.22
B	-1.09	0.42	0.44
GE	0.16	0.12	-0.64
IdF	0.06	2.38	2.69
PdL	-1.09	0.08	0.45
CVL	-0.15	-1.05	-0.70
BFC	-0.57	-0.77	-0.71
NA	-0.47	-0.17	0.19
ARA	-0.78	0.72	0.26
O	1.84	0.58	-0.20
PACA	1.21	-0.19	0.75
C	-0.89	-2.06	-1.68

Figure 3.20. *Reduced centered variables*

It should be noted that this example is essentially intended for educational purposes and, to the best of our knowledge, does not correspond to any serious study. The three criteria are expressed differently: the unemployment rate is a percentage of the working population, the student number is a percentage of the total population, and the number of movie theaters is also calculated as a percentage of the total population. With three criteria whose values are difficult to compare, reduced-centered coordinates are used. Thus, each region is represented by a point in three-dimensional space, where the coordinates correspond to the reduced-centered variables (see Figure 3.20).

Next, the distance between each pair of points is calculated, resulting in the table shown in Figure 3.21 (for convenience, the squared distance is shown).

Step 1: the smallest distance, 0.11 (orange), is identified, indicating that regions B and PdL can be merged (see Figure 3.21).

Region	HdF	N	B	GE	IdF	PdL	CVL	BFC	NA	ARA	O	PACA	C
HdF	0.00	5.07	10.33	3.21	18.66	10.41	6.31	7.54	6.70	8.32	0.25	2.68	14.87
N	5.07	0.00	1.99	0.54	16.24	1.58	0.65	0.55	0.32	1.87	4.91	2.84	5.44
B	10.33	1.99	0.00	2.83	10.25	0.11	4.33	3.01	0.80	0.22	9.01	5.76	10.69
GE	3.21	0.54	2.83	0.00	16.21	2.78	1.48	1.34	1.17	2.06	3.21	3.13	6.95
IdF	18.66	16.24	10.25	16.21	0.00	11.60	23.27	21.89	13.00	9.37	14.74	11.68	39.73
PdL	10.41	1.58	0.11	2.78	11.60	0.00	3.49	2.36	0.53	0.54	9.25	5.46	9.21
CVL	6.31	0.65	4.33	1.48	23.27	3.49	0.00	0.25	1.67	4.44	6.87	4.68	2.53
BFC	7.54	0.55	3.01	1.34	21.89	2.36	0.25	0.00	1.19	3.21	7.89	5.64	2.71
NA	6.70	0.32	0.80	1.17	13.00	0.53	1.67	1.19	0.00	0.89	6.01	3.11	7.28
ARA	8.32	1.87	0.22	2.06	9.37	0.54	4.44	3.21	0.89	0.00	7.07	5.01	11.52
O	0.25	4.91	9.01	3.21	14.74	9.25	6.87	7.89	6.01	7.07	0.00	1.88	16.59
PACA	2.68	2.84	5.76	3.13	11.68	5.46	4.68	5.64	3.11	5.01	1.88	0.00	13.81
C	14.87	5.44	10.69	6.95	39.73	9.21	2.53	2.71	7.28	11.52	16.59	13.81	0.00

Figure 3.21. *Initial stage. For a color version of this figure, see www.iste.co.uk/cochard/mathematics3.zip*

Region	HdF	N	GE	IdF	CVL	BFC	NA	ARA	O	PACA	C	B	PdL
HdF	0.00	5.07	3.21	18.66	6.31	7.54	6.70	8.32	0.25	2.68	14.87	10.33	10.41
N	5.07	0.00	0.54	16.24	0.65	0.55	0.32	1.87	4.91	2.84	5.44	1.99	1.58
B	10.33	1.99	2.83	10.25	4.33	3.01	0.80	0.22	9.01	5.76	10.69	0.00	0.11
GE	3.21	0.54	0.00	16.21	1.48	1.34	1.17	2.06	3.21	3.13	6.95	2.83	2.78
IdF	18.66	16.24	16.21	0.00	23.27	21.89	13.00	9.37	14.74	11.68	39.73	10.25	11.60
PdL	10.41	1.58	2.78	11.60	3.49	2.36	0.53	0.54	9.25	5.46	9.21	0.11	0.00
CVL	6.31	0.65	1.48	23.27	0.00	0.25	1.67	4.44	6.87	4.68	2.53	4.33	3.49
BFC	7.54	0.55	1.34	21.89	0.25	0.00	1.19	3.21	7.89	5.64	2.71	3.01	2.36
NA	6.70	0.32	1.17	13.00	1.67	1.19	0.00	0.89	6.01	3.11	7.28	0.80	0.53
ARA	8.32	1.87	2.06	9.37	4.44	3.21	0.89	0.00	7.07	5.01	11.52	0.22	0.54
O	0.25	4.91	3.21	14.74	6.87	7.89	6.01	7.07	0.00	1.88	16.59	9.01	9.25
PACA	2.68	2.84	3.13	11.68	4.68	5.64	3.11	5.01	1.88	0.00	13.81	5.76	5.46
C	14.87	5.44	6.95	39.73	2.53	2.71	7.28	11.52	16.59	13.81	0.00	10.69	9.21

Figure 3.22. *Step 1. For a color version of this figure, see www.iste.co.uk/cochard/mathematics3.zip*

The result is shown in Figure 3.22. The rows corresponding to the B and PdL regions can be crossed out in the B and PdL columns.

Step 2: the smallest distance among the unstriped boxes, 0.22 (orange boxes), is identified. This indicates that the ARA region can be added to the previous aggregate (see Figure 3.22).

The result is shown in Figure 3.23.

Region	HdF	N	GE	IdF	CVL	BFC	NA	O	PACA	C	ARA	B	PdL
HdF	0.00	5.07	3.21	18.66	6.31	7.54	6.70	0.25	2.68	14.87	8.32	10.33	10.41
N	5.07	0.00	0.54	16.24	0.65	0.55	0.32	4.91	2.84	5.44	1.87	1.99	1.58
B	10.33	1.99	2.83	10.25	4.33	3.01	0.80	9.01	5.76	10.69	0.22	0.00	0.11
GE	3.21	0.54	0.00	16.21	1.48	1.34	1.17	3.21	3.13	6.95	2.06	2.83	2.78
IdF	18.66	16.24	16.21	0.00	23.27	21.89	13.00	14.74	11.68	39.73	9.37	10.25	11.60
PdL	10.41	1.58	2.78	11.60	3.49	2.36	0.53	9.25	5.46	9.21	0.54	0.11	0.00
CVL	6,31	0,65	1,48	23.27	0.00	0.25	1.67	6.87	4.68	2.53	4.44	4.33	3.49
BFC	7.54	0.55	1.34	21.89	0.25	0.00	1.19	7.89	5.64	2.71	3.21	3.01	2.36
NA	6.70	0.32	1.17	13.00	1.67	1.19	0.00	6.01	3.11	7.28	0.89	0.80	0.53
ARA	8.32	1.87	2.06	9.37	4.44	3.21	0.89	7.07	5.01	11.52	0.00	0.22	0.54
O	0.25	4.91	3.21	14.74	6.87	7.89	6.01	0.00	1.88	16.59	7.07	9.01	9.25
PACA	2.68	2.84	3.13	11.68	4.68	5.64	3.11	1.88	0.00	13.81	5.01	5.76	5.46
C	14.87	5.44	6.95	39.73	2.53	2.71	7.28	16.59	13.81	0.00	11.52	10.69	9.21

Figure 3.23. *Step 2. For a color version of this figure, see www.iste.co.uk/cochard/mathematics3.zip*

Region	N	GE	IdF	NA	PACA	C	ARA	B	PdL	HdF	O	BFC	CVL
HdF	5.07	3.21	18.66	6,70	2.68	14.87	8.32	10.33	10.41	0.00	0.25	7.54	6.31
N	0.00	0.54	16.24	0.32	2.84	5.44	1.87	1.99	1.58	5.07	4.91	0.55	0.65
B	1.99	2.83	10.25	0,80	5.76	10.69	0.22	0.00	0.11	10.33	9.01	3.01	4.33
GE	0.54	0.00	16.21	1,17	3.13	6.95	2.06	2.83	2.78	3.21	3.21	1.34	1.48
IdF	16.24	16.21	0.00	13,00	11.68	39.73	9.37	10.25	11.60	18.66	14.74	21.89	23.27
PdL	1.58	2.78	11.60	0,53	5.46	9.21	0.54	0.11	0.00	10.41	9.25	2.36	3.49
CVL	0.65	1.48	23.27	1,67	4.68	2.53	4.44	4.33	3.49	6.31	6.87	0.25	0.00
BFC	0.55	1.34	21.89	1,19	5.64	2.71	3.21	3.01	2.36	7.54	7.89	0.00	0.25
NA	0.32	1.17	13.00	0.00	3.11	7.28	0.89	0.80	0.53	6.70	6.01	1.19	1.67
ARA	1.87	2.06	9.37	0,89	5.01	11.52	0.00	0.22	0.54	8.32	7.07	3.21	4.44
O	4.91	3.21	14.74	6,01	1.88	16.59	7.07	9.01	9.25	0.25	0.00	7.89	6.87
PACA	2.84	3.13	11.68	3,11	0.00	13.81	5.01	5.76	5.46	2.68	1.88	5.64	4.68
C	5.44	6.95	39.73	7,28	13.81	0.00	11.52	10.69	9.21	14.87	16.59	2.71	2.53

Figure 3.24. *Step 3. For a color version of this figure, see www.iste.co.uk/cochard/mathematics3.zip*

Region	GE	IdF	PACA	C	ARA	B	PdL	HdF	O	BFC	CVL	N	NA
HdF	3.21	18.66	2.68	14.87	8.32	10.33	10.41	0.00	0.25	7.54	6.31	5.07	6.70
N	0.54	16.24	2.84	5.44	1.87	1.99	1.58	5.07	4.91	0.55	0.65	0.00	0.32
B	2.83	10.25	5.76	10.69	0.22	0.00	0.11	10.33	9.01	3.01	4.33	1.99	0.80
GE	0.00	16.21	3.13	6.95	2.06	2.83	2.78	3.21	3.21	1.34	1.48	0.54	1.17
IdF	16.21	0.00	11.68	39.73	9.37	10.25	11.60	18.66	14.74	21.89	23.27	16.24	13.00
PdL	2.78	11.60	5.46	9.21	0.54	0.11	0.00	10.41	9.25	2.36	3.49	1.58	0.53
CVL	1.48	23.27	4.68	2.53	4.44	4.33	3.49	6.31	6.87	0.25	0.00	0.65	1.67
BFC	1.34	21.89	5.64	2.71	3.21	3.01	2.36	7.54	7.89	0.00	0.25	0.55	1.19
NA	1.17	13.00	3.11	7.28	0.89	0.80	0.53	6.70	6.01	1.19	1.67	0.32	0.00
ARA	2.06	9.37	5.01	11.52	0.00	0.22	0.54	8.32	7.07	3.21	4.44	1.87	0.89
O	3.21	14.74	1.88	16.59	7.07	9.01	9.25	0.25	0.00	7.89	6.87	4.91	6.01
PACA	3.13	11.68	0.00	13.81	5.01	5.76	5.46	2.68	1.88	5.64	4.68	2.84	3.11
C	6.95	39.73	13.81	0.00	11.52	10.69	9.21	14.87	16.59	2.71	2.53	5.44	7.28

Figure 3.25. *Step 4. For a color version of this figure, see www.iste.co.uk/cochard/mathematics3.zip*

Step 3: several possibilities for the shortest distance are found, with a value of 0.25 appearing four times (orange boxes). These values are distributed in pairs: HdF with O and CVL with BFC. Therefore, the HdF and O regions can be grouped together, on the one hand, and CVL and BFC, on the other (see Figure 3.23). The result is shown in Figure 3.24.

Step 4: the shortest distance is now 0.32 (orange boxes), indicating that the N and NA regions can be grouped together (see Figure 3.24). The result is shown in Figure 3.25.

Step 5: the shortest distance, 0.53 (orange boxes), merges the regions ARA, B and PdL, on the one hand, and N and NA, on the other (see Figure 3.25). The result is shown in Figure 3.26.

Region	GE	IdF	PACA	C	HdF	O	BFC	CVL	ARA	B	PdL	N	NA
HdF	3.21	18.66	2.68	14.87	0.00	0.25	7.54	6.31	8.32	10.33	10.41	5.07	6.70
N	0.54	16.24	2.84	5.44	5.07	4.91	0.55	0.65	1.87	1.99	1.58	0.00	0.32
B	2.83	10.25	5.76	10.69	10.33	9.01	3.01	4.33	0.22	0.00	0.11	1.99	0.80
GE	0.00	16.21	3.13	6.95	3.21	3.21	1.34	1.48	2.06	2.83	2.78	0.54	1.17
IdF	16.21	0.00	11.68	39.73	18.66	14.74	21.89	23.27	9.37	10.25	11.60	16.24	13.00
PdL	2.78	11.60	5.46	9.21	10.41	9.25	2.36	3.49	0.54	0.11	0.00	1.58	0.53
CVL	1.48	23.27	4.68	2.53	6.31	6.87	0.25	0.00	4.44	4.33	3.49	0.65	1.67
BFC	1.34	21.89	5.64	2.71	7.54	7.89	0.00	0.25	3.21	3.01	2.36	0.55	1.19
NA	1.17	13.00	3.11	7.28	6.70	6.01	1.19	1.67	0.89	0.80	0.53	0.32	0.00
ARA	2.06	9.37	5.01	11.52	8.32	7.07	3.21	4.44	0.00	0.22	0.54	1.87	0.89
O	3.21	14.74	1.88	16.59	0.25	0.00	7.89	6.87	7.07	9.01	9.25	4.91	6.01
PACA	3.13	11.68	0.00	13.81	2.68	1.88	5.64	4.68	5.01	5.76	5.46	2.84	3.11
C	6.95	39.73	13.81	0.00	14.87	16.59	2.71	2.53	11.52	10.69	9.21	5.44	7.28

Figure 3.26. *Step 5. For a color version of this figure, see www.iste.co.uk/cochard/mathematics3.zip*

Region	IdF	PACA	C	HdF	O	BFC	CVL	GE	ARA	B	PdL	N	NA
HdF	18,66	2.68	14.87	0.00	0.25	7.54	6.31	3.21	8.32	10.33	10.41	5.07	6.70
N	16,24	2.84	5.44	5.07	4.91	0.55	0.65	0.54	1.87	1.99	1.58	0.00	0.32
B	10,25	5.76	10.69	10.33	9.01	3.01	4.33	2.83	0.22	0.00	0.11	1.99	0.80
GE	16,21	3.13	6.95	3.21	3.21	1.34	1.48	0.00	2.06	2.83	2.78	0.54	1.17
IdF	0,00	11.68	39.73	18.66	14.74	21.89	23.27	16.21	9.37	10.25	11.60	16.24	13.00
PdL	11,60	5.46	9.21	10.41	9.25	2.36	3.49	2.78	0.54	0.11	0.00	1.58	0.53
CVL	23,27	4.68	2.53	6.31	6.87	0.25	0.00	1.48	4.44	4.33	3.49	0.65	1.67
BFC	21,89	5.64	2.71	7.54	7.89	0.00	0.25	1.34	3.21	3.01	2.36	0.55	1.19
NA	13,00	3.11	7.28	6.70	6.01	1.19	1.67	1.17	0.89	0.80	0.53	0.32	0.00
ARA	9,37	5.01	11.52	8.32	7.07	3.21	4.44	2.06	0.00	0.22	0.54	1.87	0.89
O	14,74	1.88	16.59	0.25	0.00	7.89	6.87	3.21	7.07	9.01	9.25	4.91	6.01
PACA	11,68	0.00	13.81	2.68	1.88	5.64	4.68	3.13	5.01	5.76	5.46	2.84	3.11
C	39,73	13.81	0.00	14.87	16.59	2.71	2.53	6.95	11.52	10.69	9.21	5.44	7.28

Figure 3.27. *Step 6. For a color version of this figure, see www.iste.co.uk/cochard/mathematics3.zip*

Step 6: the shortest distance, 0.54 (orange boxes), merges the GE region with the ARA, B, PdL, N and NA aggregates (see Figure 3.26). The result is shown in Figure 3.27.

Step 7: the shortest distance, 0.55 (orange boxes), merges the aggregates BFC, CVL and GE, ARA, B, PdL, N and NA (see Figure 3.27). The result is shown in Figure 3.28.

Step 8: the new shortest distance, 1.88 (orange boxes), prompts the merging of PACA with the HdF and O aggregates (see Figure 3.28). The result is shown in Figure 3.29.

Step 9: the shortest distance, now 2.53 (orange boxes), corresponds to the addition of C to the BFC, CVL, GE, ARA, B, PdL, N and NA aggregates (see Figure 3.29). The result is shown in Figure 3.30.

Region	IdF	PACA	C	HdF	O	BFC	CVL	GE	ARA	B	PdL	N	NA
HdF	18.66	2.68	14.87	0.00	0.25	7.54	6.31	3.21	8.32	10.33	10.41	5.07	6.70
N	16.24	2.84	5.44	5.07	4.91	0.55	0.65	0.54	1.87	1.99	1.58	0.00	0.32
B	10.25	5.76	10.69	10.33	9.01	3.01	4.33	2.83	0.22	0.00	0.11	1.99	0.80
GE	16.21	3.13	6.95	3.21	3.21	1.34	1.48	0.00	2.06	2.83	2.78	0.54	1.17
IdF	0.00	11.68	39.73	18.66	14.74	21.89	23.27	16.21	9.37	10.25	11.60	16.24	13.00
PdL	11.60	5.46	9.21	10.41	9.25	2.36	3.49	2.78	0.54	0.11	0.00	1.58	0.53
CVL	23.27	4.68	2.53	6.31	6.87	0.25	0.00	1.48	4.44	4.33	3.49	0.65	1.67
BFC	21.89	5.64	2.71	7.54	7.89	0.00	0.25	1.34	3.21	3.01	2.36	0.55	1.19
NA	13.00	3.11	7.28	6.70	6.01	1.19	1.67	1.17	0.89	0.80	0.53	0.32	0.00
ARA	9.37	5.01	11.52	8.32	7.07	3.21	4.44	2.06	0.00	0.22	0.54	1.87	0.89
O	14.74	1.88	16.59	0.25	0.00	7.89	6.87	3.21	7.07	9.01	9.25	4.91	6.01
PACA	11.68	0.00	13.81	2.68	1.88	5.64	4.68	3.13	5.01	5.76	5.46	2.84	3.11
C	39.73	13.81	0.00	14.87	16.59	2.71	2.53	6.95	11.52	10.69	9.21	5.44	7.28

Figure 3.28. *Step 7. For a color version of this figure, see www.iste.co.uk/cochard/mathematics3.zip*

Region	IdF	C	PACA	HdF	O	BFC	CVL	GE	ARA	B	PdL	N	NA
HdF	18.66	14.87	2.68	0.00	0.25	7.54	6.31	3.21	8.32	10.33	10.41	5.07	6.70
N	16.24	5.44	2.84	5.07	4.91	0.55	0.65	0.54	1.87	1.99	1.58	0.00	0.32
B	10.25	10.69	5.76	10.33	9.01	3.01	4.33	2.83	0.22	0.00	0.11	1.99	0.80
GE	16.21	6.95	3.13	3.21	3.21	1.34	1.48	0.00	2.06	2.83	2.78	0.54	1.17
IdF	0.00	39.73	11.68	18.66	14.74	21.89	23.27	16.21	9.37	10.25	11.60	16.24	13.00
PdL	11.60	9.21	5.46	10.41	9.25	2.36	3.49	2.78	0.54	0.11	0.00	1.58	0.53
CVL	23.27	2.53	4.68	6.31	6.87	0.25	0.00	1.48	4.44	4.33	3.49	0.65	1.67
BFC	21.89	2.71	5.64	7.54	7.89	0.00	0.25	1.34	3.21	3.01	2.36	0.55	1.19
NA	13.00	7.28	3.11	6.70	6.01	1.19	1.67	1.17	0.89	0.80	0.53	0.32	0.00
ARA	9.37	11.52	5.01	8.32	7.07	3.21	4.44	2.06	0.00	0.22	0.54	1.87	0.89
O	14.74	16.59	1.88	0.25	0.00	7.89	6.87	3.21	7.07	9.01	9.25	4.91	6.01
PACA	11.68	13.81	0.00	2.68	1.88	5.64	4.68	3.13	5.01	5.76	5.46	2.84	3.11
C	39.73	0.00	13.81	14.87	16.59	2.71	2.53	6.95	11.52	10.69	9.21	5.44	7.28

Figure 3.29. *Step 8. For a color version of this figure, see www.iste.co.uk/cochard/mathematics3.zip*

Region	IdF	PACA	HdF	O	C	BFC	CVL	GE	ARA	B	PdL	N	NA
HdF	18.66	2.68	0.00	0.25	14.87	7.54	6.31	3.21	8.32	10.33	10.41	5.07	6.70
N	16.24	2.84	5.07	4.91	5.44	0.55	0.65	0.54	1.87	1.99	1.58	0.00	0.32
B	10.25	5.76	10.33	9.01	10.69	3.01	4.33	2.83	0.22	0.00	0.11	1.99	0.80
GE	16.21	3.13	3.21	3.21	6.95	1.34	1.48	0.00	2.06	2.83	2.78	0.54	1.17
IdF	0.00	11.68	18.66	14.74	39.73	21.89	23.27	16.21	9.37	10.25	11.60	16.24	13.00
PdL	11.60	5.46	10.41	9.25	9.21	2.36	3.49	2.78	0.54	0.11	0.00	1.58	0.53
CVL	23.27	4.68	6.31	6.87	2.53	0.25	0.00	1.48	4.44	4.33	3.49	0.65	1.67
BFC	21.89	5.64	7.54	7.89	2.71	0.00	0.25	1.34	3.21	3.01	2.36	0.55	1.19
NA	13.00	3.11	6.70	6.01	7.28	1.19	1.67	1.17	0.89	0.80	0.53	0.32	0.00
ARA	9.37	5.01	8.32	7.07	11.52	3.21	4.44	2.06	0.00	0.22	0.54	1.87	0.89
O	14.74	1.88	0.25	0.00	16.59	7.89	6.87	3.21	7.07	9.01	9.25	4.91	6.01
PACA	11.68	0.00	2.68	1.88	13.81	5.64	4.68	3.13	5.01	5.76	5.46	2.84	3.11
C	39.73	13.81	14.87	16.59	0.00	2.71	2.53	6.95	11.52	10.69	9.21	5.44	7.28

Figure 3.30. *Step 9. For a color version of this figure, see www.iste.co.uk/cochard/mathematics3.zip*

Region	IdF	PACA	HdF	O	C	BFC	CVL	GE	ARA	B	PdL	N	NA
HdF	18.66	2.68	0.00	0.25	14.87	7.54	6.31	3.21	8.32	10.33	10.41	5.07	6.70
N	16.24	2.84	5.07	4.91	5.44	0.55	0.65	0.54	1.87	1.99	1.58	0.00	0.32
B	10.25	5.76	10.33	9.01	10.69	3.01	4.33	2.83	0.22	0.00	0.11	1.99	0.80
GE	16.21	3.13	3.21	3.21	6.95	1.34	1.48	0.00	2.06	2.83	2.78	0.54	1.17
IdF	0.00	11.68	18.66	14.74	39.73	21.89	23.27	16.21	9.37	10.25	11.60	16.24	13.00
PdL	11.60	5.46	10.41	9.25	9.21	2.36	3.49	2.78	0.54	0.11	0.00	1.58	0.53
CVL	23.27	4.68	6.31	6.87	2.53	0.25	0.00	1.48	4.44	4.33	3.49	0.65	1.67
BFC	21.89	5.64	7.54	7.89	2.71	0.00	0.25	1.34	3.21	3.01	2.36	0.55	1.19
NA	13.00	3.11	6.70	6.01	7.28	1.19	1.67	1.17	0.89	0.80	0.53	0.32	0.00
ARA	9.37	5.01	8.32	7.07	11.52	3.21	4.44	2.06	0.00	0.22	0.54	1.87	0.89
O	14.74	1.88	0.25	0.00	16.59	7.89	6.87	3.21	7.07	9.01	9.25	4.91	6.01
PACA	11.68	0.00	2.68	1.88	13.81	5.64	4.68	3.13	5.01	5.76	5.46	2.84	3.11
C	39.73	13.81	14.87	16.59	0.00	2.71	2.53	6.95	11.52	10.69	9.21	5.44	7.28

Figure 3.31. *Step 10. For a color version of this figure, see www.iste.co.uk/cochard/mathematics3.zip*

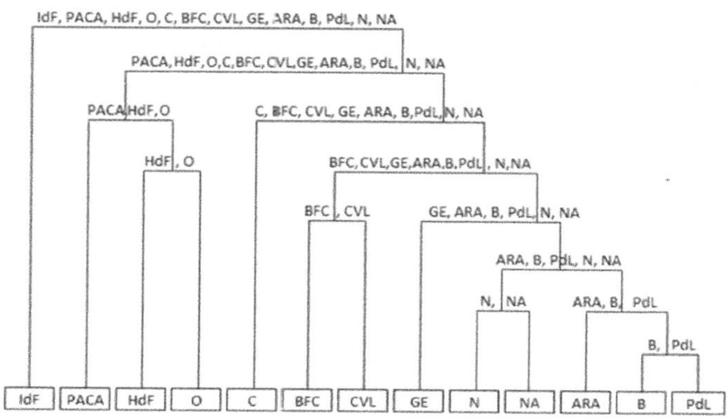

Figure 3.32. *Dendrogram*

Step 10: the shortest distance, 2.84 (orange boxes), is used to merge the two previous aggregates (see Figure 3.30). The result is shown in Figure 3.31.

Step 11: this is the final step, where the IdF region joins the aggregate comprising all regions with a distance value of 9.37 (orange boxes) (see Figure 3.31).

In these steps, the regions were grouped in an ascending fashion, starting with single regions (singletons) and ending with an aggregate comprising all regions. Reversing these steps produces the dendrogram shown in Figure 3.32.

3.5.3. *Ward's aggregation strategy*

To aggregate two classes, an aggregation measure is required to represent the degree of similarity between these classes.

One of the most commonly used measures is *Ward's measure*, calculated from the distance between individuals. Choosing an appropriate distance is therefore important. This measure is expressed as follows, referred to as the "Ward measure":

$$D^2(A,B) = \frac{d^2(g_A, g_B)}{\frac{1}{n_A} + \frac{1}{n_B}} = \frac{n_A n_B}{n_A + n_B} d^2(g_A, g_B)$$

where d represents the Euclidean distance. In this formula:

– g_A and g_B are the centers of gravity of classes A and B, respectively;

– n_A and n_B denote the sizes (number of elements) of these classes.

By assigning each center of gravity a weight equal to its size, this expression can be rewritten using the Euclidean distance. Let g represent the center of gravity of g_A and g_B. In the individual space with origin O, g_A and g_{BA} can be represented by the vectors $\boldsymbol{g_A} = \boldsymbol{O}\boldsymbol{g}_A$ and $\boldsymbol{g_B} = \boldsymbol{O}\boldsymbol{g}_B$ (with vectors shown in bold for clarity). The definition of the center of gravity $\boldsymbol{g}$ can then be expressed as follows:

$$(n_A + n_B)\boldsymbol{g} = n_A\boldsymbol{g_A} + n_B\boldsymbol{g_B}$$

From this, it follows that:

$$(n_A + n_B)(g - \boldsymbol{g_A}) = n_B(\boldsymbol{g_B} - \boldsymbol{g_A}) \quad \text{and} \quad (n_A + n_B)(\boldsymbol{g} - \boldsymbol{g_B}) = n_A(\boldsymbol{g_A} - \boldsymbol{g_B})$$

Squaring these expressions yields:

$$(n_A + n_B)^2(\boldsymbol{g} - \boldsymbol{g}_A)^2 = n_B^2(\boldsymbol{g}_B - \boldsymbol{g}_A)^2 \quad \text{and} \quad (n_A + n_B)^2(\boldsymbol{g} - \boldsymbol{g}_B)^2 = n_A^2(\boldsymbol{g}_A - \boldsymbol{g}_B)^2$$

Using the Euclidean distance yields:

$$(n_A + n_B)^2 d^2(g, g_A) = n_B^2 d^2(g_A, g_B) et (n_A + n_B)^2 d^2(g, g_B) = n_A^2 d^2(g_A, g_B)$$

The inertia of the points g_A and g_B with respect to g is given by:

$$I_g = n_A d^2(g, g_A) + n_B d^2(g, g_B)$$

Thus:

$$I_g = \frac{n_A n_B}{(n_A + n_B)} d^2(g_A, g_B)$$

Ward's measure corresponds to the inertia of the two classes relative to their common center of gravity. Minimizing $D^2(A, B)$ is therefore equivalent to minimizing the inertia I_g

EXAMPLE 3.10.– Returning to the hierarchy of regions in Example 3.9, assuming they have equal weighting, Ward's measure can be expressed for singletons ($n_A = n_B = 1$) using the reduced centered coordinates X, Y, Z (see Figure 3.33).

	HdF	N	B	GE	IdF	PdL	CVL	BFC	NA	ARA	O	PACA	C
HdF	0.00	2.54	5.16	1.61	9.33	5.21	3.16	3.77	3.35	4.16	0.12	1.34	7.43
N	2.54	0.00	0.99	0.27	8.12	0.79	0.33	0.28	0.16	0.94	2.46	1.42	2.72
B	5.16	0.99	0.00	1.41	5.12	0.06	2.17	1.50	0.40	0.11	4.51	2.88	5.35
GE	1.61	0.27	1.41	0.00	8.11	1.39	0.74	0.67	0.59	1.03	1.61	1.56	3.47
IdF	9.33	8.12	5.12	8.11	0.00	5.80	11.64	10.94	6.50	4.68	7.37	5.84	19.87
PdL	5.21	0.79	0.06	1.39	5.80	0.00	1.75	1.18	0.26	0.27	4.63	2.73	4.60
CVL	3.16	0.33	2.17	0.74	11.64	1.75	0.00	0.13	0.83	2.22	3.43	2.34	1.27
BFC	3.77	0.28	1.50	0.67	10.94	1.18	0.13	0.00	0.60	1.60	3.94	2.82	1.35
NA	3.35	0.16	0.40	0.59	6.50	0.26	0.83	0.60	0.00	0.44	3.01	1.56	3.64
ARA	4.16	0.94	0.11	1.03	4.68	0.27	2.22	1.60	0.44	0.00	3.54	2.51	5.76
O	0.12	2.46	4.51	1.61	7.37	4.63	3.43	3.94	3.01	3.54	0.00	0.94	8.30
PACA	1.34	1.42	2.88	1.56	5.84	2.73	2.34	2.82	1.56	2.51	0.94	0.00	6.90
C	7.43	2.72	5.35	3.47	19.87	4.60	1.27	1.35	3.64	5.76	8.30	6.90	0.00

Figure 3.33. *Ward's measurements. For a color version of this figure, see www.iste.co.uk/cochard/mathematics3.zip*

Ward's measure for a pair of singletons equals half the square of the distance between the two singletons. The smallest observed value is 0.06 (orange boxes), which permits us to aggregate the B and PdL regions (see Figure 3.34). To achieve this, the coordinates of the center of gravity of B and PdL are calculated (as shown in Figure 3.34). The updated table of Ward's measurements is shown in Figure 3.35. The smallest value of the Ward measure is now 0.12 (orange boxes), indicating the merging of the HdF and O regions.

Region	X	Y	Z
HdF	1.94	0.34	-0.62
N	-0.15	-0.40	-0.22
GE	0.16	0.12	-0.64
IdF	0.06	2.38	2.69
CVL	-0.15	-1.05	-0.70
BFC	-0.57	-0.77	-0.71
NA	-0.47	-0.17	0.19
ARA	-0.78	0.72	0.26
O	1.84	0.58	-0.20
PACA	1.21	-0.19	0.75
C	-0.89	-2.06	-1.68
B, PdL	-1.09	0.25	0.44

Figure 3.34. *Grouping of B and PdL*

	HdF	N	GE	IdF	CVL	BFC	NA	ARA	O	PACA	C	B, PdL
HdF	0.00	2.54	1.61	9.33	3.16	3.77	3.35	4.16	0.12	1.34	7.43	6.89
N	2.54	0.00	0.27	8.12	0.33	0.28	0.16	0.94	2.46	1.42	2.72	1.17
GE	1.61	0.27	0.00	8.11	0.74	0.67	0.59	1.03	1.61	1.56	3.47	1.85
IdF	9.33	8.12	8.11	0.00	11.64	10.94	6.50	4.68	7.37	5.84	19.87	7.26
CVL	3.16	0.33	0.74	11.64	0.00	0.13	0.83	2.22	3.43	2.34	1.27	2.59
BFC	3.77	0.28	0.67	10.94	0.13	0.00	0.60	1.60	3.94	2.82	1.35	1.77
NA	3.35	0.16	0.59	6.50	0.83	0.60	0.00	0.44	3.01	1.56	3.64	0.42
ARA	4.16	0.94	1.03	4.68	2.22	1.60	0.44	0.00	3.54	2.51	5.76	0.23
O	0.12	2.46	1.61	7.37	3.43	3.94	3.01	3.54	0.00	0.94	8.30	6.07
PACA	1.34	1.42	1.56	5.84	2.34	2.82	1.56	2.51	0.94	0.00	6.90	3.72
C	7.43	2.72	3.47	19.87	1.27	1.35	3.64	5.76	8.30	6.90	0.00	6.61
B, PdL	6.89	1.17	1.85	7.26	2.59	1.77	0.42	0.23	6.07	3.72	6.61	0.00

Figure 3.35. *Ward measurement updates. For a color version of this figure, see www.iste.co.uk/cochard/mathematics3.zip*

The reader is invited to continue the calculations, keeping the following two observations in mind:

1) The factor $\frac{n_A n_B}{n_A+n_B}$ must be considered when calculating Ward's measurements.

2) The coordinates of an aggregate's center of gravity must be recalculated at each step. If the aggregate includes one composed of n_A regions and another composed of n_B regions, its coordinates are:

$$X = \frac{n_A X_A + n_B X_B}{n_A + n_B}$$

and similarly, for Y and Z.

The final result is the dendrogram shown in Figure 3.36, where the height corresponds to the square root of the Ward measure shared by two aggregates.

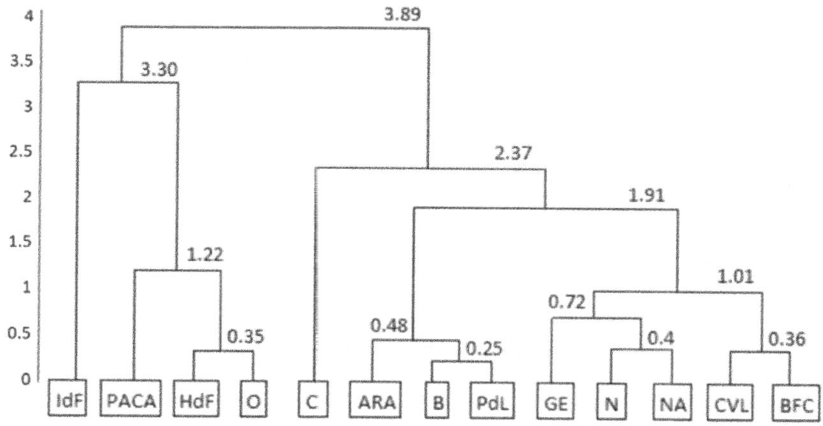

Figure 3.36. *Dendrogram*

3.6. Appendices

3.6.1. *Huygens–König theorem*

Consider a point A in space $\mathbb{R}^p$ and a cloud of n points i with a center of gravity G. The point A can be represented by a vector $\boldsymbol{x}(\text{A})$ with components $\boldsymbol{x}_1(\text{A}), \boldsymbol{x}_2(\text{A}), \dots, \boldsymbol{x}_p(\text{A})$. Similarly, the center of gravity can be represented by a vector $\boldsymbol{x}(\text{G})$ with components $x_1(\text{G}), x_2(\text{G}), \dots, \boldsymbol{x}_p(\text{G})$. Likewise, the point i corresponds to a vector $\boldsymbol{x}(i)$ with components $x_1(i), x_2(i), \dots, x_p(i)$.

Let us calculate the inertia of the points i with respect to point A using the classic definition of distance with a matrix $\boldsymbol{M}$:

$$I_A = \sum_{i=1}^{n} \omega_i d^2(i, \mathrm{A}) = \sum_{i=1}^{n} \omega_i [\boldsymbol{x}(i) - \boldsymbol{x}(\mathrm{A})^t \, \boldsymbol{M}[\boldsymbol{x}(i) - \boldsymbol{x}(\mathrm{A})]$$

Now, add and subtract $\boldsymbol{x}(\mathrm{G})$ in the square brackets:

$$I_A = \sum_{i=1}^{n} \omega_i [\boldsymbol{x}(i) - \boldsymbol{x}(\mathrm{G}) + \boldsymbol{x}(\mathrm{G}) - \boldsymbol{x}(\mathrm{A})]^t \, \boldsymbol{M}[\boldsymbol{x}(i) - \boldsymbol{x}(\mathrm{G}) + \boldsymbol{x}(\mathrm{G}) - \boldsymbol{x}(\mathrm{A})]$$

Developing the matrix product:

$$\begin{aligned} I_A = \sum_{i=1}^{n} \omega_i [\boldsymbol{x}(i) - \boldsymbol{x}(\mathrm{G})]^t \boldsymbol{M}[\boldsymbol{x}(i) - \boldsymbol{x}(\mathrm{G})] \\ + \sum_{i=1}^{n} \omega_i \, [\boldsymbol{x}(\mathrm{G}) - \boldsymbol{x}(\mathrm{A})]^t \boldsymbol{M}[\boldsymbol{x}(\mathrm{G}) - \boldsymbol{x}(\mathrm{A})] \\ + 2 \sum_{i=1}^{n} \omega_i \, [\boldsymbol{x}(i) - \boldsymbol{x}(\mathrm{G})]^t \boldsymbol{M}[\boldsymbol{x}(\mathrm{G}) - \boldsymbol{x}(\mathrm{A})] \end{aligned}$$

Since G is the center of gravity of the point cloud, the following holds:

$$\sum_{i=1}^{n} \omega_i \, [x(i) - x(\mathrm{G})] = \mathbf{0}$$

Thus, the inertia becomes:

$$I_A = \sum_{i=1}^{n} \omega_i d^2(i, \mathrm{G}) + \left(\sum_{i=1}^{n} \omega_i \right) d^2 \, (\mathrm{G}, \mathrm{A})$$

This shows that the inertia with respect to A is the sum of the inertia of points i in relation to G and the inertia of G in relation to A. This corresponds to the *Huygens-König theorem*.

Application: consider the case where there are K classes C_k representing n individuals. Let g_k denote the center of gravity of the individuals in class C_k, and g

denote the center of gravity of all n individuals. Taking g as point A and considering class C_k as a cloud of points, the previous general result leads to the following expression:

$$\sum_{i \in C_k} \omega_i d^2(i,g) = \sum_{i \in C_k} \omega_i d^2(i,g_k) + \left(\sum_{i \in C_k} \omega_i\right) d^2(g_k,g)$$

Now, summing over all classes, the result is:

$$\sum_k \sum_{i \in C_k} \omega_i d^2(i,g) = \sum_k \sum_{i \in C_k} \omega_i d^2(i,g_k) + \sum_k \left(\sum_{i \in C_k} \omega_i\right) d^2(g_k,g)$$

Alternatively:

$$\sum_{i=1}^{n} \omega_i d^2(i,g) = \sum_k \sum_{i \in C_k} \omega_i d^2(i,g_k) + \sum_k \left(\sum_{i \in C_k} \omega_i\right) d^2(g_k,g)$$

This leads to the result:

$$I_g = W + Q.$$

3.6.2. *Classification software*

Let us examine the two programs mentioned in the previous chapter.

3.6.2.1. *Tanagra software*

a) Partitioning

Tanagra software provides *k-means* clustering functionality. After loading the data table and applying the "Define status" component, the *K-Means* function can be selected in the *Clustering* section (see Figure 3.37).

After execution, the results are displayed in the right-hand window. To visualize the classes, the "*View dataset*" and "*Scatterplot with label*" functions in the *Data visualization* section can be used (see Figure 3.38).

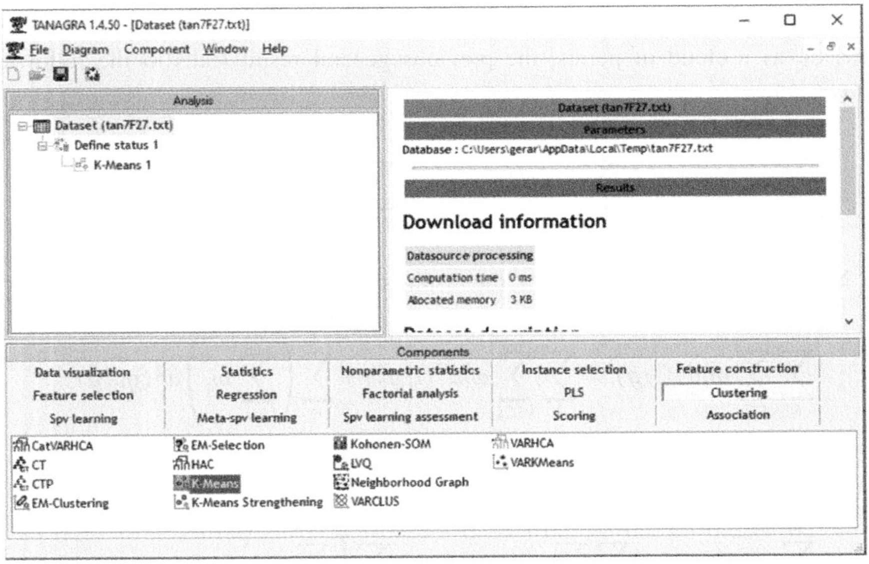

Figure 3.37. *K-means functionality. For a color version of this figure, see www.iste.co.uk/cochard/mathematics3.zip*

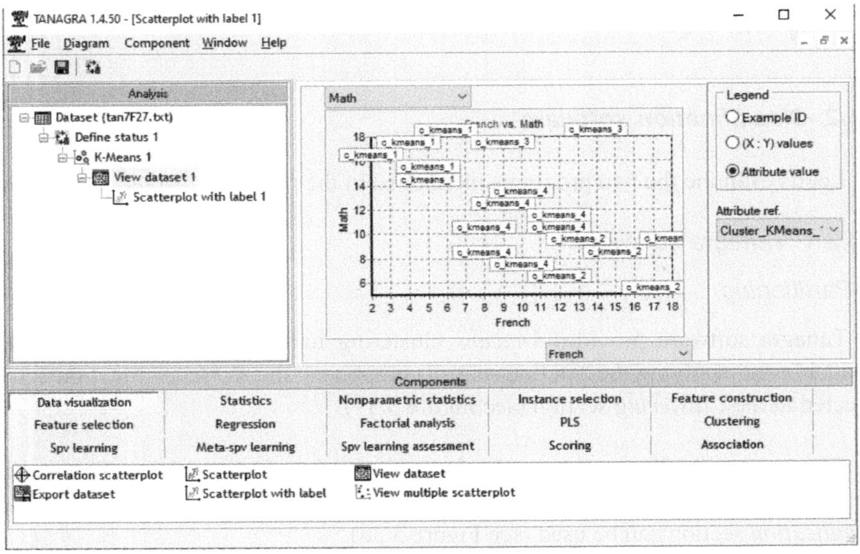

Figure 3.38. *Results. For a color version of this figure, see www.iste.co.uk/cochard/mathematics3.zip*

b) Hierarchical methods

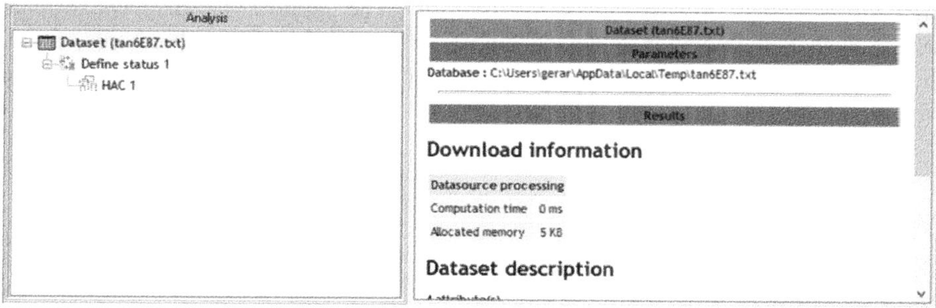

Figure 3.39. *HAC function. For a color version of this figure, see www.iste.co.uk/cochard/mathematics3.zip*

To perform hierarchical clustering, Tanagra offers the HAC (Hierarchical Agglomerative Clustering) feature. Alternatively, the *CatVARHCA* method can be used. After preparing the data file in Excel, we can load it into Tanagra. Once the file is loaded and the "*Define status*" component is added, we can access the *HAC* function in the *Clustering* section (see Figure 3.39).

In the *HAC* parameters, Tanagra allows us to select the option for automatically detecting the optimal number of classes. Additionally, we can choose to normalize variance and specify a maximum level for the tree, such as 10 (see Figure 3.40).

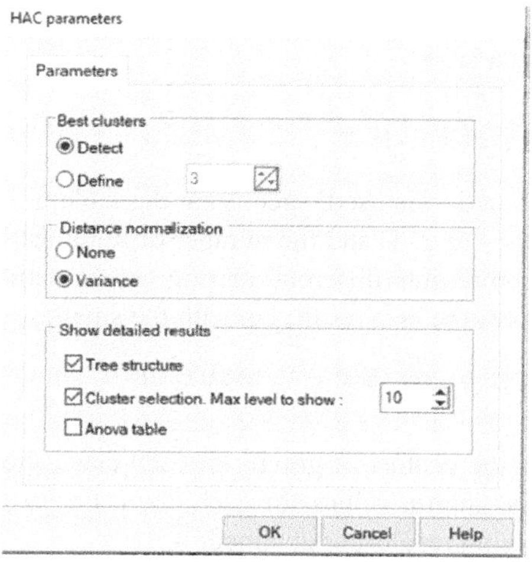

Figure 3.40. *Options*

To view the results in Tanagra, use the "*View*" option. In the right-hand window, there are two tabs: "*Report*" and "*Dendrogram*". The "*Report*" tab displays various results, such as the number of classes and the structure of the hierarchical tree, while the "*Dendrogram*" tab provides a graphical representation of the hierarchical tree (see Figure 3.41).

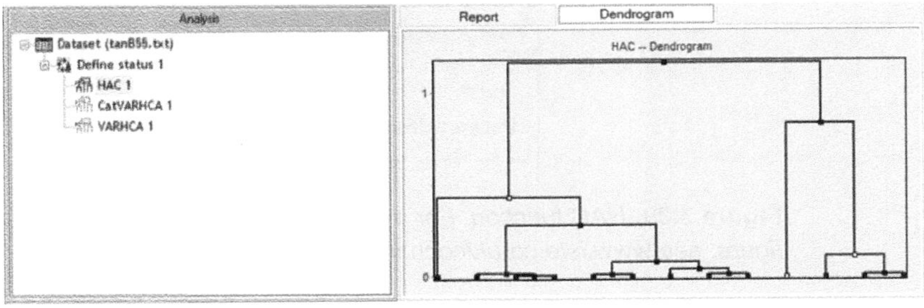

Figure 3.41. *Dendrogram tab. For a color version of this figure, see www.iste.co.uk/cochard/mathematics3.zip*

3.6.2.2. *R software*

a) Partitioning

As a reminder, the use of R software was covered in Chapter 2 for more detailed information. This section focuses mainly on the commands required for the study of this chapter.

After loading the data table:

```
> library( readxl )
> table <- read_excel ("cloud.xlsx")
```

Next, the *kmeans* function is used, specifying the table to be analyzed (*tab*), the desired number of classes (e.g. 4) and the number of initializations (*nstart*, here 10). The *nstart* parameter represents different starting configurations, and the software chooses the one that gives the best result, i.e. with the smallest value of W:

```
> tab_kmeans <- kmeans(tab, centers = 4, nstart=10)
> print(tab_kmeans)
```

The result includes the centers of gravity of each class, the composition of each class and the intra-class inertia values for each class. For example, for the data in Example 3.5, the following results are obtained:

```
Cluster means:
    French Math
1 15.000000 7.50000
2 4.400000 16.00000
3 9.857143 10.14286
4 11.500000 17.50000

Clustering vector:
[1] 1 1 3 2 2 3 1 1 3 2 2 4 3 3 3 1 3 2 4 1

Within cluster sum of squares by cluster:
[1] 39.50000 19.20000 43.71429 13.00000
 (between_SS / total_SS = 83.7%)
```

To visualize results graphically, the *factoextra* library can be used. It provides additional features for visualizing results in cluster form:

```
> fviz_cluster(tab_kmeans, data = tab)
```

The classes are presented graphically in Figure 3.42.

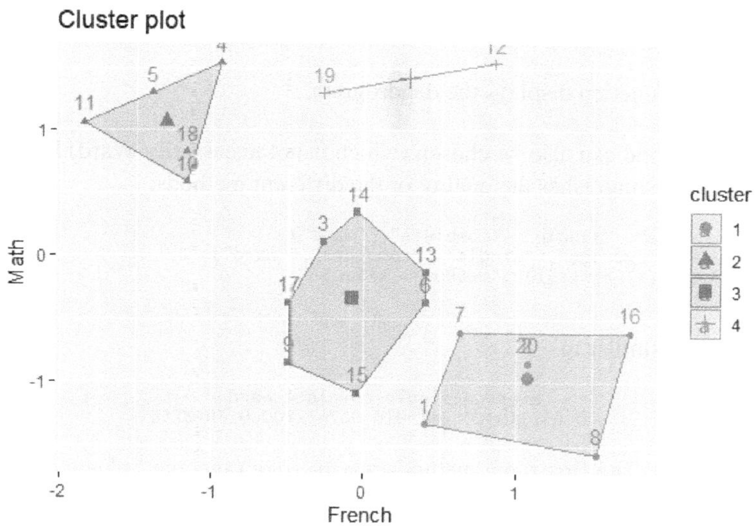

Figure 3.42. *Resulting classes. For a color version of this figure, see www.iste.co.uk/cochard/mathematics3.zip*

b) Hierarchical methods

Two function libraries are needed: *factoextra* and *cluster*. In addition, to read data from Excel, the *readxl* library is used. These libraries provide specific functions for performing clustering analyses and visualizing results efficiently.

In this case, the following commands are used:

```
> library(factoextra)
> library(cluster)
> library(readxl)
> table <- read_excel("cloud.xlsx")
```

It is convenient to work with reduced centered coordinates, which can be achieved using the *scale()* function. This function centers the data by subtracting the mean of each variable and scales them by dividing by the standard deviation of each variable:

```
> tab <- scale(table)
```

The function to be used for hierarchical clustering is *agnes()*. The main arguments for this function are the data table to be explored (in this case, *tab*) and the classification method to be used (in this case, *Ward*):

```
> clust <- agnes(tab, method = "ward")
> pltree(clust, ces = 0.6, hang = -1, main = "Dendrogram")
```

The *pltree()* function displays the dendrogram.

The best method can also be chosen (which is not necessarily Ward) by applying a criterion that distinguishes the quality of the different methods:

```
> m <- c("average", "single", "complete", "ward")
> names(m) <- c("average", "single", "complete", "ward")
> ac <- function(x){agnes(tab, method = x)$ac}
> sapply(m; ac)
```

The result is similar to

```
  average    single  complete      ward
0.6521194 0.2479916 0.7672700 0.7948758
```

in favor of Ward. The first three methods are *average* (average linkage aggregation measure), *single* (minimum linkage aggregation measure) and *complete* (maximum linkage aggregation measure).

4

Linear Programming

CONCEPTS COVERED IN THIS CHAPTER.–

Linear programming is a fundamental tool for optimizing functions subject to constraints.

This chapter provides a detailed exploration of this technique, beginning with an introductory example that illustrates the type of problems it addresses.

Next, the general formulation of linear programming and its geometric interpretation are then introduced. Over the years, several algorithms have been developed to solve linear programs, with the simplex algorithm being the most prominent and widely applied. This algorithm is described in detail, accompanied by illustrative examples.

The simplex algorithm assumes that the solution where all variables are zero is a feasible solution. When this assumption fails, the "two-phase" method becomes necessary, and its principles and applications are explained.

The concept of duality, which links two complementary formulations of the same linear program, is then examined, along with the phenomenon of degeneracy.

Finally, as an extension of linear programming over non-negative real numbers, integer linear programming is introduced, with a focus on techniques such as Gomory cuts and the Branch and Bound algorithm.

References: [BRO 82, DES 76, ECO 98, FAU 74, FAU 79, FAU 14, JAC 98, KAU 75, PAP 92, PHE 75].

4.1. An introductory example

A simple problem discussed herein serves to introduce the subject.

In a factory, there are four different machines, designated by the letters A, B, C and D. These machines are used to manufacture saucepans and frying pans, with each machine having specific features and capabilities:

– Machines A and B can produce both saucepans and frying pans.

– Machine C is limited to making saucepans.

– Machine D is limited to making frying pans.

To better understand the situation, the detailed quantitative data presented in Figure 4.1 is useful.

machine	Number of pans per hour	Number of frying pans per hour
A	500	800
B	850	400
C	450	
D		300

Figure 4.1. *The data*

The production of a saucepan requires the sequential use of machines A, B and C, while the production of a frying pan requires the sequential use of machines A, B and D.

The net income from the sale of each item is as follows:

– The sale of a saucepan earns 5 euros.

– The sale of a frying pan brings in 4 euros.

The objective is to determine the optimum quantities of saucepans and frying pans to produce in order to maximize profit, assuming that all produced items can be sold.

The mathematical formulation of the problem is described as follows:

1) Objective function: the goal is to maximize profit, represented by z. Let x_1 denote the number of saucepans to be manufactured and x_2 the number of frying pans to be manufactured. The profit can be expressed as:

$$z = 5x_1 + 4x_2$$

2) Constraints: are based on the capacities of the machines, expressed as follows:

– Machine A: takes $\frac{1}{500}$ hours to produce a saucepan and $\frac{1}{800}$ hours to produce a frying pan. For x_1 saucepans and x_2 frying pans, the total running time is less than 1 hour:

$$\frac{x_1}{500} + \frac{x_2}{800} \leq 1 \text{ or equivalently, } \quad 0.200x_1 + 0.125x_2 \leq 100 \qquad [R1]$$

– Machine B: requires $\frac{1}{850}$ hours to produce a saucepan and $\frac{1}{400}$ hours to produce a frying pan. The corresponding constraint is:

$$\frac{x_1}{850} + \frac{x_2}{400} \leq 1 \quad \text{or equivalently, } \quad 0.1176x_1 + 0.25x_2 \leq 100 \qquad [R2]$$

– Machine C: this machine only processes saucepans, requiring $\frac{1}{450}$ hours per unit. The corresponding constraint is:

$$\frac{x_1}{450} \leq 1 \quad \text{or equivalently,} \quad 0.2222x_1 \leq 100 \qquad [R3]$$

– Machine D: this machine is used for frying pans, requiring $\frac{1}{300}$ hours per unit. The corresponding constraint is:

$$\frac{x_2}{300} \leq 1 \quad \text{or equivalently,} \quad 0.3333x_2 \leq 100 \qquad [R4]$$

3) Non-negativity constraints: as this is a production problem, the decision variables must be non-negative:

$$x_1 \geq 0 \qquad [R5]$$

$$x_2 \geq 0 \qquad [R6]$$

Note on fractional and integer variables: although the decision variables are inherently integers (since fractional quantities cannot be manufactured), this formulation focuses on the fractional version of the problem. Techniques for addressing integer variables will be discussed later.

The problem can be solved graphically because both the objective function and the constraints are linear in x_1 and x_2, allowing them to be represented as straight lines on a Cartesian plane.

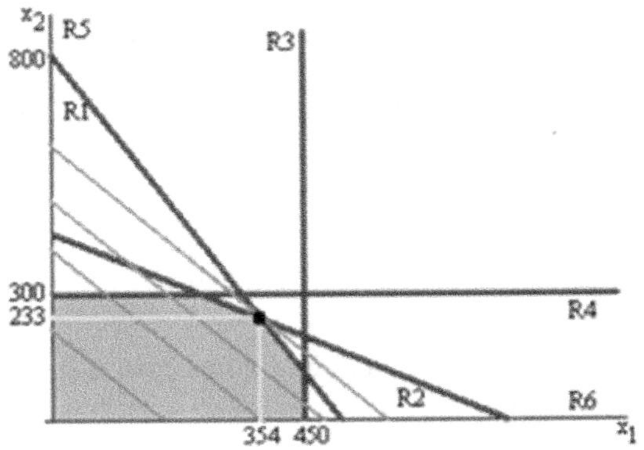

Figure 4.2. *Graphic resolution. For a color version of this figure, see www.iste.co.uk/cochard/mathematics3.zip*

The line corresponding to the objective function (shown in green) can be moved parallel to itself. This is referred to as the contour line, with all such lines sharing the same slope. The constraint lines (shown in red) define regions in the plane. Possible solutions are confined to the polygon P, whose area is shaded gray (see Figure 4.2).

As the objective function line moves from the origin (representing zero profit) towards the northeast, the profit increases. The maximum profit is reached at the vertex $(354.19, 233.29)$ of the polygon P. The optimal profit value, 2704.11 euros, is achieved when producing $x_1 = 354.19$ saucepans and $x_2 = 233.29$ frying pans.

However, as previously noted, fractional values for x_1 and x_2 are impractical since 0.19 saucepans and 0.29 frying pans have no real-world meaning.

A natural approach is to "round off" the results, yielding $x_1 = 354$ saucepans and $x_2 = 233$ frying pans, resulting in a profit of $z = 2702$ euros.

NOTE 4.1.– The rounding applied may not necessarily result in the optimal solution.

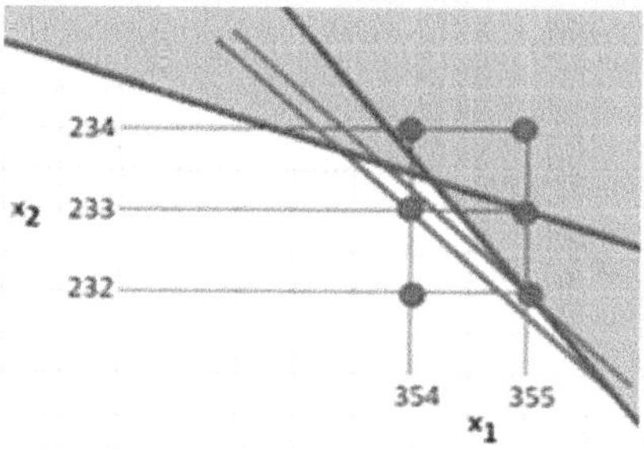

Figure 4.3. *Zoom. For a color version of this figure, see www.iste.co.uk/cochard/mathematics3.zip*

Indeed, a closer examination of the assumed values, as shown in Figure 4.3, reveals that the correct values are $x_1 = 355$ and $x_2 = 232$, resulting in $z = 2703$!

In the previous mathematical formulation, the variables x_1 and x_2 were assumed to be real, non-negative and non-integer, corresponding to a linear program (also referred to as a real-number linear program). However, to obtain the correct solution in this example, it would be necessary to solve a linear program in integers, which is more difficult to solve than the previous case. The topic of integer linear programming will be explored in section 4.8. For now, the focus remains on real-number linear programming.

4.2. General formulation

In the general case, a linear program is formulated as follows:

1) The objective function is expressed as:

$$z = \sum_{j=1}^{n} c_j x_j$$

Here, x_j represents the decision variables, while c_j denotes the associated unit "costs". Depending on the problem, the function z can be either maximized or minimized. It is important to note that minimizing z is equivalent to maximizing $-z$, and vice versa. In this study, the focus is on maximizing z.

2) There are m linear constraints:

$$\sum_{j=1}^{n} a_{ij}x_j \leq b_i \qquad \text{for } i = 1, \dots, m$$

3) The variables and constants are subject to the following conditions:

$$x_j \geq 0 \qquad \text{for } j = 1, \dots, n$$

$$b_i \geq 0 \qquad \text{for } i = 1, \dots, m$$

$$a_{ij} \in R,\ \forall i = 1, \dots, m, \forall j = 1, \dots, n$$

4) In the basic (initial) problem, the goal is to maximize z. Note that maximizing z is equivalent to minimizing $-z$.

The standard linear program, referred to as P1, is expressed in canonical form (though another canonical form is often used for minimization problems):

$$Maximize \quad z = \sum_{j=1}^{n} c_j x_j$$

Subject to $\sum_{j=1}^{n} a_{ij}x_j \leq b_i \ \ i = 1, \dots, m$

$$x_j \geq 0 \ \ j = 1, \dots, n$$

$$b_i \geq 0 \ \ i = 1, \dots, m$$

$$a_{ij} \in R \ \ \forall i = 1, \dots, m, \forall j = 1, \dots, n$$

To derive a linear system with m equations and $n + m$ unknowns, *slack variables* $x_{n+1}, x_{n+2}, \dots, x_{n+m}$ are introduced. These transform the inequality constraints into equations:

$$\begin{array}{llll} a_{11}x_1 + a_{12}x_2 + \cdots + a_{1n}x_n + x_{n+1} & & & = b_1 \\ a_{21}x_1 + a_{22}x_2 + \cdots + a_{2n}x_n & + x_{n+2} & & = b_2 \\ \vdots & & & \\ a_{m1}x_1 + a_{m2}x_2 + \cdots + a_{mn}x_n & & + x_{n+m} & = b_m \end{array}$$

In matrix form, this system is expressed as $\boldsymbol{AX} = \boldsymbol{B}$, where:

$$\boldsymbol{A} = \begin{bmatrix} a_{11} & a_{12} & \cdots & a_{1n} & 1 & 0 & \cdots & 0 \\ a_{21} & a_{22} & \cdots & a_{2n} & 0 & 1 & \cdots & 0 \\ \cdots & \cdots & \cdots & \cdots & \cdots & \cdots & \cdots & 0 \\ a_{m1} & a_{m2} & \cdots & a_{mn} & 0 & 0 & \cdots & 1 \end{bmatrix} \quad \boldsymbol{X} = \begin{bmatrix} x_1 \\ x_2 \\ \vdots \\ \vdots \\ \vdots \\ x_n \end{bmatrix} \quad \boldsymbol{B} = \begin{bmatrix} b_1 \\ b_2 \\ \vdots \\ b_m \end{bmatrix}$$

This representation is referred to as the "*standard form*" of the linear program. The addition of m slack variables corresponds directly to the number of inequality constraints. Consequently, the total number of decision variables increases by m. To solve this system, a matrix $\boldsymbol{C}$ of dimensions (m) rows and $(n + m)$ columns must be identified such that $\boldsymbol{C}.\boldsymbol{A} = \boldsymbol{I}$, where $\boldsymbol{I}$ is the $m \times m$ identity matrix. By multiplying both sides of $\boldsymbol{A}.\boldsymbol{X} = \boldsymbol{B}$ by the matrix $\boldsymbol{C}$ (if it exists), the solution is obtained as:

$$\boldsymbol{X} = \boldsymbol{C}.\boldsymbol{B}.$$

Returning to the P1 program, minimizing the objective function z is equivalent to maximizing $-z$. This modification does not after the constraints of P1, which remain unchanged.

The constraints in P1 can take different forms:

$$\sum_{j=1}^{n} a_{ij}x_j \leq b_i, \qquad i = 1, \dots, m$$

To transform an inequality into an equality, additional positive terms must be introduced. These terms add slack variables into the model:

$$a_{i1}x_1 + a_{i2}x_2 + \cdots + a_{in}x_n \leq b_i \longrightarrow a_{i1}x_1 + a_{i2}x_2 + \cdots + a_{in}x_n + x_e = b_i$$

where x_e is a slack variable. This variable appears with a coefficient of 1 in the constraint and a coefficient of 0 in the objective function.

When a constraint is expressed with the inequality sign "≥", the same approach is applied, but with a negative slack variable:

$$a_{i1}x_1 + a_{i2}x_2 + \cdots + a_{in}x_n \geq b_i \longrightarrow a_{i1}x_1 + a_{i2}x_2 + \cdots + a_{in}x_n - \boldsymbol{x_e} = b_i$$

In this case, the slack variable x_e is subtracted, appearing with a coefficient of -1 in the constraint and 0 in the objective function. However, the solution

$x_1 = x_2 = \cdots = x_n = 0$ must remain feasible. This would lead to $-1 \times x_e = b_i$, which contradicts the assumption $b_i \geq 0$.

To solve this problem, an "*artificial variable*" x_a ($x_a \geq 0$) is introduced. The constraint becomes:

$$a_{i1}x_1 + a_{i2}x_2 + \cdots . + a_{in}x_n \geq b_i \longrightarrow a_{i1}x_1 + a_{i2}x_2 + \cdots . + a_{in}x_n - x_e + \boldsymbol{x_a} = b_i$$

The artificial variable x_a has a coefficient of $+1$ in the constraint and 0 in the objective function.

When the constraint is expressed as an equality ("="), introducing an artificial variable is also necessary:

$$a_{i1}x_1 + a_{i2}x_2 + \cdots . + a_{in}x_n = b_i \longrightarrow a_{i1}x_1 + a_{i2}x_2 + \cdots . + a_{in}x_n + x_a = b_i$$

In this case, this artificial variable x_a is expected to equal zero in the final solution. Artificial variables are introduced purely to facilitate calculations. For constraints of the "≥" or "=" type, a method called the "two-phase method" is typically used to eliminate artificial variables. This method will be examined in greater detail in section 4.5.

4.3. Geometry of a linear program

Some key mathematical results related to linear programming are as follows:

– When $n = m$, the system of linear equations has exactly one solution.

– When $n < m$, the system has infinitely many solutions. Among these, there exists a subset $\{x_j\}$ where $x_j \geq 0$ for $j = 1, \ldots, n + m$. These solutions are referred to as "possible solutions".

– When $n \leq 3$, a graphical representation of the possible solutions is feasible.

– When $n > 3$, a graphical solution becomes impractical. In this case, the "region" of possible solutions forms a hyperpolyhedron, as shown in Figure 4.4. This hyperpolyhedron is intersected by a hyperplane corresponding to the objective function. However, several mathematical results have been established for problems of this nature. While detailed demonstrations are beyond the scope of this section, these results form the basis of linear programming techniques.

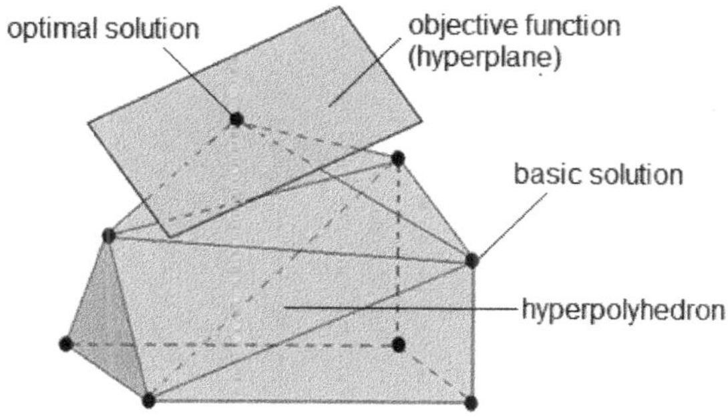

Figure 4.4. *Objective function and basic solutions. For a color version of this figure, see www.iste.co.uk/cochard/mathematics3.zip*

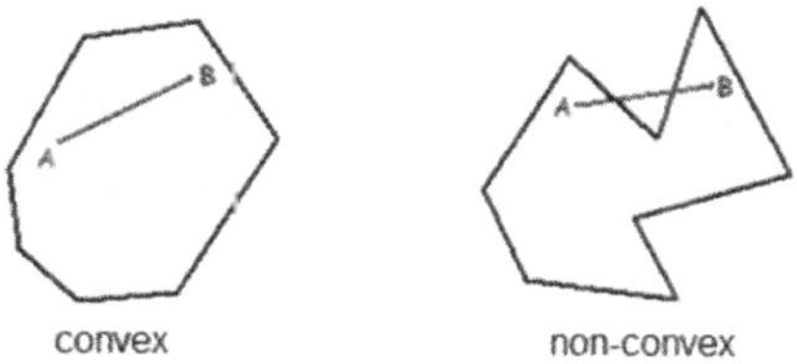

Figure 4.5. *Convexity*

– The hyperpolyhedra generated by the system are convex. A geometric set E is convex if, for any points A and B with E, the entire line segment AB lies within E (as shown in Figure 4.5).

– The vertices of the hyperpolyhedron are the "basic" solutions.

– The desired solution, except in rare cases, is located at one of these basic solutions.

– A basic solution includes at most m positive variables, with the remaining variables equal to zero.

– The solution process involves transitioning from one basic solution to another in a manner that increases the value of z.

These results are essential for solving the linear programming problem efficiently.

These results can be validated using the introductory example depicted in Figure 4.6.

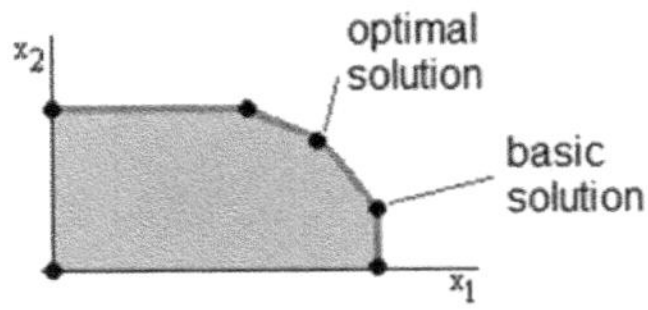

Figure 4.6. *Application to the introductory example*

4.4. Simplex algorithm

Various algorithms have been developed to solve linear programming problems, but the most widely used is the "*simplex algorithm*", introduced by George Dantzig in 1947. While the theoretical foundations of the algorithm will not be detailed here, its practical application and core concept are explained below.

The simplex algorithm operates by transitioning from one basic solution to another within an m-dimensional space, where m represents the number of constraints in the problem. It starts with an initial solution, which may not necessarily be optimal, and iteratively improves the solution until an optimal one is reached.

$$\begin{array}{cccccc} V_1 & V_2 & V_3 & V_4 & V_5 & V_6 \end{array}$$

$$\begin{bmatrix} 0.2000 & 0.1250 & 1 & 0 & 0 & 0 \\ 0.1176 & 0.2500 & 0 & 1 & 0 & 0 \\ 0.2222 & 0.0000 & 0 & 0 & 1 & 0 \\ 0.0000 & 0.3333 & 0 & 0 & 0 & 1 \end{bmatrix} \begin{bmatrix} x_1 \\ x_2 \\ x_3 \\ x_4 \\ x_5 \\ x_6 \end{bmatrix} = \overset{B}{\begin{bmatrix} 100 \\ 100 \\ 100 \\ 100 \end{bmatrix}}$$

Figure 4.7. *Matrix representation*

Now, consider applying the simplex algorithm to the introductory example, which includes two decision variables and four constraints (along with two additional integrity constraints on the decision variables). The initial problem can be represented in matrix form $\boldsymbol{AX} = \mathbf{B}$ (known as the "*simplex table*"), as shown in Figure 4.7. The vectors $\mathbf{V_1}$ and $\mathbf{V_2}$ correspond to the decision variables, while $\mathbf{V}_3$, $\mathbf{V}_4$, $\mathbf{V}_5$ and $\mathbf{V}_6$ represent the slack variables.

An obvious solution to the problem is: $x_1 = 0, x_2 = 0, x_3 = x_4 = x_5 = x_6 = 100$, which gives $z = 5x_1 + 4x_2 = 0$. This solution is the known initial solution.

By examining the columns of the matrix **A** ($\mathbf{V_1}, \mathbf{V_2}, \mathbf{V_3}, \mathbf{V_4}, \mathbf{V_5}, \mathbf{V_6}$) and the second member **B**, it is evident that they are vectors of $\mathbb{R}^4$. The vectors $\mathbf{V_3}, \mathbf{V_4}, \mathbf{V_5}$ and $\mathbf{V_6}$ form a basis of $\mathbb{R}^4$. Thus, the vectors (columns) $\mathbf{V_1}$ and $\mathbf{V_2}$ can be expressed in terms of this basis:

$$\mathbf{V_1} = 0.200\mathbf{V_3} + 0.1176\mathbf{V_4} + 0.2222\mathbf{V_5}$$

$$\mathbf{V_2} = 0.125\mathbf{V_3} + 0.250\mathbf{V_4} + 0.3333\mathbf{V_6}$$

In addition, the second member **B** can be expressed as follows:

$$\mathbf{B} = 100(\mathbf{V_3} + \mathbf{V_4} + \mathbf{V_5} + \mathbf{V_6})$$

These equations allow the columns of the matrix **A** and the second member **B** to be represented in terms of the basis vectors (columns) $\mathbf{V_3}, \mathbf{V_4}, \mathbf{V_5}$ and $\mathbf{V_6}$. To improve the current solution (with $z = 0$), a basis change will be performed:

$$\{\mathbf{V_3}, \mathbf{V_4}, \mathbf{V_5}, \mathbf{V_6}\} \rightarrow \{\mathbf{V_3}, \mathbf{V_4}, \mathbf{V_1}, \mathbf{V_6}\}$$

To do this, it is checked that the determinant $\det(\mathbf{V_3}, \mathbf{V_4}, \mathbf{V_1}, \mathbf{V_6})$ is non-zero, which would indicate that the vectors $\mathbf{V_3}, \mathbf{V_4}, \mathbf{V_1}$ and $\mathbf{V_6}$ are linearly independent. Indeed, if the determinant is zero, this would mean that there is a linear combination of the vectors $\mathbf{V_3}, \mathbf{V_4}, \mathbf{V_1}$ and $\mathbf{V_6}$ that results in the zero vector. Calculating the determinant, the following is obtained:

$$\begin{vmatrix} 1 & 0 & 0.2000 & 0 \\ 0 & 1 & 0.1176 & 0 \\ 0 & 0 & 0.2222 & 0 \\ 0 & 0 & 0.0000 & 1 \end{vmatrix} = 0.2222 \neq 0$$

The new basis $\{\mathbf{V_3}, \mathbf{V_4}, \mathbf{V_1}, \mathbf{V_6}\}$ can be chosen. In this case, $\mathbf{V_5}$ leaves the basis, and $\boldsymbol{V_1}$ enters the new basis. The form of the new equation $\mathbf{AX} = \mathbf{B}$ in this basis change is determined (see Figure 4.8).

In the new basis $\{\mathbf{V_3}, \mathbf{V_4}, \mathbf{V_1}, \mathbf{V_6}\}$, $\mathbf{V_5}$ can be expressed in terms of the other vectors in the basis. Since $\mathbf{V_1} = 0.2\mathbf{V_3} + 0.1176\mathbf{V_4} + 0.2222\mathbf{V_5}$, it follows that $\mathbf{V_5} = 4.5005\mathbf{V_1} - 0.9001\mathbf{V_3} - 0.5293\mathbf{V_4}$. Hence, $\mathbf{V_2}$ remains unchanged, depending only on $\mathbf{V_3}, \mathbf{V_4}$ and $\mathbf{V_6}$.

V_1	V_2	V_3	V_4	V_5	V_6	X		B
						x_1		
0	0.1250	1	0	-0.9001	0	x_2		9.99
0	0.2500	0	1	-0.5293	0	x_3	=	47.07
1	0.0000	0	0	4.5005	0	x_4		450.05
0	0.3333	0	0	0.0000	1	x_5		100.00
						x_6		

Figure 4.8. *Base change*

The second member **B** can also be rewritten according to this new basis:

$$\mathbf{B} = 100(\mathbf{V_3} + \mathbf{V_4} + \mathbf{V_5} + \mathbf{V_6}) = 9.99\mathbf{V_3} + 47.07\mathbf{V_4} + 450.05\mathbf{V_1} + 100\mathbf{V_6}$$

The equation $\mathbf{AX} = \mathbf{B}$ in the new basis thus takes the form shown in Figure 4.8. By performing the base change, a new obvious solution arises:

$$x_1 = 450.05,\ x_2 = 0,\ x_3 = 9.99,\ x_4 = 47.07,\ x_5 = 0,\ x_6 = 100,$$

which gives a value for z equal to 2250 (with a rounding error).

In this way, the value of z was improved with this base change. It is important to note that replacing $\mathbf{V_5}$ with $\mathbf{V_1}$ in the base was not done at random. Dantzig proposed two criteria (to be explained in this section) for selecting the incoming and outgoing vectors.

	V_1	V_2	V_3	V_4	V_5	V_6	B
V_3	0.2000	0.1250	1	0	0	0	100
V_4	0.1176	0.2500	0	1	0	0	100
V_5	0.2222	0.0000	0	0	1	0	100
V_6	0 0000	0.3333	0	0	0	1	100
	5.0000	4.0000	0	0	0	0	0

Figure 4.9. *Practical table*

A closer look will be taken at how to build the new foundations and how the solution gradually improves. First, the problem is presented in its initial version in the form of a table, as shown in Figure 4.9. The matrix **A** and the vector **B** are presented, with each row accompanied by a corresponding base vector (column), indicated by a 1 in the row. The last row represents the coefficients c_j of the objective function. Finally, the box at the bottom right indicates the value of $-z$ for the given base, which is equal to 0 in the initial phase.

In this representation, the indices of the table elements (including the last row and column) must be specified. Columns are always numbered $j = 1, 2, 3, \ldots, p$ and correspond to vectors $\mathbf{V_1}, \mathbf{V_2}, \ldots, \mathbf{V_p}$. Rows, on the other hand, are numbered with the index of the base vectors. In Figure 4.9, the index i runs from top to bottom, taking the values 3, 4, 5 and 6. For example, $a_{42} = 0.25,\ b_5 = 100\ and\ c_2 = 4$.

First Dantzig criterion: *select the vector (column)* $\mathbf{V_j}$ *to be included in the basis by choosing the one with the highest* c_j *coefficient.*

For this problem, $c_1 = 5$, so the (column) vector $\mathbf{V_1}$ is likely to enter the basis.

Second Dantzig criterion: determine the vector (column) $\mathbf{V_i}$ *to remove from the basis, select the one corresponding to the smallest positive ratio* b_i/a_{ij} *(with* $a_{ij} > 0$*).*

In this case, the ration $b_3/a_{31} = 100/0.2222$ gives the smallest ratio, so the vector (column) $\mathbf{V_5}$ leaves the basis.

Basis change: after selecting the entering and leaving vectors, the components of the matrix are adjusted using two operations:

– For the outgoing vector i: divide the row corresponding to $\mathbf{V_i}$ (including the column element **B**) by the pivot a_{ij} (where j is the "incoming/entering" column):

$$a_{ik} \rightarrow a_{ik}/a_{ij}$$

$$b_i \rightarrow b_i/a_{ij}$$

– For the other rows: perform the following adjustments for each coefficient:

$$a_{kl} \rightarrow a_{kl} - (a_{kj} \times a_{il})/a_{ij}$$

$$b_k \rightarrow b_k - (a_{kj} \times b_i)/a_{ij}$$

$$c_l \rightarrow c_l - (c_j \times a_{il})/a_{ij}$$

After applying these operations, the line corresponding to $\mathbf{V_5}$ becomes the line corresponding to $\mathbf{V_1}$ with the values 1 0 0 0 4.5 0 | 450. The line corresponding to $\mathbf{V_3}$ becomes 0 0.125 1 0 -0.9 0 | 10. This table is updated to reflect the changes, as shown in Figure 4.10.

	V_1	V_2	V_3	V_4	V_5	V_6	B
V_3	0	0.1250	1	0	-0.9000	0	10.00
V_4	0	0.2500	0	1	-0.5294	0	47.06
V_1	1	0.0000	0	0	4.5000	0	450.00
V_6	0	0.3333	0	0	0.0000	1	100.00
	0	4.0000	0	0	-22.5000	0	-2250.00

Figure 4.10. *V_1 enters the base, V_5 leaves*

The value of z has increased to 2250 (the value -2250 reads $z - 2250 = 0$).

Repeat the process: the highest c_j coefficient is 4, so the vector $\mathbf{V_2}$ is added to the basis. The lowest ratio b_k/a_{k2} is 80, corresponding to the first row, which means the vector $\mathbf{V_3}$ is removed from the basis. The necessary calculations for the basis change result in the new table shown in Figure 4.11.

	V_1	V_2	V_3	V_4	V_5	V_6	B
V_2	0	1	8,0000	0	-7.2000	0	80.00
V_4	0	0	-2.0000	1	1.2706	0	27.06
V_1	1	0	0.0000	0	4.5000	0	450.00
V_6	0	0	-2.6667	0	2.4000	1	73.33
	0	0	-32.0000	0	6.3000	0	-2570.00

Figure 4.11. *V_4 enters the base, V_3 leaves*

	V_1	V_2	V_3	V_4	V_5	V_6	B
V_2	0	1	-3.33333	5.66667	0	0	233.33
V_5	0	0	-1.57407	0.78704	1	0	21.30
V_1	1	0	7.08333	-3.5417	0	0	354.17
V_6	0	0	1.11111	-1.8889	0	1	22.22
	0	0	-22.0833	-4.9583	0	0	-2704.17

Figure 4.12. *V_5 enters the base, V_4 leaves*

The value of z has increased again, and is now worth 2,570.

Continuing the process: the highest c_j coefficient is 6.3, which means the vector $\mathbf{V_5}$ is added to the basis. The lowest b/a_{k5} ratio is 27.06, which indicates that the vector $\mathbf{V_4}$ is removed from the basis. The necessary calculations for the basis change result in a new table shown in Figure 4.12.

There is no longer any positive c_j coefficient, indicating that the optimum value of z has been reached. Since integer values are expected for the decision variables, the solutions obtained are approximations: $x_1 \approx 354, \quad x_2 \approx 233, \quad$ and $z \approx 2702$. Despite rounding errors, this result is consistent with that obtained at the beginning of this section by graphical resolution.

In fact, the simplex algorithm is designed for *real* variables, not *integer* variables. Thus, it can be concluded that an *approximate* solution of the optimal solution has been obtained. The problem has been solved in its "relaxed" form, using real instead of integer variables. To obtain an exact solution, integer linear programming must be used, which will be covered later.

NOTE 4.2.– In the simplex method, the Dantzig criterion, which favors the coefficient with the highest absolute value in the objective row, is a classic but not mandatory rule. Alternative approaches, such as random, lexicographic or heuristic criteria, can be used to avoid cycles and adapt the method to specific situations.

NOTE 4.3.– The discussion here implicitly considers a linear program of the "Maximize z" type with:

$$\sum_{j=1}^{n} a_{ij}x_j \leq b_i, \qquad i = 1, \dots, m, \qquad \text{with} \quad b_i \geq 0.$$

However, other, more complex formulations exist. Alternative forms of linear constraints will be explored in section 4.5.

Note that practical programs are available for obtaining solutions to linear programs. A few examples include:

– For a small number of variables:

- PHPSimplex (http://www.phpsimplex.com/fr/).

- Excel Solver.

– For a large number of variables:

- IBM's CPLEX, a free download for university students.

- Gurobi Optimizer (https://www.gurobi.com/solutions/gurobi-optimizer/).

- Xpress Solver (https://www.solver.com/xpress-solver-engine).

However, to fully understand the simplex mechanism, the following examples will continue with "by hand" calculations (preferably using a spreadsheet program).

EXAMPLE 4.1.– Return to the introductory example of this chapter. The initial table of the simple algorithm is given in Figure 4.13.

	V_1	V_2	V_3	V_4	V_5	V_6	B
V_3	0.2	0.125	1	0	0	0	100
V_4	0.1176	0.25	0	1	0	0	100
V_5	0.2222	0	0	0	1	0	100
V_6	0	0.3333	0	1	0	1	100
	5	4	0	0	0	0	0

Figure 4.13. *Initial table*

The Dantzig criteria indicate that the vector $\mathbf{V_1}$ must enter the basis, and the vector $\mathbf{V_5}$ must leave (see Figure 4.14).

	V_1	V_2	V_3	V_4	V_5	V_6	B
V_3	0.2	0.125	1	0	0	0	100
V_4	0.1176	0.25	0	1	0	0	100
V_5	0.2222	0	0	0	1	0	100
V_6	0	0.3333	0	1	0	1	100
	5	4	0	0	0	0	0

Figure 4.14. *V_2 enters the base, V_5 leaves*

This gives Figure 4.15. The Dantzig criteria indicate that $\mathbf{V_2}$ must enter the basis, while $\mathbf{V_3}$ must leave the basis (see Figure 4.16).

	V_1	V_2	V_3	V_4	V_5	V_6	B
V_3	0	0.125	1	0	-0.9001	0	9.9910
V_4	0	0.25	0	1	-0.5293	0	47.0747
V_1	1	0	0	0	4.5005	0	450.0450
V_6	0	0.3333	0	1	0	1	100.0000
	0	4	0	0	-22.502	0	-2250.2250

Figure 4.15. *Base change*

	V_1	V_2	V_3	V_4	V_5	V_6	B
V_3	0	0.125	1	0	-0.9001	0	9.9910
V_4	0	0.25	0	1	-0.5293	0	47.0747
V_1	1	0	0	0	4.50045	0	450.0450
V_6	0	0.3333	0	1	0	1	100
	0	4	0	0	-22.502	0	-2250.2250

Figure 4.16. *V_2 enters the base, V_3 leaves*

	V_1	V_2	V_3	V_4	V_5	V_6	B
V_2	0	1	8	0	-7.2007	0	79.9280
V_4	0	0	-2	1	1.2709	0	27.0927
V_1	1	0	0	0	4.5005	0	450.0450
V_6	0	0	-2.6664	1	2.4	1	73.36
	0	0	-32	0	6.3006	0	-2569.9370

Figure 4.17. *Base change*

After changing the basis, the result is shown in Figure 4.17. The Dantzig criteria indicate that $\mathbf{V_5}$ must enter the basis and then $\mathbf{V_4}$ must leave (see Figure 4.18).

	V_1	V_2	V_3	V_4	V_5	V_6	B
V_2	0	1	8	0	-7.2007	0	79.9280
V_4	0	0	-2	1	1.2709	0	27.0927
V_1	1	0	0	0	4.5005	0	450.0450
V_6	0	0	-2.6664	1	2.4	1	73.36
	0	0	-32	0	6.3006	0	-2569.937

Figure 4.18. *V_5 enters the base, V_4 leaves*

After applying the basis change formulas, the result is shown in Figure 4.19.

	V_1	V_2	V_3	V_4	V_5	V_6	B
V_2	0	1	-3.3314	5.6657	0	0	233.4278
V_5	0	0	-1.5737	0.7868	1	0	21.3173
V_1	1	0	7.0822	-3.5411	0	0	354.1076
V_6	0	0	1.1104	-0.8884	0	1	22.1985
	0	0	-22.085	-4.9575	0	0	-2704.2493

Figure 4.19. *Base change*

Dantzig's first criterion can no longer be applied, signifying that the optimal solution has been reached with $x_1 = 354.1076$ (from row $\mathbf{V_1}$ and column **B**), $x_2 = 233.4278$ (from row $\mathbf{V_2}$ and column **B**). The other variables are zero. The result matches the graphical solution, except for rounding errors.

EXAMPLE 4.2.– This example is taken from a Diploma of Higher Accounting exam. The manager of a Pro-Mer factory has decided to launch the production of diving suits: the Shorty model, denoted by S, and the Long John model, denoted by L. The diving suits are manufactured successively by three workshops: A, B and C. For each workshop, the machines are used by operators S and L for specific times (in minutes, in this case). For each workshop, the machines are used by operators S and L for specific times (in minutes, in this case). The table in Figure 4.20 summarizes the times allocated to S and L for each workshop, as well as the monthly time available for each workshop.

workshop	model S	model L	monthly available time
A	20	25	36000
B	20	30	45000
C	15	15	24000

Figure 4.20. *Manufacturing times*

Economic information is also grouped together in the table shown in Figure 4.21.

elements	model S	model L
unit selling price	500 €	700 €
unit manufacturing cost	350 €	500 €

Figure 4.21. *Economic information*

Profit is calculated by subtracting the manufacturing cost from the selling price (i.e. selling price – manufacturing cost). The goal is to determine the quantities x_1 (of S combinations) and x_2 (of L combinations) to be produced each month in order to achieve maximum profit. However, there are two market limitations: a maximum of 1,000 S combinations and 700 L combinations that can be absorbed each month.

The problem can be formulated as follows: the decision variables are x_1 and x_2 (positive or zero). The objective function to be maximized is:

$$z = (500-350)x_1 + (700-500)x_2 = 150x_1 + 200x_2$$

For each workshop, the constraints are:

$$20x_1 + 25x_2 \leq 36000$$

$$20x_1 + 30x_2 \leq 45000$$

$$15x_1 + 15x_2 \leq 24000$$

Finally, the commercial constraints are:

$$x_1 \leq 1000$$

$$x_2 \leq 700$$

The initial simplex table is shown in Figure 4.22 (which requires five slack variables).

	V_1	V_2	V_3	V_4	V_5	V_6	V_7	B
V_3	20	25	1	0	0	0	0	36000
V_4	20	30	0	1	0	0	0	45000
V_5	15	15	0	0	1	0	0	24000
V_6	1	0	0	0	0	1	0	1000
V_7	0	1	0	0	0	0	1	700
	150	200	0	0	0	0	0	0

Figure 4.22. *Initial table*

The first Dantzig criterion indicates that the vector $\mathbf{V_2}$ enters the basis because 200 is the largest positive number in the last row.

The second Dantzig criterion shows that the $700/1$ ratio is the smallest of all ratios $\frac{b_i}{a_{i2}}$. Hence, the vector $\mathbf{V_7}$ leaves the basis (see Figure 4.23).

	V_1	V_2	V_3	V_4	V_5	V_6	V_7	B
V_3	20	25	1	0	0	0	0	36000
V_4	20	30	0	1	0	0	0	45000
V_5	15	15	0	0	1	0	0	24000
V_6	1	0	0	0	0	1	0	1000
V_7	0	1	0	0	0	0	1	700
	150	200	0	0	0	0	0	0

Figure 4.23. *V_2 enters the base, V_7 leaves*

Apply the basis change relations (see Figure 4.24).

	V_1	V_2	V_3	V_4	V_5	V_6	V_7	B
V_3	20	0	1	0	0	0	-25	18500
V_4	20	0	0	1	0	0	-30	24000
V_5	15	0	0	0	1	0	-15	13500
V_6	1	0	0	0	0	1	0	1000
V_2	0	1	0	0	0	0	1	700
	150	0	0	0	0	0	-200	-140000

Figure 4.24. *Base change*

Once again, Dantzig's first criterion indicates that it is the vector $\mathbf{V_1}$ that enters the basis.

The second Dantzig criterion reveals that the ratio $13500/15$ is the smallest of the ratios $\frac{b_i}{a_{i1}}$, meaning that the vector $\mathbf{V_5}$ leaves the basis (see Figure 4.25).

	V_1	V_2	V_3	V_4	V_5	V_6	V_7	B
V_3	20	0	1	0	0	0	-25	18500
V_4	20	0	0	1	0	0	-30	24000
V_5	15	0	0	0	1	0	-15	13500
V_6	1	0	0	0	0	1	0	1000
V_2	0	1	0	0	0	0	1	700
	150	0	0	0	0	0	-200	-140000

Figure 4.25. *V_1 enters the base, V_5 leaves*

Apply the basis change relations (see Figure 4.26).

	V_1	V_2	V_3	V_4	V_5	V_6	V_7	B
V_3	0	0	1	0	-1.33	0	-5	500
V_4	0	0	0	1	-1.33	0	-10	6000
V_1	1	0	0	0	0.067	0	-1	900
V_6	0	0	0	0	-0.07	1	1	100
V_2	0	1	0	0	0	0	1	700
	0	0	0	0	-10	0	-50	-275000

Figure 4.26. *Base change*

Since the first Dantzig criterion is no longer applicable, the optimization process is complete. The values of x_1 and x_2 can be read in the **B** on the rows corresponding to $\mathbf{V_1}$ and $\mathbf{V_2}$: $x_1 = 900$, $x_2 = 700$, and $z = 275000$.

4.5. Two-phase method

As explained above, when there are constraints with the signs "≥" or "=", artificial variables are introduced, which must then be reduced to zero. This approach is known as the "*two-phase method*", because it involves applying the simplex method twice.

Phase 1 aims to minimize the sum of the artificial variables. This minimization must lead to the reduction of these variables to zero (if this is not the case, the problem has no solution) and to obtaining an initial solution. Phase 2 involves returning to the initial problem, using the initial solution obtained and considering the artificial variables as zero.

Let us illustrate the process with an example. Consider the following linear program:

$$\text{Max } z = 4x_1 + 3x_2 + 2x_3$$

$$\text{s.t. (subject to):}$$

$$3x_1 + 2x_2 + x_3 \leq 1200$$

$$2x_1 + 3x_2 + 2x_3 \geq 1400$$

$$x_1 + x_2 + x_3 = 600$$

$$x_1 + x_2 - x_3 \leq 400$$

$$x_1, x_2, x_3 \geq 0$$

It is immediately clear that the solution $x_1 = x_2 = x_3 = 0$ does not satisfy the initial constraints (as shown by the second and third constraints). Let us rewrite the linear program into a standard form, introducing the slack variables $e_1, e_2,\ e_3$ and the artificial variables $a_1,\ a_2$:

$$\text{Max}\ \ z = 4x_1 + 3x_2 + 2x_3 + 0.e_1 + 0.e_2 + 0.e_3 + 0.a_1 + 0.a_2$$

s. t.

$$3x_1 + 2x_2 + x_3 + e_1 = 1200$$

$$2x_1 + 3x_2 + 2x_3 - e_2 + a_1 = 1400$$

$$x_1 + x_2 + x_3 + a_2 = 600$$

$$x_1 + x_2 - x_3 + e_3 = 400$$

$$x_1, x_2, x_3, e_1, e_2, e_3, a_1, a_2 \geq 0$$

Phase 1: minimization of the sum of artificial variables.

The standard form of the linear program is almost the same as the one previously presented. Only the objective function changes:

$$\text{Min}\ \ z' = a_1 + a_2 \quad \text{or} \quad \text{Max}\ \ z'' = -z' = -a_1 - a_2$$

The expression for z'' is derived from the equations of the standard form:

$$a_1 = 1400 - 2x_1 - 3x_2 - 2x_3 + e_2$$

$$a_2 = 600 - x_1 - x_2 - x_3$$

Thus, $z'' = -2000 + 3x_1 + 4x_2 + 3x_3 - e_2$, and maximizing z'' is equivalent to maximizing $w = 3x_1 + 4x_2 + 3x_3 - e_2$ with $w = z'' + 2000$.

Figure 4.27 presents the equations in tabular form for easier visualization (the notation has been adjusted to clearly distinguish between slack and artificial variables).

	V_1	V_2	V_3	E_1	E_2	E_3	A_1	A_2	B
E_1	3	2	1	1	0	0	0	0	1200
A_1	2	3	2	0	-1	0	1	0	1400
A_2	1	1	1	0	0	0	0	1	600
E_3	1	1	-1	0	0	1	0	0	400
	3	4	3	0	-1	0	0	0	0

Figure 4.27. *Initial table for phase 1*

To apply Dantzig's criteria: in this case, the vector $\mathbf{V_2}$ has the highest positive coefficient, so it is the vector that will enter the basis, and the vector $\mathbf{E_3}$ has the smallest ratio, so it leaves the basis (see Figure 4.28).

	V_1	V_2	V_3	E_1	E_2	E_3	A_1	A_2	B
E_1	3	2	1	1	0	0	0	0	1200
A_1	2	3	2	0	-1	0	1	0	1400
A_2	1	1	1	0	0	0	0	1	600
E_3	1	1	-1	0	0	1	0	0	400
	3	4	3	0	-1	0	0	0	0

Figure 4.28. *V_2 enters the base, E_3 leaves*

This leads to a modification of the basis, as shown in Figure 4.29 after the basis change.

	V_1	V_2	V_3	E_1	E_2	E_3	A_1	A_2	B
E_1	1	0	3	1	0	-2	0	0	400
A_1	-1	0	5	0	-1	-3	1	0	200
A_2	0	0	2	0	0	-1	0	1	200
V_2	1	1	-1	0	0	1	0	0	400
	-1	0	7	0	-1	-4	0	0	-1600

Figure 4.29. *Base change*

The Dantzig criteria indicate that $\mathbf{V_3}$ enters the basis and $\mathbf{A_1}$ leaves the basis (see Figure 4.30).

	V_1	V_2	V_3	E_1	E_2	E_3	A_1	A_2	B
E_1	1	0	3	1	0	-2	0	0	400
A_1	-1	0	5	0	-1	-3	1	0	200
A_2	0	0	2	0	0	-1	0	1	200
V_2	1	1	-1	0	0	1	0	0	400
	-1	0	7	0	-1	-4	0	0	-1600

Figure 4.30. *V_3 enters the base, A_1 leaves*

	V_1	V_2	V_3	E_1	E_2	E_3	A_1	A_2	B
E_1	1.6	0	0	1	0.6	-0.2	-0.6	0	280
V_3	-0.2	0	1	0	-0.2	-0.6	0.2	0	40
A_2	0.4	0	0	0	0.4	0.2	-0.4	1	120
V_2	0.8	1	0	0	-0.2	0.4	0.2	0	440
	0.4	0	0	0	0.4	0.2	-1.4	0	-1880

Figure 4.31. *Base change*

	V_1	V_2	V_3	E_1	E_2	E_3	A_1	A_2	B
E_1	1.6	0	0	1	0.6	-0.2	-0.6	0	280
V_3	-0.2	0	1	0	-0.2	-0.6	0.2	0	40
A_2	0.4	0	0	0	0.4	0.2	-0.4	1	120
V_2	0.8	1	0	0	-0.2	0.4	0.2	0	440
	0.4	0	0	0	0.4	0.2	-1.4	0	-1880

Figure 4.32. *V_1 enters the base, E_1 leaves*

After the basis change, the results are obtained as shown in Figure 4.31. According to the Dantzig criteria, it is now shown that $\mathbf{V_1}$ enters the base and $\mathbf{E_1}$ leaves (note that $\mathbf{E_2}$ could also have entered the base, but a choice was made) (see Figure 4.32).

After the new basis change, the results are obtained as shown in Figure 4.33. According to the Dantzig criteria, it is again shown that $\mathbf{E_2}$ enters the basis and $\mathbf{A_2}$ leaves (note that $\mathbf{E_3}$ could also have entered the base, as could $\mathbf{A_2}$, but a choice was made) (see Figure 4.34).

	V_1	V_2	V_3	E_1	E_2	E_3	A_1	A_2	B
V_1	1	0	0	0.625	0.375	-0.13	-0.38	0	175
V_3	0	0	1	0,125	-0.13	-0.63	0.125	0	75
A_2	0	0	0	-0,25	0.25	0.25	-0.25	1	50
V_2	0	1	0	-0,5	-0.5	0.5	0.5	0	300
	0	0	0	-0,25	0.25	0.25	-1.25	0	-1950

Figure 4.33. *Base change*

	V_1	V_2	V_3	E_1	E_2	E_3	A_1	A_2	B
V_1	1	0	0	0.625	0.375	-0.13	-0.38	0	175
V_3	0	0	1	0.125	-0.13	-0.63	0.125	0	75
A_2	0	0	0	-0.25	0.25	0.25	-0.25	1	50
V_2	0	1	0	-0.5	-0.5	0.5	0.5	0	300
	0	0	0	-0.25	0.25	0.25	1.25	0	-1950

Figure 4.34. ***E**$_2$ enters the base, **A**$_2$ leaves*

After the basis change, the results are obtained as shown in Figure 4.35.

	V_1	V_2	V_3	E_1	E_2	E_3	A_1	A_2	B
V_1	1	0	0	1	0	-0.5	0	-1.5	100
V_3	0	0	1	0	0	-0.5	0	0.5	100
E_2	0	0	0	-1	1	1	-1	4	200
V_2	0	1	0	-1	0	1	0	2	400
	0	0	0	0	0	0	-1	-1	-2000

Figure 4.35. *Base change*

Since the first Dantzig criterion can no longer be applied, the optimization process for phase 1 is complete. The following initial solution is obtained:

$$x_1 = 100,\ x_2 = 400,\ x_3 = 100,\ e_1 = 0,\ e_2 = 200,\ e_3 = 0,\ a_1 = a_2 = 0,$$

and therefore $z' = 0$.

The target value for this initial solution is therefore $z = 1800$. Note that the artificial variables have been correctly reduced to zero, in row with the objective. Furthermore, the corresponding vectors are no longer part of the basis vectors, consistent with the simplex approach.

Phase 2. Elimination of artificial variables.

The previous table is modified as follows:

a) Columns of artificial variables $\mathbf{A_1}$ and $\mathbf{A_2}$ are deleted.

b) The economic function from the initial program $z = 4x_1 + 3x_2 + 2x_3$ is taken, but now expressed by replacing x_1, x_2 and x_3, which correspond to the basis vectors $\mathbf{V_1}, \mathbf{V_2}$and $\mathbf{V_3}$, with expressions in terms of the other variables.

	V_1	V_2	V_3	E_1	E_2	E_3	B
V_1	1	0	0	1	0	-0.5	100
V_3	0	0	1	0	0	-0.5	100
E_2	0	0	0	-1	1	1	200
V_2	0	1	0	-1	0	1	400
	0	0	0	-1	0	0	-1800

Figure 4.36. *Initial table for phase 2*

Standard program equations (with artificial variables cancelled out):

$$3x_1 + 2x_2 + x_3 + e_1 = 1200$$

$$2x_1 + 3x_2 + 2x_3 - e_2 = 1400$$

$$x_1 + x_2 + x_3 = 600$$

$$x_1 + x_2 - x_3 + e_3 = 400$$

using the first three equations:

$$x_1 = 200 - \frac{e_1}{2} - \frac{e_2}{2}$$

$$x_2 = 200 + e_2$$

$$x_3 = 200 + \frac{e_1}{2} - \frac{e_2}{2}$$

Thus,

$$z = 4x_1 + 3x_2 + 2x_3 = 1800 - e_1$$

Therefore, $z - 1800 = -e_1$.

The table for the simplex algorithm is shown in Figure 4.36. Since the first Dantzig criterion cannot be applied, the optimal solution has already been reached (which was also the initial solution obtained in phase 1). Had this not been the case, the simplex algorithm would have been continued until an optimal solution was found. Thus, the following values are obtained:

$$x_1 = 100,\ x_2 = 400,\ x_3 = 100,\ e_1 = 0,\ e_2 = 200,\ e_3 = 0, \text{ and } z = 1800.$$

Note that the first three equations were chosen to express x_1, x_2 and x_3 in terms of the variables corresponding to the vectors not in the basis. However, their expression involves e_2, which is a base variable. The fourth equation allows for the evaluation of e_2 as a function of e_1 and e_3, and the result of z remains unchanged.

4.6. Duality

The general case of problem (P_1), recently addressed, involves decision variables that can be defined as positive or arbitrary:

$$(P_1)\begin{cases} \text{Maximize } z_1 = \sum_{j=1}^{n} c_j x_j \\ \text{s.t. } \sum_{j=1}^{n} a_{ij} x_j \le b_i \text{ for } i = 1, \dots, m \end{cases}$$

This can be compared to the following problem (P_2):

$$(P_2)\begin{cases} \text{Minimize } z_2 = \sum_{i=1}^{m} b_i y_i \\ \text{s.t. } \sum_{i=1}^{m} a_{ij} y_i \ge c_j \text{ for } j = 1, \dots, n \end{cases}$$

Problems (P_1) and (P_2) are referred to as the *primal* and the *dual* of the same linear program. Transitioning between the primal and the dual involves the following transformations:

1) Variable exchange: the primal variables x_j ($j = 1, ..., n$) are exchanged with the dual variables y_i (i = $1, ..., m$).

2) Constant exchange: the primal constants c_j ($j = 1, ..., n$) are exchanged with the dual constants b_i ($i = 1, ..., m$).

3) Change of inequality sign: primal constraints expressed with inequality signs ($\leq, \geq$) are transformed into dual constraints with the opposite inequality sign ($\geq, \leq$).

4) Exchange of maximization and minimization: a primal maximization problem corresponds to a dual minimization problem, and vice versa.

These transformations establish the equivalence between the primal and the dual problems. The dual provides an alternative perspective on the primal, highlighting the marginal costs associated with the constraints and allowing the derivation of lower or upper bounds on the optimal value.

To provide a concrete example, consider a linear program with two decision variables ($n = 2$), $x_1 \geq 0$ and $x_2 \geq 0$, and four constraints ($m = 4$). This can be represented using a table, as shown in Figure 4.37.

Primal	Dual
Variables :·x_1, x_2	Variables :·y_1, y_2, y_3, y_4
Constraints $a_{11}x_1 + a_{12}x_2 \leq b_1$ $a_{21}x_1 + a_{22}x_2 \leq b_2$ $a_{31}x_1 + a_{32}x_2 \leq b_3$ $a_{41}x_1 + a_{42}x_2 \leq b_4$	Constraints $a_{11}y_1 + a_{21}y_2 + a_{31}y_3 + a_{41}y_4 \geq c_1$ $a_{12}y_1 + a_{22}y_2 + a_{32}y_3 + a_{42}y_4 \geq c_2$
Objective function $z_1 = c_1x_1 + c_2x_2$	Objective function $z_2 = b_1y_1 + b_2y_2 + b_3y_3 + b_4y_4$

Figure 4.37. *Primal/dual comparison*

It is shown that solving the primal yields the solution of the dual and vice versa. More precisely:

– The optimum value of z_2 is equal to the optimum value of z_1.

– A constraint satisfied as an equality in the primal corresponds to a strictly positive variable in the dual, and vice versa.

– At optimum, the $i-$ th dual variable is equal (to the nearest sign) to the marginal values of the $i-$ th primal slack variable.

EXAMPLE 4.3.– Consider the following linear program (primal) with two decision variables x_1 and x_2, and with the following four constraints:

$$2x_1 + x_2 \leq 1000$$

$$x_1 + x_2 \leq 800$$

$$x_1 \leq 400$$

$$x_2 \leq 700$$

The objective function is: $z_1 = 20x_1 + 30x_2$ to be *maximized.*

The optimal solution to this problem is: $x_1 = 100,\ x_2 = 700.$

The dual program corresponding to the primal program described above is as follows: it has four decision variables y_1, y_2, y_3 and y_4, and the following two dual constraints:

$$2y_1 + y_2 + y_3 \geq 20$$

$$y_1 + y_2 + y_4 \geq 30$$

The objective function is:

$$z_2 = 1000y_1 + 800y_2 + 400y_3 + 700y_4 \text{ to be } \textit{minimized.}$$

To verify the announced result: the optimal value of z_2 is 23,000. The initial and optimal states for the maximization problem are shown in Figure 4.38.

initial state

	variables		slack variables				
	x_1	x_2	x_3	x_4	x_5	x_6	
3	2	1	1	0	0	0	1000
4	1	1	0	1	0	0	800
5	1	0	0	0	1	0	400
6	0	1	0	0	0	1	700
	20	30	0	0	0	0	0

optimal state

	variables		slack variables				
	x_1	x_2	x_3	x_4	x_5	x_6	
3	0	0	1	-2	0	1	100
4/1	1	0	0	1	0	-1	100
5	0	0	0	-1	1	1	300
6/2	0	1	0	0	0	1	700
	0	0	0	-20	0	-10	23000

Figure 4.38. *Simplex solution*

The optimal solution, yielding $z_1 = 23000$, is:

$$x_1 = 100,\ x_2 = 700,\ x_3 = 100,\ x_4 = 0,\ x_5 = 300, x_6 = 0$$

For the optimal solution, the primal constraints are:

$$900 \leq 1000,$$

$$800 = 800, y_2 \text{ strictly positive},$$

$$100 \leq 400,$$

$$700 = 700, y_4 \text{ strictly positive}.$$

From the result on the slack variables, it is deduced that $y_2 = 20$ and $y_4 = 10$, which leads to the result:

$$z_2 = 800 \times 20 + 700 \times 10 = 23000.$$

The reader can verify the result of the dual program by using the simplex algorithm with the two-phase method.

With the two-phase method, a standard form of the primal program has been used. However, in more general terms, the rules for transitioning from primal to dual are shown in Figure 4.39, where the various quantities are defined as follows:

$$\boldsymbol{C} = \begin{bmatrix} c_1 \\ c_2 \\ \vdots \\ c_n \end{bmatrix} \boldsymbol{A} = \begin{bmatrix} a_{11} & a_{12} & \cdots & a_{1n} \\ a_{21} & a_{22} & \cdots & a_{2n} \\ \vdots & \vdots & \ddots & \vdots \\ a_{m1} & a_{m2} & \cdots & a_{mn} \end{bmatrix} \boldsymbol{X} = \begin{bmatrix} x_1 \\ x_2 \\ \vdots \\ x_n \end{bmatrix} \boldsymbol{B} = \begin{bmatrix} b_1 \\ b_2 \\ \vdots \\ b_m \end{bmatrix} \boldsymbol{Y} = \begin{bmatrix} y_1 \\ y_2 \\ \vdots \\ y_m \end{bmatrix}$$

primal	dual
Minimize $z = \mathbf{C}^T\mathbf{X}$ subject to constraints $\mathbf{AX} \geq \mathbf{B}$ $\mathbf{X} \geq 0$	Maximize $w = \mathbf{B}^T\mathbf{Y}$ subject to constraints $\mathbf{A}^T\mathbf{Y} \leq \mathbf{C}$ $\mathbf{Y} \geq 0$
Minimize $z = \mathbf{C}^T\mathbf{X}$ subject to constraints $\mathbf{AX} = \mathbf{B}$ $\mathbf{X} \geq 0$	Maximize $w = \mathbf{B}^T\mathbf{Y}$ subject to constraints $\mathbf{A}^T\mathbf{Y} \leq \mathbf{C}$
Maximize $z = \mathbf{C}^T\mathbf{X}$ subject to constraints $\mathbf{AX} = \mathbf{B}$ $\mathbf{X} \geq 0$	Minimize $w = \mathbf{B}^T\mathbf{Y}$ subject to constraints $\mathbf{A}^T\mathbf{Y} \geq \mathbf{C}$

Figure 4.39. *The different cases*

4.7. Degeneracy

It may occur that two quantities c_j are equal, leading to uncertainty about which column should be included in the basis. In such cases, an arbitrary choice must be made to determine which column enters the basis.

There may also be indeterminacy regarding which columns should be removed from the basis. This implies that the problem admits an infinite number of optimal solutions, and this indeterminacy must be considered when interpreting the results.

A simple case of degeneracy arises when the hyperplane representing the objective function is parallel to a face of the feasible region (the polyhedron) that contains an optimal solution. In this case, all the points on this face correspond to optimal solutions, leading to indeterminacy in the selection of the solution. There are an infinite number of solutions that satisfy the constraints and optimize the objective function, and this must be taken into account when analyzing the problem.

EXAMPLE 4.4.– Consider the following linear program: the decision variables are x_1 and x_2, with the following constraints:

$$x_1 \leq 4$$

$$x_1 + x_2 \leq 6$$

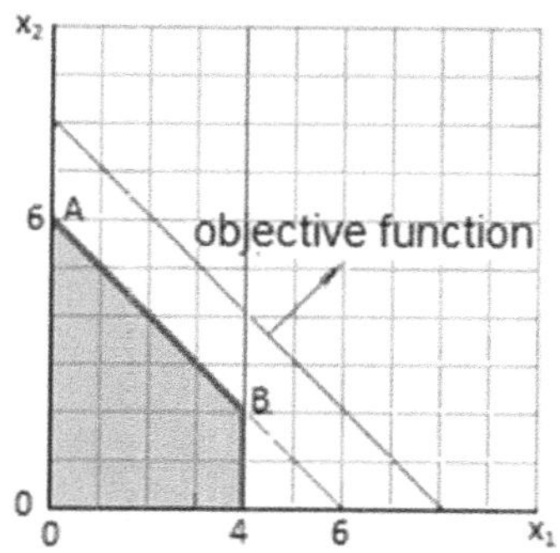

Figure 4.40. *Graphical resolution. For a color version of this figure, see www.iste.co.uk/cochard/mathematics3.zip*

The objective function is as follows:

$$z = x_1 + x_2 \quad \text{to be } \textit{maximized.}$$

The graphical solution of the problem (see Figure 4.40) shows the degeneracy. All points on segment AB correspond to optimal solutions.

4.8. Introduction to integer linear programming

The simplex algorithm typically provides real, often fractional, solutions for a linear program (P). When integer solutions are required, an initial phase called relaxation is performed, which consists of solving (P) while ignoring the integrality constraints.

From the (real) solution obtained, methods such as "*Gomory cuts*" or the "*Branch and Bound*" algorithm are used to find an integer solution. These techniques ensure an efficient exploration of the solution space, taking into account the integrality constraints into account to meet the requirements of the problem (P).

4.8.1. *Gomory cuts*

Consider an integer linear program (P) defined by:

$$(\text{P})\begin{cases} \text{Max z} = c_1x_1 + c_2x_2 + \cdots + c_nx_n \\ \quad s.t. \qquad \boldsymbol{Ax} \leq \boldsymbol{B} \\ \qquad\qquad \boldsymbol{x} \in \text{N}^\text{n} \end{cases}$$

To solve this problem, it is replaced with the relaxed linear program (P') identical to (P), but with $\boldsymbol{x} \in \mathbb{R}^n$

lines		x_1	x_2	...	x_k	...	x_n	,...	x_p	b
1	x_{f1}	α_{11}	α_{12}	...	0	...	α_{1n}	...	α_{1p}	β_1
...	...	...	...	...	...	...	...	...	...	...
i	x_k	α_{k1}	α_{k2}	...	1	...	α_{kn}	...	α_{kp}	β_i
...	...	...	...	...	...	...	...	...	...	...
n	x_{fn}	α_{n1}	α_{n2}	...	0	...	α_{nn}	...	α_{np}	β_n
		c_1	c2	...	c_k	...	c_n	...	c_p	-z

Figure 4.41. *Simplex table at the optimality stage*

The simplex algorithm is then applied to (P′), resulting in the optimal table, as shown in Figure 4.41.

The base variables x_k follow the equation:

$$x_k + \sum_{j \in HB} \alpha_{ij} x_j = \beta_i \tag{4.1}$$

where *HB* represents the indices of the non-base variables. For any solution (real or integer), each coefficient can be decomposed into an integer part and a fractional part:

$$\alpha_{ij} = \lfloor \alpha_{ij} \rfloor + F(\alpha_{ij}) \quad \text{and} \quad \beta_i = \lfloor \beta_i \rfloor + F(\beta_i),$$

where $F(a_{ij})$ and $F(\beta_i)$ represent the fractional parts, with $0 \leq F < 1$. Substituting these expressions into equation [4.1] gives:

$$x_k + \sum_{j \in HB} \lfloor \alpha_{ij} \rfloor x_j + \sum_{j \in HB} F(\alpha_{ij}) x_j = \lfloor \beta_i \rfloor + F(\beta_i)$$

Since $\sum_{j \in HB} F(\alpha_{ij}) x_j$ is non-negative, it follows that:

$$x_k + \sum_{j \in HB} \lfloor \alpha_{ij} \rfloor x_j \leq \lfloor \beta_i \rfloor + F(\beta_i) \tag{4.2}$$

Given that x_k and x_i are integers, the terms:

$$x_k + \sum_{j \in HB} \lfloor \alpha_{ij} \rfloor x_j \quad \text{and} \quad \lfloor \beta_i \rfloor$$

are integers, while $F(\beta_i)$ remains fractional. This leads to a specific constraint for integer solutions.

By removing [4.1] from [4.2]:

$$-\sum_{j \in HB} F(\alpha_{ij}) x_j \leq -F(\beta_i) \text{ or } \sum_{j \in HB} F(\alpha_{ij}) x_j \geq F(\beta_i) \tag{4.3}$$

The inequality [4.3] is an additional constraint that any integer solution must satisfy. It acts as a limitation on the solution space of the relaxed program (P'), reducing this space through "*cuts*". These additional constraints are at the heart of the "*Gomory cuts*" method, also called Gomory truncations.

EXAMPLE 4.5.– Apply the method to the introductory example of this chapter. Consider the following relaxed linear program:

Maximize $z = 5x_1 + 4x_2$

$$\text{s.t.}$$

$$0.2x_1 + 0.125x_2 + x_3 = 100$$

$$0.1176x_1 + 0.25x_2 + x_4 = 100$$

$$0.2222x_1 + x_5 = 100$$

$$0.3333x_2 + x_6 = 100$$

$$x_1, x_2 \in \mathbb{R}$$

where x_3, x_4, x_5 *and* x_6 are slack variables. The non-integer solution obtained is:

$$x_1 = 354.1076, \quad x_2 = 233.4278, \quad z = 2704.2493.$$

At optimality, the simplex table is shown in Figure 4.42, where the row corresponding to $\mathbf{V_1}$ **is** singularized for further analysis.

	V_1	V_2	V_3	V_4	V_5	V_6	B
V_2	0	1	-3.3314	5.6657	0	0	233.4278
V_5	0	0	-1.5737	0.7868	1	0	21.3173
V_1	1	0	7.0822	-3.5411	0	0	354.1076
V_6	0	0	1.1104	-0.8884	0	1	22.1985
	0	0	-22.085	-4.9575	0	0	-2704.2493

Figure 4.42. *Optimality simplex table*

In this example, apply equation [4.3] to the simplex table. The whole and fractional parts of the relevant values are as follows:

$$\lfloor 7.0822 \rfloor = 7, \quad F(7.0822) = 0.0822,$$

$$\lfloor -3.5411 \rfloor = -4, \quad F(-3.5411) = 0.4589,$$

$$\lfloor 354.1076 \rfloor = 354, \quad F(354.1076) = 0.1076.$$

This results in the inequality:

$$0.1076 \leq 0.0822x_3 + 0.4589x_4.$$

By substituting x_3 and x_4 with their respective expressions in terms of x_1 and x_2:

$$x_3 = 100 - 0.2x_1 - 0{,}125x_2 \quad \text{and} \quad x_4 = 100 - 0.1176x_1 - 0.25x_2,$$

the inequality becomes:

$$0.1076 \leq 0.0822x_3 + 0.4589x_4$$

By replacing x_3 and x_4 with their respective functions as a function of x_1 and x_2 we obtain:

$$x_3 = 100 - 0.2x_1 - 0.125x_2 \quad \text{and} \quad x_4 = 100 - 0.1176x_1 - 0.25x_2.$$

Expanding and simplifying:

$$0.1076 \leq 0.0822(100 - 0.2x_1 - 0.125x_2) + 0.4589(100 - 0.1176x_1 - 0.25x_2).$$

After combining terms, this simplifies to:

$$0.1304x_1 + 0.2315x_2 \leq 100$$

	V_1	V_2	V_3	V_4	V_5	V_6	V_7	B
V_3	0.2	0.125	1	0	0	0	0	100
V_4	0.1176	0.25	0	1	0	0	0	100
V_5	0.2222	0	0	0	1	0	0	100
V_6	0	0.3333	0	0	0	1	0	100
V_7	0.1304	0.2315	0	0	0	0	1	100
	5	4	0	0	0	0	0	0

	V_1	V_2	V_3	V_4	V_5	V_6	V_7	B
V_3	0	0.125	1	0	-0.9	0	0	9.991
V_4	0	0.25	0	1	-0.529	0	0	47.075
V_1	1	0	0	0	4.5005	0	0	450.05
V_6	0	0.3333	0	0	0	1	0	100
V_7	0	0.2315	0	0	-0.587	0	1	41.314
	0	4	0	0	-22.5	0	0	-2250

	V_1	V_2	V_3	V_4	V_5	V_6	V_7	B
V_2	0	1	8	0	-7.201	0	0	79.928
V_4	0	0	-2	1	1.2709	0	0	27.093
V_1	1	0	0	0	4.5005	0	0	450.05
V_6	0	0	-2.666	0	2.4	1	0	73.36
V_7	0	0	-1.852	0	1.0801	0	1	22.811
	0	0	-32	0	6.3006	0	0	-2570

	V_1	V_2	V_3	V_4	V_5	V_6	V_7	B
V_2	0	1	-4.347	0	0	0	6.6667	232
V_4	0	0	0.1792	1	0	0	-1.177	0.252
V_1	1	0	7.7167	0	0	0	-4.167	355
V_6	0	0	1.4487	0	0	1	-2.222	22.674
V_5	0	0	-1.715	0	1	0	0.9258	21.119
	0	0	-21.2	0	0	0	-5.833	-2703

Figure 4.43. *Simplex solution. For a color version of this figure, see www.iste.co.uk/cochard/mathematics3.zip*

The constraint derived from the Gomory cut is added to the relaxed linear program, resulting in a new linear program!

$$\text{Maximize } z = 5x_1 + 4x_2$$

s.t.

$$0.2x_1 + 0.125x_2 + x_3 = 100$$

$$0.1176x_1 + 0.25x_2 + x_4 = 100$$

$$0.2222x_1 + x_5 = 100$$

$$0.3333x_2 + x_6 = 100$$

$$0.1304x_1 + 0.2315x_2 + x_7 = 100$$

The resolution of this linear program, after applying the Gomory cut, yields an integer solution:

$$x_1 = 355, \quad x_2 = 232, \quad z = 2703.$$

The added constraint, *e*, is represented graphically along with the other constraints. This representation removes allowing the light gray area (see Figure 4.44). The new constraint eliminates any ambiguity regarding the integer solution sought, ensuring that the solution is entirely clear and leaving no doubt about its validity.

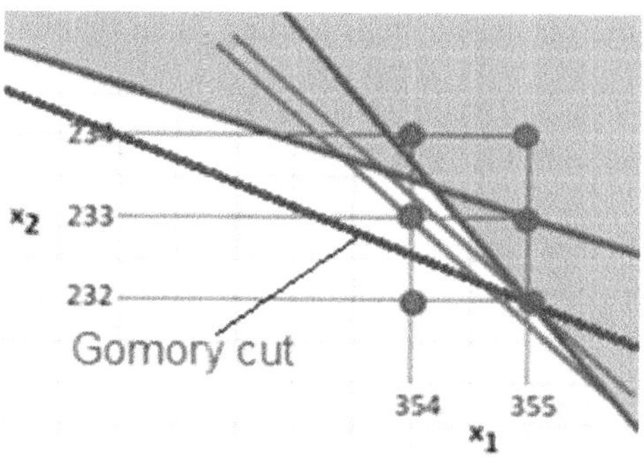

Figure 4.44. *Graphic resolution. For a color version of this figure, see www.iste.co.uk/cochard/mathematics3.zip*

EXAMPLE 4.6.– Consider the following integer linear program (P):

$$\text{Maximize } z = 7x_1 + 9x_2$$

$$\text{s.t.}$$

$$x_1 + 3x_2 \leq 6$$

$$7x_1 + x_2 \leq 35$$

$$x_1, x_2 \in \mathbb{N}$$

To begin, the simplex algorithm is applied to solve the relaxed program (P′), defined as:

$$\text{Maximize } z = 7x_1 + 9x_2$$

$$\text{s.t.}$$

$$x_1 + 3x_2 \leq 6$$

$$7x_1 + x_2 \leq 35$$

$$x_1, x_2 \in \mathbb{R}$$

Figure 4.45 shows the resolution steps leading to an optimal value of z, which corresponds to:

$$x_1 = 4.95, \quad x_2 = 0.35, \quad z = 37.8.$$

To obtain a Gomory cut, consider the row corresponding to $\mathbf{V_2}$. The fractional parts of the values are computed as follows:

$$\lfloor 0.35 \rfloor = 0, \quad F(0.35) = 0.35,$$

$$\lfloor -0.05 \rfloor = -1, \quad F(-0.05) = 0.95,$$

$$\lfloor 0.35 \rfloor = 0, \quad F(0.35) = 0.35.$$

Using these values, equation [4.3] is expressed as:

$$0.35x_3 + 0.95x_4 \geq 0.35.$$

	V_1	V_2	V_3	V_4	B
V_3	1	3	1	0	6
V_4	7	1	0	1	35
	7	9	0	0	0

	V_1	V_2	V_3	V_4	B
V_2	0.333	1	0.333	0	2
V_4	6.667	0	-0.333	1	33
	4	0	-3	0	-18

	V_1	V_2	V_3	V_4	B
V_2	0	1	0.35	-0.05	0.35
V_1	1	0	-0.05	0.15	4.95
	0	0	-2.8	-0.6	-37.8

Figure 4.45. *Program resolution (P')*

Expression of x_3 and x_4 using the equations derived from the constraints:

$$x_1 + 3x_2 + x_3 = 6 \quad \text{gives} \quad x_3 = 6 - x_1 - 3x_2,$$

$$7x_1 + x_2 + x_4 = 35 \quad \text{gives} \quad x_4 = 35 - 7x_1 - x_2.$$

Substituting these expressions in the Gomory equation results in the additional constraint:

$$7x_1 + 2x_2 \leq 35.$$

Defining the updated program (P′), this constraint is added to the relaxed program (P′) to form the new linear program (P″):

$$\text{Maximize } z = 7x_1 + 9x_2$$

s.t.

$x_1 + 3x_2 \leq 6$

$7x_1 + x_2 \leq 35$

$7x_1 + 2x_2 \leq 35$

$x_1, x_2 \in \mathbb{R}$

Solving (P"), as shown in Figure 4.46, gives a non-integer solution:

$x_1 = 4.895, \quad x_2 = 0.368.$

	V_1	V_2	V_3	V_4	V_5	B
V_3	1	3	1	0	0	6
V_4	7	1	0	1	0	35
V_5	7	2	0	0	1	35
	7	9	0	0	0	0

	V_1	V_2	V_3	V_4	V_5	B
V_2	0.333	1	0.333	0	0	2
V_4	6.667	0	-0.333	1	0	33
V_5	6.333	0	-0.667	0	1	31
	4	0	-3	0	0	-18

	V_1	V_2	V_3	V_4	V_5	B
V_2	0	1	0.368	0	-0.053	0.368
V_4	0	0	0.368	1	-1.053	0.368
V_1	1	0	-0.105	0	0.158	4.895
	0	0	-2.579	0	-0.632	-37.58

Figure 4.46. *Program resolution (P")*

To refine the solution, a new Gomory cut is added by considering the row $\mathbf{V_1}$:

$$\lfloor -0.105 \rfloor = -1, \quad F(-0.105) = 0.895,$$

$$\lfloor 0.158 \rfloor = 0, \quad F(0.158) = 0.158,$$

$$\lfloor 4.895 \rfloor = 4, \quad F(4.895) = 0.895.$$

Using the values derived, relation [4.3] is expressed as:

$$0.895x_3 + 0.158x_5 \geq 0.4895.$$

Substituting x_3 and x_5:

$$x_3 = 6 - x_1 - 3x_2,$$

$$x_5 = 35 - 7x_1 - 2x_2,$$

into the inequality results in the following Gomory cut:

$$2x_1 + 3x_2 \leq 10.$$

A new program (P‴) is obtained, by adding the above constraint:

$$\text{Maximize } z = 7x_1 + 9x_2$$

s. t.

$$x_1 + 3x_2 \leq 6$$

$$7x_1 + x_2 \leq 35$$

$$7x_1 + 2x_2 \leq 35$$

$$2x_1 + 3x_2 \leq 10$$

x_1, x_2 real numbers

	V_1	V_2	V_3	V_4	V_5	V_6	B
V_3	1	3	1	0	0	0	6
V_4	7	1	0	1	0	0	35
V_5	7	2	0	0	1	0	35
V_6	2	3	0	0	0	1	10
	7	9	0	0	0	0	0

	V_1	V_2	V_3	V_4	V_5	V_6	B
V_2	0.3333	1	0.3333	0	0	0	2
V_4	6.6667	0	-0.333	1	0	0	33
V_5	6.3333	0	-0.667	0	1	0	31
V_6	1	0	-1	0	0	1	4
	4	0	-3	0	0	0	-18

	V_1	V_2	V_3	V_4	V_5	V_6	B
V_2	0	1	0.6667	0	0	-0.3333	0.666667
V_4	0	0	6.3333	1	0	-6.6667	6.333333
V_5	0	0	5.6667	0	1	-6.3333	5.666667
V_1	1	0	-1	0	0	1	4
	0	0	1	0	0	-4	-34

	V_1	V_2	V_3	V_4	V_5	V_6	B
V_2	0	1	0	-0.105	0	0.36842	0
V_3	0	0	1	0.1579	0	-1.0526	1
V_5	0	0	0	-0.895	1	-0.3684	0
V_1	1	0	0	0.1579	0	-0.0526	5
	0	0	0	-0.158	0	-2.9474	-35

Figure 4.47. *Program resolution (P‴). For a color version of this figure, see www.iste.co.uk/cochard/mathematics3.zip*

Figure 4.47 presents the steps in the simplex algorithm for solving the program (P‴).

This time, optimality is achieved with integer values for the decision variables:

$$x_1 = 5, \quad x_2 = 0, \quad z = 35.$$

This result was obtained after the addition of two Gomory cuts.

4.8.2. *Branch and Bound algorithm*

The Branch and Bound algorithm solves integer linear programming problems by exploring a tree of possible solutions in a structured manner. The first step is to solve the relaxed linear program to obtain an optimal solution, even if it is not integer. Then, the tree is built by dividing the problem into subproblems by imposing additional constraints, allowing for the exclusion of certain branches and thus reducing the search time.

Suppose a linear maximization program with two integer decision variables, x_1 and x_2, provides the following relaxed solution:

$$x_1 = 3.14 \text{ and } x_2 = 5.47.$$

To find the desired integer solution, additional constraints are imposed. For example, for x_1, the hypotheses are tested:

$$x_1 \leq 3 \text{ or } x_1 \geq 4.$$

To solve the initial problem using the Branch and Bound algorithm, assumptions are introduced to explore subdomains of integer solutions. Consider a linear maximization program (P) with two integer decision variables, x_1 and x_2, which provides a relaxed solution:

$$x_1 = 3.14 \text{ and } x_2 = 5.47.$$

The process can be outlined as follows:

1) *Division into subproblems*

For x_1, two branches are created by testing the following additional constraints:

– (P1): program (P) with the additional constraint $x_1 \leq 3$;

– (P2): program (P) with the additional constraint $x_1 \geq 4$.

2) *Solving subproblems*

Each subproblem is solved by applying the simplex algorithm to the new constraints.

3) *Selection criteria*

The solution is checked to see if it is integer or if a branch can be eliminated (for instance, in the case of infeasibility or if it cannot improve the overall solution).

4) *Recursive exploration*

These steps are repeated for each subproblem until all the solutions respect the integrality constraints.

5) *Stopping criterion*

The exploration of branches stops when all variables have integer values or when a branch cannot improve the solution.

Note that the case $3 < x_1 < 4$ is not considered, as x_1 must be an integer. This observation simplifies the tree structure of the Branch and Bound algorithm by limiting the subproblems to cases where $x_1 \leq 3$ and $x_1 \geq 4$. These hypotheses ensure that each branch respects the integrality constraint, facilitating the progression towards an integer optimal solution.

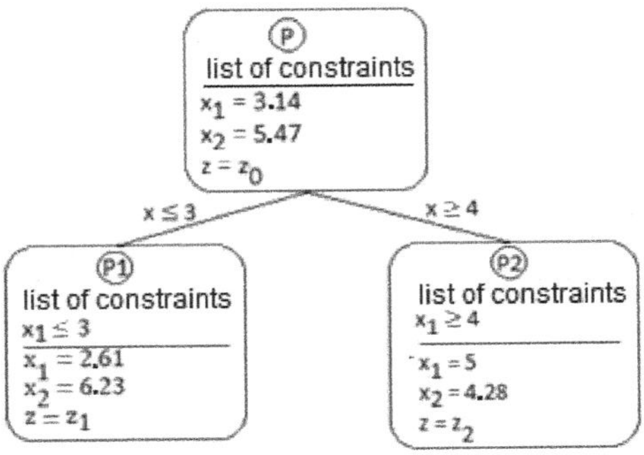

Figure 4.48. *Start of a tree structure*

Consider z_0, z_1 and z_2, which correspond to the values of z obtained from the relaxed linear programs (P), (P1) and (P2), respectively. These values allow the creation of an initial tree structure, as shown in Figure 4.48. This structure facilitates the exploration of sub-domains in the Branch and Bound algorithm by testing the additional constraints $x_1 \leq 3$ and $x_1 \geq 4$. This helps us to identify an optimal integer solution while reducing the search space.

If $z_2 \geq z_1$, it becomes worthwhile to explore the program (P2). This leads to the creation of two additional sub-programs, (P21) and (P22), as represented in Figure 4.49.

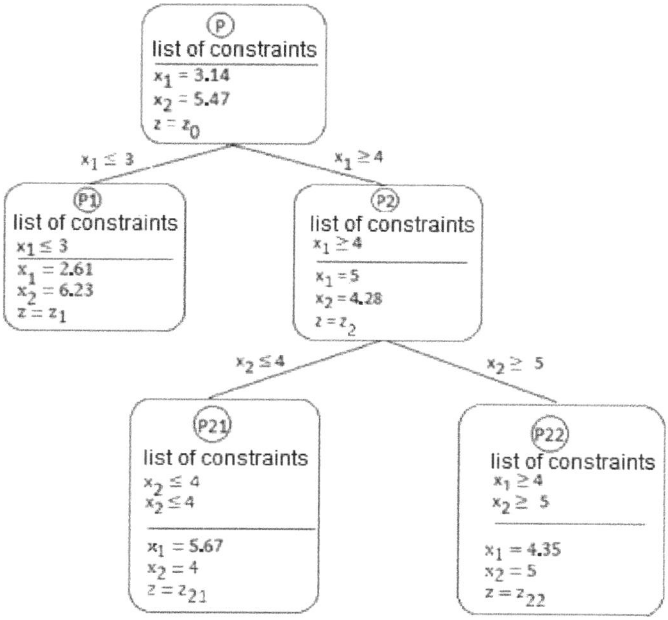

Figure 4.49. *Two new subprograms, P21 and P22*

The comparison among z_1, z_{21} and z_{22} determines the next direction to follow when developing the tree structure. This method, which relies on branching (separation) and results analysis (evaluation), is why the Branch and Bound technique is also referred to as the separation–evaluation method.

Not all branches of the tree are explored. Branches that are deemed *sterile* or are *pruned* correspond to the following cases:

– No feasible solution exists within the branch.

– The solution obtained is feasible, meaning all variables gave integer values, so further branching is unnecessary.

– The value of z obtained is lower than the current lower bound (in the case of maximization), meaning the branch is not promising for finding an optimal solution.

EXAMPLE 4.7.– Revisiting the introductory example from this chapter, the solution to the relaxed linear program (P) is as follows:

$$x_1 = 354.1076, \quad x_2 = 233.4278, \quad z = 2704.2493.$$

To continue the search for an integer solution, program (P) is divided into two sub-programs by introducing the constraints:

$$x_1 \leq 354 \quad \text{and} \quad x_1 \geq 355.$$

Figure 4.50 shows the initial tree structure corresponding to this separation.

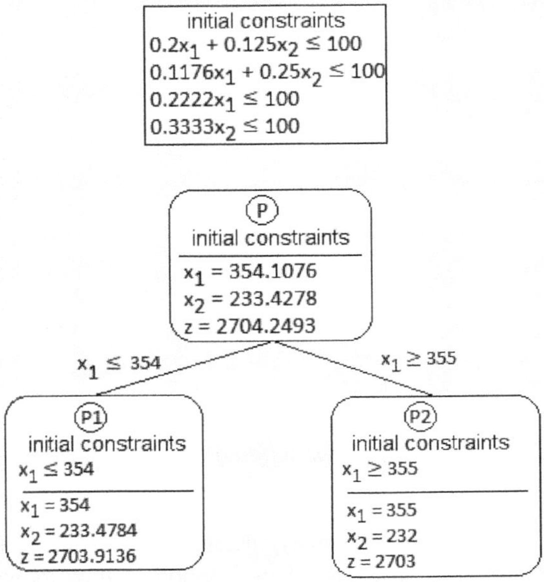

Figure 4.50. *Separation into two sub-programs (P1) and (P2)*

Program (P2) provides an integer solution with $z = 2703$. Since further separation is unnecessary, this program is retained.

Program (P1), however, results in a non-integer solution with $z = 2703.91$. It can be divided (separated) into two sub-programs, (P3) and (P4), as shown in Figure 4.51.

(P3) yields an integer solution, but with $z = 2702 < 2703$.

(P4) produces a non-integer solution with $z = 2700.46 < 2703$.

Consequently, an optimal solution is obtained from program (P2).

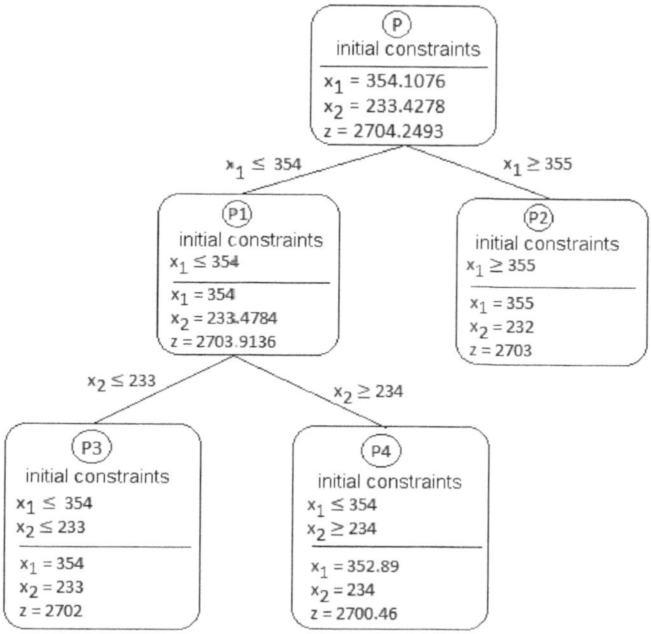

Figure 4.51. *Separation into two sub-programs (P3) and (P4)*

EXAMPLE 4.8.– Knapsack problem. This problem involves optimizing the total value of objects placed in a bag while respecting a maximum capacity constraint W_{max} (e.g. a weight limit). Each object is characterized by its weight w_i and its value v_i. The goal is to determine which objects to include in the bag to maximize the total value without exceeding the maximum capacity W_{max} (see Figure 4.52). This problem is a classic in combinatorial optimization.

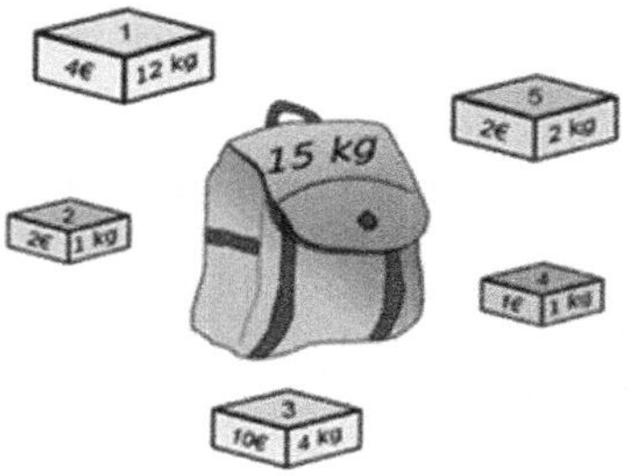

objects	1	2	3	4	5
weight w_i	12	1	4	1	2
value v_i	4	2	10	1	2

$W_{max} = 15$ $V_{max} = ?$

Figure 4.52. *The knapsack problem*

The knapsack problem is formulated as an integer linear program that maximizes the total value of objects:

$$z = \sum_{i=1}^{n} x_i v_i$$

where x_i is a Boolean variable (integer), such that:

$$x_i = \begin{cases} 1 & \text{if object } i \text{ is in the knapsack} \\ 0 & \text{otherwise} \end{cases}$$

The capacity constraint limits the total weight and is expressed as:

$$\sum_{i=1}^{n} x_i w_i \leq W_{max}$$

For the given data, the integer linear program (P) becomes:

Maximize $z = 4x_1 + 2x_2 + 10x_3 + x_4 + 2x_5$

subject to $12x_1 + x_2 + 4x_3 + x_4 + 2x_5 \leq 15$

where $x_i \in \{0,1\}, \forall i = 1, \dots ,5$.

These constraints are implicitly handled in the simplex algorithm by the condition $0 \leq x_i \leq 1$, for each i, $i \in \{1, \dots ,5\}$.

Upon solving the relaxed linear program (P′) using the simplex algorithm, the following solution is obtained:

$$x_1 = 0.583, \quad x_2 = x_3 = x_4 = x_5 = 0, \quad z = 17.333.$$

This solution is not valid because x_1 is not integer. The relaxed linear program (P′) can be divided into two sub-programs:

– (P1): adding the constraint $x_1 \leq 0$, which fixes $x_1 = 0$. The solution obtained is integer: $x_1 = 0,\ x_2 = x_3 = x_4 = x_5 = 1,\ z = 15$.

– (P2): adding the constraint $x_1 \geq 1$. The solution is non-integer: $x_1 = 0$, $x_2 = 0,\ x_3 = 0.75,\ x_4 = x_5 = 0,\ z = 11.5$.

There is no need to separate (P2), as $z = 11.5 < 15$. Therefore, an optimal solution is provided by (P1).

EXAMPLE 4.9.– Let the linear program (P*) be

$$\text{Maximize } z = 8x_1 + 5x_2$$

s. t.

$$x_1 + x_2 \leq 6$$

$$9x_1 + 5x_22 \leq 45$$

$$x_1, x_2 \in \mathbb{N}$$

The relaxed version (P′) of (P) gives the solution:

$$x_1 = 3.75,\ x_2 = 2.25,\ z = 41.25.$$

To obtain an integer solution, (P′) is divided into two sub-programs:

– (P1) with the constraint $x_1 \leq 3$, giving $x_1 = 3,\ x_2 = 3$ and $z = 39$.

– (P2) with the constraint $x_1 \geq 4$, giving $x_1 = 4,\ x_2 = 1.8$ and $z = 41$.

The value $z = 41 > 39$ suggests exploring (P2), which is divided into:

– (P3) with the constraint $x_2 \leq 1$, giving $x_1 = 4.4,\ x_2 = 1$ and $z = 40.5$.

– (P4) with the constraint $x_2 \geq 2$, which has no solution and is therefore abandoned.

Since $z = 40.5 > 39$ in (P3), (P3) is further divided into:

– (P5) with the constraint $x_1 \leq 4$, giving $x_1 = 4,\ x_2 = 1$ and $z = 37$.

– (P6) with the constraint $x_1 \geq 5$, giving $x_1 = 5,\ x_2 = 0$ and $z = 40$.

The solution of (P6), where $z = 40$, is better than the solution of (P1) and (P5). It is therefore an optimal solution.

5

Elements of Graph Theory

CONCEPTS COVERED IN THIS CHAPTER.–

Graphs serve as powerful tools for modeling a broad spectrum of problems. Their origins trace back to 1741 with Euler's solution to the Königsberg bridge problem. Over time, graph theory has been significantly advanced by numerous mathematicians, including König, Cayley, Menger, Berge, Erdös and others.

This chapter introduces the fundamental concepts of graph theory, with applications to be explored in subsequent chapters.

It begins by defining a graph, examining its graphical and tabular representations, and introducing a range of specialized terminology (which is not always consistent across the literature).

The discussion then moves to the transitive closure of a graph and its decomposition into strongly connected components of directed graphs.

A section focuses on specific types of graphs and trees, exploring the concept of spanning trees.

The chapter concludes with an exploration of extremum spanning trees, featuring a discussion of prominent algorithms, including those of Dijkstra, Sollin and Kruskal.

References: [DRO 87, FAU 79, MOU 80, PHE 75].

5.1. Definition and representations of a graph

A *graph* G is generally defined as a pair (X, U), where X is a set of vertices (or nodes) and U is a set of edges, represented by ordered pairs of elements from X. Formally, $G = (X, U)$ can be expressed as follows:

$$G = (x_i, u_j),\ x_i \in X,\ u_j \in X \times X$$

5.1.1. *Graphical representation*

The elements of the set X are represented as *points* or *vertices*, while the elements of the set U are represented as *segments*, *branches* or *arcs* connecting the vertices.

EXAMPLE 5.1.– Figure 5.1 shows a graph with seven vertices and 10 arcs.

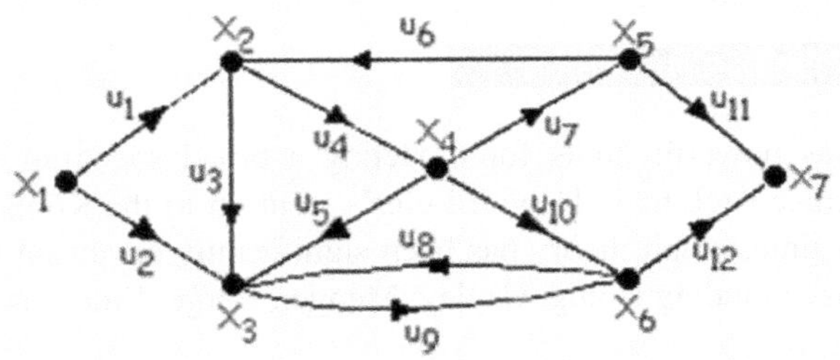

Figure 5.1. *Example of a graph*

A graph is referred to as a *directed graph* when each arc has a specified direction (see Figure 5.2). In this case, the term *arc* means that there is an orientation associated with the connection.

Figure 5.2. *Arc of a directed graph*

Conversely, a graph is described as *undirected graphs* when its arcs lack a specific direction (see Figure 5.3). In such cases, the connections are referred to simply as *edges*.

Figure 5.3. *Edge of an undirected graph*

Note that the graph in Figure 5.1 is a directed graph.

It is often necessary to assign each arc or edge one or more numerical values, such as travel cost or capacity, when the graph represents a transport network. In such cases, the result is called a *valued graph*.

Additionally, multiple arcs or edges connect a pair of vertices, corresponding to several possible means of transport between them.

5.1.2. *Tables associated with a graph*

A graph can be represented using various data structures, with several possible representations available.

Following or preceding a vertex

This representation, also known as a *graph dictionary*, involves listing the vertices that directly follow or precede each vertex in the graph.

EXAMPLE 5.2.– Representation of the following and previous tables: Figure 5.4 shows the following and preceding tables for the graph in Figure 5.1.

dictionary of successors

	successors
X1	X2, X3
X2	X3, X4
X3	X6
X4	X3, X5, X6
X5	X2, X7
X6	X3, X7
X7	-

dictionary of predecessors

	predecessors
X1	-
X2	X1, X5
X3	X1, X2, X4, X6
X4	X2
X5	X4
X6	X3, X4
X7	X5, X6

Figure 5.4. *Dictionaries*

Adjacency matrix

An adjacency matrix is a *Boolean matrix* where both rows and columns correspond to vertices. Each cell of the matrix contains a value of 1 or 0, indicating the presence or absence of an arc from the vertex corresponding to the row to the vertex corresponding to the column.

EXAMPLE 5.3.– The adjacency matrix of the graph shown in Figure 5.1 is presented in Figure 5.5.

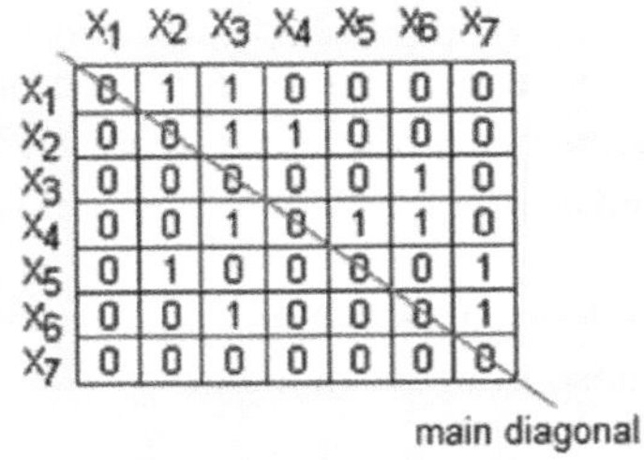

Figure 5.5. *Adjacency matrix. For a color version of this figure, see www.iste.co.uk/cochard/mathematics3.zip*

Reading the matrix from row to column provides the dictionary of successors, while reading it from column to row provides the dictionary of predecessors. In particular, elements on the main diagonal indicate the presence of loops, which is not the case in Example 5.1.

The adjacency matrix has the following characteristics:

– For an undirected graph, the matrix is symmetrical.

– If the edges are valued, the 1s are replaced by the numerical values associated with the corresponding edge. In this case, the matrix transitions from being Boolean to a *cost matrix*.

– It is also possible to represent the matrix by leaving empty cells where a 0 would otherwise be placed.

5.2. Main concepts and technology

This section distinguishes between concepts specific to directed graphs and those specific to undirected graphs.

However, it is important to note that any undirected graph can be equivalently represented as a directed graph by replacing each edge with two arcs of opposite directions connecting the same vertices.

5.2.1. *Elements of a graph*

Elementary components

The constituent elements of a graph are referred to as *vertices*, whether for a directed or undirected graph. However, the terms "*arcs*" and "*edges*" are used differently depending on the graph type. For a directed graph, the term "arc" designates connections between vertices. In contrast, for undirected graphs, the term "edge" is preferred to represent connections between vertices.

Additionally, a branch whose origin and end coincide is called a "*loop*" (see Figure 5.6).

Figure 5.6. *A loop*

Combining these components

1) In a directed graph,

– A "*path*" is a sequence of adjacent arcs that allows movement from one vertex to another.

– A "*circuit*" is a path whose initial vertex coincides with its final vertex.

– An "*elementary path*" is one in which all vertices are distinct.

– A "*Hamiltonian path*" is a path that visits each vertex of the graph exactly once.

– A "*Hamiltonian circuit*" is a circuit that traverses all the vertices of the graph exactly once.

2) In an undirected graph,

– A "*chain*" is a sequence of adjacent edges that allows movement from one vertex to another.

– A "*cycle*" is a chain where the initial and final vertices coincide.

– An "*elementary chain*" is one in which all vertices are distinct.

– A "*Eulerian chain*" is a chain that uses each edge of the graph exactly once.

– A "*Eulerian cycle*" is a chain that traverses all the edges of the graph exactly once.

EXAMPLE 5.4.– The “Königsberg bridge problem”, also known as Kaliningrad bridge problem, is a famous problem in graph theory solved by Euler.

The city is divided by the “Pregolya River” and is connected by seven bridges linking four districts: North (N), Center (C), South (S) and East (E) (see Figure 5.7). The challenge is to determine whether a walker can complete a tour by crossing each bridge exactly once.

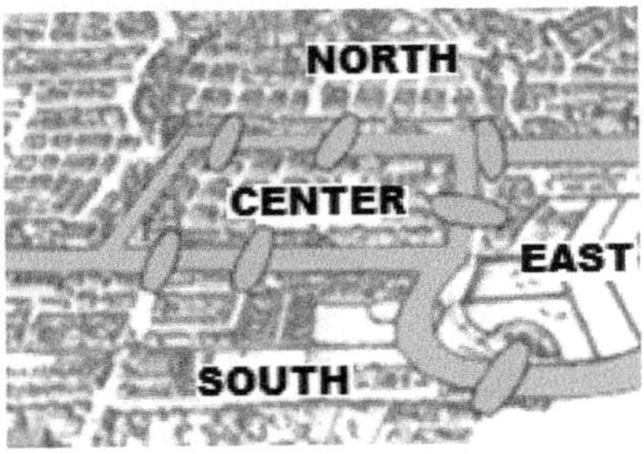

Figure 5.7. *Königsberg bridges. For a color version of this figure, see www.iste.co.uk/cochard/mathematics3.zip*

The situation of Königsberg’s bridges can be represented by a graph (see Figure 5.8), where the edges represent the bridges and the vertices represent the districts: N for North, C for Center, S for South and E for East. This representation also helps to clarify the connections between neighborhoods and bridges. There are two bridges connecting the North (N) and Center (C) districts, as well as two bridges linking the Center (C) and South (S) districts.

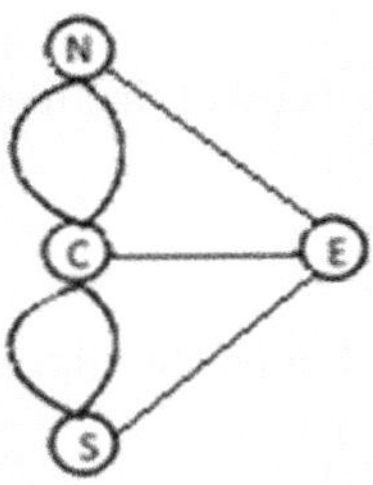

Figure 5.8. *Problem graph*

The problem at hand is to find the "*Eulerian cycles*" in the graph. Given the simplicity of the graph, it is possible to list all possible cycles in order to check if an *Eulerian cycle* exists (see Figure 5.9).

As shown, none of the cycles listed meets the criteria for an Eulerian cycle in the Königsberg bridge graph. Specifically, none of these cycles traverse each edge exactly once or return to the starting point (see Figure 5.9).

Therefore, the problem of finding an Eulerian cycle in this graph has no solution.

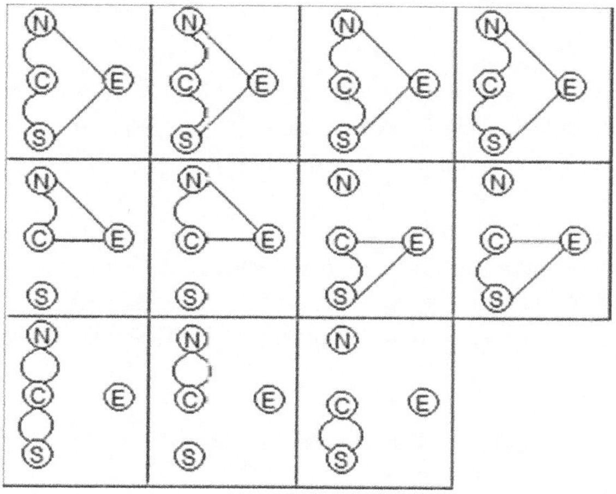

Figure 5.9. *List of possible cycles*

The following theorem is stated (Theorem 5.1).

THEOREM 5.1 (EULER–HIERHOLZER).–

A connected undirected graph G with even degree for all vertices ⇔ ***G*** admits an Eulerian cycle.

For a directed graph, the following two propositions are equivalent:

– The graph has an Eulerian circuit.

– The graph is strongly connected, and each vertex is both the origin and the end of the same number of arcs.

EXAMPLE 5.5.– Consider the undirected graph shown in Figure 5.10.

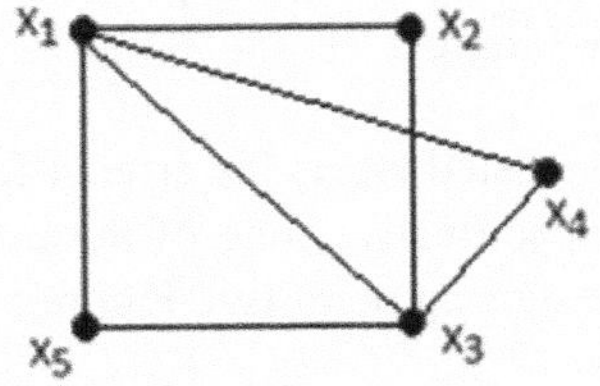

Figure 5.10. *Eulerian cycle search*

Each vertex of this graph has an even degree, either 2 or 4. Consequently, this graph admits an Eulerian cycle. An example of an Eulerian cycle in this graph can be seen by following the vertex sequence: $X_1 - X_2 - X_3 - X_1 - X_5 - X_3 - X_4 - X_1$.

EXAMPLE 5.6.– Consider the directed graph shown in Figure 5.11. It can be seen that there is an Eulerian circuit: $X_1 - X_2 - X_3 - X_4 - X_5 - X_3 - X_1$. All vertices have one origin and one endpoint, except for X_3, which has two origins and two endpoints.

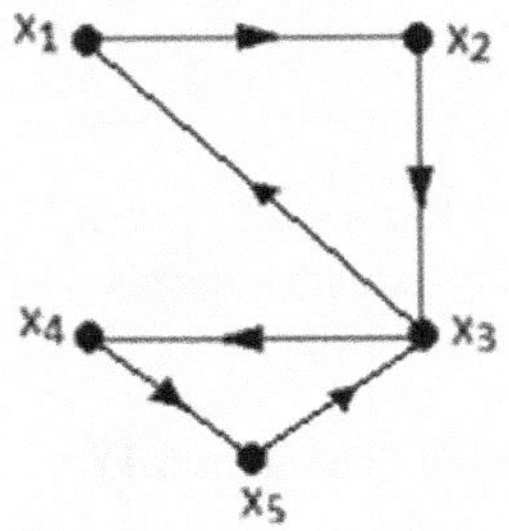

Figure 5.11. *Eulerian cycle search*

Other definitions

The "*degree*" of a vertex in an undirected graph is defined as the number of edges having one of their endpoints at this vertex. Each loop is counted twice. The sum of the degrees of all the vertices in a graph is equal to twice the number of edges in the graph.

In the case of a directed graph, the *exterior half-degree* of a vertex corresponds to the number of arcs originating at the vertex in question (see Figure 5.12).

Figure 5.12. *Exterior half-degree = 2*

The *interior half-degree* of a vertex corresponds to the number of arcs ending at the vertex in question (see Figure 5.13).

Figure 5.13. *Interior half-degree = 2*

Main types of graphs

A connected graph (or weakly connected for a directed graph) is a graph in which there is at least one chain connecting each pair of vertices (x_i, x_j) of the graph. Figure 5.14 shows this property.

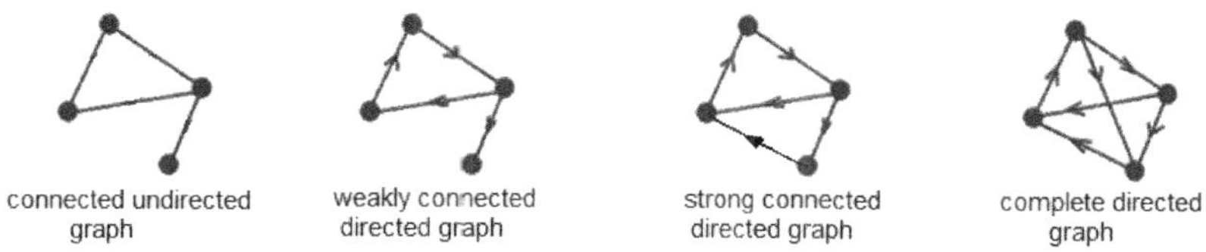

Figure 5.14. *Connectedness*

Weak connectivity is an equivalence relation on the set of vertices of the graph, satisfying the following properties:

– Reflexivity: a vertex X_i is connected to itself.

– Symmetry: if the vertex X_i is connected to vertex X_j, then there is a chain linking vertex X_j to vertex X_i.

– Transitivity: if the vertex X_i is connected to vertex X_j and vertex X_j is connected to vertex X_k, then there is a chain connecting vertex X_i to vertex X_k.

This equivalence relation allows the partitioning of the set of vertices into related components, which are disjoint parts of the set of vertices. The union of all related components gives the complete set of vertices in the graph.

A strongly connected directed graph is one in which there is at least one path connecting each pair of vertices (X_i, X_j) in both directions: from X_i to X_j and from X_j to X_i. Unlike weak connectivity, connections between vertices here are made via directed paths. The difference lies in the use of directed paths instead of chains. Strong connectivity is also an equivalence relation on all the vertices of the graph, with the properties of reflexivity, symmetry and transitivity. Strongly connected components are a partition of the set of vertices in the graph.

A complete directed graph is one in which there is always an arc between any two vertices. In other words, in a complete graph, if the arc (X_i, X_j) does not belong to the graph, then the arc (X_j, X_i) belongs to the graph. This means that every pair of vertices is connected by an edge.

For an undirected graph, *a tree is a cycle-free connected graph.* This means that there is a unique chain between each pair of vertices, and no cycle is present in the graph. For a directed graph, the definition is the same, provided "chain" is replaced by "path", "connected" by "weakly connected" and "cycle" by "circuit".

5.2.2. *Analysis of graph structure*

The following sections provide key concepts that simplify graph solving methods.

Finding circuits in a directed graph

Loops are eliminated as elementary circuits, either directly on the graph or on the Boolean matrix (indicated by the presence of non-zero elements on the main diagonal).

All vertices that are either origin-only (see Figure 5.12) or endpoint-only (see Figure 5.13) are progressively eliminated.

If, with this procedure, the graph is deleted (reduced to an empty set of vertices), then the graph contains no circuits.

EXAMPLE 5.7.– Consider the directed graph shown in Figure 5.15.

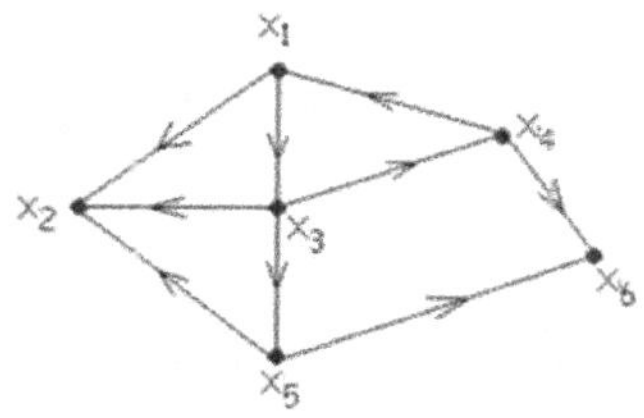

Figure 5.15. *Directed graph*

From the graph in Figure 5.15, eliminate X_2, which is an arrival vertex, then X_6 for the same reason, and finally X_5 for the same reason (see Figure 5.16).

From the Boolean adjacency matrix (see Figure 5.17):

– X_2: null line (X_2 is only an output); elimination of row and column X_2.

– X_6: null row (X_6 is only an output): elimination of row and column X_6.

– X_5: becomes a null row (i.e. an output); elimination of row and column X_5.

This leaves X_1, X_3 and X_4 with null rows, which form a circuit.

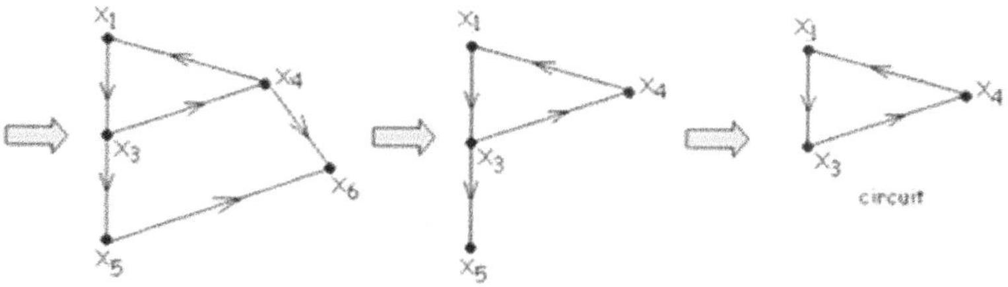

Figure 5.16. *Elimination process*

	X1	X2	X3	X4	X5	X6
X1	0	1	1	0	0	0
X2	0	0	0	0	0	0
X3	0	1	0	1	0	0
X4	1	0	0	0	0	1
X5	0	0	0	0	0	1
X6	0	0	0	0	0	0

⇒

	X1	X2	X3	X4	X5	X6
X1	0	1	1	0	0	0
X2	0	0	0	0	0	0
X3	0	1	0	1	0	0
X4	1	0	0	0	0	1
X5	0	0	0	0	0	1
X6	0	0	0	0	0	0

⇒

	X1	X2	X3	X4	X5	X6
X1	0	1	1	0	0	0
X2	0	0	0	0	0	0
X3	0	1	0	1	0	0
X4	1	0	0	0	0	1
X5	0	0	0	0	0	1
X6	0	0	0	0	0	0

⇒

	X1	X3	X4
X1	0	1	0
X3	0	0	1
X4	1	0	0

Figure 5.17. *Elimination using the adjacency matrix*

Level decomposition of a directed graph

Level decomposition is a technique used to order the vertices of a connected directed graph without circuits, in order to avoid backtracking.

Two techniques are presented for performing this decomposition:

1) *From the graph*: this method consists of eliminating, at each iteration k, all vertices that have no predecessors. These vertices form level N_k. Initially, the first level consists of vertices with no predecessors. Then, at each iteration, vertices with no predecessors in the current graph are eliminated and placed in the next level. This process is repeated until all vertices have been assigned to their respective levels.

2) *From the dictionary of predecessors*: this method uses a predecessor dictionary, which associates each vertex with the vertices directly connected to it. Vertices with no predecessor constitute the first level. Then, at each iteration k, vertices belonging to previous levels are removed from the predecessor dictionary. Vertices with no predecessor in the dictionary at iteration k are placed in level N_k.

EXAMPLE 5.8.– Consider the graph in Figure 5.18.

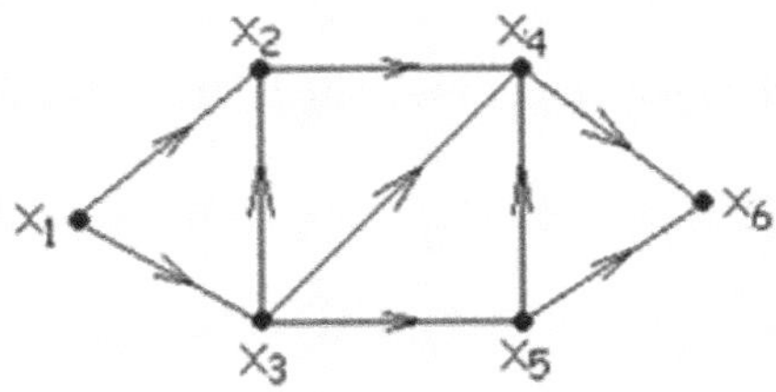

Figure 5.18. *Graph to explore*

Decomposition from the graph (see Figure 5.19) and decomposition from the dictionary of predecessors (see Figure 5.20) both lead to the graph shown in Figure 5.21, which is redrawn according to the levels.

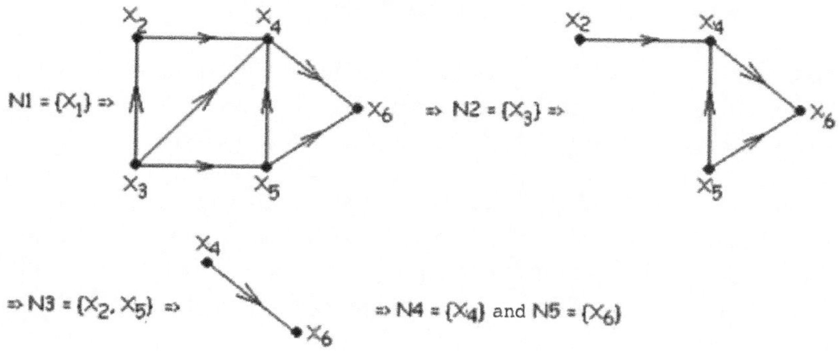

Figure 5.19. *Decomposition from the graph*

dictionary of predecessors

nodes	predecessors	N1 = {X_1}	N2 = {X_3}	N3 = {X_2, X_5}	N4 = {X_4}	N5 = {X_6}
X_1	-					
X_2	X_1, X_3	X_3	-			
X_3	X_1, X_3	-				
X_4	X_2, X_5	X_2, X_5	X_2, X_5	-		
X_5	X_3	X_3	-			
X_5	X_4, X_5	X_4, X_5	X_4, X_5	X_4	-	

Figure 5.20. *Decomposition from the dictionary of predecessors*

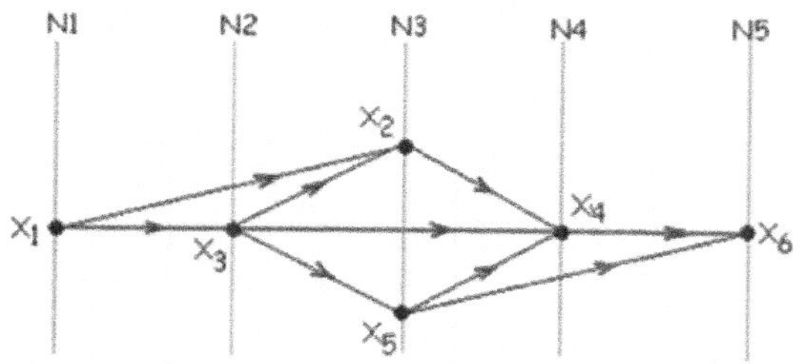

Figure 5.21. *Representation of the graph by levels*

5.3. Transitive closure of a graph's vertices

The *transitive closure* of a vertex X_i in a graph is the subset of vertices in the graph, "including X_i", such that there is a path from X_i to each of them. The Boolean adjacency matrix $\boldsymbol{A}$ is helpful in finding paths between two vertices.

Calculating $\boldsymbol{A}^2 = \boldsymbol{A} \times \boldsymbol{A}$ provides paths of length 2. The matrix multiplication refers to "logical" matrix multiplication, which uses "logical" multiplication (identical to arithmetic multiplication) and logical addition (distinct from arithmetic addition, where $1 + 1 = 1$). Similarly, $\boldsymbol{A}^3$ represents paths of length 3, etc.

By superimposing, i.e. logically adding $\boldsymbol{A}, \boldsymbol{A}^2, \boldsymbol{A}^3, \ldots, \boldsymbol{A}^{n-1}$, all possible paths between two vertices (indicated by 1's) in a graph with n vertices are obtained.

Adding the identity matrix $\mathbf{1}$ (with 1's on the main diagonal and 0's elsewhere) represents the path from a vertex X_i to itself.

As a result, the matrix $\boldsymbol{G} = \mathbf{1} + \boldsymbol{A} + \boldsymbol{A}^2 + \ldots + \boldsymbol{A}^{n-1}$ provides the graph's transitive closure. The row of $\boldsymbol{G}$ corresponding to vertex X_i indicates the transitive closure of the vertex X_i, with 1's marking reachable vertices.

EXAMPLE 5.9.– Consider the Boolean adjacency matrix A from Example 5.8.

$$\boldsymbol{A} = \begin{bmatrix} 1 & 1 & 1 & 0 & 0 & 0 \\ 0 & 1 & 0 & 1 & 0 & 0 \\ 0 & 1 & 1 & 1 & 1 & 0 \\ 0 & 0 & 0 & 1 & 0 & 1 \\ 0 & 0 & 0 & 1 & 1 & 1 \\ 0 & 0 & 0 & 0 & 0 & 1 \end{bmatrix}.$$

Calculate $\boldsymbol{A}^2$, $\boldsymbol{A}^3, \boldsymbol{A}^4, \boldsymbol{A}^5$.

$$\boldsymbol{A}^2 = \boldsymbol{A} \times \boldsymbol{A} = \begin{bmatrix} 1 & 1 & 1 & 1 & 1 & 0 \\ 0 & 1 & 0 & 1 & 0 & 1 \\ 0 & 1 & 1 & 1 & 1 & 1 \\ 0 & 0 & 0 & 1 & 0 & 1 \\ 0 & 0 & 0 & 1 & 1 & 1 \\ 0 & 0 & 0 & 0 & 0 & 1 \end{bmatrix} \quad \boldsymbol{A}^3 = \boldsymbol{A} \times \boldsymbol{A}^2 = \begin{bmatrix} 1 & 1 & 1 & 1 & 1 & 1 \\ 0 & 1 & 0 & 1 & 0 & 1 \\ 0 & 1 & 1 & 1 & 1 & 1 \\ 0 & 0 & 0 & 1 & 0 & 1 \\ 0 & 0 & 0 & 1 & 1 & 1 \\ 0 & 0 & 0 & 0 & 0 & 1 \end{bmatrix}$$

$$\boldsymbol{A}^4 = \boldsymbol{A}^2 \times \boldsymbol{A}^2 = \begin{bmatrix} 1 & 1 & 1 & 1 & 1 & 1 \\ 0 & 1 & 0 & 1 & 0 & 1 \\ 0 & 1 & 1 & 1 & 1 & 1 \\ 0 & 0 & 0 & 1 & 0 & 1 \\ 0 & 0 & 0 & 1 & 1 & 1 \\ 0 & 0 & 0 & 0 & 0 & 1 \end{bmatrix} = \boldsymbol{A}^3$$

$$A^5 = A^2 \times A^3 = \begin{bmatrix} 1 & 1 & 1 & 1 & 1 & 1 \\ 0 & 1 & 0 & 1 & 0 & 1 \\ 0 & 1 & 1 & 1 & 1 & 1 \\ 0 & 0 & 0 & 1 & 0 & 1 \\ 0 & 0 & 0 & 1 & 1 & 1 \\ 0 & 0 & 0 & 0 & 0 & 1 \end{bmatrix} = A^3$$

$\mathbf{1} + A^3 = A^3$ provides all transitive closures:

– Transitive closure of X_1: $\{X_1, X_2, X_3, X_4, X_5, X_6\}$

– Transitive closure of X_2 : $\{X_2, X_4, X_6\}$

– Transitive closure of X_3 : $\{X_2, X_3, X_4, X_5, X_6\}$

– Transitive closure of X_4 : $\{X_4, X_6\}$

– Transitive closure of X_5 : $\{X_4, X_5, X_6\}$

– Transitive closure of X_6 : $\{X_6\}$

5.4. Decomposition of a directed graph into strongly connected components

Several techniques can be used to decompose a directed graph into strongly connected components. The simplest method involves determining, for any given vertex X, the list of all its predecessors (both immediate or distant) and the list of all its successors (both immediate or distant). The vertices that appear in both lists form a strongly connected component. Thus, the intersection of these two lists represents the strongly connected component to which the vertex X belongs.

EXAMPLE 5.10.– Consider the graph shown in Figure 5.22.

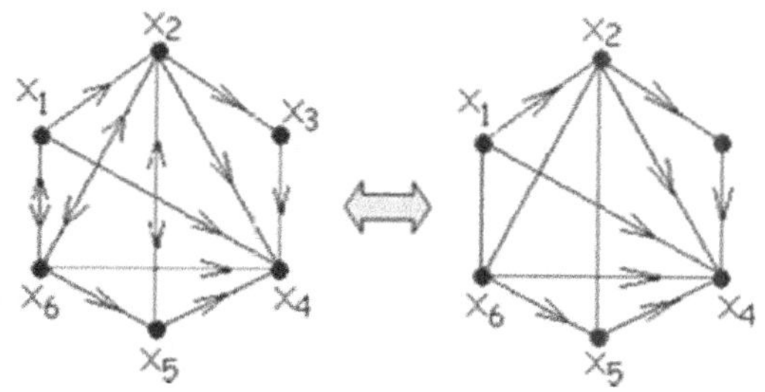

Figure 5.22. *Graph to explore*

For X_1:

– List of predecessors: $\{X_1, X_6, X_2, X_5\}$

– List of successors: $\{X_1, X_2, X_3, X_4, X_5, X_6\}$

– Strongly connected component: $\{X_1, X_2, X_5, X_6\}$

Two vertices remain X_3 and X_4.

For X_3:

– List of predecessors: $\{X_3, X_2, X_1, X_5, X_6\}$

– List of successors: $\{X_3, X_4\}$

– Strongly connected component: $\{X_3\}$

For X_4:

– List of predecessors: $\{X_4, X_1, X_2, X_3, , X_5, X_6\}$

– List of successors: $\{X_4\}$

– Strongly connected component: $\{X_4\}$

This results in the three strongly connected components of the graph:

– $A = \{X_1, X_2, , X_5, X_6\}$,

– $B = \{X_3\}$,

– $C = \{X_4\}$

as shown in Figure 5.23.

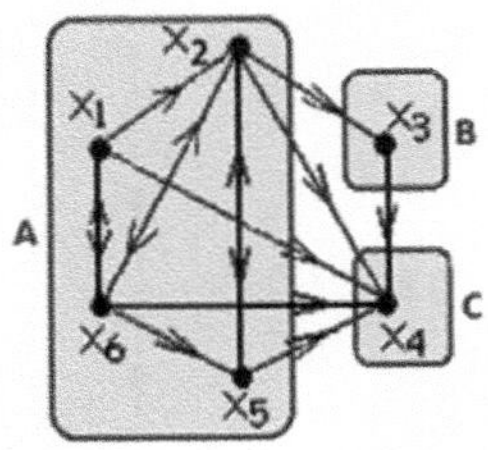

Figure 5.23. *Strongly related components*

NOTE 5.1.– This result can be obtained from the graph's transitive closure matrix by placing the vertices in the corrected order.

$A^4 =$

	X_1	X_2	X_5	X_6	X_3	X_4
X_1	1	1	1	1	1	1
X_2	1	1	1	1	1	1
X_5	1	1	1	1	1	1
X_6	1	1	1	1	1	1
X_3	0	0	0	0	1	1
X_4	0	0	0	0	0	1

Figure 5.24. *Strongly related components*

Indeed, on $\boldsymbol{A}^4$, when reordered, the strongly connected components can be clearly seen (highlighted in gray in Figure 5.24).

5.5. Trees

5.5.1. *Introduction*

Let $G = (X, U)$ be an undirected finite graph. Each edge $u \in U, u = (x_i, x_j)$, is associated with a number $d(u) = d_{ij}$, which can be positive, negative or zero, and is called *length*. This length can represent various parameters, such as distance, travel time, transport cost, hourly capacity, reliability index, etc.

In this graph, the objective is to find a subset of edges that provides a direct or indirect link between every pair of vertices. There are generally several such subsets that satisfy this condition. Among these, the goal is to find the one that minimizes (or maximizes) an objective function that depends on the lengths of the selected edges. Typically, the values on the edges correspond to the values of this objective function

This problem is known as *extremum spanning tree* (minimum or maximum) and is frequently encountered in networks.

5.5.2. *Trees in a graph*

In a graph, there is a relationship between the number of vertices n, the number of edges m and the number of related components p, which is stated here without proof:

$$n - p \leq m$$

The number $n(G)$, called the *cyclomatic number,* is defined as:

$$n(G) = m - n + p,$$

This number is non-negative ($n(G) \geq 0$) and plays an important role in the study of graphs. It has several interesting properties. A theorem, also presented without proof, highlights the significance of this number.

THEOREM 5.2.– The cyclomatic number $n(G)$ of a graph G is equal to the number of independent cycles.

The cyclomatic number $n(G)$ is an essential concept in the study of graphs and their topological properties. It provides information on the connectivity and structure of the graph and is widely used in the fields such as networks, optimization, algorithmics and more.

DEFINITION 5.1.– A ***tree*** is a finite, connected, acyclic (cycle-free) graph.

This is the simplest structure with these properties. Figure 5.25 shows some examples of trees.

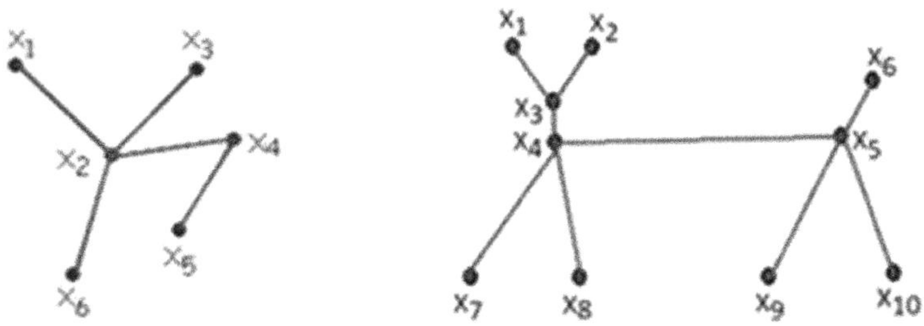

Figure 5.25. *Some trees*

THEOREM 5.3.– A graph G of order n (with n vertices) is a tree if and only if one of the following six equivalent properties holds:

1) G is connected and acyclic;

2) G is acyclic and has exactly $(n-1)$ edges;

3) G is connected and has exactly $(n-1)$ edges;

4) G is connected, and deleting an edge makes it unconnected;

5) G is acyclic, and adding an edge between two non-adjacent vertices creates exactly one cycle;

6) any pair of vertices is connected by exactly one chain.

These six properties are equivalent and describe different characteristics of a graph that qualify it as a tree.

Trees are widely used in various disciplines and fields to organize and represent information. They play a key role in classification, decision processes, computer architecture, language structure (such as sentence decomposition), distribution networks and many other areas.

5.5.3. *Spanning tree in a graph*

A spanning tree of a graph G is a partial graph that contains *all the vertices* of G, but *only some of its edges*, and has a tree structure.

THEOREM 5.4.– A necessary and sufficient condition for a graph G to have a spanning tree is that it must be connected.

In other words, if the graph G is not connected, it consists of several disjoint connected components and cannot have a spanning tree. On the other hand, if G is connected, a spanning tree can be found as follows:

1) Search for an edge in G whose removal does not disconnect the graph. If no such edge exists, G itself is a tree, in accordance with property 4 of Theorem 5.3.

2) If such an edge exists, remove it from the graph G and continue searching for another edge to remove in the remaining graph. The goal is to progressively eliminate edges that are not necessary to maintain the graph's connectivity.

3) Repeat this process until no more edges can be removed without disconnecting the graph. At this point, the result is a spanning tree of G that retains the connectivity of the original graph.

In summary, if the graph G is connected, a spanning tree can be constructed by progressively removing non-essential edges while maintaining the graph's connectivity. This theorem characterizes the existence of a spanning tree in a graph and provides a method for constructing it.

EXAMPLE 5.11.– Consider the graph shown in Figure 5.26.

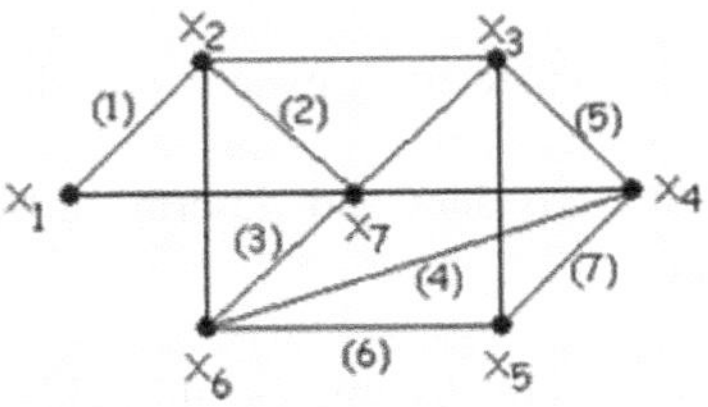

Figure 5.26. *Explore graph*

Removing edges (1), (2), (3), (4), (5), (6) and (7), in any order, produces the tree shown in Figure 5.27, which can be simplified (see Figure 5.28). This tree is not unique; another spanning tree is shown in Figure 5.29.

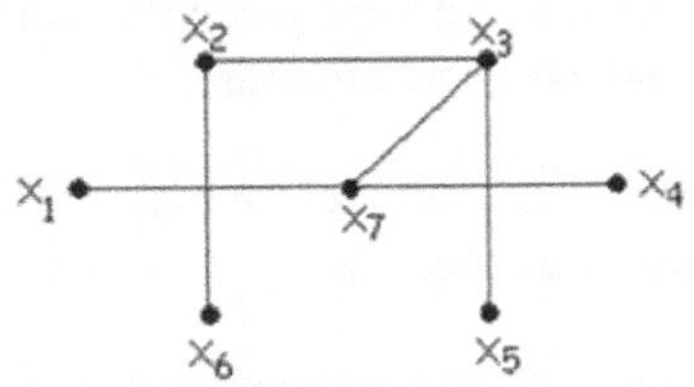

Figure 5.27. *Spanning tree*

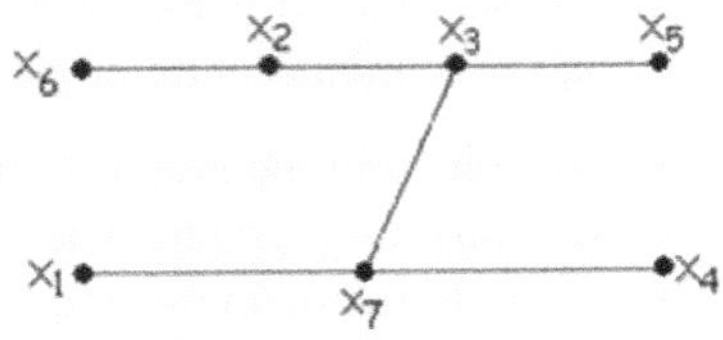

Figure 5.28. *Another drawing of the spanning tree*

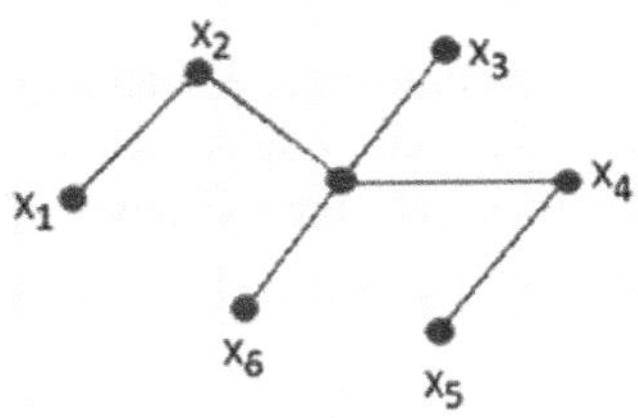

Figure 5.29. *Another spanning tree*

5.6. Finding a fundamental system of independent cycles of a connected graph

Some problems, such as the study of electrical networks, require finding a fundamental system of independent cycles in a given graph. Although the tree is a commonly used method for solving this problem, other approaches also exist.

Suppose the graph G is connected. Begin by constructing a spanning tree (X, U_{n-1}), where $u_1, u_2, \ldots, u_{m-(n-1)}$ are the edges of U that are not present in U_{n-1}. When one of these *edges* u_k is added to the spanning tree (X, U_{n-1}), a single cycle P_k is created (in accordance with property 5 of Theorem 5.3). The cycles thus formed, $P_1, P_2, \ldots, P_k$, are independent of each other, since each contains an edge that is absent from the others. Since $\mathrm{n}(G) = m - n + 1$ (because the graph is connected), a fundamental system of *n(G)* independent cycles is obtained.

EXAMPLE 5.12.– Consider the graph shown in Figure 5.30.

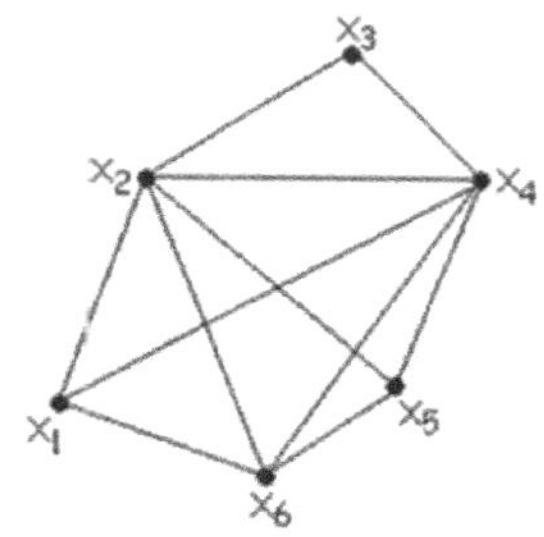

Figure 5.30. *Graph to explore*

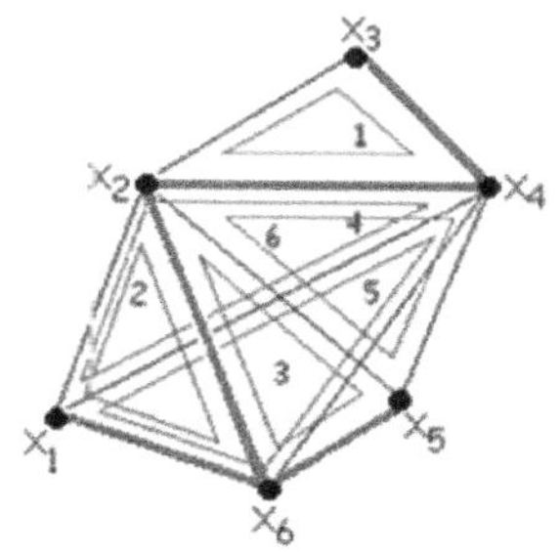

Figure 5.31. *Existence of six independent cycles. For a color version of this figure, see www.iste.co.uk/cochard/mathematics3.zip*

In this case, $(G) = 11 - 6 + 1 = 6$. Therefore, there are six independent cycles. The spanning tree in Figure 5.31 is drawn with red lines, and the cycles obtained are numbered from 1 to 6.

5.7. Extremum spanning tree

5.7.1. *General information*

Of all the spanning trees that can be determined in a given graph, the one of primary interest is typically the one that minimizes or maximizes an objective function involving edge length.

A common application is in telecommunications, where n cities are connected by cables or transmitters, allowing communication between any pair of locations. The goal is to find the links that minimize the total length of cables or the number of transmitters required. Other applications involve connecting roads, railroads, pipelines, canals, telephone lines, etc.

5.7.2. *Extremum spanning tree search algorithms*

Several search algorithms exist. The Prim and Dijkstra, Solin and Kruskal algorithms are presented in what follows.

Prim and Dijkstra algorithm

1) Select an arbitrary vertex.

2) Select the shortest or longest edge from this vertex, depending on whether the objective is to find a minimal or maximal spanning tree.

3) The selected edge and the two vertices it connect define a connected component of the graph.

4) Add the nearest neighbor of the vertices within this component and the edge with the smallest or largest corresponding value.

5) Gradually extend the connected component in this way.

6) Stop when the component contains all the vertices in the graph.

EXAMPLE 5.13.– Consider the graph shown in Figure 5.32.

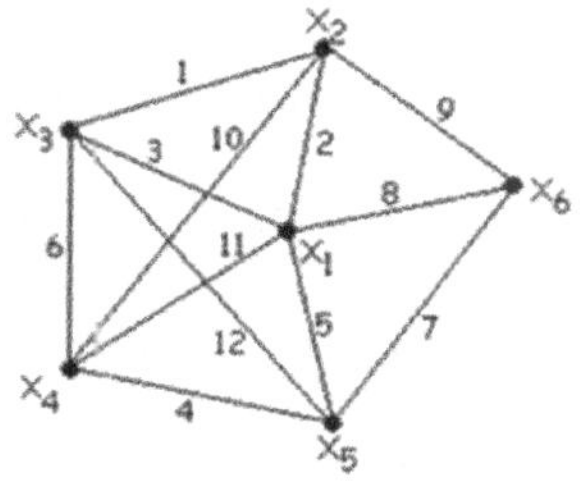

Figure 5.32. *Graph to explore*

– Choose X_1 as the starting vertex. Its nearest neighbor is X_2, forming the component $\{X_1, X_2\}$.

– The nearest vertex to this component is X_3, forming the component $\{X_1, X_2, X_3\}$.

– The nearest vertex to this component is X_5, forming the component $\{X_1, X_2, X_3, X_5\}$.

– The nearest vertex to this component is X_4, forming the component $\{X_1, X_2, X_3, X_5, X_4\}$.

– The nearest vertex to this component is (obviously) X_6, forming the component $\{X_1, X_2, X_3, X_5, X_4, X_6\}$ which is a spanning tree of minimum length (see Figure 5.33).

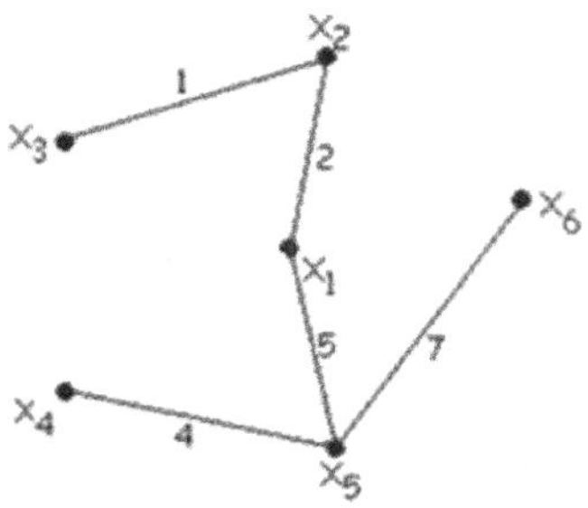

Figure 5.33. *Minimal spanning tree*

An analogous method can also be used to find the maximum spanning tree.

Sollin's algorithm

Sollin's algorithm works as follows:

1) For each vertex, select the edge that connects it to the nearest vertex. This enables sub-trees.

2) Treat these subtrees as vertices and repeat the process until the subtrees forms a complete graph tree.

Using the minimum value for selection results in the minimum spanning tree, while using the maximum value results in the maximum spanning tree.

EXAMPLE 5.14.– Take the graph from Figure 5.32 as a double-entry table (see Figure 5.34).

	X_1	X_2	X_3	X_4	X_5	X_6
X_1		[2]	3	11	5	8
X_2	2		[1]	10	∞	9
X_3	3	[1]		6	12	∞
X_4	11	10	6		[4]	∞
X_5	5	∞	12	[4]		7
X_6	8	9	∞	∞	[7]	

Figure 5.34. *Graph table*

The symbol "∞" is used to represent an indirect connection, i.e. the absence of a direct edge between two vertices, or the presence of a path passing through several vertices.

The numerical values in the graph boxes represent the lengths of the corresponding edges.

Boxed values indicate minimum edge values. These minimum values are used to find the minimum tree. A similar approach can be used to find the maximum tree:

– For X_1, the nearest vertex is X_2.

– For X_2, the nearest vertex is X_3.

– For X_3, the nearest vertex is X_2.

This results in the first sub-tree (see Figure 5.35):

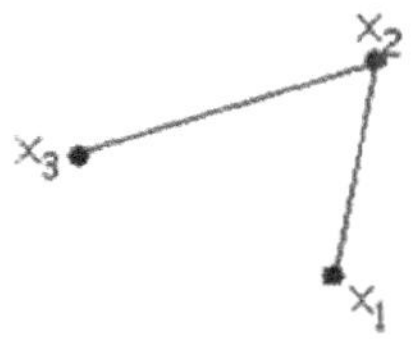

Figure 5.35. *First sub-tree*

– For X_4, the nearest vertex is X_5.

– For X_5, the nearest vertex is X_4.

– For X_6, the nearest vertex is X_5.

This results in the second sub-tree (see Figure 5.36).

Figure 5.36. *Second sub-tree*

All the vertices have been visited.

The smallest distance between the two sub-trees is sought. This is the distance between X_1 and X_5, which are connected. This produces the minimal spanning tree of length 19 (see Figure 5.37).

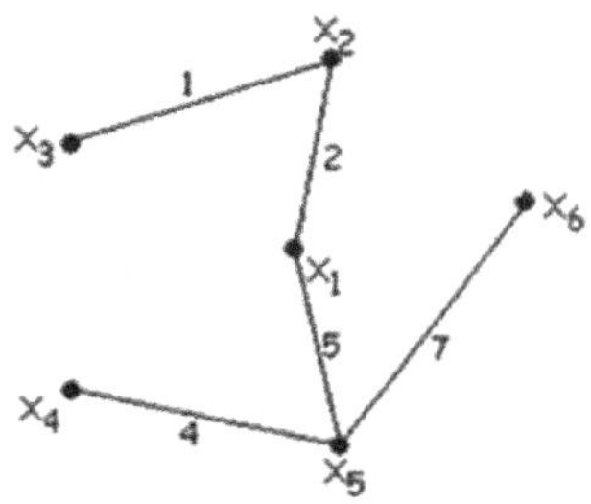

Figure 5.37. *Minimal spanning tree*

Kruskal's algorithm

Kruskal's algorithm for finding a spanning tree of minimum weight can be summarized in several steps:

1) *Edge sorting*: first, sort the edges of the graph in ascending order of weight (or length). This ensures that edges with the lowest weight are considered first when building the spanning tree (with the lowest weight).

2) *Going through the sorted edges*: next, go through the sorted edges in ascending order of weight. For each edge, check whether it creates a cycle in the spanning tree built so far. If not, add it to the spanning tree.

3) *Building the spanning tree*: repeat the previous step until all vertices are included in the spanning tree. At each stage, add an edge that does not create a cycle in the spanning tree. The result is a spanning tree of minimum weight.

Note that Kruskal's algorithm guarantees the construction of a minimum weight spanning tree when the graph is weighted and connected. Additionally, the algorithm can be applied to disconnected graphs by considering the components separately.

EXAMPLE 5.15.– Consider the graph shown in Figure 5.32. To rank the distances in ascending order, here is the sorted list of edges with their corresponding weights:

– X_2X_3: 1

– X_1X_2: 2

– X_1X_3: 3

– X_4X_5: 4

– X_1X_5: 5

– X_3X_4: 6

– X_5X_6: 7

– X_1X_6: 8

– X_2X_6: 9

– X_2X_4: 10

– X_1X_4: 11

– X_2X_5: 12

1) Start with the edges in ascending order:

The first two edges $X_2\,X_3(1)$ and $X_1X_2(2)$ are added to the tree, as they do not form a cycle (see Figure 5.38(a)).

2) Add the next smallest edge:

The edge $X_1X_3(3)$ is considered, but it is discarded because it would create a cycle with the already included edges X_1X_2 and $X_2\,X_3$.

3) Proceed to the next smallest edges:

X_4X_5 (4) and $X_1X_5(5)$ are added to the three because they do not form any cycle (see Figure 5.38(b)).

4) Next edge to consider:

X_3X_4 (6) is considered, but it is discarded because it would create a cycle with the edges $X_1X_5$and X_4X_5

5) Next edge:

X_5X_6 (7) is added to the tree (see Figure 5.38(c)), as it does not form a cycle.

6) Remaining edges:

All remaining edges $(X_1X_6\ (8), X_2X_6\ (9), X_2X_4\ (10), X_1X_4\ (11), X_2X_5\ (12))$ are discarded because they would all create cycles with the edges already included in the three.

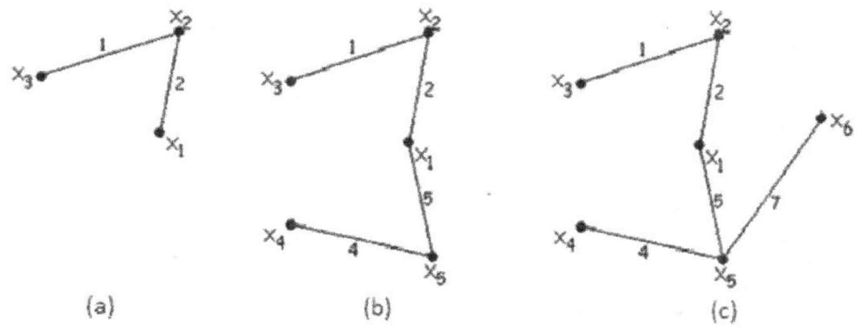

Figure 5.38. *Successive steps*

Finally, the spanning tree is obtained as shown in Figure 5.37.

Of course, for graphs with a large number of vertices, solving graph problems efficiently requires computers and programming algorithms. While the previous examples were provided for illustration purposes, handling large-scale graphs requires efficient algorithms and adequate computational resources.

6

Path Optimization

CONCEPTS COVERED IN THIS CHAPTER.–

This chapter presents a first application of graph theory: finding the shortest or longest path.

Several solution methods are explored, including the level method, enumeration method, Bellman–Ford algorithm, Bellman–Kalaba algorithm and Dijkstra algorithm.

References: [BRO 82, DRO 87, FAU 74, FAU 14, MOU 80].

The term "traffic and transport problems" covers a wide variety of problems. The following is a brief overview:

– Travel problems: optimizing routes for efficient travel.

– Transportation problems: transporting large quantities of goods at the lowest possible cost.

– Maximum flow problems: maximizing the flow through a transport network to meet demand while accounting for resource availability.

Assignment problems are also related to traffic issues, as they involve optimal matching, such as allocating "resources" to "tasks" in the most efficient way. As will be shown, this category of problems shares similarities with the previous ones, particularly in their reliance on graph-based approaches.

In this chapter, the focus is on path optimization.

6.1. Extremal-length paths

6.1.1. *General information*

Let G be any directed graph, and let d_{ij} represent the length associated with the arc (X_i, X_j) or $(\mathrm{X_i}, \mathrm{X_j})$. For any path P, the path length $D(P)$ is given by:

$$D(P) = \sum_{u \in P} d(u)$$

where u is an arc belonging to the path P, and $d(u) = d_{ij}$ is the length of the arc u, which joins two consecutive vertices X_i and X_j of the path P.

The problem addressed here is the find paths (subject to certain constraints) whose length is extremal, i.e. either minimum or maximum.

The nature of the problem of finding extremal paths varies depending on the specific context that led to the modeling of the graph and the constraints imposed on the desired path. However, the search for an extremal path is typically the final step in solving a broader problem.

For instance:

– In "scheduling problems", the arc lengths may represent the "estimated" durations of tasks or operations, which are inherently challenging to predict.

– In "transport problems", these lengths often correspond to generalized costs, a function of distance, transport costs, etc., and are similarly difficult to define precisely.

In such cases, relying solely on the shortest or longest calculated path makes no sense, as it is unlikely to yield the true extremal path, especially when paths of nearly equivalent lengths exist. Instead, it is often more meaningful to identify all paths whose lengths deviate by at most a given amount ε from the length of the extremal path. These paths are refereed as ε-extremal paths.

6.1.2. *Solving algorithms*

This section explores several algorithms, including some historical methods, for identifying the extremal path between two vertices in a directed graph. These algorithms will be illustrated through their application to a specific case study (Example 6.1).

EXAMPLE 6.1.– Consider the directed graph shown in Figure 6.1.

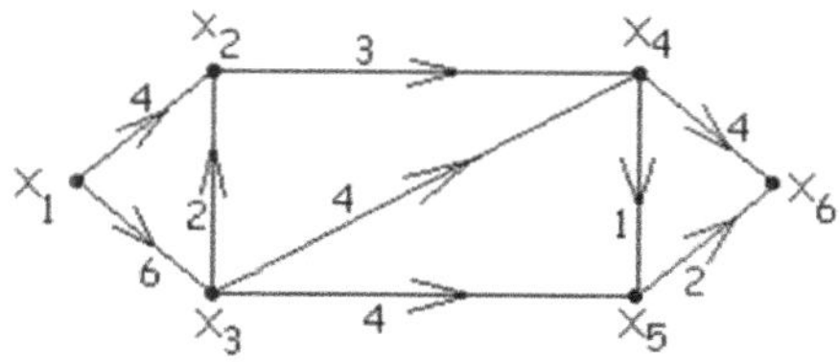

Figure 6.1. *Directed graph for exploration. For a color version of this figure, see www.iste.co.uk/cochard/mathematics3.zip*

The objective is to determine the shortest path between X_1 and X_6.

Level method

The procedure involves decomposing the graph into levels to present it in an ordered form.

Starting from the initial vertex (which has no predecessors), the subsequent vertices are marked with the shortest (or longest) length of the arc or path connecting them to the current vertex. The process begins with the graph shown in Figure 6.2.

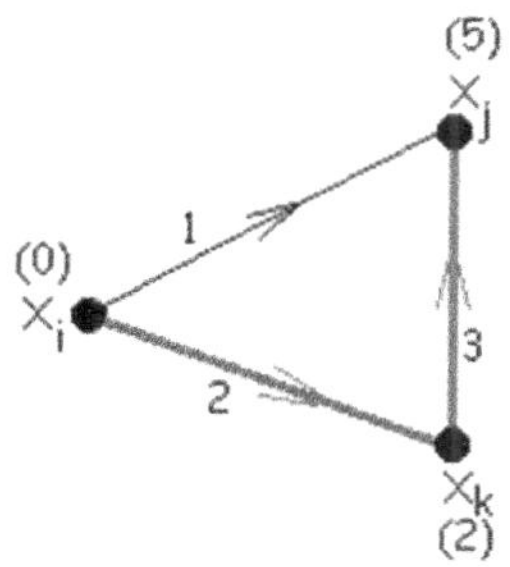

Figure 6.2. *Application of the level method*

If X_i has no predecessor, it is marked with 0. For the shortest path between X_i and X_j, X_k is marked with $0 + 2 = 2$, and X_j is marked with $0 + 1 = 1$.

For the longest path between X_i and X_j, X_j is marked with $0 + 2 + 3 = 5$. The corresponding arcs are represented by "red lines". Thus, for the longest path between X_i and X_j, the "red-line" path has a total length of 5.

To find the extremal path between start and end points (as in the example), the previous phase is applied progressively to all the vertices of the graph.

EXAMPLE 6.2.– The graph considered is free of circuits.

The decomposition into levels yields the results shown in Figure 6.3.

nodes	predecessors	N1	N2	N3	N4, N5, N6
X_1					
X_2	X_1, X_3	X_3	-		
X_3	X_1, X_3	-			
X_4	X_2, X_3	X_2, X_3	X_2	-	
X_4	X_3, X_4	X_3, X_4	X_4	X_4	-
X_5	X_4, X_5	X_4, X_5	X_4, X_5	X_4, X_5	X_5

N1 = $\{X_1\}$ N2 = $\{X_3\}$ N3 = $\{X_2\}$ N4 = $\{X_4]$ N5 = $\{X_5\}$ N6 = $\{X_6\}$

Figure 6.3. *Decomposition into levels*

From this decomposition, the ordered graph shown in Figure 6.4 is obtained.

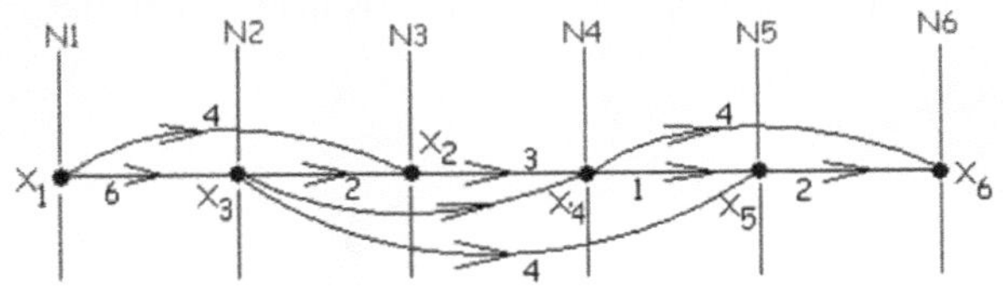

Figure 6.4. *Ordered graph*

The shortest and longest paths are then easily deduced, as shown in Figure 6.5.

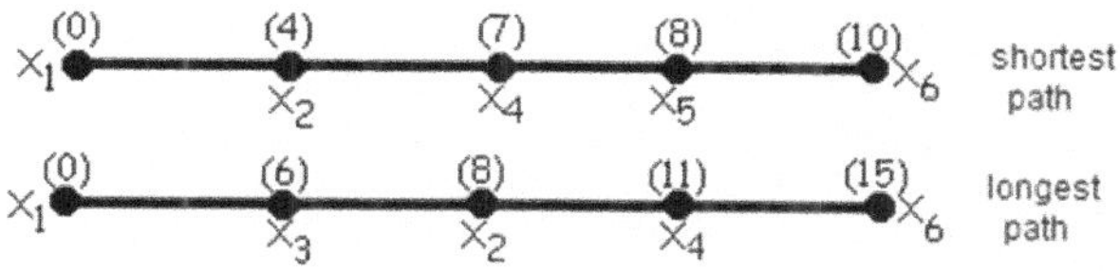

Figure 6.5. *Shortest and longest paths*

Applying the procedure produces the diagram shown in Figure 6.6, which represents the shortest path with a value of 10.

The diagram in Figure 6.7 shows the longest path with a value of 15.

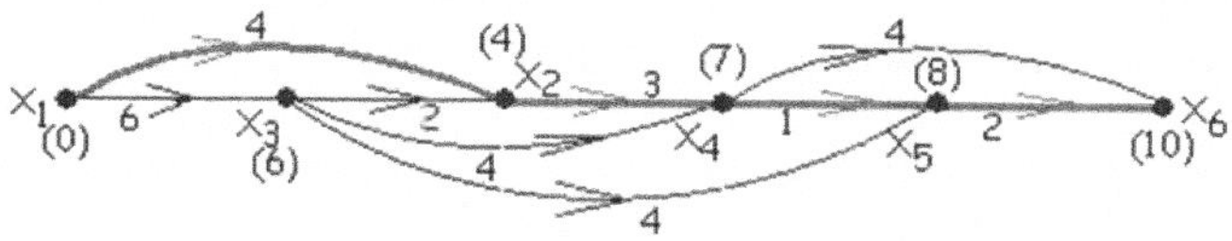

Figure 6.6. *Shortest path. For a color version of this figure, see www.iste.co.uk/cochard/mathematics3.zip*

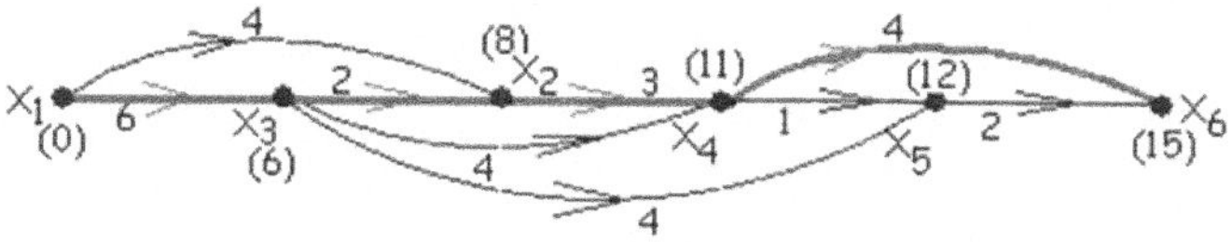

Figure 6.7. *Longest path. For a color version of this figure, see www.iste.co.uk/cochard/mathematics3.zip*

Enumeration method

This method is suitable only for graphs with a limited number of vertices. It involves listing all possible paths and comparing their lengths. However, as the number of vertices and paths increases, the approach becomes computationally expensive and impractical due to the exhaustive nature of the exploration.

EXAMPLE 6.3.– Enumerating the paths from X_1 to X_6 produces the tree shown in Figure 6.8.

The levels of this tree, labeled from $N1$ to $N6$, are clearly visible.

A total of seven possible paths have been identified:

– $C1 = \{X_1, X_2, X_4, X_3, X_5, X_6\}$, length 11

– $C2 = \{X_1, X_2, X_4, X_5, X_6\}$, length 10

– $C3 = \{X_1, X_2, X_4, X_6\}$, length 13

– $C4 = \{X_1, X_3, X_2, X4, X_6\}$, length 15

– $C5 = \{X_1, X_3, X_4, X_5, X_6\}$, length 13

– $C6 = \{X_1, X_3, X_4, X_6\}$, length 14

– $C7 = \{X_1, X_3, X_5, X_6\}$, length 12

This enumeration allows the classification of paths, revealing the shortest path with a length of 10 and the longest with a length of 15.

However, it is important to note that this method becomes increasingly tedious and impractical as the number of vertices grows.

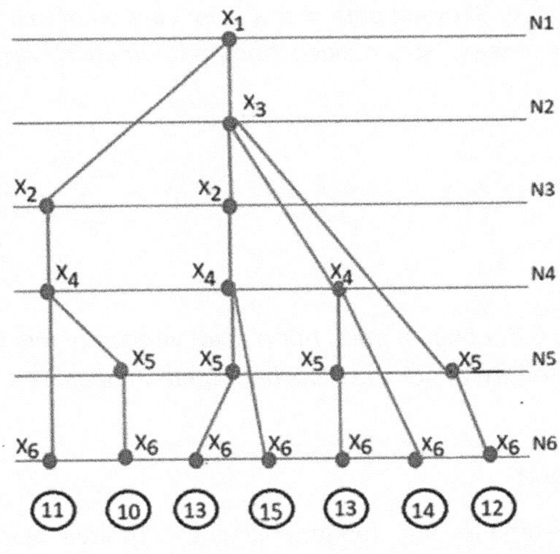

Figure 6.8. *Enumeration of all paths*

Bellman–Ford algorithm

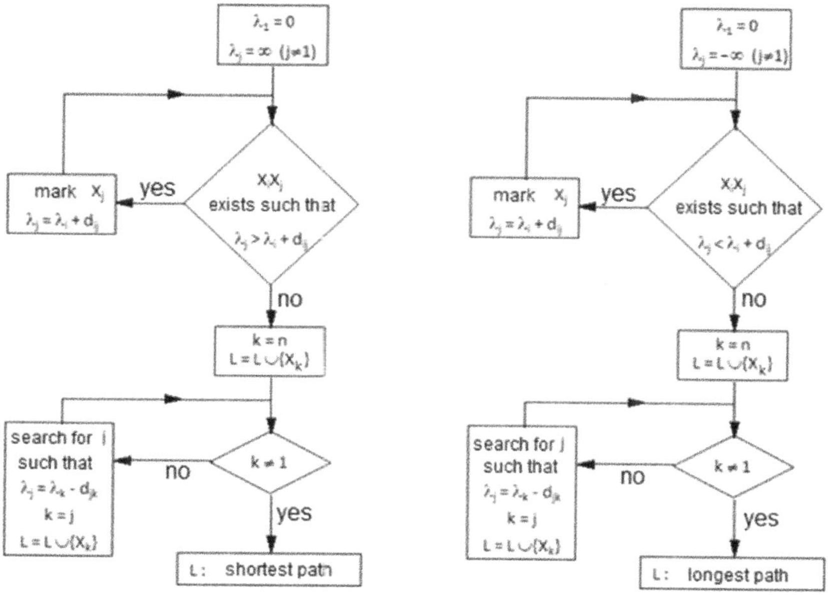

Figure 6.9. *Flowcharts of a Bellman–Ford algorithm*

The Bellman–Ford algorithm was historically the first algorithm developed to optimize the search for an extremal path. While more efficient algorithms have since been developed, studying this algorithm is valuable due to its significant influence on subsequent advancements. The Bellman–Ford algorithm can be used to find either a minimum or an extremal path.

The principle of the algorithm involves assigning weights to the vertices of a graph. These weights are progressively adjusted, decreased for a minimum path or increased for a maximum path.

To illustrate the process for finding a minimum path, all vertices are initially assigned an infinite weight (∞), except for the starting vertex (X_1), which is assigned a weight of 0. The operations of the algorithm are shown in the flowcharts in Figure 6.9: the left flowchart represents the minimization, and the right represents the maximization. L denotes an ordered list.

The algorithm will now be applied to Example 6.1 to determine the minimum path.

EXAMPLE 6.4.– Bellman–Ford algorithm: Starting with the graph shown in Figure 6.1, the initialization is shown in Figure 6.10.

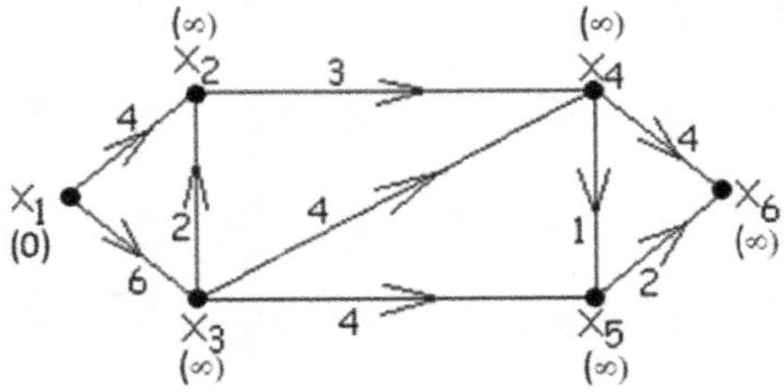

Figure 6.10. *Initialization*

Step 1: The weights of vertices X_2 and X_3, which are directly connected to X_1, are updated accordingly (see Figure 6.11).

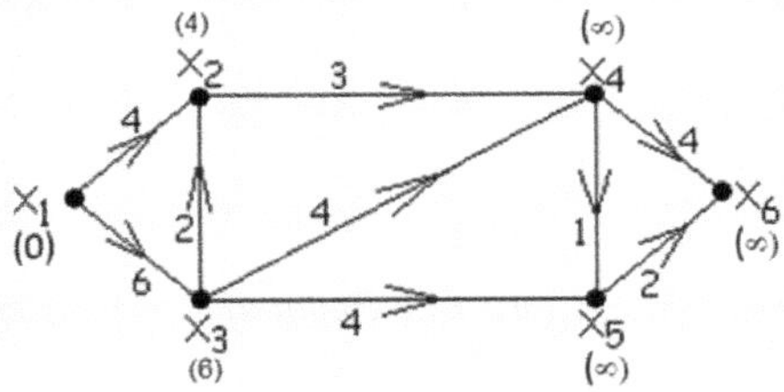

Figure 6.11. *Step 1*

Step 2: The weight of vertex weight X_4 is adjusted (see Figure 6.12).

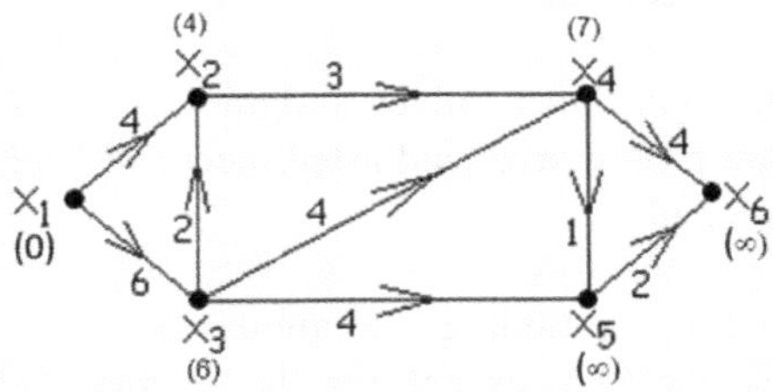

Figure 6.12. *Step 2*

Step 3: The weight of X_4 is updated through the link $X_3 - X_4$, as 7 is less than $6 + 4$.

Similarly, the weight of X_5 is adjusted via the link $X_4 - X_5$, resulting in a weight of 8 (see Figure 6.13).

Using the $X_3 - X_5$ connection would result in a higher weight (10).

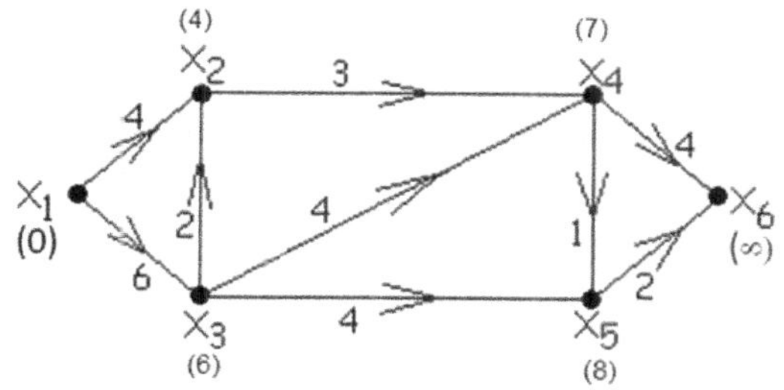

Figure 6.13. *Step 3*

Step 4: The only vertex to be uploaded is X_6, which receives a weight of 10 via the connection $X_5 - X_6$ (see Figure 6.14).

Using the $X_4 - X_6$ connection would result in a higher weight of 11.

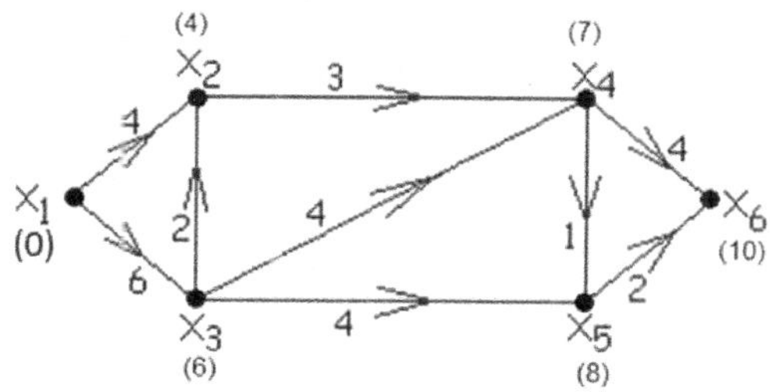

Figure 6.14. *Step 4*

The process has reached a point where no further modifications to the weights are possible.

Next, the second part of the algorithm is applied:

- $L = \{X_6\}$
- $L = \{X_6, X_5\}$
- $L = \{X_6, X_5, X_4\}$

$-L = \{X_6, X_5, X_4, X_2\}$

$-L = \{X_6, X_5, X_4, X_2, X_1\}$

The minimum path found is $X_1 - X_2 - X_4 - X_5 - X_6$, with a total length of 10.

Bellman–Kalaba algorithm

The fundamental concept of the Bellman–Kalaba algorithm is to progressively consider paths originating from X_1, increasing the number of arcs step by step.

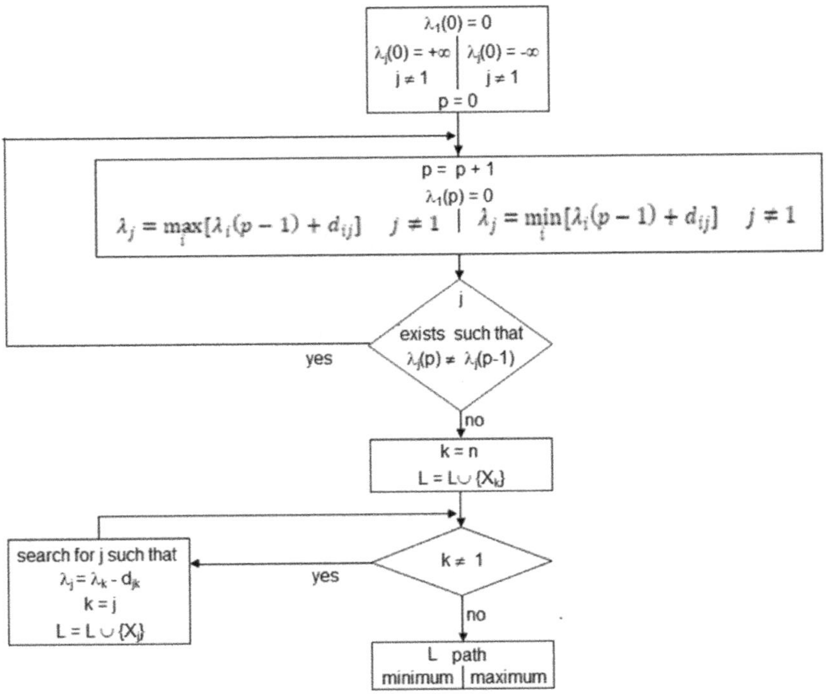

Figure 6.15. *Bellman–Kalaba algorithm*

Vertices are assigned weights, similar to the Bellman–Ford algorithm. The Bellman–Kalaba algorithm also consists of two parts, with the second part identical to the first. Figure 6.15 shows the algorithm's flowchart, with minimization represented on the left and maximization on the right.

The algorithm is now applied to Example 6.1 to determine the minimum path.

EXAMPLE 6.5.– Bellman–Kalaba algorithm: Initialization begins with the graph in Figure 6.1 (see Figure 6.16).

Step $p = 0$: At this stage, all vertices are assigned infinite weight (∞) (see Figure 6.16).

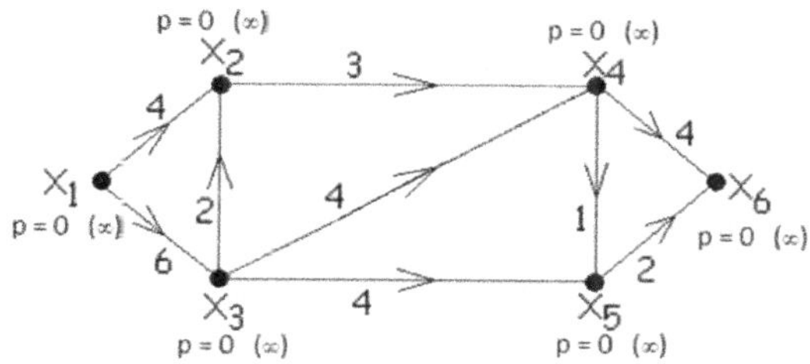

Figure 6.16. *Initialization*

Step $p = 1$: The weights of X_1, X_2, and X_3 are updated (see Figure 6.17).

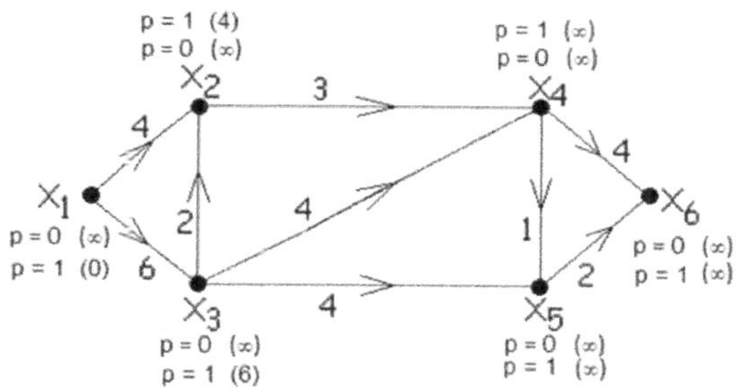

Figure 6.17. *p = 1*

Step $p = 2$: Update the weights of X_4 and X_5 (see Figure 6.18).

Step $p = 3$: Update the weights of X_5 and X_6 (see Figure 6.19).

Step $p = 4$: Update the weight of X_6 (see Figure 6.20).

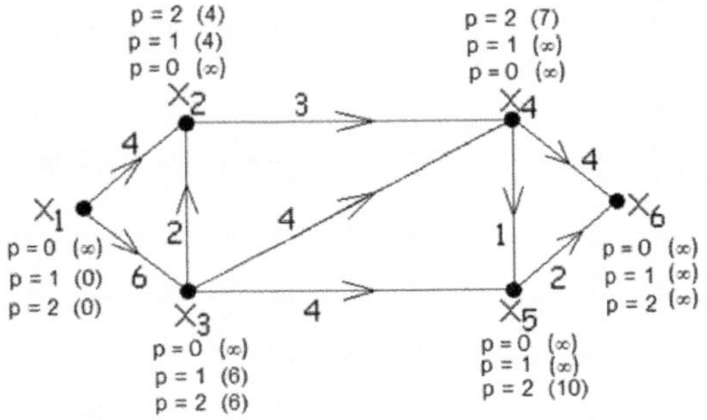

Figure 6.18. *p = 2*

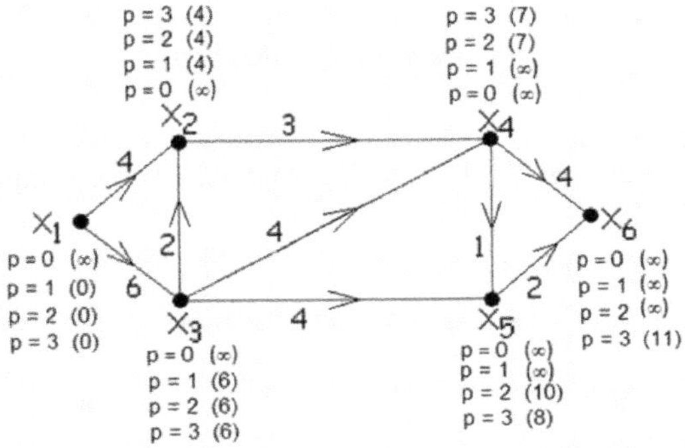

Figure 6.19. *p = 3*

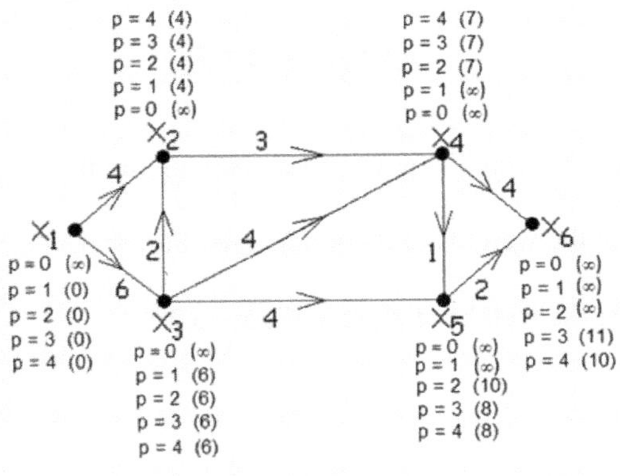

Figure 6.20. *p = 4*

At this stage, it is evident that all weights for $p = 4$ are identical to those for $p = 3$, except for X_6. However, an additional iteration for $p = 5$ would result in a weight of 10. Consequently, the first part of the algorithm can be considered complete.

For the second part, the vertices are successively determined as follows:

- $L = \{X_6\}$
- $L = \{X_6, X_5\}$ because $10 - 2 = 8$
- $L = \{X_6, X_5, X_4\}$ because $8 - 1 = 7$
- $L = \{X_6, X_5, X_4, X_2\}$ because $7 - 3 = 4$
- $L = \{X_6, X_5, X_4, X_2, X_1\}$ because $4 - 4 = 0$

Thus, the minimum path is $X_1 - X_2 - X_4 - X_5 - X_6$, with the graph as described in Example 6.4.

Dijkstra's algorithm

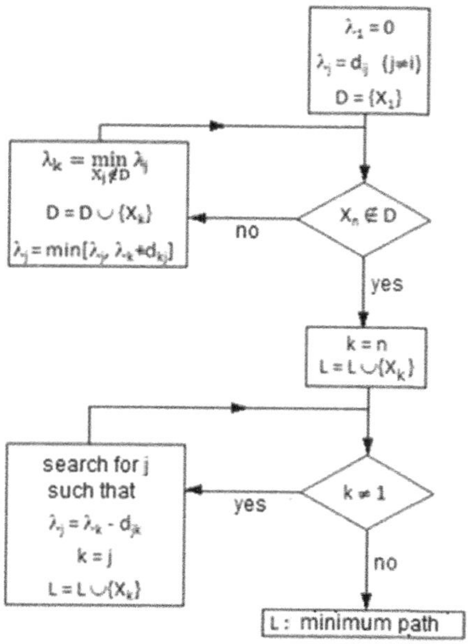

Figure 6.21. *Dijkstra's algorithm*

Also referred to as the Moore-Dijkstra algorithm, Dijkstra's algorithm is more efficient than its predecessors and is specifically designed to identify paths of minimum length. It has wide application in route minimization and is extensively used in Global Positioning System (GPS) navigation.

The starting point of Dijkstra's algorithm differs from that of the Bellman–Ford and Bellman–Kalaba algorithms.

When $\lambda_1 = 0$, the other λ_j values are set to d_{1j}. If there is no direct arc connects vertex 1 to vertex j, λ_j is set to ∞. In addition, Dijkstra's algorithm maintains an up-to-date list D of vertices.

The algorithm consists of two parts, with the second part identical to that of the previous algorithms (see Figure 6.21). A key feature of this algorithm is that iterations do not revisit vertices that have already been marked and added to the list D. These vertices are often referred to as "marked vertices".

The algorithm will now be applied to Example 6.1.

EXAMPLE 6.6.– Dijkstra's algorithm: Initialization begins with the graph shown in Figure 6.1 (shown in Figure 6.22).

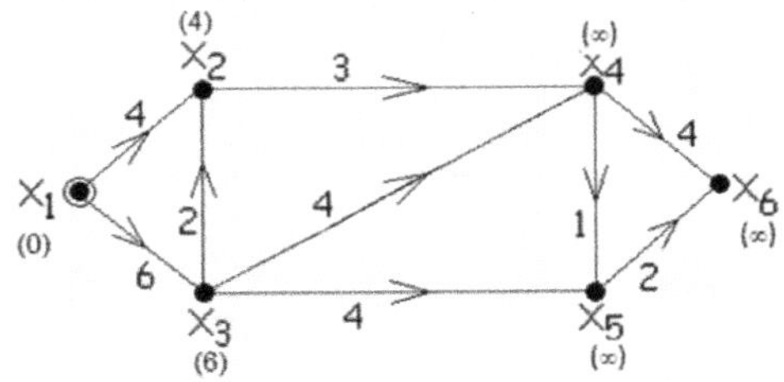

Figure 6.22. *Initialization*

$D = \{X_1\}$. Among all vertices other than X_1, the vertex X_2 has the lowest weight. Therefore, the vertex X_2 is added to the list D, resulting in $D = \{X_1, X_2\}$ (see Figure 6.23). The weights are updated as follows: $\lambda_3 = 6$ (unchanged), $\lambda_4 = 7$, while the remaining weights stay unchanged.

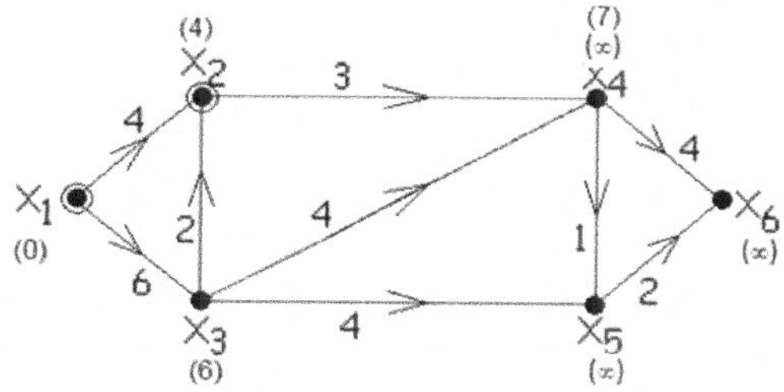

Figure 6.23. *Step 1*

Among the four vertices X_3, X_4, X_5, and X_6, vertex X_3 has the lowest weight. Vertex X_3 is added to the list D, resulting in $D = \{X_1\ X_2, X_3\}$ (see Figure 6.24). The weights are updated as follows: $\lambda_4 = 7$ (unchanged) and $\lambda_5 = 10$.

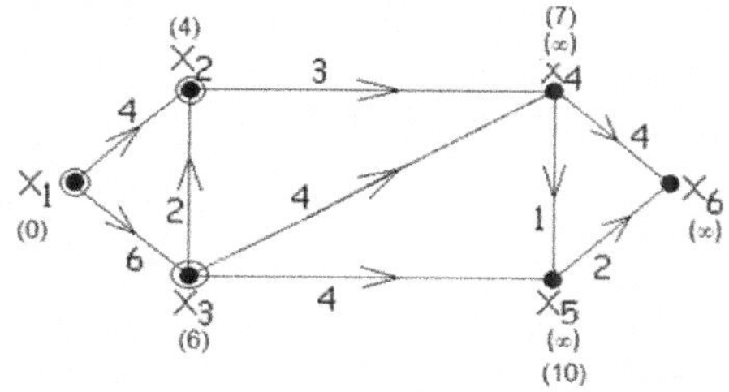

Figure 6.24. *Step 2*

Among the three remaining vertices X_4, X_5, and X_6, the vertex X_4 has the lowest weight. Therefore, the vertex X_4 is added to the list D, resulting in $D = \{X_1, X_2, X_3, X_4\}$ (see Figure 6.25). The weights are updated as follows: $\lambda_5 = 8$ and $\lambda_6 = 11$.

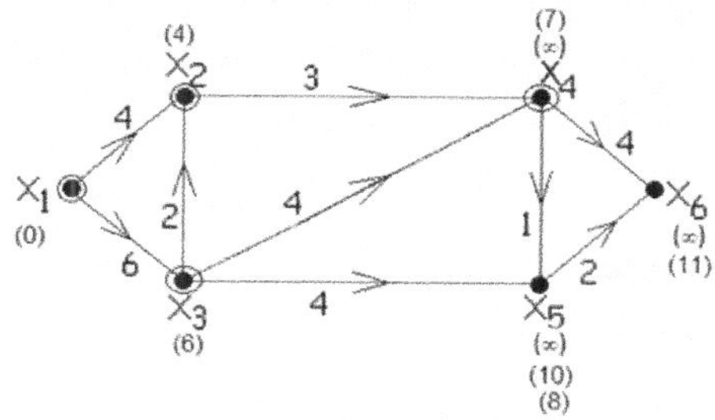

Figure 6.25. *Step 3*

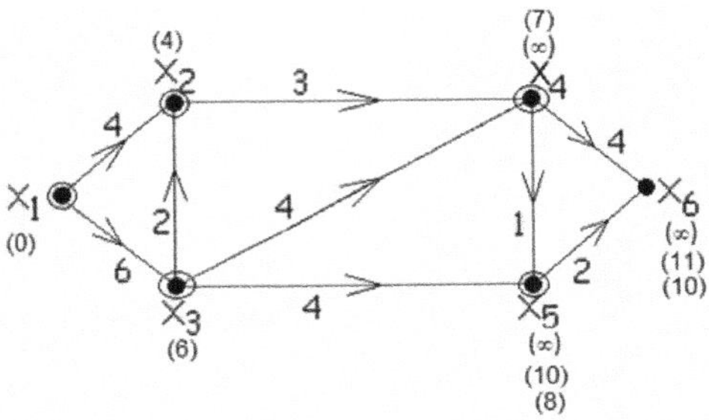

Figure 6.26. *Step 4*

Among the two remaining vertices X_5 and X_6, vertex X_5 has the lowest weight. Thus, the vertex X_5 is added to the list D, resulting in $D = \{X_1, X_2, X_3, X_4, X_5\}$ (see Figure 6.26). The weight is updated as follows: $\lambda_6 = 10$.

The final unmarked vertex, X_6, has the lowest weight and is marked. The list becomes $D = \{X_1, X_2, X_3, X_4, X_5, X_6\}$ (see Figure 6.27).

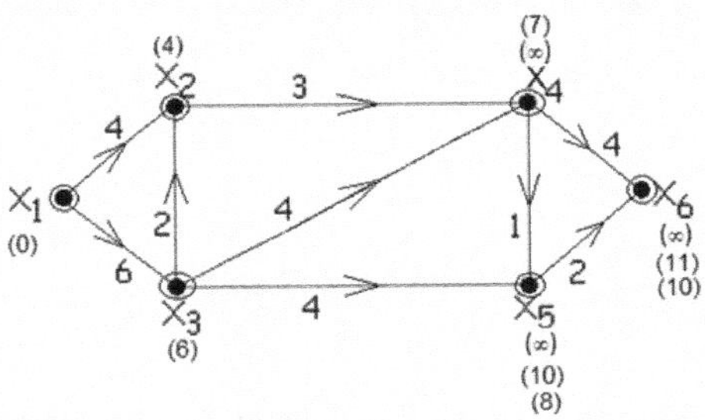

Figure 6.27. *Step 5*

All the vertices in the graph have been marked, as the list D contains all the vertices in the graph. The second part of the algorithm can now begin. The path construction proceeds as follows:

– $L = \{X_6\}$

– $L = \{X_6, X_5\}$ because $10 - 2 = 8$

– $L = \{X_6, X_5, X_4\}$ because $8 - 1 = 7$

– $L = \{X_6, X_5, X_4, X_2\}$ because $7 - 3 = 4$

– $L = \{X_6, X_5, X_4, X_2, X_1\}$ because $4 - 4 = 0$

This gives the minimum path: $X_1 \rightarrow X_2 \rightarrow X_4 \rightarrow X_5 \rightarrow X_6$, with a length of 10.

In practice, it is convenient to use a table, as shown in Figure 6.28.

steps	X_1	X_2	X_3	X_4	X_5	X_6
1	0	4 - X_1	6 - X_1			
2		4 - X_1		7 - X_2		
3			6 - X_1	10 - X_3	10 - X_3	
4				7 - X_2	8 - X_4	11 - X_4
5					8 - X_4	10 - X_5
6						10 - X_5

Figure 6.28. *Practical table*

How to use the table:

Step 1: Start at the vertex X_1. Since this vertex will not be revisited, eliminate its corresponding column (in dark gray). From X_1, X_2 or X_3 can be reached. In the columns for X_2 and X_3, the vertex from which the path came, i.e. X_1, is used to calculate the distances:

– From X_1 to X_2: $0 + 4 = 4$.

– From X_1 to X_3: $0 + 6 = 6$.

These values are added to the respective columns. Then, the smallest value, which is 4, is selected, and X_2 is marked.

Step 2: The column for X_2 is now marked with the value $4 - X_1$. Revisiting this column is not necessary. From X_2, X_4 is the only reachable vertex. In the column for X_4, mark the value $7 - X_2$ (since $7 = 4 + 3$). Now, between $6 - X_1$ and $7 - X_1$, the smallest value, $6 - X_1$, is chosen, marking the column for X_3.

Step 3: The column for X_3 is marked with the value $6 - X_1$, and revisiting this column is not necessary. From X_3, X_4 and X_5 are reachable, giving the values $10 - X_3$ and $10 - X_3$ for these columns. Between $7 - X_2$, $10 - X_3$, and $10 - X_3$, the smallest value $7 - X_2$ is selected, marking X_4.

Step 4: The column for X_4 is marked with the value $7 - X_2$. Revisiting this column is not necessary. From X_4, X_5 and X_6 are reachable, resulting in the values $8 - X_4$ and $11 - X_4$. Between $10 - X_3$, $8 - X_4$, and $11 - X_4$, the smallest value, $8 - X_4$, is selected, marking the column for X_5.

Step 5: The column for X_5 is marked with the value $8 - X_4$. Revisiting this column is not necessary. From X_5, the only reachable vertex is X_6, giving the value $10 - X_5$. Between $11 - X_4$ and $10 - X_5$, the smallest value, $10 - X_5$, is selected, marking the column for X_6.

Step 6: All vertices have now been explored.

To obtain the minimum path, start from the destination point X_6.

– From X_6, the previous vertex is X_5 (because of the value $10 - X_5$).

– From X_5, the previous vertex is X_4.

– From X_4, the previous vertex is X_2.

– From X_2, the previous vertex is X_1.

Thus, the minimum path is $X_1 \rightarrow X_2 \rightarrow X_4 \rightarrow X_5 \rightarrow X_6$, with a total length of 10.

6.1.3. *Searching for ε-extremal paths*

As previously discussed, the imprecision in determining arc lengths often needs to be considered. In such cases, the goal is not only to find the optimal or extremal path length but also to identify all neighboring paths whose lengths differ by no more than a small margin, denoted as ε, from the optimal path length.

This approach helps manage uncertainties in the system and offers alternative routes. It is not always beneficial to route all goods via the shortest path, as this can lead to congestion and longer journey times. Instead, it is effective to diversify the paths taken by using paths of similar lengths.

The procedure is relatively simple: start by searching for the optimal path between two vertices or between the starting point (input) and the endpoint (output) of the graph. Next, search for neighboring paths whose lengths differ by at most ε from the length of the optimal path.

EXAMPLE 6.7.– Let us return to Example 6.43, where path enumeration provided the result shown in Figure 6.8.

To obtain the two-minimal paths, the length of these paths must not exceed 12 (10 + 2). In addition to the minimum path with a length of 10, two other two-minimal paths with lengths of 11 and 12 are also found.

6.2. Hamiltonian path search

Recall the following definitions of a directed graph with vertices $X_1, X_2, \dots, X_n$:

1) A *Hamiltonian path* $(X_{i1}, X_{i2}, \dots, X_{in})$ is a path that passes through each vertex of the graph exactly once.

2) A *Hamiltonian circuit* $(X_{i1}, X_{i2}, \dots, X_{in}, X_{i1})$ is a circuit that passes through each vertex of the graph exactly once, with the exception for X_{i1}, which is visited both at the beginning and the end.

There are simple necessary conditions for a graph to have a Hamiltonian path:

– If a directed graph is complete, then there is at least one Hamiltonian path.

– If a directed graph is both complete and strongly connected, then at least one Hamiltonian circuit exists.

– Any strongly connected directed graph without loops, composed of n vertices, and whose degree of each vertex is at least equal to n, admits a Hamiltonian circuit.

– A symmetric, connected, loop-free graph composed of n vertices, with the degree of each vertex at least equal to $\frac{n}{2}$, admits a Hamiltonian circuit.

These properties can also be useful:

– If a graph G contains a Hamiltonian path, then G must be connected.

– If a graph G contains a Hamiltonian circuit, then every vertex of G must have a degree of at least 2.

Several methods can be used to find Hamiltonian paths. The following are explanations of a few methods.

6.2.1. *Decomposition into strongly connected components*

Once the strongly connected components of a graph have been identified, it becomes possible to find the Hamiltonian paths. Indeed, if the directed graph G is made up of several strongly connected components, such as A, B and C, then a Hamiltonian path must connect these components, since they constitute a partition of G. In other words, for a path to be Hamiltonian, it must pass through at least one vertex of each strongly connected component of the graph.

EXAMPLE 6.8.– Consider the graph shown in Figure 6.29, which is made up of three strongly connected components: A, B and C (as shown in Figure 6.30).

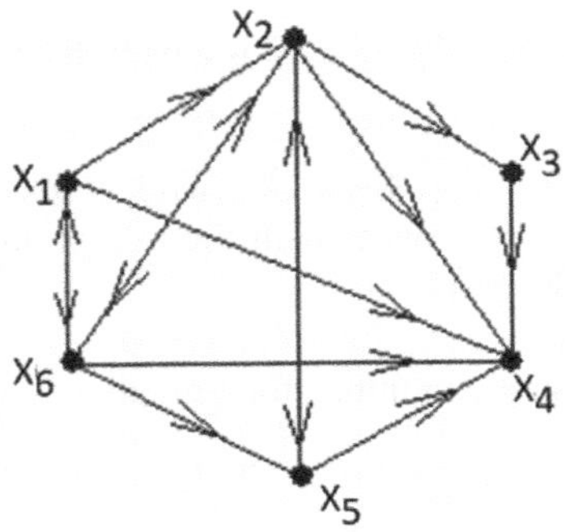

Figure 6.29. *Graph to explore*

It is obvious that the Hamiltonian paths link the three components and follow the pattern $A \rightarrow B \rightarrow C$, as no arc leaves component C.

All that remains is to list the Hamiltonian paths of the component A, which must end at X_2 (since only the arc $X_2 \rightarrow X_3$ allows the transition from component A to component B). There is really only one possible path: $X_1 \rightarrow X_6 \rightarrow X_5 \rightarrow X_2$.

Thus, the only Hamiltonian path in the graph is: $X_1 \rightarrow X_6 \rightarrow X_5 \rightarrow X_2 \rightarrow X_3 \rightarrow X_4$.

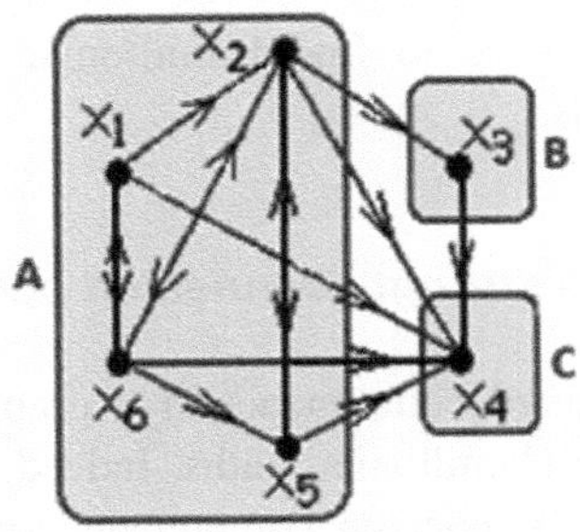

Figure 6.30. *Strongly connected components*

6.2.2. *Branch and Bound algorithm*

The classic Traveling Salesman Problem (TSP) involves finding a minimum-length Hamiltonian circuit in a complete graph. The objective is to find a path that visits each vertex exactly once, with the starting and ending vertex being the same, while minimizing the total travel cost. In other words, the goal is to identify a Hamiltonian circuit that minimizes the overall distance or travel cost.

Consider a complete graph, symmetrical or not, with n vertices, where each arc (X_i, X_j) is associated with a cost d_{ij}, represented in a cost matrix $\boldsymbol{D}$. The objective is to find a circuit that visits all the vertices while minimizing the sum of the costs along this circuit. If the graph is not complete or symmetrical, edges of infinite length can be added between unconnected vertices, thus searching for Hamiltonian circuits.

To illustrate these concepts, here is Example 6.9.

EXAMPLE 6.9.– The traveling salesman must visit cities 1, 2, 3 and 4 exactly once, starting at city 1 and returning to city 1 after completing the tour. Figure 6.31 shows the corresponding graph (not to scale).

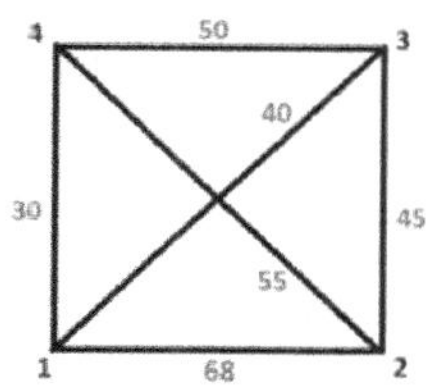

Figure 6.31. *Graph to explore*

To find the minimum-length Hamiltonian circuit, several methods are available, some of which allow for an exact (optimal) solution to be found. These include integer linear programming, Branch and Bound (BB), and dynamic programming. There are also methods that provide approximate solutions, known as heuristics and metaheuristics.

To begin with, the simplest method is to list all possible circuits.

EXAMPLE 6.10.– This list corresponds to the tree structure shown in Figure 6.32.

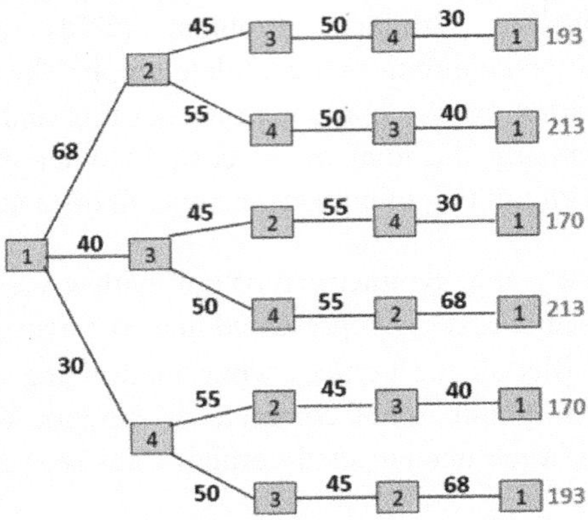

Figure 6.32. *Route enumeration*

This process leads to solving the problem, which is circuit $1 - 3 - 2 - 4 - 1$ with a length of 170. It is important to note that circuit $1 - 4 - 2 - 3 - 1$ is exactly the same Hamiltonian cycle as the previous one. In fact, all circuits go in pairs, since a circuit run in the opposite direction is also a circuit of the same length.

This method has significant limitations. For a graph of n vertices, there are approximately $\frac{(n-1)!}{2}$ possible Hamiltonian cycles. In the previous example with only three vertices, there were three possible cycles. However, as the number of vertices increases to 100, for example, enumeration becomes impossible. It is therefore necessary to find ways of reducing the tree of possible cycles. A common approach is to use the BB method. This method has already been encountered in the case of integer linear programming.

The BB method is based on the following observations: For each node i in the tree structure, a value E_i is associated, which represents either a lower bound (in the case of minimization) or an upper bound (in the case of maximization). The value E_i increases as the tree is traversed downward for minimization and decreases for maximization. In the case of minimization, if a solution value E is already known and $E_i > E$, the branch corresponding to node i can be discarded, as it will not be possible to obtain a solution better than E. The inequality is reversed in the case of maximization.

To make these concepts more concrete, let us apply the BB algorithm to the specific example in Figure 6.31, using its practical implementation.

EXAMPLE 6.11.– a) To begin with, the distance matrix is drawn up, with impossible paths replaced by the symbol ∞ (see Figure 6.33).

	1	2	3	4
1	∞	68	40	30
2	68	∞	45	55
3	40	45	∞	50
4	30	55	50	∞

Figure 6.33. *Distance matrix*

b) For each line, the minimum value is identified and subtracted from the elements in that row (see Figure 6.34).

	1	2	3	4	
1	∞	68	40	30	30
2	68	∞	45	55	45
3	40	45	∞	50	40
4	30	55	50	∞	30
					145

⇨

	1	2	3	4
1	∞	38	10	0
2	23	∞	0	10
3	0	5	∞	10
4	0	25	20	∞

Figure 6.34. *After line subtraction*

c) For each column of the new matrix, the smallest element is identified and subtracted from the elements in that column (see Figure 6.35). The result is recorded in the bottom right corner.

	1	2	3	4	
1	∞	38	10	0	
2	23	∞	0	10	
3	0	5	∞	10	
4	0	25	20	∞	
	0	5	0	0	5

⇨

1	1	2	3	4	
1	∞	33	10	0	
2	23	∞	0	10	
3	0	0	∞	10	
4	0	20	20	∞	
					150

Figure 6.35. *Column subtraction. For a color version of this figure, see www.iste.co.uk/cochard/mathematics3.zip*

This results in the reduced matrix corresponding to node 1 (number framed top left) and the value $E_1 = 150$ (the sum of the smallest elements found).

This node is noted as shown in Figure 6.36.

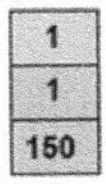

Figure 6.36. *The root. For a color version of this figure, see www.iste.co.uk/cochard/mathematics3.zip*

In the first box, the node number is shown; in the second box, the graph vertex number (note that the tree node number should not be confused with the graph vertex number); and in the third box, the value of E_1.

Starting from vertex 1, three branches are considered: going to vertex 2, going to vertex 3, or going to vertex 4. This is shown in Figure 6.37.

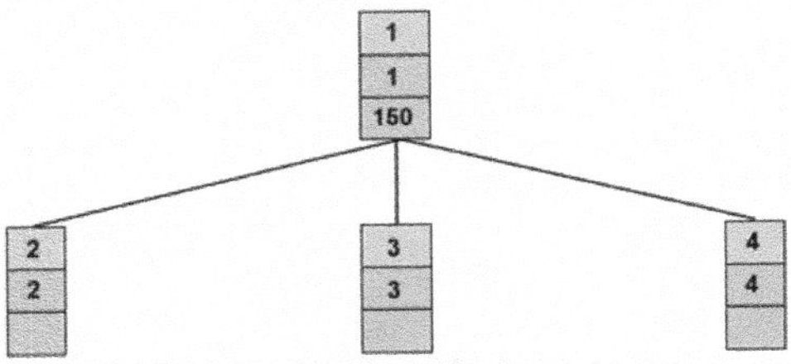

Figure 6.37. *The three branches to consider. For a color version of this figure, see www.iste.co.uk/cochard/mathematics3.zip*

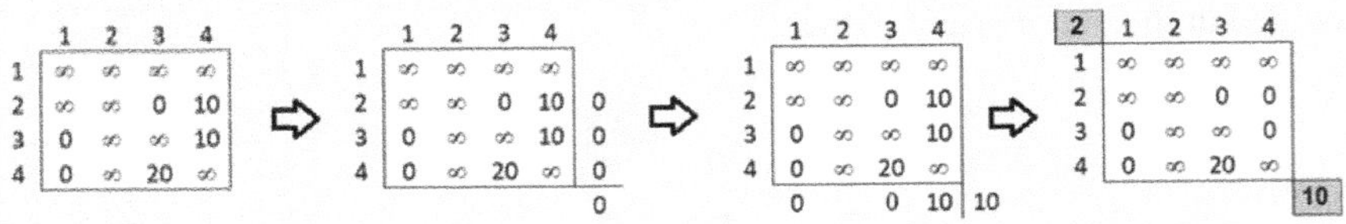

Figure 6.38. *Processing node 2. For a color version of this figure, see www.iste.co.uk/cochard/mathematics3.zip*

To calculate the values of E_2, E_3, and E_4, the reduced matrices for nodes 2, 3 and 4 are derived from the reduced matrix of node 1.

For node 2, Figure 6.38 is obtained.

The boxes corresponding to row 1 and column 2 are marked as impossible, as vertices 1 and 2 can no longer be used. In addition, the path 2 – 1 is marked as "impossible", as returning is not allowed. The aforementioned steps (b) and (c) are then applied. The same process is followed for node 3 (see Figure 6.39). Finally, for node 4, Figure 6.40 is obtained.

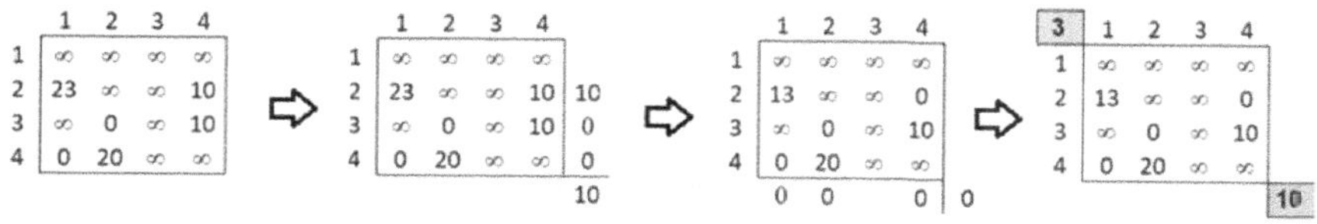

Figure 6.39. *Processing node 3. For a color version of this figure, see www.iste.co.uk/cochard/mathematics3.zip*

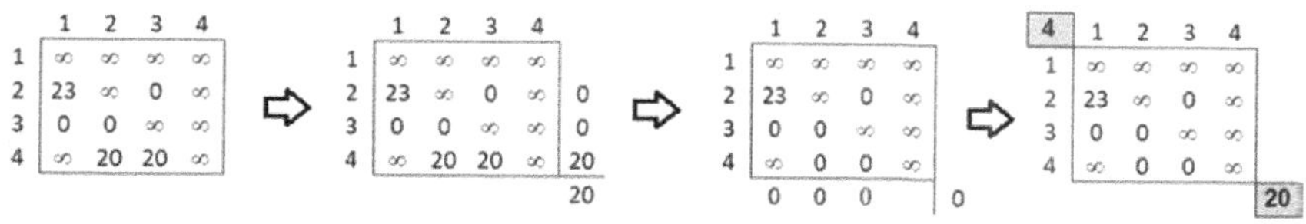

Figure 6.40. *Processing node 4. For a color version of this figure, see www.iste.co.uk/cochard/mathematics3.zip*

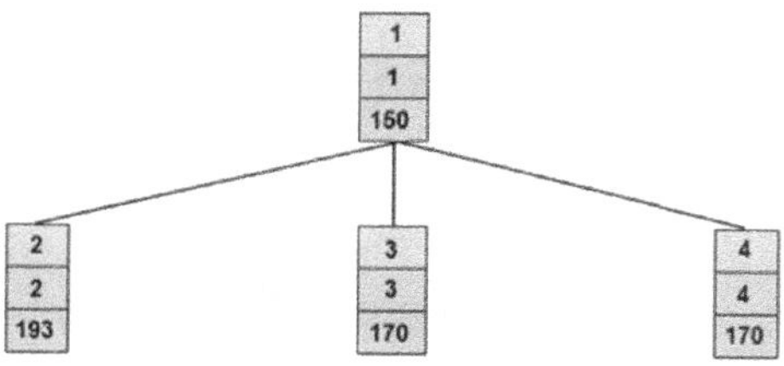

Figure 6.41. *Current situation. For a color version of this figure, see www.iste.co.uk/cochard/mathematics3.zip*

The value of E_2 is calculated using the general relationship $E_i = E_j + d^j(a,b) + \gamma_i$, where j is the "parent" node of node i, d^j is a distance calculated with the node matrix j, (a,b) is the path involved in the "node(j)-vertex a" to "node(i)-top b", and γ_i is the sum of the minimum node costs for node i. Here,

$$E_2 = E_1 + d^1(1,2) + \gamma_2 = 150 + 33 + 10 = 193$$

Similarly,

$$E_3 = E_1 + d^1(1,3) + \gamma_3 = 150 + 10 + 10 = 170$$

$$E_4 = E_1 + d^1(1,4) + \gamma_4 = 150 + 0 + 20 = 170$$

This gives the situation shown in Figure 6.41.

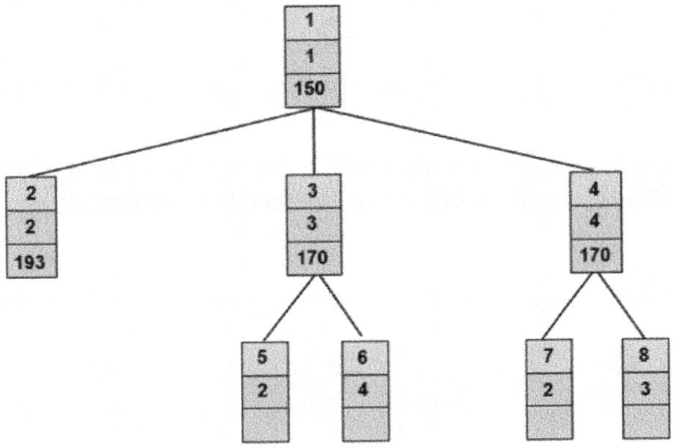

Figure 6.42. *New routes to examine. For a color version of this figure, see www.iste.co.uk/cochard/mathematics3.zip*

For the moment, branch $1-2$ (node 2) can be temporarily discarded, and the focus is shifted to branches $1-3$ and $1-4$ (nodes 3 and 4), which have two equal values.

Therefore, the paths $3-2, 3-4,\ 4-2$, and $4-3$, corresponding to nodes 5, 6, 7 and 8, respectively, need to be examined. These are shown in Figure 6.42.

The reduced matrices for nodes 5, 6, 7 and 8 will now be calculated.

Node 3 to node 5, or vertex 3 to vertex 2, is shown in Figure 6.43.

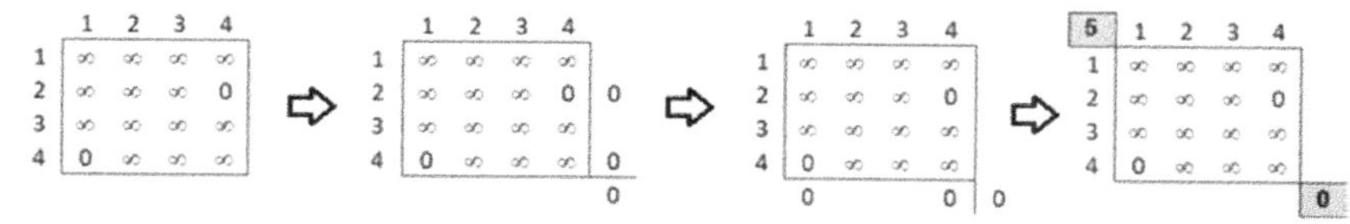

Figure 6.43. *Processing node 3 to node 5. For a color version of this figure, see www.iste.co.uk/cochard/mathematics3.zip*

Node 3 to node 6, or vertex 3 to vertex 4, is shown in Figure 6.44.

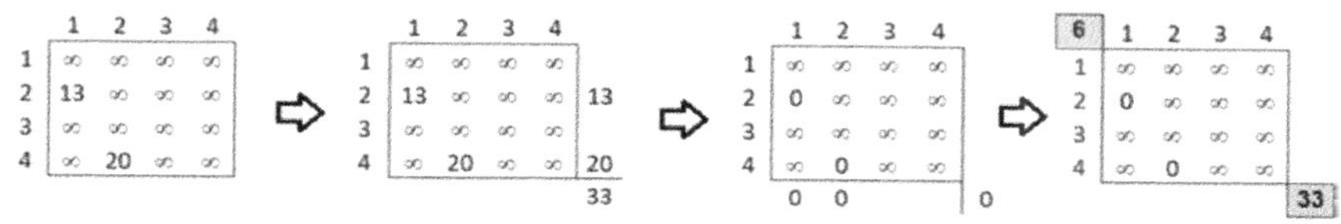

Figure 6.44. *Processing node 3 to node 6. For a color version of this figure, see www.iste.co.uk/cochard/mathematics3.zip*

Node 4 to node 7, or vertex 4 to vertex 2, is shown in Figure 6.45.

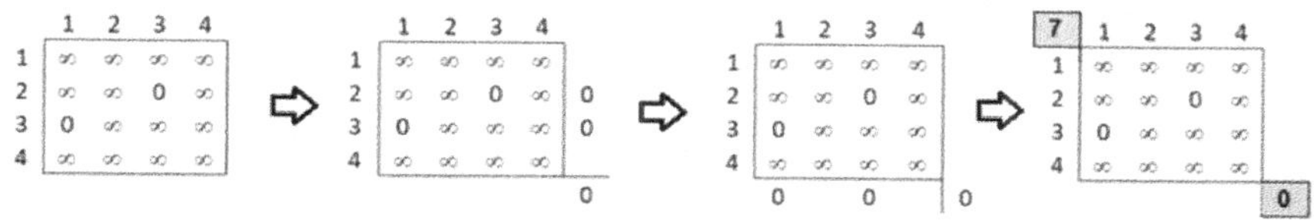

Figure 6.45. *Processing node 4 to node 7. For a color version of this figure, see www.iste.co.uk/cochard/mathematics3.zip*

Node 4 to node 8, or vertex 4 to vertex 3, is shown in Figure 6.46.

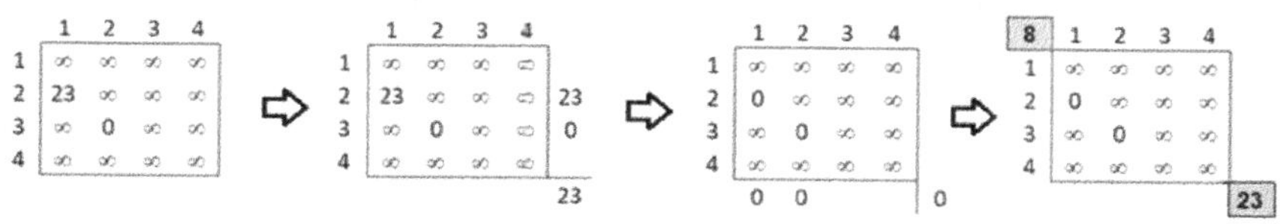

Figure 6.46. *Processing node 4 to node 8. For a color version of this figure, see www.iste.co.uk/cochard/mathematics3.zip*

This gives the result shown in Figure 6.47.

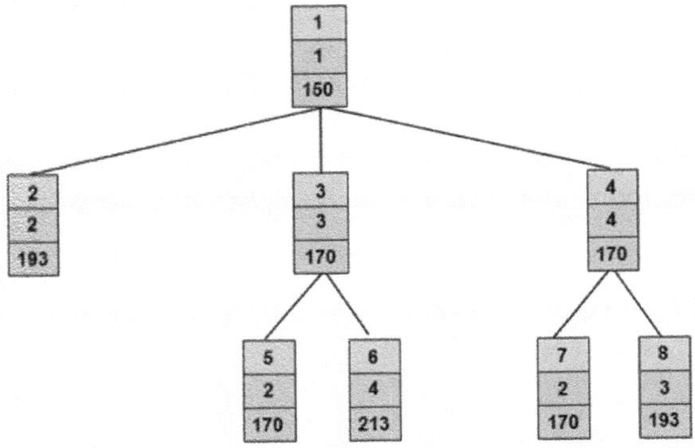

Figure 6.47. *Processing results. For a color version of this figure, see www.iste.co.uk/cochard/mathematics3.zip*

The best values are at nodes 5 and 7. Therefore, the other branches are temporarily discarded, and the branches from 5 and 7 are explored.

There is little choice left (see Figure 6.48).

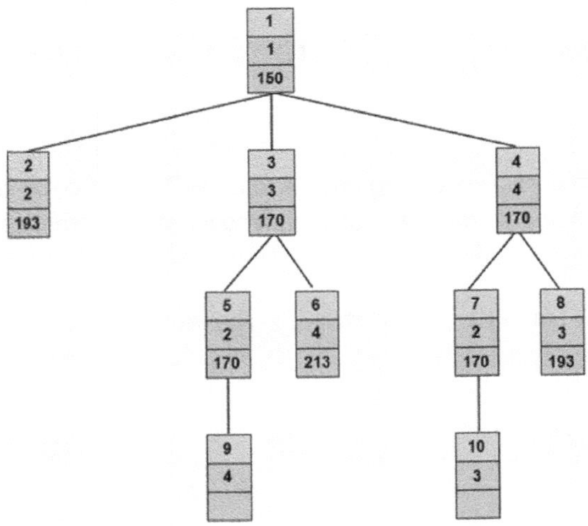

Figure 6.48. *The current situation. For a color version of this figure, see www.iste.co.uk/cochard/mathematics3.zip*

The values of E_9 and E_{10} are determined as follows:

– Node 5 to node 9, or vertex 2 to vertex 4, is shown in Figure 6.49.

– Node 7 to node 10, or vertex 2 to vertex 3, is shown in Figure 6.50.

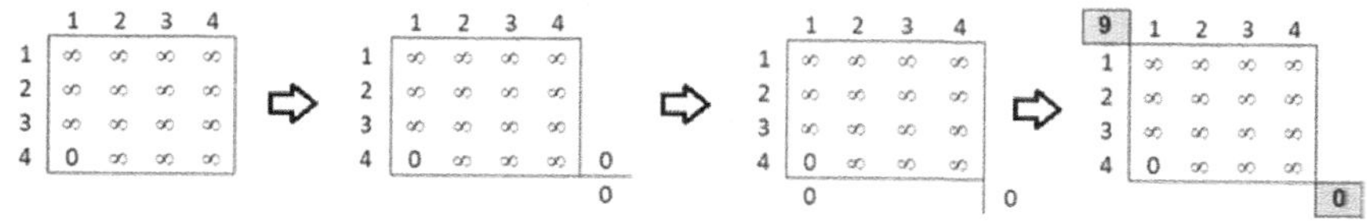

Figure 6.49. *Processing node 5 to node 9. For a color version of this figure, see www.iste.co.uk/cochard/mathematics3.zip*

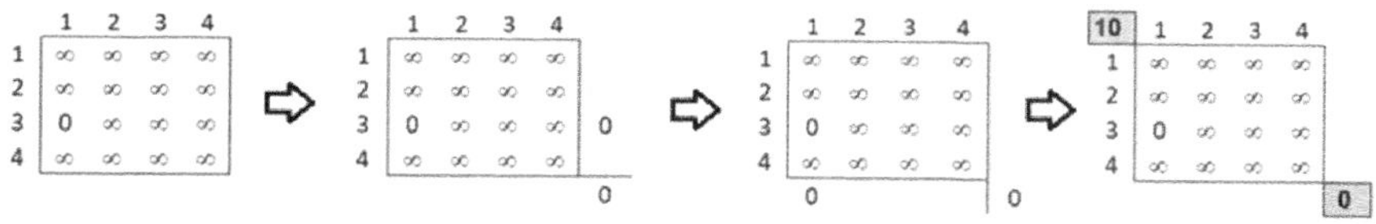

Figure 6.50. *Processing node 7 to node 10. For a color version of this figure, see www.iste.co.uk/cochard/mathematics3.zip*

This leads to the situation shown in Figure 6.51 (note that paths 4 – 1 and 3 – 1 have not been forbidden, as 1 is the last vertex to be reached: the return to the starting point is allowed).

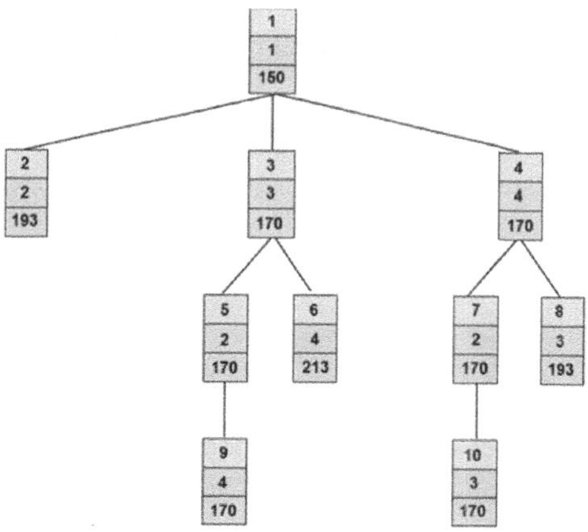

Figure 6.51. *Current situation. For a color version of this figure, see www.iste.co.uk/cochard/mathematics3.zip*

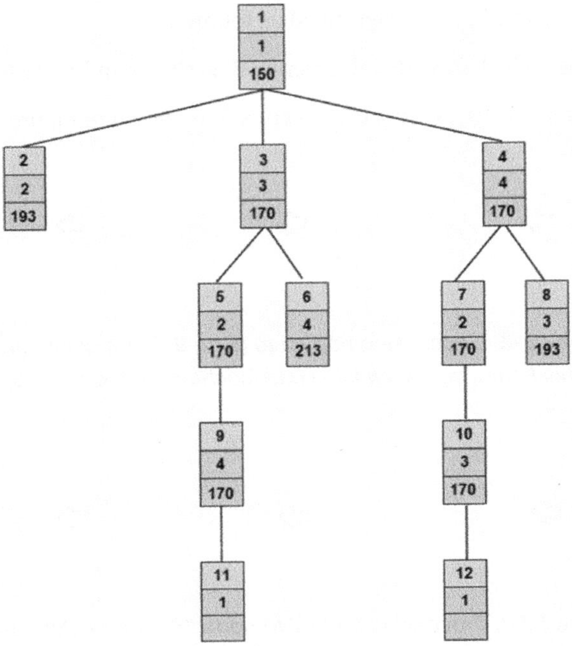

Figure 6.52. *Current result. For a color version of this figure, see www.iste.co.uk/cochard/mathematics3.zip*

All that remains is to finish by returning to vertex 1 (see Figure 6.52).

– Node 9 to node 11, or vertex 4 to vertex 1, is shown in Figure 6.53.

– Node 10 to node 12, or vertex 3 to vertex 1, is shown in Figure 6.54, with $E_{11}1 = 170$ and $E_{12} = 170$ (see Figure 6.55).

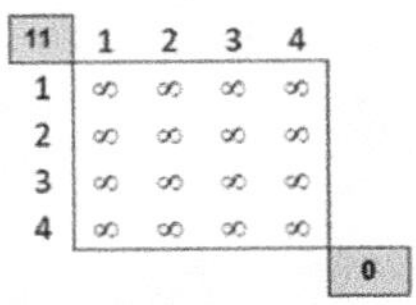

Figure 6.53. *Processing node 9 to node 11. For a color version of this figure, see www.iste.co.uk/cochard/mathematics3.zip*

12	1	2	3	4	
1	∞	∞	∞	∞	
2	∞	∞	∞	∞	
3	∞	∞	∞	∞	
4	∞	∞	∞	∞	
					0

Figure 6.54. *Processing node 10 to node 12. For a color version of this figure, see www.iste.co.uk/cochard/mathematics3.zip*

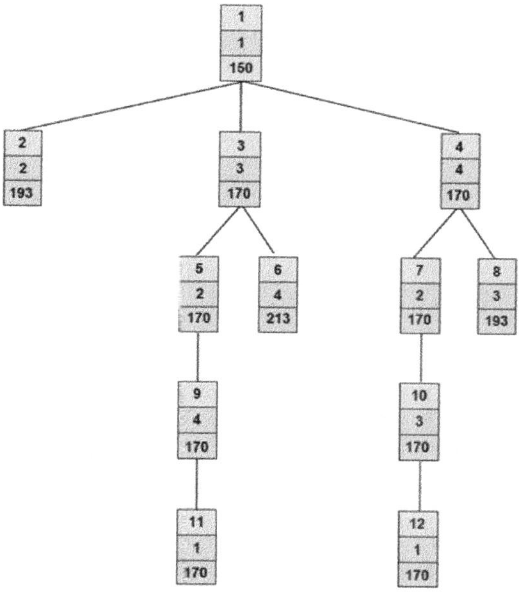

Figure 6.55. *Processing result. For a color version of this figure, see www.iste.co.uk/cochard/mathematics3.zip*

This results in two solutions: 1 − 3 − 2 − 4 − 1 and 1 − 4 − 2 − 3 − 1. In fact, the second solution is simply the reverse of the first. The value 170 represents the minimum distance.

7

Transportation Problems

CONCEPTS COVERED IN THIS CHAPTER.–

This chapter discusses optimization methods applied to transportation or traffic problems. Three types of problems are studied.

The maximum flow problem: passing a maximum flow of materials through a network whose arcs have limited capacities. The Ford–Fulkerson algorithm, which solves this problem, is examined in detail.

The minimum-cost transport problem: minimizing transport costs across a network. Methods such as the Northwest Corner, Least Cost and Balas-Hammer are presented to obtain an initial solution, followed by the stepping stone algorithm and the potential method to find an optimal solution.

The assignment problem: finding a cost-minimizing bijection between two sets of n elements. The Hungarian algorithm is used to solve this problem.

References: [BRO 82, DES 76, DRO 87, FAU 79, FAU 74, FAU 14, PHE 75].

Under this heading, different types of problems are covered. A concise list is provided as follows:

– *Travel problems*: optimizing a route to get from one point to another. This type of problem was addressed in Chapter 6.

– *Maximum flow problems*: routing a maximum flow in a transport network to meet a demand, considering the available capacity (goods, liquids, information, etc.).

– *Transport cost optimization problems*: minimizing the costs of transporting goods between multiple sites, particularly in logistics and distribution.

– *Assignment problems*: determining the optimum match between "means" and "tasks", such as assigning employees to projects or resources to activities.

These problems often rely on graph algorithms to model and solve constraints, providing optimized solutions.

7.1. Maximum flow

7.1.1. *General*

Let $G = (X, U)$ be *an antisymmetric* directed graph with n vertices. In this graph, if an arc $X_i \longrightarrow X_j$ exists, then the arc $X_j \longrightarrow X_i$ does not exist. Among the vertices, two particular vertices are distinguished: X_1 and X_n.

– X_1 *is* the *entry vertex* and has no predecessors. The set Γ^- of predecessors of X_1 is empty: $\Gamma^-(X_1) = \emptyset$.

– X_n is the *exit vertex* and has no successors. The set Γ^+ of successors to X_n is empty: $\Gamma^+(X_n) = \emptyset$.

– Each arc of G is associated with a capacity $c_{ij} > 0$.

A *flow* in this graph is a set of non-negative quantities Φ_{ij} associated with each arc ij. A flow is considered *feasible* if it satisfies the following constraints:

1) Capacity constraints: $\Phi_{ij} \leq c_{ij},\ for\ all\ arcs\ ij \in U.$

2) Flow conservation constraints: for vertices other than X_1 and X_n, the sum of flows entering a vertex is equal to the sum of flows leaving that vertex (see Figure 7.1):

$$\sum_{X_j \in \Gamma^-(X_i)} \Phi_{ji} = \sum_{X_k \in \Gamma^+(X_i)} \Phi_{ik}$$

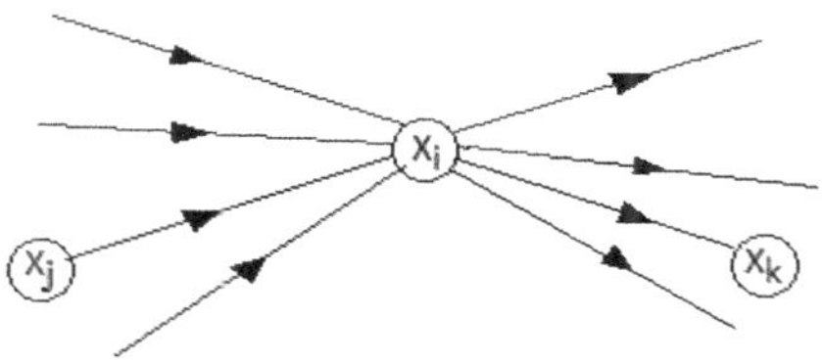

Figure 7.1. *Flow conservation*

3) Flow conservation constraint for vertices X_1 and X_n (see Figure 7.2):

$$\sum_{X_k \in \Gamma^+(X_1)} \Phi_{1k} = \sum_{X_j \in \Gamma^-(X_n)} \Phi_{jn} = F$$

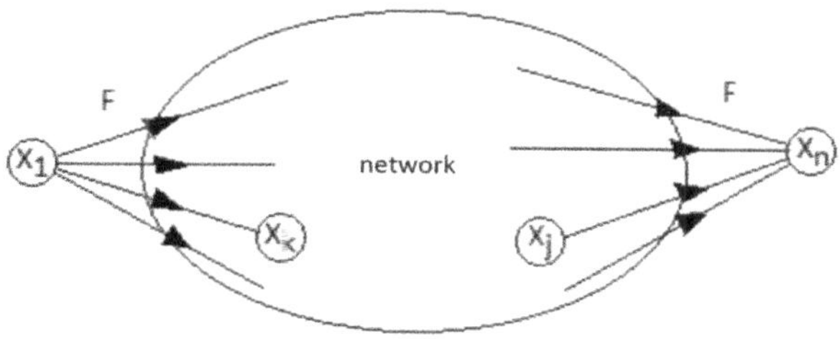

Figure 7.2. *Flow conservation at the entry and exit vertices*

The *maximum value* of F, called *maximum flow*, is examined. This value is not necessarily unique. Several methods can be used to solve this problem, including linear programming. However, the Ford–Fulkerson algorithm is particularly suited to this type of problem.

The maximum flow problem involves transport networks represented by acyclic graphs, with sender and receiver nodes. The arcs of the graph have maximum capacities, which represent, for example, the limits of freight transport. The objective is to route as many flows as possible while respecting two key constraints: the *capacity* (constraint 1) and the *flow conservation constraint* (constraint 2).

Sender nodes have "availabilities", and receiver nodes have "requests". It is essential that the total availabilities *used* equals the total of requests *received*. To represent this network as a graph G, a single input node X_1 and a single output node X_n are introduced. The outgoing arcs of X_1 have capacities equal to availabilities, while the incoming arcs to X_n have capacities corresponding to demands. This structure ensures compliance with the flow conservation constraint (constraint 3).

EXAMPLE 7.1.– Suppose there are three stores and four customers to serve. The table in Figure 7.3 shows the possible routes between stores and customers, along with the associated availabilities and requests.

stores \ customers	4	5	6	7	availability
1	80	30	40	0	**140**
2	70	0	30	10	**100**
3	0	80	70	50	**200**
requests	**145**	**110**	**130**	**55**	

Figure 7.3. *Transportation constraints*

The situation described corresponds to the graph shown in Figure 7.4, which highlights the connections between stores (1, 2, 3) and customers (4, 5, 6, 7). The arcs between stores and customers are assigned maximum capacity.

A fictitious vertex E (representing the starting vertex X_1) has been added and linked to stores 1, 2 and 3 using arcs, with capacities determined by the availabilities. Similarly, a fictitious vertex S (representing the arrival vertex X_n) has been added, with arcs linking customers (4, 5, 6, 7) to this vertex. The capacities on these arcs correspond to the respective demands.

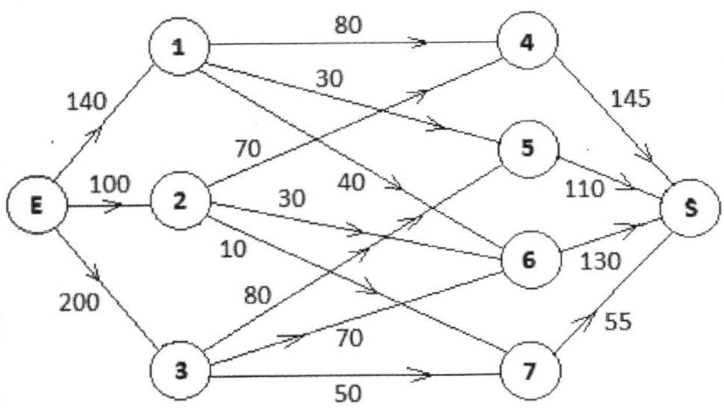

Figure 7.4. *The problem graph*

7.1.2. Ford–Fulkerson theorem

A "cut" C in a graph G is a partition of the set of vertices into two disjoint subsets, A and B, such that $X_1 \in A$ (the source vertex) and $X_n \in B$ (the sink vertex), as shown in Figure 7.5. The directed arcs of A to B form the cut. The capacity of the cut is defined as:

$$c(C) = \sum_{X_i \in A,\ X_j \in B} c_{ij}$$

In this expression, C represents the "cut" (A, B), where A contains the source vertex X_1 and B contains the sink vertex X_n. The arcs considered are those from A to B.

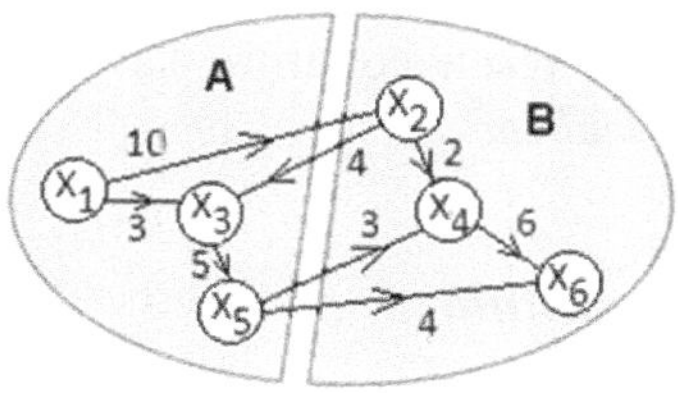

Figure 7.5. *A C-cut with value c(C) = 10 + 3 + 4 = 17*

Let F be a feasible flow. The following quantities are defined:

– $r_{ij} = c_{ij} - \Phi_{ij}$ and $r_{ji} = \Phi_{ij}$ for any arc $u = (i, j)$. These quantities are commonly referred to as residual capacities.

– The value r_{ij} represents the maximum possible increase in flow through the arc (i, j). The flow ϕ_{ij} can be increased from its current value until it reaches the capacity c_{ij}.

– The value r_{ji} represents the minimum possible decrease in flow through the arc (i, j). The flow ϕ_{ij} can be decreased from its current value until it reaches 0.

The following theorem is admitted.

THEOREM 7.1 (FORD–FULKERSON).– Let $\mathfrak{F}$ be the family of feasible flows and $\mathfrak{C}$ the family of cuts in a graph. Let $F_{max} = \max\{F \mid F \in \mathfrak{F}\}$ and $F_{min} = \min\{c(C) \mid C \in \mathfrak{C}\}$. Then, the following holds:

$$F \leq c_{min} \quad \text{and} \quad F_{max} = c_{min}.$$

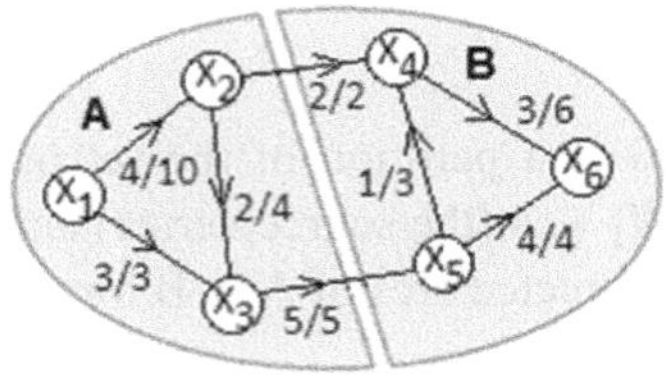

Figure 7.6. *Flow/capacity notation*

In Figure 7.6, the arcs are annotated in "flow/capacity" form. The cut shown in this figure has a minimum capacity, which can be verified, by $c(C) = 2 + 5 = 7$.

In addition, the flow F in the graph is calculated as follows: $F = 3 + 4 = 7$.

Thus, $F_{max} = F = 7$. This result confirms that "*finding a maximal flow*" is equivalent to "*finding a minimal cut*".

7.1.3. *Ford–Fulkerson algorithm*

The algorithm relies on the construction of a "*residual graph* H", based on the residual capacities of the arcs. This residual graph H contains the same vertices as the original graph G, but arcs are added or removed according to the residual capacities, as shown in Figure 7.7:

– If the residual capacity $r_{ij} > 0$ (meaning that the arc $u = X_iX_j$ in G is not saturated), the arc X_iX_j is included in H with residual capacity $r_{ij} = c_{ij} - \phi_{ij}$.

– If the residual capacity $r_{ji} > 0$ (indicating a positive flow from X_i to X_j), the arc $u' = X_jX_i$ is included in H with the value $r_{ji} = \phi_{ij}$.

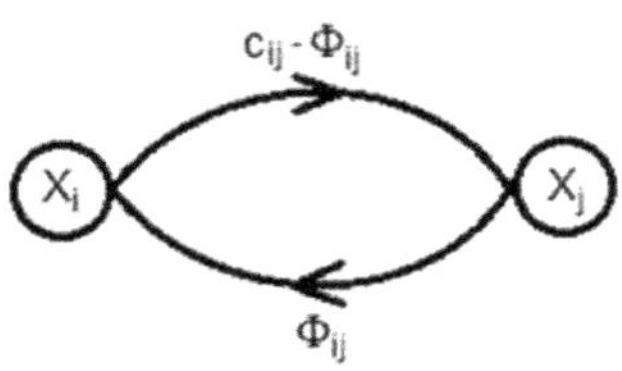

Figure 7.7. *Residual capacities*

When one of the two residual arc values is zero, the corresponding arc is excluded from the residual graph H. Note that in the second case, the arc (j, i) does not belong to the graph G because the graph is antisymmetric. However, it is included in the residual graph H.

The following example, based on Example 7.1, illustrates how these operations lead to the solution of the maximal flow.

EXAMPLE 7.2.– Let us start by passing a null flow ($F = 0$), which is always possible, as shown in Figure 7.8.

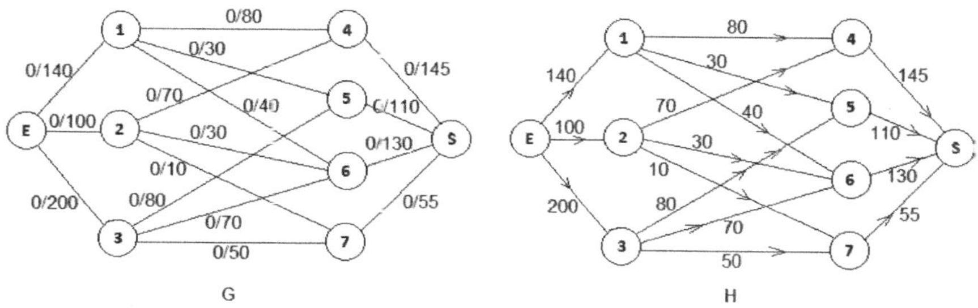

Figure 7.8. *Flow graph G and residual graph H*

To simplify the presentation of the flow graph (see Figure 7.8), the arrows on the arcs have been omitted, as this does not pose a problem since all arcs are oriented from left to right. With this initial flow, all residual capacities r_{ij} are positive, and $r_{ii} = 0$. Therefore, the residual graph is equivalent to the graph G but with capacities only.

The arrows in the residual graph indicate the possible flow progression from vertex E (entry) to vertex S (exit).

To increase the flow, an increasing path is identified in H, i.e. a path that allows an additional flow to be transferred. For example, by following the path $E - 3 - 7 - S$, the arc $3 - 7$ can be saturated (see Figure 7.9), which modifies the flows on arcs $E - 3, 3 - 7$, and $7 - S$. The path $E - 3 - 7$ - $- S$ is an "augmenting" path. After this step, the total flow becomes $F = 50$.

The new residual graph, recalculated according to the values of r_{ij} and r_{ii}, is shown in Figure 7.9. Saturated arcs in the flow graph are represented by "thick red lines". On the arcs $E - 3$ and $7 - S$, the updated values imply the appearance of pairs of opposite arcs. For $3 - 7$, the orientation of the arc is reversed.

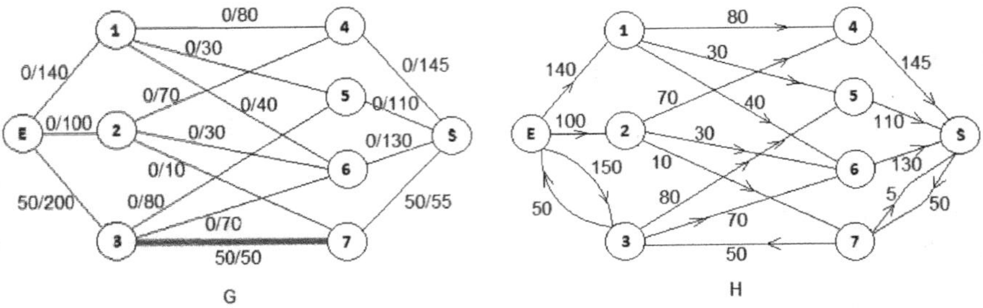

Figure 7.9. *Flow graph G and residual graph H. For a color version of this figure, see www.iste.co.uk/cochard/mathematics3.zip*

The exploration of the residual graph H continues to identify an augmenting path linking E to S. At this stage, several paths remain available. For example, by following the path $E - 3 - 5 - S$, it is possible to increase the flow by 80, leading to saturation of the arc $3 - 5$. The result of this update is depicted in the flow graph, as shown in Figure 7.10. After this step, the total flow now reaches $F = 130$.

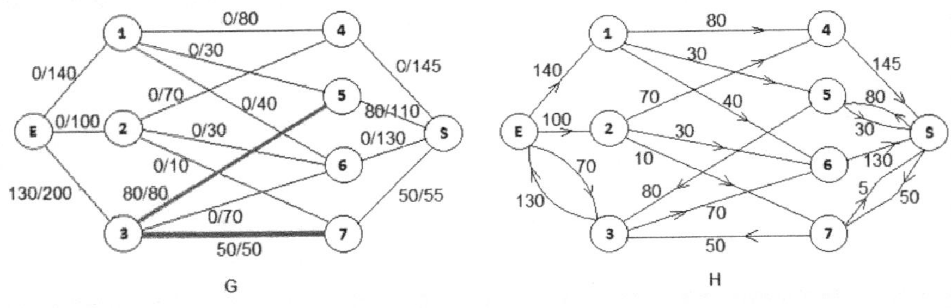

Figure 7.10. *Flow graph G and residual graph H. For a color version of this figure, see www.iste.co.uk/cochard/mathematics3.zip*

Figure 7.10 shows the residual graph H after increasing the flow to $F = 130$. Several potential augmenting paths remain in the graph H. By following $E - 1 - 4 - 5$, the arc $1 - 4$ can be saturated, increasing the flow by 80. This update is reflected in Figure 7.11, with the total flow no reaching $F = 210$.

Next, by following the path $E - 3 - 6 - S$, both arcs $E - 3$ and $3 - 6$ are saturated simultaneously. This results in the configuration shown in Figure 7.12 for the flow graph.

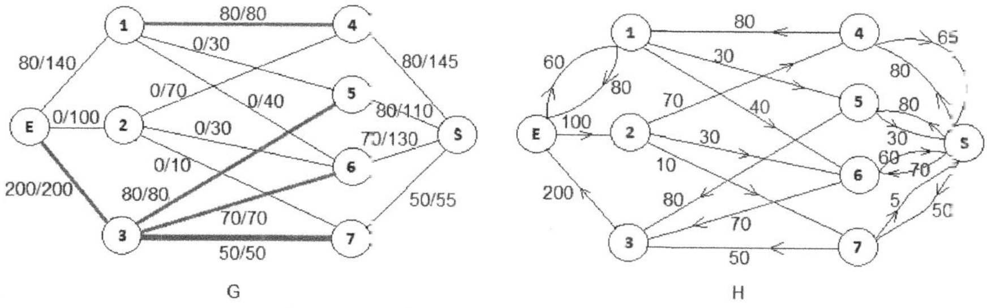

Figure 7.11. *Flow graph G and residual graph H. For a color version of this figure, see www.iste.co.uk/cochard/mathematics3.zip*

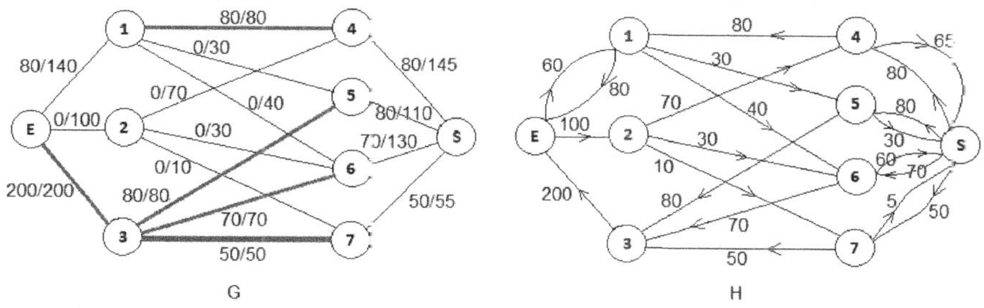

Figure 7.12. *Flow graph G and residual graph H. For a color version of this figure, see www.iste.co.uk/cochard/mathematics3.zip*

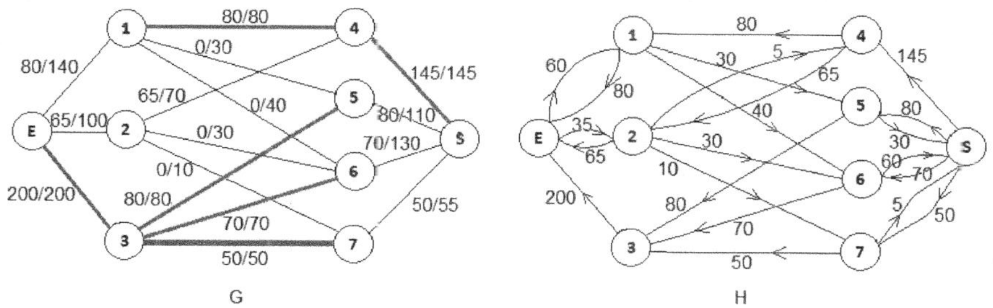

Figure 7.13. *Flow graph G and residual graph H. For a color version of this figure, see www.iste.co.uk/cochard/mathematics3.zip*

The flow F now reaches 280 units. The resulting residual graph in Figure 7.12 still allows additional augmenting paths. By selecting the path $E-2-4-S$, arc $4-S$ becomes saturated, increasing the flow to 345 units.

At this stage, the flow is $F = 345$. The updated residual graph H, as shown in Figure 7.13, continues to provide possible augmenting paths.

Next, along the path $E - 2 - 6 - S$, arc $2 - 6$ reaches saturation. Figure 7.14 represents the revised flow graph, where the total flow increases to $F = 375$ units.

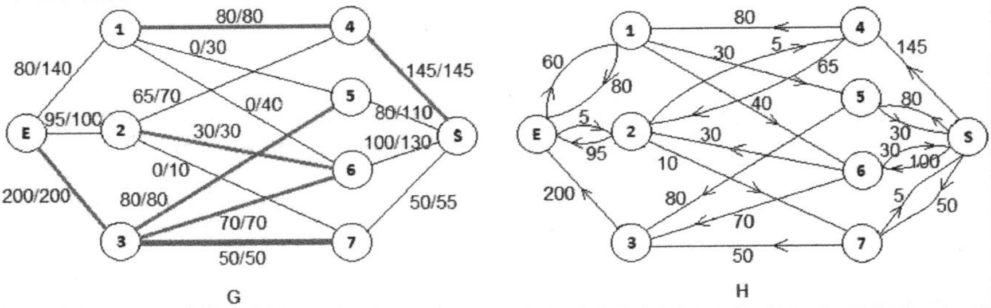

Figure 7.14. *Flow graph G and residual graph H. For a color version of this figure, see www.iste.co.uk/cochard/mathematics3.zip*

In the residual graph shown in Figure 7.14, the path $E - 1 - 5 - S$ is selected to further increase the flow. This operation results in the saturation of both arc $1 - 5$ and arc $5 - S$.

The update configuration of the flow graph is presented in Figure 7.15, where the total flow has now reached $F = 405$ units.

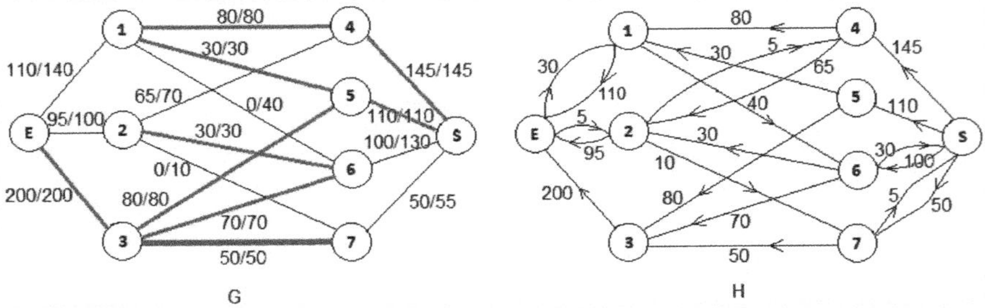

Figure 7.15. *Flow graph G and residual graph H. For a color version of this figure, see www.iste.co.uk/cochard/mathematics3.zip*

In the residual graph H (see Figure 7.15), the available paths from E to S become limited. The path $E - 1 - 6 - S$ is selected, resulting in the saturation of arcs $E - 1$ and $6 - S$, bringing the total flow to $F = 435$ (see Figure 7.16).

In the updated residual graph H (see Figure 7.16), the only remaining feasible path is $E-2-7-S$. By saturating arcs $E-2$ and $7-S$, a final flow increase of 5 units is achieved, leading to $F=440$.

Figure 7.17 shows this final configuration.

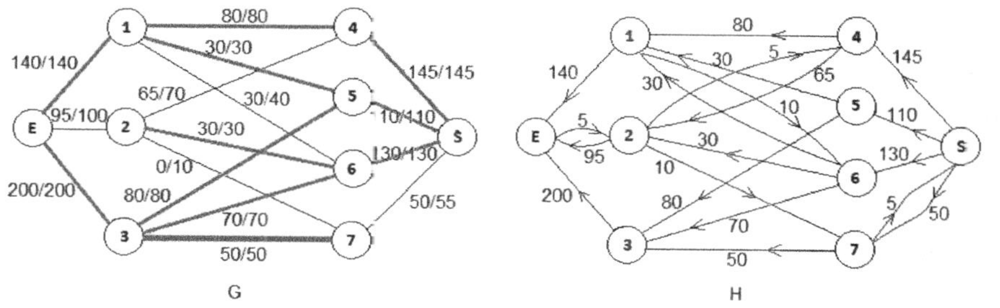

Figure 7.16. *Flow graph G and residual graph H. For a color version of this figure, see www.iste.co.uk/cochard/mathematics3.zip*

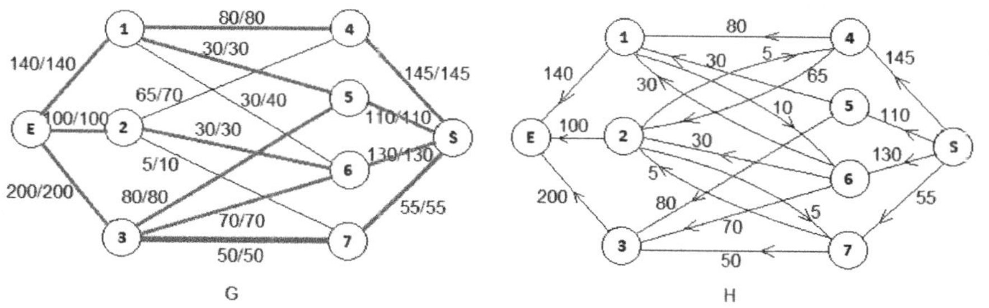

Figure 7.17. *Flow graph G and residual graph H. For a color version of this figure, see www.iste.co.uk/cochard/mathematics3.zip*

As shown in the final residual graph shows, no path from E to S remains available, indicating that the optimal solution has been reached with a maximum flow of $F\ =\ 440$ units.

This process highlights the fact that the choice of augmenting paths can be arbitrary. However, a strategic selection of these paths can lead to a faster convergence to the optimal solution, minimizing the number of iterations required to achieve the result.

7.1.4. *Practical solution method*

The process illustrated in Example 7.2 follows the Ford–Fulkerson algorithm. This method can be reformulated in a more practical way by following these steps:

1) *Initialization*: start with an arbitrary feasible flow F that satisfies all constraints (1), (2) and (3), i.e. capacity, flow conservation and network structure.

2) *Enhancement (optional)*: enhance the initial flow so that any path from X_1 to X_n contains at least one fully saturated arc X_iX_j (i.e. an arc where the maximum quantity is transported: $\phi_{ij} = c_{ij}$). This flow is then considered *complete.*

This step can sometimes lead directly to the optimal solution but is not always sufficient.

3) *Iteration*: repeat the following steps.

a) Mark the entry vertex E.

b) For each marked vertex x:

i) mark adjacent vertices y for which the arc xy is unsaturated (i.e. $\phi_{xy} < c_{xy}$), using the notation $+x$;

ii) mark adjacent vertices y for which the arc yx carries a positive flow (i.e. $\phi_{yx} > 0$), using the notation $-x$.

c) If the exit vertex S is marked, adjust the flow accordingly.

4) Termination: the process stops when S can no longer be marked, indicating that the maximum flow has been reached.

This iterative method uses markings to identify augmenting paths efficiently, optimizing the computation of the maximum flow.

Let us apply the algorithm, in its new form, to Example 7.1.

EXAMPLE 7.3.–

Step 1: the process begins with the initial flow configuration shown in Figure 7.18. This initial flow is obtained manually, without applying any forced optimization.

– Saturated arcs (where $\phi_{ij} = c_{ij}$) are highlighted in red.

– Null arcs (where $\phi_{ij} = 0$) are marked in blue.

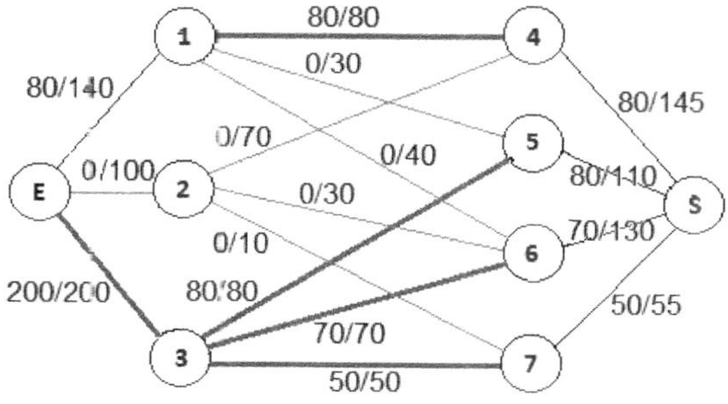

Figure 7.18. *Starting flow. For a color version of this figure, see www.iste.co.uk/cochard/mathematics3.zip*

Note: This initial flow is not complete. The following paths: $E-1-5-S, E-1-6-S, E-2-4-S, E-2-6-S, E-2-7-S$ do not contain any saturated arcs.

A complete flow would require that at least one arc in every path from E to S at least be saturated ($\phi_{ij} = c_{ij}$). At this stage, the total flow is 280 units.

Step 2: vertex marking (see Figure 7.19).

Note that a vertex that has already been marked is not marked again. Multiple paths may exist to reach the exit vertex *S*. Once the vertex *S* is reached, additional markings are unnecessary.

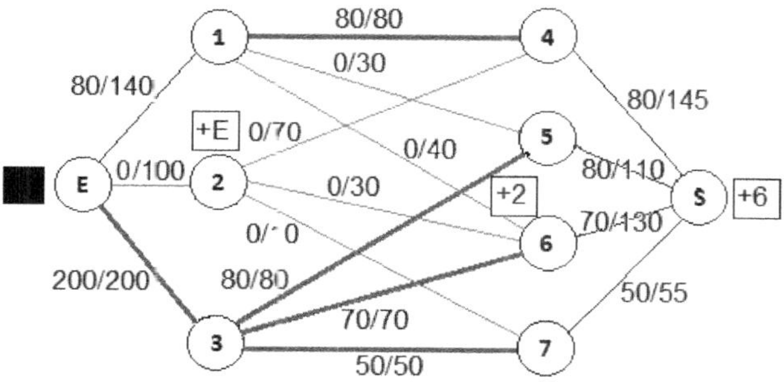

Figure 7.19. *Marking process. For a color version of this figure, see www.iste.co.uk/cochard/mathematics3.zip*

In the case of the marking in Figure 7.19, the vertex S has been marked with the path $E-2-6-S$. This path is identified as an augmenting path using the previous vertex markings. By improving this path by 30 units, the arc $2-6$ becomes saturated (see Figure 7.20). As a result, the total flow increases to 310 units.

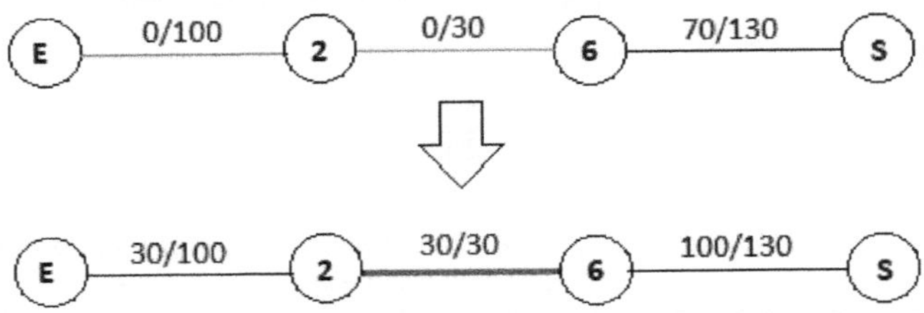

Figure 7.20. *Flow enhancement. For a color version of this figure, see www.iste.co.uk/cochard/mathematics3.zip*

Step 2 is repeated with the new flow shown in Figure 7.21(a). Based on the unsaturated arcs, for example, the path $E-1-5-S$ is selected (there are several possible choices, as shown in Figure 7.21(b).

This path saturates the arcs $1-5$ and $5-S$, resulting in a flow increase of 30 units (see Figure 7.22).

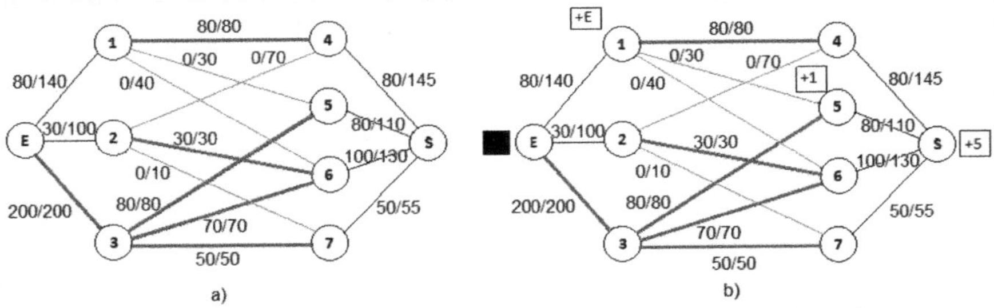

Figure 7.21. *a) Flow graph and b) marking. For a color version of this figure, see www.iste.co.uk/cochard/mathematics3.zip*

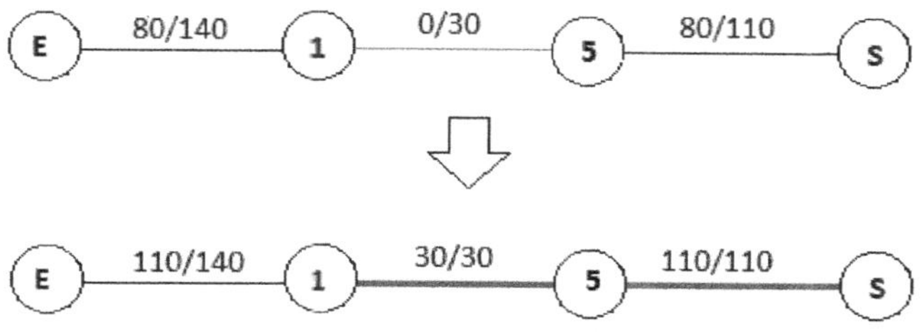

Figure 7.22. *Flow enhancement. For a color version of this figure, see www.iste.co.uk/cochard/mathematics3.zip*

The flow increases to 340 units. Figure 7.23(a) shows the updated graph.

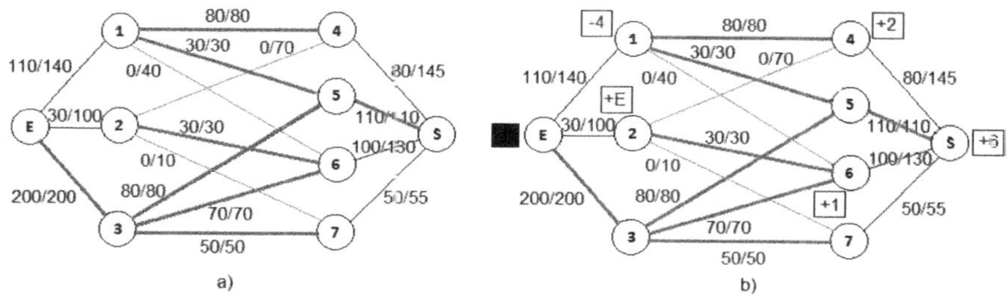

Figure 7.23. *a) Flow graph and b) marking. For a color version of this figure, see www.iste.co.uk/cochard/mathematics3.zip*

The marking shown in Figure 7.23(b) corresponds to the path $E - 2 - 4 - 1 - 6 - S$, as shown in Figure 7.24.

The possible increase is 30 units, added in the $E \longrightarrow S$ direction or subtracted in the $S \longrightarrow E$ direction, in order to respect the equality of incoming and outgoing flows for each vertex. This indicates that the arc $1 - 4$ is no longer saturated. The flow is now 370 units.

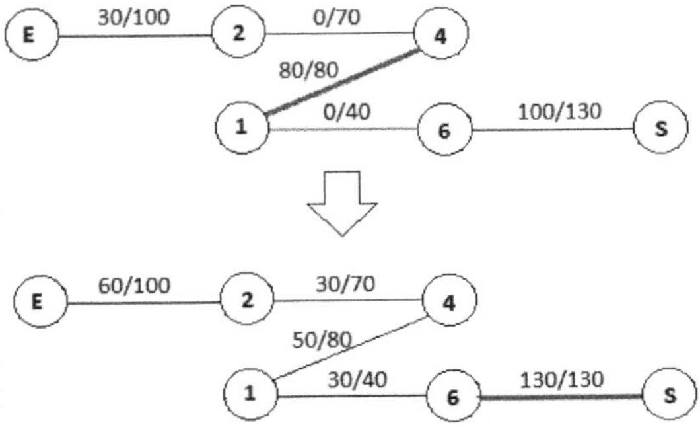

Figure 7.24. *Flow enhancement. For a color version of this figure, see www.iste.co.uk/cochard/mathematics3.zip*

Figure 7.25(a) shows the updated graph. There are still possible markings, such as the one in Figure 7.25(b), which corresponds to the path $E - 2 - 7 - S$.

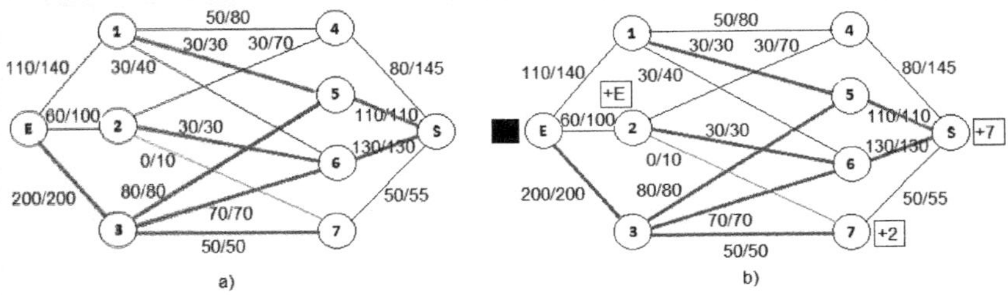

Figure 7.25. *a) Flow graph and b) marking. For a color version of this figure, see www.iste.co.uk/cochard/mathematics3.zip*

This path can be increased by 5 units (see Figure 7.26), increasing the flow to 375 units (see Figure 7.27(a)).

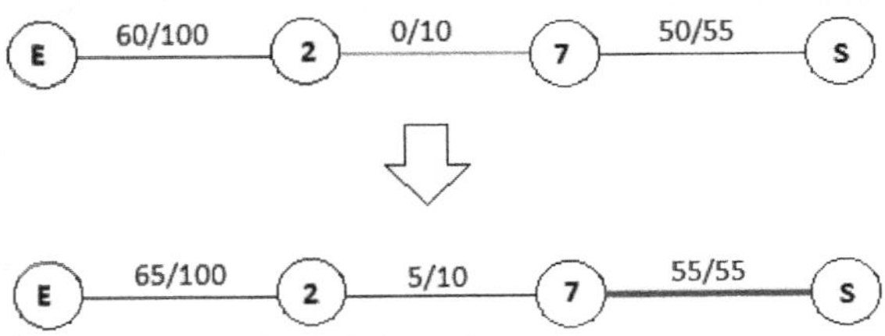

Figure 7.26. *Flow enhancement. For a color version of this figure, see www.iste.co.uk/cochard/mathematics3.zip*

The marking now chosen is that shown in Figure 7.27(b), corresponding to the path $E - 1 - 4 - S$, which can be increased by 30 units (see Figure 7.28). This results in the saturation of the arcs $E - 1$ and $1 - 4$.

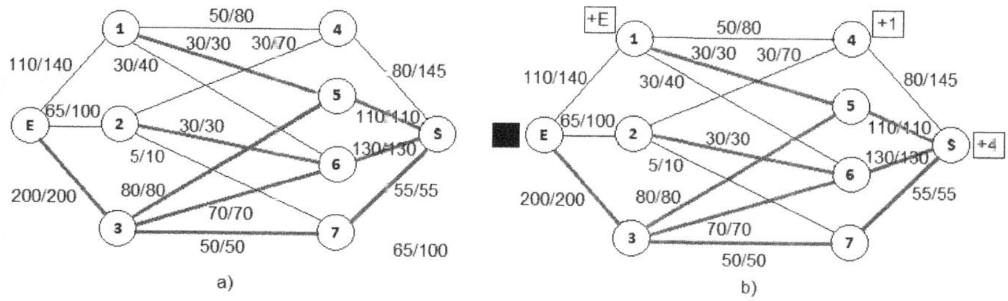

Figure 7.27. *a) Flow graph and b) marking. For a color version of this figure, see www.iste.co.uk/cochard/mathematics3.zip*

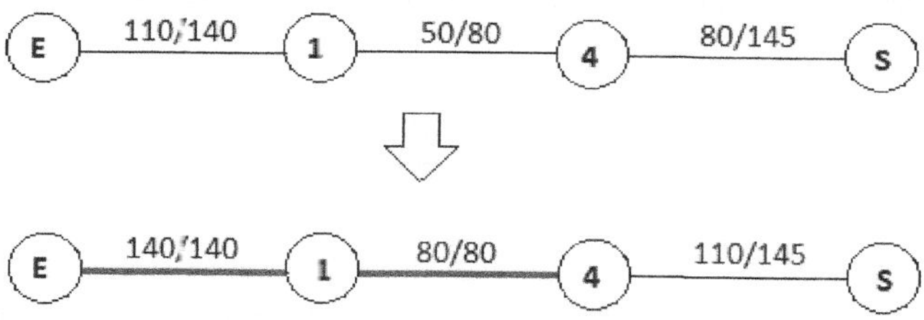

Figure 7.28. *Flow enhancement. For a color version of this figure, see www.iste.co.uk/cochard/mathematics3.zip*

The flow is now 405 units. The new graph is shown in Figure 7.29(a).

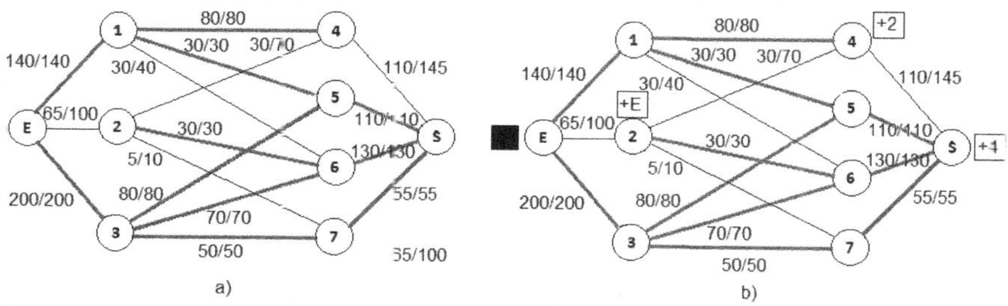

Figure 7.29. *a) Flow graph and b) marking. For a color version of this figure, see www.iste.co.uk/cochard/mathematics3.zip*

In Figure 7.29(b), it is observed that since E, a direct connection between vertices 1 and 3, is no longer possible. By marking 2, then 4 and finally S, the path $E-2-4-S$ can increase the flow by 35 units, saturating the arcs $E-2$ and $4-S$ (see Figure 7.30).

As a result, the flow increases to 440 units. The new graph shown in Figure 7.31 shows that none of the three vertices 1, 2 or 3 can be marked from E. Consequently, it becomes impossible to reach S, indicating that optimality has been achieved with a maximum flow of $F = 440$ units.

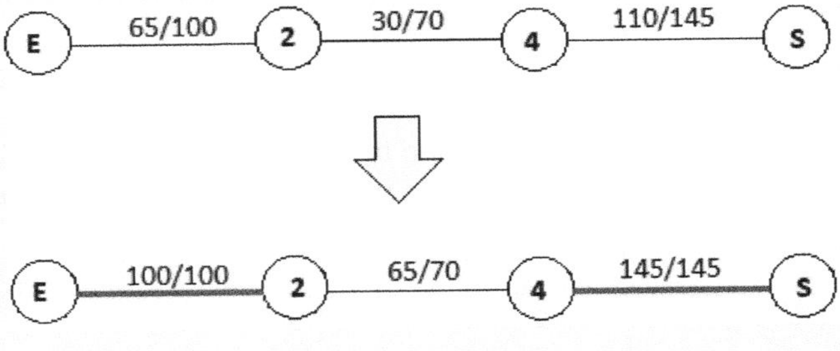

Figure 7.30. *Flow enhancement. For a color version of this figure, see www.iste.co.uk/cochard/mathematics3.zip*

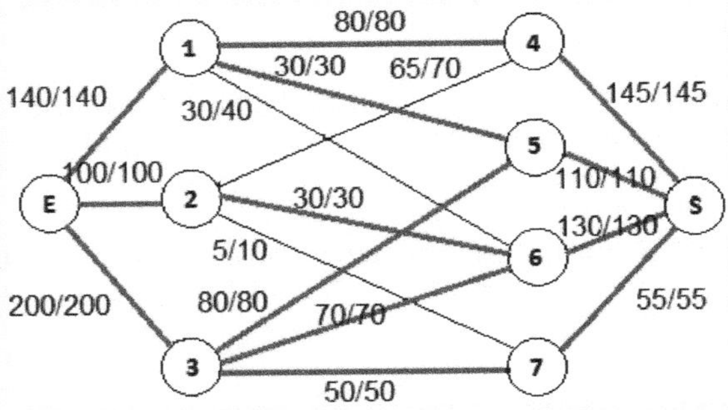

Figure 7.31. *Flow graph. For a color version of this figure, see www.iste.co.uk/cochard/mathematics3.zip*

7.2. Least cost transportation

7.2.1. *Issues*

The goal is to transport goods from m sources to n destinations while minimizing transport costs. This problem can be represented as a transportation model, where the cost of moving goods along different routes must be optimized to minimize the total cost.

EXAMPLE 7.4.– Let I, II, III and IV be the sources, and 1, 2, 3, 4, 5 and 6 be the destinations.

destinations

sources	1	2	3	4	availability
I	83	27	35	61	26
II	65	39	42	78	14
III	53	56	54	92	18
requests	14	11	5	28	58

Figure 7.32. *Problem data*

The source–destination cost matrix is shown in Figure 7.32.

This problem can be formulated as a linear program with the objective of minimizing the following total cost:

$$z = \sum_{i=1}^{m} \sum_{j=1}^{n} c_{ij} x_{ij}$$

where c_{ij} represents the coefficients of the cost matrix (unit costs), and x_{ij} is a variable representing the quantities transported on the route from source i to destination j.

There are three constraints to consider. First, the relationship that expresses the equality between supply (a_i, representing the availability at source i) and demand (b_j, representing the demand at destination j) is:

$$\sum_{i=1}^{m} a_i = \sum_{j=1}^{n} b_j$$

In addition, the following constraints ensure that the sum of the quantities transported on the routes from each source i is equal to the availability at the source a_i, and the sum of the quantities transported on the routes to each destination j is equal to the demand at that destination b_j:

$$\sum_{j=1}^{n} x_{ij} = a_i \qquad \forall i = 1, \dots, m$$

$$\sum_{i=1}^{m} x_{ij} = b_j \qquad \forall j = 1, \dots, n$$

In addition to linear programming, there are algorithms for solving this problem, which can be divided into two categories: those that obtain an initial solution and those that improve the solution until optimality is reached.

Among the most popular algorithms for obtaining an initial solution are the Northwest Corner Method, the Least Cost Method and the Balas-Hammer Method (also known as Vogel's Method).

For improving an initial solution, the *Stepping Stone Method* and the Potential Method are commonly used.

7.2.2. Northwest Corner algorithm

The *Northwest Corner Algorithm* is used to find an initial solution to the transportation problem. The decision variables are the quantities x_{ij}, which must satisfy a set of $n + m + 1$ independent constraints. A feasible solution must therefore have $nm - (n + m + 1) = (m - 1)(n - 1)$ zero variables. For instance, in Example 7.4, there will be $(3 - 1)(4 - 1) = 6$ zero variables.

To find an acceptable solution using the Northwest Corner algorithm, start with the table of transported quantities (i.e. the first source and destination) and saturate the availability of the first source from left to right. Then, move on to the second source and proceed in the same way. This process becomes clearer with the example provided.

EXAMPLE 7.5.–

Northwest corner

	1	2	3	4	avail.
I					26
II					14
III					18
req.	14	11	5	28	58

Figure 7.33. *The Northwest Corner*

Starting at the Northwest Corner of the matrix (see Figure 7.33), i.e. cell (I,1), 14 units are allocated to satisfy the demand of destination 1 (14), which fully satisfies its demand. Continuing along the same row of the matrix, 11 units are allocated to satisfy the demand of destination 2 (11), which fully satisfies its demand. This leaves an availability of 1 unit, which is allocated to destination 3. Thus, the initial availability of 26 at resource I has been fully used (see Figure 7.34).

	1	2	3	4	avail.
I	14	11	1		26
II					14
III					18
req.	14	11	5	28	58

Figure 7.34. *Processing the first row*

Moving to the new Northwest Corner, i.e. cell (II,3), 4 units are allocated to fully satisfy destination 3's demand, thus saturating it. The remaining availability of 10 units at source II is then allocated to partially satisfy the demand of destination 4 (see Figure 7.35).

	1	2	3	4	avail.
I	14	11	1		26
II			4	10	14
III					18
req.	14	11	5	28	58

Figure 7.35. *Processing the second row*

Moving to the new Northwest Corner, i.e. cell (III,4), the only unexplored cell, destination 4 is allocated the total availability of source III (18), which saturates its demand (10 + 18 = 28) (see Figure 7.36).

	1	2	3	4	avail.
I	14	11	1		26
II			4	10	14
III				18	18
req.	14	11	5	28	58

Figure 7.36. *Processing the third row*

The resulting solution has a cost of: $z = 14 \times 83 + 11 \times 27 + 1 \times 35 + 4 \times 42 + 10 \times 78 + 18 \times 92 = 4{,}098$.

7.2.3. *Least cost method*

The Least Cost method, which is more efficient than the Northwest Corner method (since it does not take costs into account), involves progressively filling the cells of the quantity table based on the lowest cost. Let us return to Example 7.5.

EXAMPLE 7.6.–

Let us create a table (see Figure 7.37) showing both quantities (still unknown) and unit costs. The costs are displayed at the top left of each cell.

	1	2	3	4	avail.
I	83	27	35	61	26
II	65	39	42	78	14
III	53	56	54	92	18
req.	14	11	5	28	58

Figure 7.37. *Table with unit costs*

The cell with the lowest cost is identified. In this case, cell (I,2) has the lowest cost, which is 27. Therefore, the demand of destination 2 can be satisfied with a quantity of 11, reducing the availability of source I and cancelling out the demand of destination 2. This way, there is no need to return to column 2 for further allocations (see Figure 7.38).

	1	2	3	4	avail.
I	83	27 / 11	35	61	15
II	65	39	42	78	14
III	53	56	54	92	18
req.	14	0	5	28	47

Figure 7.38. *Least cost: 27*

Of the remaining cells, cell (I,3) has the lowest cost, at 35. Therefore, the demand of destination 3 can be satisfied with a quantity of 5, which reduces the availability of source I and cancels out the demand of destination 3. This way, there is no need to return to column 3 for further allocations (see Figure 7.39).

	1	2	3	4	avail.
I	83	27 11	35 5	61	10
II	65	39	42	78	14
III	53	56	54	92	18
req.	14	0	0	28	42

Figure 7.39. *Least cost: 35*

The lowest cost among the remaining cells is 53, found in cell (III,1). The demand of destination 1 can be completely satisfied by allocating a quantity of 14, which reduces the availability of source III and saturates the demand of destination 2. As a result, there is no need to return to column 1 for further allocations (see Figure 7.40).

	1	2	3	4	avail.
I	83	27 11	35 5	61	10
II	65	39	42	78	14
III	53 14	56	54	92	4
req.	0	0	0	28	28

Figure 7.40. *Least cost: 53*

The lowest cost among the remaining cells is 61, found in cell (I,4). Therefore, a quantity of 10 is allocated to destination 4, exhausting the availability of source I. There will be no need to return to the first row (source I) later (see Figure 7.41).

	1	2	3	4	avail.
I	83	27 / 11	35 / 5	61 / 10	0
II	65	39	42	78	14
III	53 / 14	56	54	92	4
req.	0	0	0	18	18

Figure 7.41. *Least cost: 61*

The lowest cost among the remaining cells is 78, found in cell (II,4). Therefore, 14 units are allocated to partially satisfy the demand of destination 4, saturating the availability of source II. There will be no need to return to row II (see Figure 7.42).

All that remains is to treat the final cell (III,4). The demand for destination 4 is fully satisfied by assigning the 4 units it was missing, completely exhausting the availability of source III (see Figure 7.43).

	1	2	3	4	avail.
I	83	27 / 11	35 / 5	61 / 10	0
II	65	39	42	78 / 14	0
III	53 / 14	56	54	92	4
req.	0	0	0	4	4

Figure 7.42. *Least cost: 78*

	1	2	3	4	avail.
I	83	27 / 11	35 / 5	61 / 10	0
II	65	39	42	78 / 14	0
III	53 / 14	56	54	92 / 4	0
req.	0	0	0	0	0

Figure 7.43. *End of processing*

Ultimately, the total cost is $z = 11 \times 27 + 5 \times 35 + 10 \times 61 + 14 \times 78 + 14 \times 53 + 4 \times 92 = 3{,}284$, which provides a better cost solution compared to the Northwest Corner method.

7.2.4. *Balas-Hammer or Vogel's algorithm*

Another commonly used method for obtaining an initial solution is the *Balas-Hammer* algorithm, also known as the *Vogel* approximation algorithm. What makes this method interesting is that, in many cases, the initial solution obtained is also the optimal one.

The algorithm works as follows: the differences between the smallest element and the next largest (or equal) element in each row and column of the unit cost matrix are calculated. The largest of these differences is then selected. This maximum difference can be found either in a row or a column.

Next, the smallest element in the corresponding row or column is chosen, and an attempt is made to satisfy the demand, taking the corresponding availability into account. This step may result in either cancelation of a request (and a reduction in availability) or the cancellation of availability (and a reduction in demand).

This process is repeated until all requests have been satisfied, and all availabilities have been exhausted. Let us apply this method to Example 7.5.

EXAMPLE 7.7.– At each iteration, two tables are updated: the difference table and the delivery table (see Figure 7.44).

	1	2	3	4	avail.	DL
I	83	27	35	61	26	8
II	65	39	42	78	14	3
III	53	56	54	92	18	1
req.	14	11	5	28	58	
DC	12	12	7	17		

	1	2	3	4	avail.
I				26	0
II					14
III					18
req.	14	11	5	2	32

Figure 7.44. *Difference table and delivery table*

On the left-hand side of the table, the *DC* row (for column differences) and the *DL* column (for row differences) have been added. For row I, the smallest cost value is 27, and the next highest value is 35, so $DL = 8$. Similarly, for column 3, the smallest cost value is 35, and the next highest value is 42, so $DC = 7$.

Having filled in the DC row and DL column, the biggest difference is found in the DC row, with a value of 17. The smallest element in the corresponding column (4) is 61. Therefore, the demand of destination 4, which requires 28 units, can be satisfied using the availability of source I. All of the availability, 26 units, is allocated to destination 4. With the availability of source I exhausted, there is no need to return to row I (see Figure 7.44).

After recalculating the differences, the largest difference of 17 is found in column 2. In this column, the smallest value is 39 in cell (II,2). The demand of destination 2 can be fully satisfied with the availability of source II. Thus, there is no need to return to column 2 again (see Figure 7.45).

	1	2	3	4	avail.	DL
I	83	27	35	61	26	
II	65	39	42	78	14	3
III	53	56	54	92	18	1
req.	14	11	5	28	58	
DC	12	17	12	14		

	1	2	3	4	avail.
I				26	0
II		11			3
III					18
req.	14	0	5	2	21

Figure 7.45. *Largest difference DC = 17*

After recalculating the differences, the largest difference of 23 is found in row II. On this row, the smallest value is 42 in the cell (II,3). Destination 3 requires 5 units, but the remaining availability of source II is 3 units. Therefore, 3 units are allocated for destination 3. This operation exhausts the availability of source II, and there is no need to return to row II (see Figure 7.46).

	1	2	3	4	avail.	DL
I	83	27	35	61	26	
II	65	39	42	78	14	23
III	53	56	54	92	18	1
req.	14	11	5	28	58	
DC	12		12	14		

	1	2	3	4	avail.
I				26	0
II		11	3		0
III					18
req.	14	0	2	2	18

Figure 7.46. *Largest difference DL = 23*

After recalculating the differences for DC, and in the case of row III, simply transferring the costs, the largest difference of 92 is found in column 4. The smallest value in this column is 92 (the only value) in cell (III,4). The remaining 2 units needed by destination 4 can be assigned, thus saturating its request. There is no need to return to column 4 (see Figure 7.47).

	1	2	3	4	avail.	DL
I	83	27	35	61	26	
II	65	39	42	78	14	
III	53	56	54	92	18	1
req.	14	11	5	28	58	
DC	53		54	92		

	1	2	3	4	avail.
I				26	0
II		11	3		0
III				2	16
req.	14	0	2	0	16

Figure 7.47. *Largest difference DC = 92*

After recalculation of the differences, the largest difference of 54 is found in column 3. The smallest (and only) value in this column is 54 in cell (III,3). The remaining 2 units are assigned to destination 3, thus saturating its request. There is no need to return to column 3 (see Figure 7.48).

	1	2	3	4	avail.	DL
I	83	27	35	61	26	
II	65	39	42	78	14	
III	53	56	54	92	18	1
req.	14	11	5	28	58	
DC	53		54			

	1	2	3	4	avail.
I				26	0
II		11	3		0
III			2	2	14
req.	14	0	0	0	14

Figure 7.48. *Largest difference DC = 54*

All that remains is to satisfy destination 1's demand by assigning it the 14 units from source III. Its demand is then satisfied (see Figure 7.49).

	1	2	3	4	avail.	DL
I	83	27	35	61	26	
II	65	39	42	78	14	
III	53	56	54	92	18	53
req.	14	11	5	28	58	
DC	53		54			

	1	2	3	4	avail.
I				26	0
II		11	3		0
III	14		2	2	0
req.	0	0	0	0	0

Figure 7.49. *Finalization*

Now that all destinations have been delivered, the total cost is calculated as:

$$z = 26 \times 61 + 11 \times 39 + 3 \times 42 + 14 \times 53 + 2 \times 54 + 2 \times 92 = 3{,}175$$

The solution with this cost is already better than those obtained using the Northwest Corner method or the Least Cost method.

7.2.5. Stepping stone algorithm

Now that an initial solution has been obtained, the next step is to improve it, if possible. Assume the initial solution was derived using the Northwest Corner method, resulting in a total cost of $z = 4{,}098$. The stepping stone algorithm can now be explored. The basic principle of this algorithm is to attempt to fill empty cells with appropriate quantities.

The quantity matrix for the initial solution includes both occupied and empty cells. Let m represents the number of sources, and n represent the number of destinations. The expression $m + n - 1$ indicates the expected structure of the solution. If the number of occupied cells, denoted no, satisfies the equation $m + n - 1 = no$, then the solution is non-degenerate. If not, the solution is degenerate, which will be discussed later.

Returning to the previous example, where the solution was obtained using the Northwest Corner method, the unit costs are placed at the top left to avoid using multiple matrices (see Figure 7.50). Occupied cells are highlighted in gray. In this case, $m + n - 1 = 3 + 4 - 1 = 6$, and $no = 6$. Therefore, the solution is non-degenerate.

	1	2	3	4	avail.
I	83 / 14	27 / 11	35 / 1	61	26
II	65	39	42 / 4	78 / 10	14
III	53	56	54	92 / 18	18
req.	14	11	5	28	58

Figure 7.50. *Northwest Corner solution*

To improve the initial solution, it is necessary to fill the empty cells. However, such filling requires a reduction in the quantities of the occupied cells in the same row and column. To maintain equilibrium, a circuit must be found that includes both an empty cell and already occupied cells.

Consider Figure 7.51 as an example.

For cell (I,4), the circuit (I,4)⟶(I,3) ⟶ (II,3) ⟶ (II,4) adds 1 to cell (I,4), subtracts 1 from cell (I,3), adds 1 to cell (II,3) and subtracts 1 from cell (II,4). This operation modifies the cost of the quantity $\Delta z = 1 \times (61 - 35 + 42 - 78) = -10$, improving the initial solution.

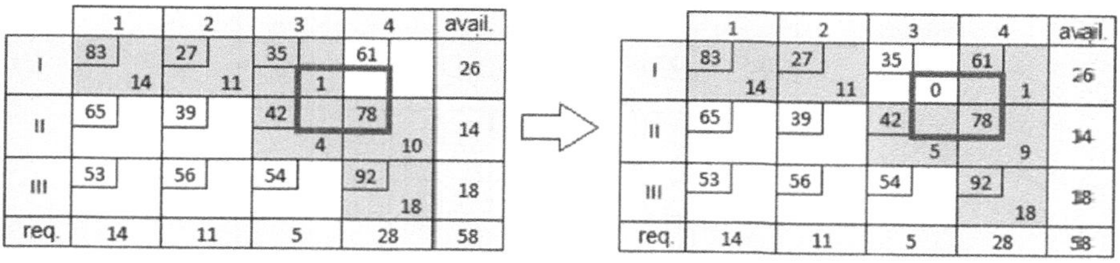

Figure 7.51. *Proposed circuit. For a color version of this figure, see www.iste.co.uk/cochard/mathematics3.zip*

Now consider the unoccupied cell (II,2) (see Figure 7.52).

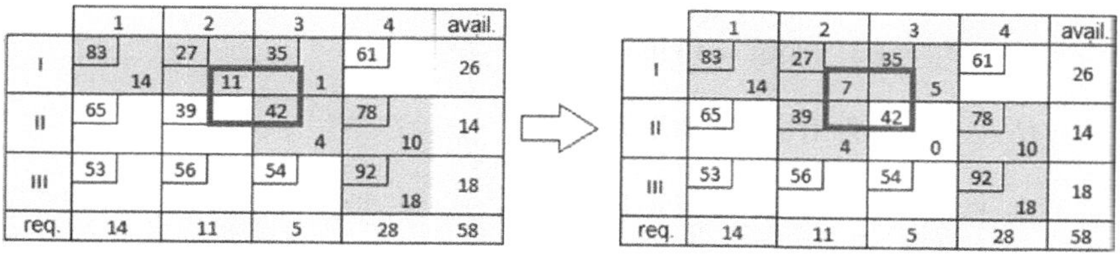

Figure 7.52. *Alternative circuit. For a color version of this figure, see www.iste.co.uk/cochard/mathematics3.zip*

With the circuit shown in Figure 7.52, 4 can be added to cell (II,2), 4 subtracted from cell (II,3), 4 added to cell (I,3) and 4 subtracted from cell (I,2). The change in cost is then $\Delta z = 4 \times (39 - 42 + 35 - 27) = 20$, which does not improve the total cost.

This is where the potential method (or UV method), which systematically explores all empty cells to find the best improvement. This method will be explained in the following, using the same example.

EXAMPLE 7.8.– Starting from the initial solution obtained by the Northwest Corner method ($z = 4{,}098$).

To apply the potentials method, a column U and a row V are added to the initial solution table (see Figure 7.53). A potential $U_I = 0$ is arbitrarily set at source I. Then, for each affected cell (marked in dark gray), the potentials U_i and V_j are calculated using the following relationship [P1]:

$$U_I + V_j = c_{ij} \qquad [P1]$$

	1	2	3	4	disp.	U
I	83 14	27 11	35 1	61	26	0
II	65	39	42 4	78 10	14	7
III	53	56	54	92 18	18	21
dem.	14	11	5	28	58	
V	83	27	35	71		

Figure 7.53. *U and V potentials*

So:

$$U_I + V_1 = 83, \text{ from which } V_1 = 83$$

$$U_I + V_2 = 27, \text{ from which } V_2 = 27$$

$$U_I + V_3 = 35, \text{ from which } V_3 = 35$$

$$U_{II} + V_3 = 42, \text{ from which } U_{II} = 7$$

$$U_{II} + V_4 = 78, \text{ from which } V_4 = 71$$

$$U_{III} + V_4 = 92, \text{ from which } U_{III} = 21$$

Next, the reduced costs of the empty cells are calculated using the formula:

$$\Delta_{ij} = U_i + V_j - c_{ij} \qquad \text{[P2]}$$

This gives:

$$\Delta_{I,4} = 0 + 71 - 61 = 10$$

$$\Delta_{ii,1} = 83 + 7 - 65 = 25$$

$$\Delta_{II,2} = 27 + 7 - 39 = -5$$

$$\Delta_{III,1} = 83 + 21 - 53 = 51$$

$$\Delta_{III,2} = 27 + 21 - 56 = -8$$

$$\Delta_{III,3} = 35 + 21 - 54 = 2$$

The positive Δ_{ij} values correspond to cell (III,1). For this cell, a circuit is drawn as shown in Figure 7.54. This circuit is more complex than the previous ones, as it must pass through occupied cells.

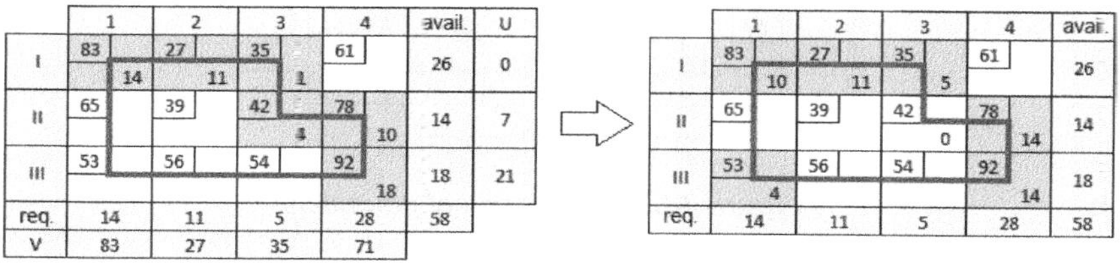

Figure 7.54. *Improvement circuit. For a color version of this figure, see www.iste.co.uk/cochard/mathematics3.zip*

It is possible to add 4 units to cell (III,1), resulting in the removal of 4 units from cell (III,4), the addition of 4 units to cell (II,4), the removal of 4 units from cell (II,3), the addition of 4 units to cell (I,3) and the removal of 4 units from cell (I,1). This operation leads to a variation in cost:

$$\Delta z = 4 \times (53 - 92 + 78 - 42 + 35 - 83) = -204.$$

Thus, the initial solution improves, and the cost is reduced to:

$$z = 4\,098 - 204 = 3{,}894.$$

The table on the right of Figure 7.54 shows the new solution. It is now necessary to recalculate the potentials, always taking $U_I = 0$, as follows (see Figure 7.55):

$$U_I + V_1 = 83, \text{ therefore } V_1 = 83$$

$$U_I + V_2 = 27, \text{ therefore } V_2 = 27$$

$$U_I + V_3 = 35, \text{ therefore } V_3 = 35$$

$$U_{III} + V_1 = 53, \text{ therefore } U_{III} = -30$$

$$U_{III} + V_4 = 92, \text{ therefore } V_4 = 122$$

$$U_{II} + V_4 = 78, \text{ therefore } U_{II} = -44$$

	1	2	3	4	avail.	U
I	83 / 10	27 / 11	35 / 5	61	26	0
II	65	39	42	78 / 14	14	-44
III	53 / 4	56	54	92 / 14	18	-30
req.	14	11	5	28	58	
V	83	27	35	122		

Figure 7.55. *Calculation of potentials*

Next, the Δ_{ij} values for unoccupied cells are calculated:

$$\Delta_{I,4} = 122 - 61 = 61$$

$$\Delta_{II,1} = 83 - 44 - 65 = -26$$

$$\Delta_{II,2} = 27 - 44 - 39 = -56$$

$$\Delta_{II,3} = 35 - 44 - 42 = -51$$

$$\Delta_{III,2} = 27 - 30 - 56 = -59$$

$$\Delta_{III,3} = 35 - 30 - 54 = -49$$

The largest positive value corresponds to cell (I,4). Starting from this cell, a cycle is performed to fill it, as shown in Figure 7.56.

	1	2	3	4	avail.	U
I	83 / 10	27 / 11	35 / 5	61	26	0
II	65	39	42	78 / 14	14	-44
III	53 / 4	56	54	92 / 14	18	-30
req.	14	11	5	28	58	
V	83	27	35	122		

⇨

	1	2	3	4	avail.
I	83 / 0	27 / 11	35 / 5	61 / 10	26
II	65	39	42	78 / 14	14
III	53 / 14	56	54	92 / 4	18
req.	14	11	5	28	58

Figure 7.56. *Enhancement circuit*

A gain of $\Delta z = 10 \times (61 - 83 + 53 - 92) = -610$ is obtained, which results in a new solution with a total cost of $z = 3{,}284$c.

Now, the same steps are repeated on the new solution obtained: calculating the potentials and the Δ_{ij} values (see Figure 7.57):

$$U_i + V_2 = 27, \text{ therefore } V_2 = 27$$

$$U_I + V_3 = 35, \text{ therefore } V_3 = 35$$

$$U_I + V_4 = 61, \text{ therefore } V_4 = 61$$

$$U_{II} + V_4 = 78, \text{ therefore } U_{II} = 17$$

$$U_{III} + V_4 = 92, \text{ therefore } U_{III} = 31$$

$$U_{III} + V_1 = 53, \text{ therefore } V_1 = 22$$

	1	2	3	4	avail.	U
I	83	27 (11)	35 (5)	61 (10)	26	0
II	65	39	42	78 (14)	14	17
III	53 (14)	56	54	92 (4)	18	31
req.	14	11	5	28	58	
V	22	27	35	61		

Figure 7.57. *Calculation of potentials*

Let us calculate the Δ_{ij} values for the unoccupied cells:

$$\Delta_{I,1} = 22 - 83 = -61$$

$$\Delta_{II,1} = 22 + 17 - 65 = -26$$

$$\Delta_{II,2} = 27 + 17 - 39 = 5$$

$$\Delta_{II,3} = 35 + 17 - 42 = 10$$

$$\Delta_{III,2} = 27 + 31 - 56 = 2$$

$$\Delta_{III,3} = 35 + 31 - 54 = 12$$

The largest positive value corresponds to cell (III,3). The circuit established (see Figure 7.58) from this cell gives it 4 units.

	1	2	3	4	avail.	U
I	83	27 (11)	35 (5)	61 (10)	26	0
II	65	39	42	78 (14)	14	17
III	53 (14)	56	54	92 (4)	18	31
req.	14	11	5	28	58	
V	22	27	35	61		

⇨

	1	2	3	4	avail.
I	83	27 (11)	35 (1)	61 (14)	26
II	65	39	42	78 (14)	14
III	53 (14)	56	54 (4)	92 (0)	18
req.	14	11	5	28	58

Figure 7.58. *Improvement circuit. For a color version of this figure, see www.iste.co.uk/cochard/mathematics3.zip*

A gain of $\Delta z = 4 \times (54 - 92 + 61 - 35) = -48$ is obtained, which leads to the new solution with a total cost of $z = 3{,}236$.

Next, the potentials and Δ_{ij} are recalculated according to the same operations (see Figure 7.59):

$$U_I + V_2 = 27, \text{ therefore } V_2 = 27$$

$$U_I + V_3 = 35, \text{ therefore } V_3 = 35$$

$$U_I + V_4 = 61, \text{ therefore } V_4 = 61$$

$$U_{II} + V_4 = 78, \text{ therefore } U_{II} = 17$$

$$U_{III} + V_3 = 54, \text{ therefore } U_{III} = 19$$

$$U_{III} + V_1 = 53, \text{ therefore } V_1 = 34$$

	1	2	3	4	avail.	U
I	83	27 (11)	35 (1)	61 (14)	26	0
II	65	39	42	78 (14)	14	17
III	53 (14)	56	54 (4)	92	18	19
req.	14	11	5	28	58	
V	34	27	35	61		

Figure 7.59. *Calculation of potentials*

The calculations for the unoccupied cells are as follows:

$$\Delta_{I,1} = 34 - 83 = -49$$

$\Delta_{II,1} = 34 + 17 - 65 = -14$

$\Delta_{II,2} = 27 + 17 - 39 = 5$

$\Delta_{II,3} = 35 + 17 - 42 = 10$

$\Delta_{III,2} = 27 + 19 - 56 = -10$

$\Delta_{III,4} = 61 + 19 - 92 = -12$

The largest positive value corresponds to cell (II,3). For this cell, a circuit is drawn as shown in Figure 7.60. This circuit adds 1 unit to cell (II,3).

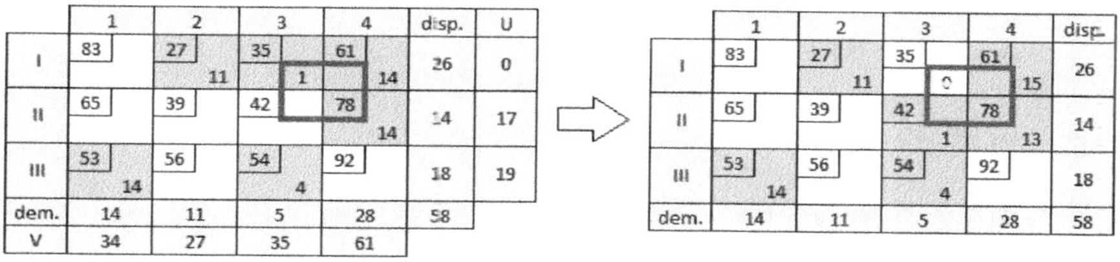

Figure 7.60. *Enhancement circuit. For a color version of this figure, see www.iste.co.uk/cochard/mathematics3.zip*

The gain obtained is $\Delta z = 1 \times (42 - 78 + 61 - 35) = -10$. This result corresponds to a new solution with cost of $z = 3{,}226$.

Continuing with the same operations on this solution, the new potentials and the Δ_{ij} values are calculated (see Figure 7.61):

$U_I + V_2 = 27$, therefore $V_2 = 27$

$U_i + V_4 = 61$, therefore $V_4 = 61$

$U_{II} + V_4 = 78$, therefore $U_{II} = 17$

$U_{II} + V_3 = 42$, therefore $V_3 = 25$

$U_{III} + V_3 = 54$, therefore $U_{III} = 29$

$U_{III} + V_1 = 53$, therefore $V_1 = 24$

	1	2	3	4	avail.	U
I	83	27 / 11	35	61 / 15	26	0
II	65	39	42 / 1	78 / 13	14	17
III	53 / 14	56	54 / 4	92	18	29
req.	14	11	5	28	58	
V	24	27	25	61		

Figure 7.61. *Calculation of potentials*

For unoccupied cells, the $\Delta_{i,j}$ are calculated as follows:

$$\Delta_{I,1} = 24 - 83 = -59$$

$$\Delta_{I,3} = 25 - 35 = -10$$

$$\Delta_{II,1} = 24 + 17 - 65 = -24$$

$$\Delta_{II,2} = 27 + 17 - 39 = 5$$

$$\Delta_{III,2} = 27 + 29 - 56 = 0$$

$$\Delta_{III,4}\ 61 + 29 - 92 = -2$$

The largest (and only) positive value is 5, which corresponds to cell (II,2). From this cell, the circuit shown in Figure 7.62 is drawn, filling the cell with 11 units.

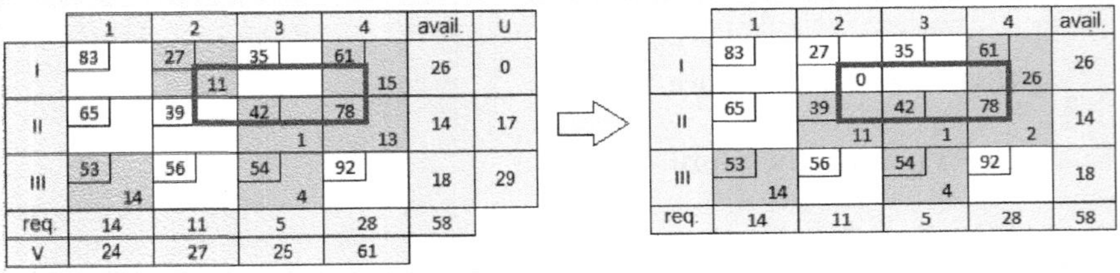

Figure 7.62. *Improvement circuit. For a color version of this figure, see www.iste.co.uk/cochard/mathematics3.zip*

This operation leads to a gain of $\Delta z = 11 \times (39 - 27 + 61 - 78) = -55$, resulting in a new solution with a cost of $z = 3{,}171$.

Next, the new potentials and Δ_{ij} are calculated for this updated solution (see Figure 7.63).

	1	2	3	4	avail.	U
I	83	27 / 0	35	61 / 26	26	0
II	65	39 / 11	42 / 1	78 / 2	14	17
III	53 / 14	56	54 / 4	92	18	29
req.	14	11	5	28	58	
V	24	22	25	61		

Figure 7.63. *Calculation of potentials*

$U_I + V_4 = 61,$ therefore $V_4 = 61$

$U_{II} + V_4 = 78,$ therefore $U_{II} = 17$

$U_{II} + V_3 = 42,$ therefore $V_3 = 25$

$U_{II} + V_2 = 39,$ therefore $V_2 = 22$

$U_{III} + V_3 = 54,$ therefore $U_{III} = 29$

$U_{III} + V_1 = 53,$ therefore $V_1 = 24$

For unoccupied cells, the $\Delta_{i,j}$ are calculated as follows:

$\Delta_{I,1} = 24 - 83 = -59$

$\Delta_{I,2} = 22 - 27 = -5$

$\Delta_{I,3} = 25 - 35 = -10$

$\Delta_{II,1} = 24 + 17 - 65 = -24$

$\Delta_{III,2} = 22 + 29 - 56 = -5$

$\Delta_{III,4} = 61 + 29 - 92 = -2$

All Δ_{ij} are negative, satisfying the optimality criterion of the method of potentials. Therefore, the final solution obtained is optimal.

It is observed that the initial solution derived using the Balas-Hammer method is close to the optimal solution.

However, a few important points still need to be addressed: the inequality between supply and demand, and the case of an unconnected graph.

7.2.6. *Inequality of supply and demand*

Where total demand differs from total supply, steps must be taken to balance them. This can be achieved by introducing fictitious sources or destinations with zero-unit transport costs:

– If total demand (D) exceeds total supply (S), there is insufficient supply to fully meet demand. To address this, a fictitious source is created with an availability equal to the difference ($D - S$). This fictitious source represents the additional quantity required to balance supply and demand.

– Conversely, if total demand (D) is less than total supply (S), there is a surplus of supply over demand. To resolve this imbalance, a fictitious destination is introduced with a demand equal to the difference between ($S - D$). This fictitious destination absorbs the excess quantity, ensuring supply and demand are balanced.

EXAMPLE 7.9.– Consider the following situation, as shown by the cost and quantity tables in Figure 7.64.

costs

	1	2	3
I	5	12	10
II	10	20	15
III	6	10	5

quantities

	1	2	3	avail.
I				15
II				20
III				25
req.	10	20	15	60/45

Figure 7.64. *Unit cost table and quantity table*

The total of supply is 60, while the total of demands is 45. To close this gap of 15 (60 – 45), a fictitious requester 4 is added with a demand of 15.

By assigning a zero cost to all routes leading to requester 4, the following situation is obtained after applying the Northwest Corner method (see Figure 7.65).

costs

	1	2	3	4
I	5	12	10	0
II	10	20	15	0
III	6	10	5	0

quantities

	1	2	3	4	avail.
I	10	5			15
II		15	5		20
III			10	15	25
req.	10	20	15	15	60

Figure 7.65. *Application of the Northwest Corner method*

The stepping stone algorithm is now applied. Following its steps, a solution with a total cost of z = 370 is obtained.

7.2.7. *Unconnected graph and degeneration*

The relationships between sources and recipients can be represented as a bipartite graph. In Example 7.4, the graphs corresponding to the quantities transported, both for the initial Northwest Corner solution and the optimal solution obtained using the stepping stone algorithm, are shown in Figure 7.66.

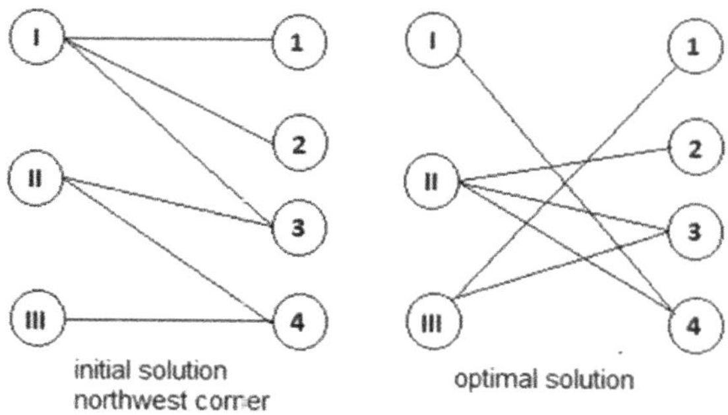

Figure 7.66. *Solution graphs*

These graphs are both connected and acyclic. The potential method described earlier applies only to connected and acyclic graphs for calculating potentials.

It is important to note that, in the graph shown in Figure 7.66, the edges represent the occupied cells from the previous tables. The equation $m + n - 1 = no$ (here, 6) holds, indicating that there is no degeneration in this case.

However, if the quantity graph is not connected, it must be artificially connected by adding a link with a small quantity $\varepsilon > 0$.

EXAMPLE 7.10.– Consider the following problem, for which an initial solution is provided, as shown in Figure 7.67. This solution corresponds to the total cost of $z = 3{,}053$.

	1	2	3	4	avail.
I	27	53	35	61 26	26
II	65	39 11	42 5	78 2	18
III	48 14	56	32	92	14
req.	14	11	5	28	58

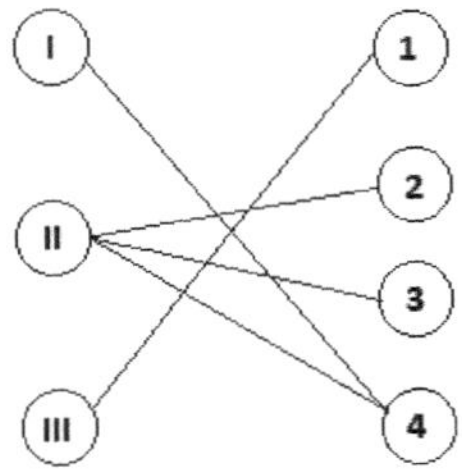

Figure 7.67. *Initial solution*

Looking at the table, it can be observed that there are five occupied cells, whereas the equation $m + n - 1 = 6$ indicates that there should be six occupied cells. This suggests a situation of degeneration. Furthermore, the corresponding graph has two distinct connected components: {III,1} and {I, II, 2, 3, 4}.

To replace an occupied cell, the one with the lowest cost is chosen. This is cell (I,1), which has a cost of 27. Starting from this cell, it is impossible to draw a circuit passing through occupied cells. To resolve this, a value of $\varepsilon > 0$ units is assigned to cell (I,1), resulting in the situation shown in Figure 7.68.

	1	2	3	4	avail.
I	27	53	35	61 26	26
II	65	39 11	42 5	78 2	18
III	48 14	56	32	92	14
req.	14	11	5	28	58

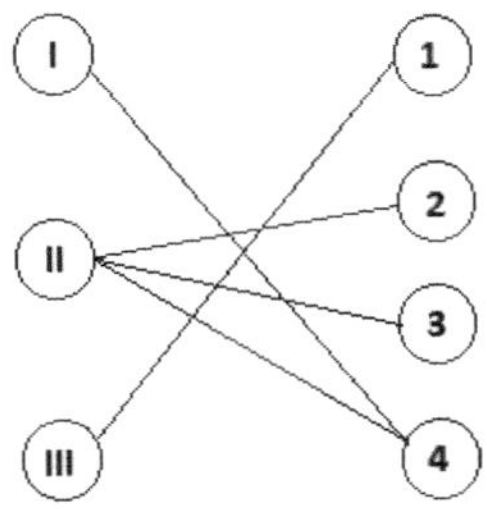

Figure 7.68. *Using the* ε *value*

	1	2	3	4	avail.	U
I	27 / ε	53	35	61 / 26	26+ε	0
II	65	39 / 11	42 / 5	78 / 2	18	17
III	48 / 14	56	32	92	14	21
req.	14+ε	11	5	28	58+ε	
V	27	22	25	61		

Figure 7.69. *Calculation of potentials*

Now, with $m + n - 1 = no = 6$, and after the addition of the edge $I - 1$, the corresponding graph has become connected. The method of potentials can now be used to improve upon the previous solution (see Figure 7.69).

For occupied cells:

$$U_I + V_1 = 27, \text{ therefore } V_1 = 27$$

$$U_I + V_4 = 61, \text{ therefore } V_4 = 61$$

$$U_{II} + V_4 = 78, \text{ therefore } U_2 = 17$$

$$U_{II} + V_3 = 42, \text{ therefore } V_3 = 25$$

$$U_{II} + V_2 = 39, \text{ therefore } V_2 = 22$$

$$U_{III} + V_1 = 48, \text{ therefore } U_{III} = 21$$

For unoccupied cells:

$$\Delta_{I,2} = 22 - 53 = -31$$

$$\Delta_{I,3} = 25 - 35 = -10$$

$$\Delta_{II,1} = 27 + 17 - 65 = -21$$

$$\Delta_{III,2} = 22 + 21 - 56 = -13$$

$$\Delta_{III,3} = 25 + 21 - 32 = 14$$

$$\Delta_{III,4} = 61 + 21 - 92 = -10$$

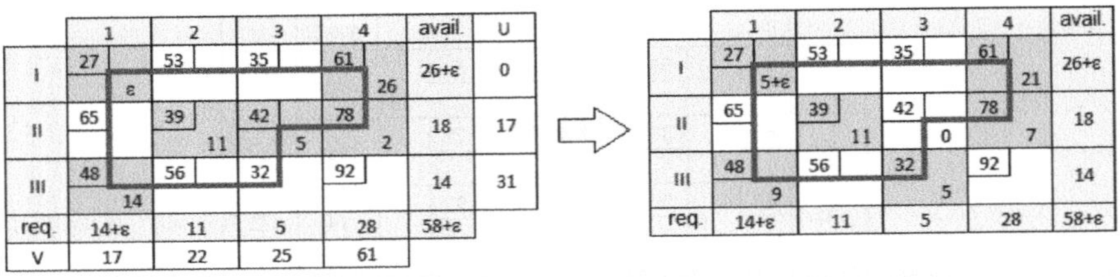

Figure 7.70. *Improvement circuit. For a color version of this figure, see www.iste.co.uk/cochard/mathematics3.zip*

	1	2	3	4	avail.	U
I	27; 5+ε	53	35	61; 21	26+ε	0
II	65	39; 11	42; 0	78; 7	18	17
III	48; 9	56	32; 5	92	14	21
req.	14+ε	11	5	28	58+ε	
V	27	22	11	61		

Figure 7.71. *Calculation of potentials*

The only positive value, 14, corresponds to cell (III,3), from which an improving circuit is drawn (see Figure 7.70).

The cost improvement is $\Delta z = -70$; hence, $z = 2{,}983$. In this new configuration (see Figure 7.71), the potentials are recalculated, followed by the calculation of the Δ_{ij}:

$$\Delta_{I,2} = 22 - 53 = -31$$

$$\Delta_{I,3} = 11 - 35 = -24$$

$$\Delta_{II,1} = 27 + 17 - 65 = -21$$

$$\Delta_{II,3} = 11 + 17 - 42 = -14$$

$$\Delta_{III,2} = 22 + 21 - 56 = -13$$

$$\Delta_{III,4} = 61 + 21 - 92 = -10$$

All values are negative, indicating that the optimal solution has been reached. The final step is to make ε tend towards 0 (see Figure 7.72).

	1	2	3	4	avail.
I	27 / 5	53	35	61 / 21	26
II	65	39 / 11	42	78 / 7	18
III	48 / 9	56	32 / 5	92	14
req.	14	11	5	28	58

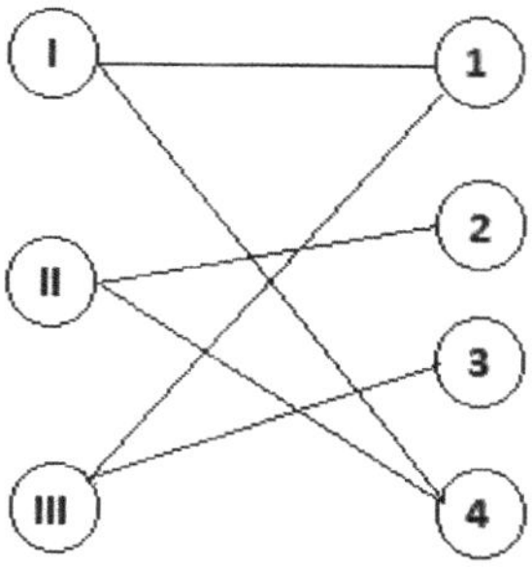

Figure 7.72. *Optimum solution*

7.2.8. *Potentials and dual program*

In the method of potentials, a legitimate question is what the potentials correspond to and why they are used. To answer this, the concept of linear programming is revisited.

The linear program is formulated as follows:

Minimize:

$$z = \sum_{i=1}^{m} \sum_{j=1}^{n} c_{ij}\, x_{ij}$$

Subject to the constraints:

$$\sum_{j=1}^{n} x_{ij} = a_i \qquad i = 1, \ldots, m$$

$$\textstyle\sum_{i=1}^{m} x_{ij} = b_j \qquad j = 1, \ldots, n,$$

where the variables x_{ij} are non-negative.

The dual program of this linear program can be written as:

Maximize:

$$w = \sum_{i=1}^{m} a_i U_i + \sum_{j=1}^{n} b_j V_j$$

Subject to the constraints:

$$U_i + V_j \leq c_{ij}, \quad i = 1, \dots, m, \quad j = 1, \dots, n$$

where U_i and V_j can take any sign.

To explain the transition from the linear program to its dual, consider the following example.

EXAMPLE 7.11.– Consider the transportation problem shown in Figure 7.73.

	1	2	3	avail.
I	c_{11}	c_{12}	c_{13}	a_1
II	c_{21}	c_{22}	c_{23}	a_2
req.	b_1	b_2	b_3	

Figure 7.73. *Transportation problem*

The linear program is:

$$\text{minimize } z = c_{11}x_{11} + c_{12}x_{12} + c_{13}x_{13} + c_{21}x_{21} + c_{22}x_{22} + c_{23}x_{23}$$

s.t.

$$c_{11}x_{11} + c_{12}x_{12} + c_{13}x_{13} = a_1$$

$$c_{21}x_{21} + c_{22}x_{22} + c_{23}x_{23} = a_2$$

$$c_{11}x_{11} + c_{21}x_{21} = b_1$$

$$c_{12}x_{12} + c_{22}x_{22} = b_2$$

$$c_{13}x_{13} + c_{23}x_{23} = b_3$$

$$x_{ij} \geq 0, \quad i = 1,2 \quad j = 1,2,3$$

There are five constraints, so for the dual program, five variables are introduced: U_1, U_2, V_1, V_2, V_3, in the order corresponding to the constraints.

The dual program is then written as follows:

$$\text{maximize } w = a_1U_1 + a_2U_2 + b_1V_1 + b_2V_2 + b_3V_3$$

s.t.

$$U_1 + V_1 \leq c_{11}$$

$$U_1 + V_2 \leq c_{12}$$

$$U_1 + V_3 \leq c_{13}$$

$$U_2 + V_1 \leq c_{21}$$

$$U_2 + V_2 \leq c_{22}$$

$$U_2 + V_3 \leq c_{23}$$

This results in the optimality condition $U_i + V_j - c_{ij} \leq 0$, which enables our interpretation of the variables U_i and V_j as the potentials used in the enhancement algorithm.

7.3. Assignment problems

7.3.1. *Issues*

Objective: Determine the best bijective match between two sets, where "the best" may refer to the most profitable, least costly or otherwise most efficient match.

EXAMPLE 7.12.– Five teachers (a, b, c, d, e) work in a school with five classes (1, 2, 3, 4, 5). At the beginning of the year, the school principal asks each teacher to rank the classes from 1 to 5, in descending order of preference (see Figure 7.89). The "cost" of each assignment can be evaluated by summing the ranking values. To best satisfy the teachers, the goal is to minimize the total cost.

The graph in Figure 7.74 presents a possible solution with a cost of $z = 1 + 2 - 2 + 4 + 3 = 12$. Is this the best solution?

classrooms

teachers	1	2	3	4	5
a	1	2	3	4	5
b	1	4	2	5	3
c	3	2	1	5	4
d	1	2	3	5	4
e	2	1	4	3	5

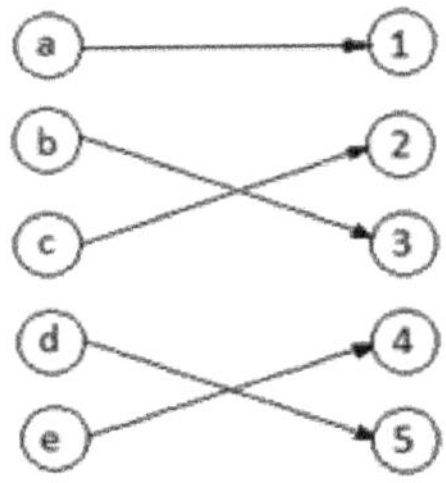

Figure 7.74. *A possible solution*

An analogy can be made with the transportation problem, where both supply and demand are equal to 1, and the maximum capacity of the arcs is 1. In fact, this represents a class of *linear problems*, known as the "allocation problem", where n resources must be assigned to n tasks.

This problem can be formulated as a linear integer program, where the decision variables represent the assignments of teachers to classes, and the constraints ensure that each teacher is assigned to exactly one class and each class is assigned exactly one teacher.

Minimize the objective function:

$$z = \sum_{i=1}^{n} \sum_{j=1}^{n} c_{ij} x_{ij}$$

Subject to the constraints:

$$\sum_{j=1}^{n} x_{ij} = 1 \quad i = 1, \dots, n$$

$$\sum_{i=1}^{n} x_{ij} = 1 \quad j = 1, \dots, n$$

$$x_{ij} = \begin{cases} 1 \text{ if the link } ij \text{ exists} \\ 0 \text{ otherwise} \end{cases}$$

EXAMPLE 7.13.– Consider the introductory Example 7.12. Starting from the initial solution shown in Figure 7.74, the stepping stone algorithm with potentials is applied. The problem is essentially a minimum-cost transportation problem. In this case, the availabilities correspond to the number of teachers to be assigned, while the demands represent the number of teachers needed by each class, as summarized in the table in Figure 7.75.

	1	2	3	4	5	avail.
a	1 (1)	2	3	4	5	1
b	1	4	2 (1)	5	3	1
c	3	2 (1)	1	5	4	1
d	1	2	3	5	4 (1)	1
e	2	1	4	3 (1)	5	1
req.	1	1	1	1	1	5

Figure 7.75. *The problem to be solved*

The cost of the initial solution is $z = 12$. As noted, there are five occupied cells, whereas nine are needed to apply the method of potentials. To address this, an "emergency" solution is applied by adding a quantity ε to the cells where the cost is 1, increasing the number of occupied cells to nine. Then, the potential method is applied (see Figure 7.76).

	1	2	3	4	5	avail.	U
a	1 (1)	2	3	4	5	1	0
b	1 (ε)	4	2 (1)	5	3	1+ε	0
c	3	2 (1)	1 (ε)	5	4	1+ε	-1
d	1 (ε)	2	3	5	4 (1)	1+ε	0
e	2	1 (ε)	4	3 (1)	5	1+ε	-2
req.	1+2ε	1+ε	1+ε	1	1	5+4ε	
V	1	3	2	5	4		

Figure 7.76. *Calculation of potentials*

For unoccupied cells:

$$\Delta_{a2} = 1,\ \Delta_{a3} = -1,\ \Delta_{a4} = 1,\ \Delta_{a5} = -1,\ \Delta_{b2} = -1,\ \Delta_{b4} = 0,$$

$$\Delta_{b5} = 1,\ \Delta_{c1} = -3,\ \Delta_{c4} = -1,\ \Delta_{c5} = -1,\ \Delta_{d2} = 1,\ \Delta_{d3} = -1,$$

$$\Delta_{d4} = 0,\ \Delta_{e1} = -3,\ \Delta_{e3} = -4 \text{ and } \Delta_{e5} = -3$$

The largest positive value of Δ_{ij} is 1, which corresponds to several cells. Let us choose the cell $(a, 2)$ and draw an enhancement circuit (see Figure 7.77).

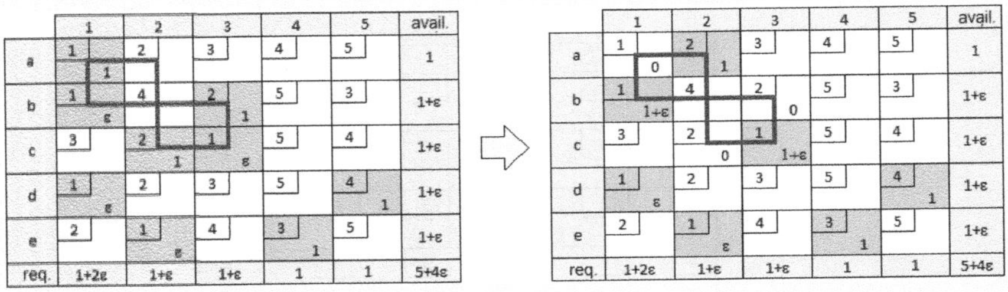

Figure 7.77. *Enhancement circuit. For a color version of this figure, see www.iste.co.uk/cochard/mathematics3.zip*

The cost saving is $\Delta z = 2 - 1 + 1 - 2 + 1 - 2 = -1$; hence, $z = 11$. However, the resulting solution is degenerate, as it corresponds to seven occupied cells instead of nine. Cell (c,3) is alone in its row and column. We add a fictitious quantity ε to cells (c,2) and (b,3) to arrive at a total of nine occupied cells. Then, we apply the potential method (see Figure 7.78).

For unoccupied cells:

$$\Delta_{a1} = -1,\ \Delta_{a3} = -2,\ \Delta_{a4} = 0,\ \Delta_{a5} = -2,\ \Delta_{b2} = -1,\ \Delta_{b4} = 0,$$

$$\Delta_{b5} = 1,\ \Delta_{c1} = -3,\ \Delta_{c4} = -1,\ \Delta_{c5} = -1, \Delta_{d2} = 1, \Delta_{d3} = -1,$$

$$\Delta_{d4} = 0,\ \Delta_{e1} = -3,\ \Delta_{e3} = -4 \text{ and } \Delta_{e5} = -3$$

	1	2	3	4	5	avail.	U
a	1	2 (1)	3	4	5	1	0
b	1 (1+ε)	4	2 (ε)	5	3	1+2ε	1
c	3	2 (ε)	1 (1+ε)	5	4	1+2ε	0
d	1 (ε)	2	3	5	4 (1)	1+ε	1
e	2	1 (ε)	4	3 (1)	5	1+ε	-1
req.	1+2ε	1+2ε	1+2ε	1	1	5+6ε	
V	0	2	1	4	3		

Figure 7.78. *Calculation of potentials*

The largest positive value of Δ_{ij} is 1, which corresponds to several cells. Let us choose (b,5) and, starting from this cell, draw an enhancement circuit (see Figure 7.79).

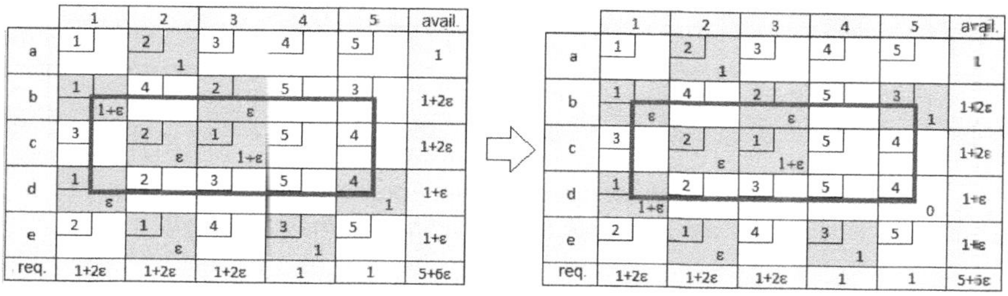

Figure 7.79. *Enhancement circuit. For a color version of this figure, see www.iste.co.uk/cochard/mathematics3.zip*

The cost saving is $\Delta z = 3 - 1 + 1 - 4 = -1$, resulting in $z = 10$. The method of potentials is then applied to the new solution obtained (see Figure 7.80).

For unoccupied cells:

$$\Delta_{a1} = -1,\ \Delta_{a3} = -2,\ \Delta_{a4} = 0,\ \Delta_{a5} = -3,\ \Delta_{b2} = -1,\ \Delta_{b4} = 0,$$

$$\Delta_{c1} = -3,\ \Delta_{c4} = -1,\ \Delta_{c5} = -2, \Delta_{d2} = 1,\ \Delta_{d3} = -1,\ \Delta_{d4} = 0,$$

$$\Delta_{d5} = -1, \Delta_{e1} = -3, \Delta_{e3} = -4 \text{ and } \Delta_{e5} = -4$$

The only positive value corresponds to cell (d,2). Starting from this cell, we draw an enhancement circuit (see Figure 7.81).

	1	2	3	4	5	avail.	U
a	1	2 / 1	3	4	5	1	0
b	1 / ε	4	2 / ε	5	3 / 1	1+2ε	1
c	3	2 / ε	1 / 1+ε	5	4	1+2ε	0
d	1 / 1+ε	2	3	5	4 / 0	1+ε	1
e	2	1 / ε	4	3 / 1	5	1+ε	-1
req.	1+2ε	1+2ε	1+2ε	1	1	5+6ε	
V	0	2	1	4	2		

Figure 7.80. *Calculation of potentials*

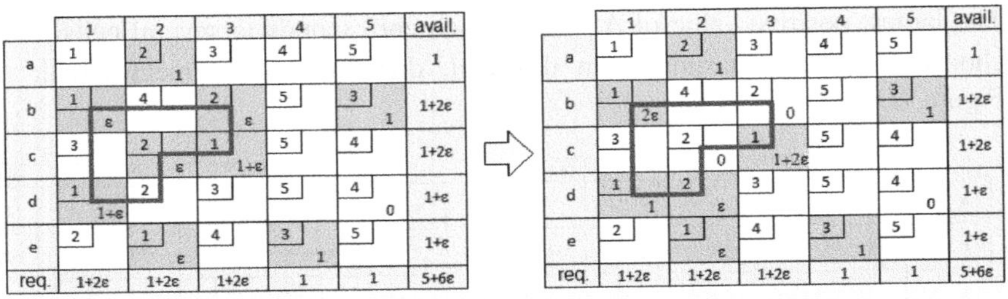

Figure 7.81. *Enhancement circuit. For a color version of this figure, see www.iste.co.uk/cochard/mathematics3.zip*

The cost saving is $\Delta z = \varepsilon \times (2 - 1 + 1 - 2 + 1 - 2) = -\varepsilon$, resulting in $z = 10 - \varepsilon$. However, the resulting solution is degenerate, as it has only eight occupied cells. Cell (c,3) is isolated in its row and column. To resolve this, a quantity ε is added to cell (b,3), bringing the total number of occupied cells to nine. The potential method is then applied (see Figure 7.82).

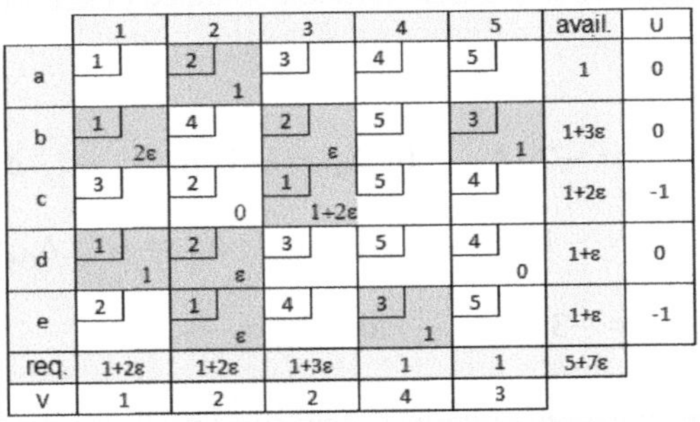

Figure 7.82. *Calculation of potentials*

For unoccupied cells:

$$\Delta_{a1}= 0,\ \Delta_{a3}= -1,\ \Delta_{a4}= 0,\ \Delta_{a5}= -2,\ \Delta_{b2}= -2,\ \Delta_{b4}= -1,$$

$$\Delta_{c1}= -3,\ \Delta_{c2}= -1,\ \Delta_{c4}= -2,\ \Delta_{c5}= -2,\ \Delta_{d3}= -1,\ \Delta_{d4}= -1,$$

$$\Delta_{d5}= -1,\ \Delta_{e1}= -2,\ \Delta_{e3}= -3 \text{ and } \Delta_{e5}= -3$$

All values are negative, indicating that optimality has been reached with a value of $z = 10 - \varepsilon$. Next, ε is cancelled. Figure 7.83 shows the graph corresponding to the solution obtained.

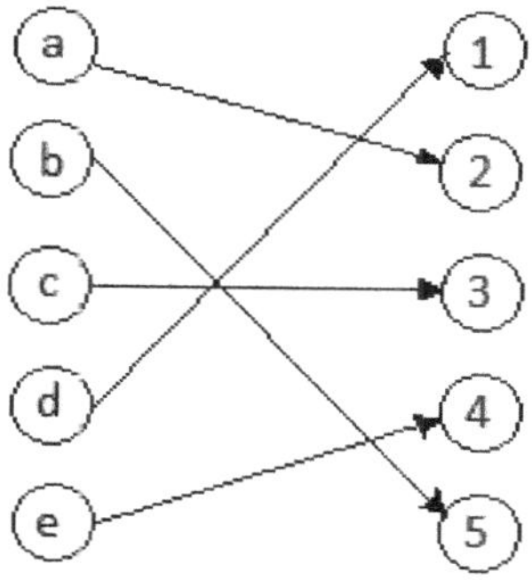

Figure 7.83. *Optimum solution*

Note that the graph is not connected and has five related components $\{a, 2\}, \{b, 5\}, \{c, 3\}, \{d, 1\}$ and $\{e, 4\}$, which is normal for a bijection.

In addition to linear programming and minimum-cost transport algorithms, other algorithms are also suitable for this type of problem. The best known of these is the Hungarian algorithm, which is described in section 7.3.2.

7.3.2. *Hungarian algorithm*

In practice, this type of problem is usually solved using the Hungarian algorithm, named after its original authors: Egervary, König, Kuhn and Munkres. To illustrate the algorithm, it is applied to Example 7.13.

Phase 1: the problem is modified by transforming the cost matrix as follows:

– Subtract the smallest element from each row of the matrix.

– Subtract the smallest element from each column of the matrix.

These adjustments are shown in Figure 7.84.

	1	2	3	4	5
a	1	2	3	4	5
b	1	4	2	5	3
c	3	2	1	5	4
d	1	2	3	5	4
e	2	1	4	3	5

costs matrix

	1	2	3	4	5
a	0	1	2	3	4
b	0	3	1	4	2
c	2	1	0	4	3
d	0	1	2	4	3
e	1	0	3	2	4

line per line

	1	2	3	4	5
a	0	1	2	1	2
b	0	3	1	2	0
c	2	1	0	2	1
d	0	1	2	2	1
e	1	0	3	0	2

column per column

	1	2	3	4	5
a	0				
b	0				0
c			0		
d	0				
e		0		0	

highlighting matches

Figure 7.84. *Phase 1*

The last table shows that a bijective match is not achieved, as one row can correspond to multiple columns and vice versa. However, a choice can be made to solve this problem (see Figure 7.85).

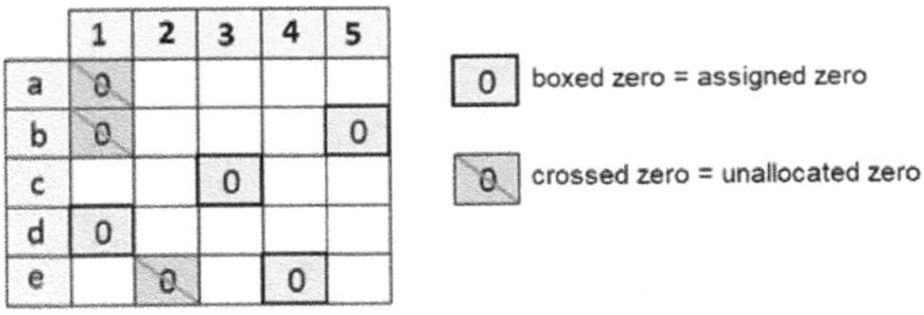

Figure 7.85. *Boxed zeros and crossed zeros. For a color version of this figure, see www.iste.co.uk/cochard/mathematics3.zip*

Phase 2: crossed zeros and boxed zeros.

– Mark all rows that do not contain a boxed zero.

– Mark all columns that contain a crossed zero in a marked row.

– Mark all rows that contain a boxed zero in a marked column.

The steps are repeated, starting from the second, as long as marking is possible (see Figure 7.86).

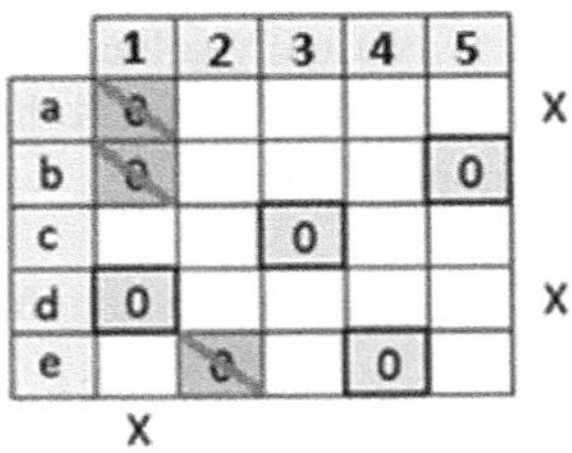

Figure 7.86. *Marking. For a color version of this figure, see www.iste.co.uk/cochard/mathematics3.zip*

– Unmarked rows and marked columns are crossed out (see Figure 7.87).

– The smallest element of the remaining array is identified (in this case, 1).

– This element is subtracted from all not striped elements and added to the doubly striped elements (see Figure 7.88).

	1	2	3	4	5	
a	0	1	2	1	2	X
b	0	3	1	2	0	
c	2	1	0	2		
d	0	1	2	2	1	X
e	1	0	3	0	2	
	X					

Figure 7.87. *Striped lines. For a color version of this figure, see www.iste.co.uk/cochard/mathematics3.zip*

	1	2	3	4	5
a	0	0	1	0	1
b	1	3	1	2	0
c	3	1	0	2	1
d	0	0	1	1	0
e	2	0	3	0	2

Figure 7.88. *Subtraction/addition operation*

By applying the method of crossed zeros and boxed zeros, it becomes possible to assign one zero per row and column. This results in three equivalent solutions, as shown in Figure 7.89.

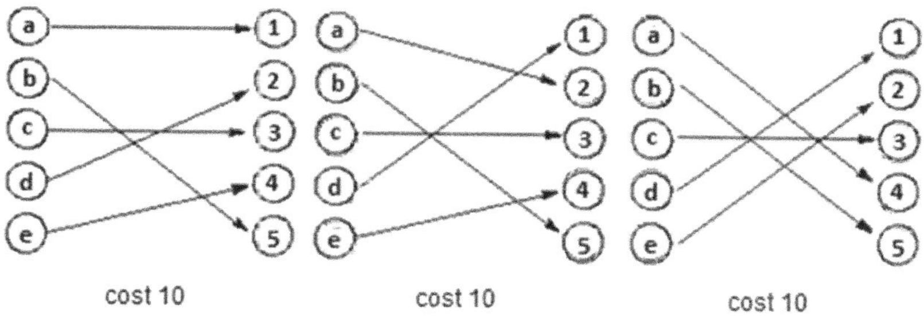

Figure 7.89. *Optimum solutions*

EXAMPLE 7.14.– Consider a scenario where five delivery personnel (A, B, C, D, E) must serve five customers (a, b, c, d, e). The objective is to minimize the total distance traveled by the drivers. The table of distances between drivers and customers is shown in Figure 7.90.

	a	b	c	d	e
A	10	12	21	30	25
B	8	15	22	9	18
C	16	24	31	18	17
D	5	15	20	28	32
E	23	13	24	17	11

Figure 7.90. *Distance table*

Let us now apply the algorithm to solve the problem. Begin by subtracting the smallest element from each row of the distance matrix, as shown in Figure 7.91.

	a	b	c	d	e
A	0	2	11	20	15
B	0	7	14	1	10
C	0	8	15	2	1
D	0	10	15	23	27
E	12	2	13	6	0

Figure 7.91. *Subtracting the smallest element from each line*

Then proceed by subtracting the smallest element from each column of the distance matrix, column by column, as shown in Figure 7.92.

	a	b	c	d	e
A	0	0	0	19	15
B	0	5	3	0	10
C	0	6	4	1	1
D	0	8	4	22	27
E	12	0	2	5	0

Figure 7.92. *Subtraction of the smallest element in each column*

At this point, it can be observed that there is at least one null element (0) in each row and column of the matrix.

An assignment choice will now be made (which is not necessarily the best one), as shown in Figure 7.93.

Now, mark the rows that do not have a framed zero (0), as shown in Figure 7.94.

	a	b	c	d	e
A	~~0~~	[0]	~~0~~	19	15
B	~~0~~	5	3	[0]	10
C	[0]	6	4	1	1
D	~~0~~	8	4	22	27
E	12	~~0~~	2	5	[0]

Figure 7.93. *Assignment choice. For a color version of this figure, see www.iste.co.uk/cochard/mathematics3.zip*

	a	b	c	d	e	
A	~~0~~	[0]	~~0~~	19	15	
B	~~0~~	5	3	[0]	10	
C	[0]	6	4	1	1	
D	~~0~~	8	4	22	27	x
E	12	~~0~~	2	5	[0]	

Figure 7.94. *Line marking. For a color version of this figure, see www.iste.co.uk/cochard/mathematics3.zip*

Next, mark the columns that have a crossed zero (0) on the only marked row, as shown in Figure 7.95.

	a	b	c	d	e	
A	~~0~~	[0]	~~0~~	19	15	
B	~~0~~	5	3	[0]	10	
C	[0]	6	4	1	1	
D	~~0~~	8	4	22	27	x
E	12	~~0~~	2	5	[0]	
	x					

Figure 7.95. *Column marking. For a color version of this figure, see www.iste.co.uk/cochard/mathematics3.zip*

Now, mark the rows that have a zero (0) boxed in a marked column, as shown in Figure 7.96.

	a	b	c	d	e	
A	0	0	0	19	15	
B	0	5	3	0	10	
C	0	6	4	1	1	x
D	0	8	4	22	27	x
E	12	0	2	5	0	
	x					

Figure 7.96. *Continuation of the marking process. For a color version of this figure, see www.iste.co.uk/cochard/mathematics3.zip*

The marking process can be repeated, but in this case, no new marks will be obtained. Therefore, cross out the unmarked rows and marked columns, as shown in Figure 7.97.

	a	b	c	d	e	
A	0	0	0	19	15	
B	0	5	3	0	10	
C	0	6	4	1	1	x
D	0	8	4	22	27	x
E	12	0	2	5	0	
	x					

Figure 7.97. *Striped rows and columns. For a color version of this figure, see www.iste.co.uk/cochard/mathematics3.zip*

The smallest remaining element in the array is 1. Therefore, subtract 1 from the elements that are not crossed out and add 1 to the elements that are crossed out twice (the other elements remain unchanged), as shown in Figure 7.98.

	a	b	c	d	e
A	1	0	0	19	15
B	1	5	3	0	10
C	0	5	3	0	0
D	0	7	3	21	26
E	13	0	2	5	0

Figure 7.98. *Subtraction/addition operation*

Now, a solution with a zero in each row and column can be found. It can also be checked if there is another equivalent solution. This is shown in Figure 7.99.

	a	b	c	d	e
A	1	0	0	19	15
B	1	5	3	0	10
C	0	5	3	0	0
D	0	7	3	21	26
E	13	0	2	5	0

Figure 7.99. *Solution obtained*

The total cost of this solution is $C = 5 + 13 + 21 + 9 + 17 = 65$.

The Hungarian algorithm can also be applied to assignment problems with *maximum cost*. To show how the maximization problem can be converted into a minimization problem, let us return to the linear program. Clearly, the following holds:

$$\max(z) = -\min(-z),$$

where z is the objective function of the maximization problem and $-z$ is the equivalent objective function of the minimization problem. By taking the opposite of the costs in the distance table, the maximization problem can be reformulated as an equivalent minimization problem. The objective function can then be rewritten as follows:

$$\max \mathbf{z} = \sum_{i=1}^{n}\sum_{j=1}^{n} c_{ij}x_{ij} \quad \Leftrightarrow \quad \min z' = -z = -\sum_{i=1}^{n}\sum_{j=1}^{n} c_{ij}x_{ij}$$

It is also true that $\min z'$ is equivalent to $\min(z' + C)$, where C is a positive constant.

Let M be the largest element of c_{ij}. Then,

$$\sum_{i=1}^{n}\sum_{j=1}^{n} Mx_{ij} = M\sum_{i=1}^{n}(\sum_{j=1}^{n} x_{ij}) = Mn \quad \text{and thus} \quad \sum_{j=1}^{n} x_{ij} = 1$$

Choose $C = Mn$. The problem now becomes minimizing:

$$z' + C = -\sum_{i=1}^{n}\sum_{j=1}^{n} c_{ij}x_{ij} + Mn = \sum_{i=1}^{n}\sum_{j=1}^{n}(M - c_{ij})x_{ij}$$

Simply apply the Hungarian algorithm to the table $M - c_{ij}$.

EXAMPLE 7.15.– Take array 7.90 from Example 7.14, assuming the goal is finding a cost-maximizing assignment. The largest element in the initial array is 32.

To reformulate the problem as a minimization problem, perform the transformation $M - c_{ij}$ on each element of the table, as shown in Figure 7.100.

	a	b	c	d	e
A	22	20	11	2	7
B	24	17	10	23	14
C	16	8	1	14	15
D	27	17	12	4	0
E	9	19	8	15	21

Figure 7.100. *Transformation $M - c_{ij}$*

Continue by subtracting the smallest element in each row from all the elements in that row, as shown in Figure 7.101.

	a	b	c	d	e
A	20	18	9	0	5
B	14	7	0	13	4
C	15	7	0	13	14
D	27	17	12	4	0
E	1	11	0	7	13

Figure 7.101. *Subtracting the smallest element from each line*

Similarly, continue by subtracting the smallest element in each column from all the elements in that column, as shown in Figure 7.102.

	a	b	c	d	e
A	19	11	9	0	5
B	13	0	0	13	4
C	14	0	0	13	14
D	26	10	12	4	0
E	0	4	0	7	13

Figure 7.102. *Subtracting the smallest element in each column*

Now, choose from the unmarked elements, as shown in Figure 7.103.

	a	b	c	d	e
A	19	11	9	[0]	5
B	13	~~0~~	[0]	13	4
C	14	[0]	~~0~~	13	14
D	26	10	12	4	[0]
E	[0]	4	~~0~~	7	13

Figure 7.103. *Choice of assignment. For a color version of this figure, see www.iste.co.uk/cochard/mathematics3.zip*

This time, a solution with a zero in every row and column has been found. Therefore, there is no need to continue the algorithm (no row marking is possible), as the optimal solution has been found. It can be checked that there is another equivalent solution.

Hence, the total cost of this solution is $C = 23 + 24 + 22 + 30 + 32 = 131$.

8

Scheduling Problems

CONCEPTS COVERED IN THIS CHAPTER.–

Scheduling problems involve finding the best solution for organizing different tasks over time, considering constraints between tasks. This chapter discusses two types of problems: project planning and workshop scheduling.

Section 8.1 covers project planning, introducing a general resolution method called the earliest and latest dates method. It also explains the concept of PERT graphs, MPM graphs and Gantt charts.

For workshop scheduling, two standard problems are addressed: the flow-shop and the job-shop. For the flow-shop problem, where the tasks of different jobs follow the same order on the shop floor machines, Johnson's algorithm is detailed. In the job-shop problem, where the tasks are not executed in the same order, the solution is more complex. An example is provided to illustrate how to solve the problem using the earliest and latest dates method.

References: [BRO 82, DER 16, ESQ 99, FAU 14, HIL 17, PHE 75].

Mathematics for Digital Science 3,
by Gérard-Michel COCHARD and Mhand HIFI. © ISTE Ltd 2025.

8.1. Planning a project

8.1.1. *Introduction*

A project is a collection of interdependent activities that lead to specific results. Project planning involves organizing operations with respect to deadlines and resources.

Initially, it is important to assess the scope of the project in terms of workload and duration. Next, optimizing the sequence of tasks allows for a schedule to be established for executing operations. Throughout the project's development, regular progress checks must be conducted, with adjustments made to the schedule as needed.

In the late 1950s, methods were developed to tackle task scheduling problems, aiming to reduce project duration and costs. Two main methods emerged:

– The American CPM method (Critical Path Method), along with its better-known variant, PERT (Program Evaluation and Review Technique), which accounts for randomness in task durations.

– The French MPM method (*Méthode des Potentiels Métra*), also referred to as the potential method.

The MPM method closely resembles to PERT, with the primary distinction being their graphical representations. In PERT, events, such as the completion of a task, are represented by vertices, while tasks themselves are represented by edges (see Figure 8.1). In contrast, the MPM method constructs the graph differently: each vertex represents a specific task, and an edge signifies a dependency or constraint between tasks (see Figure 8.2).

Figure 8.1. *PERT formalism*

Figure 8.2. *MPM formalism*

The MPM representation is adopted in the remainder of this discussion. In this method, links between tasks can take various forms:

– *End→ Start*: the next task can only begin once the previous task has been completed.

– *End→ End*: the next task ends at the same time as the previous task.

– *Start→ Start*: the start of the previous task triggers the start of the next task.

– *Start→ End*: the start of the previous task marks the end of the next task.

Links between tasks may also include numerical values, known as valuated links, to indicate specific deadlines or constraints (see Figure 8.3).

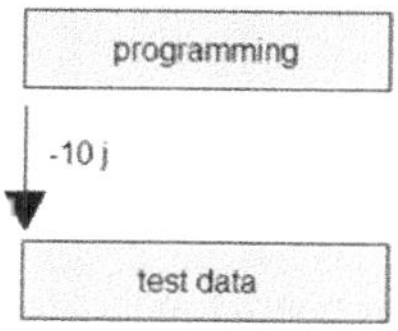

Figure 8.3. *An example of a validated link*

Figure 8.3 shows that test set production begins 10 days before programming. This represents *Start → Start constraint*, with a negative value on the link, indicating that test sets production must start 10 days prior to the start of programming.

In an MPM graph, of the *critical path* is the path that connects *critical tasks* – those whose delay would directly affect the project's overall duration. Critical tasks play an essential role in project management, as their timely completion is essential to maintaining the project schedule.

The constraints in scheduling problems can generally be classified into three categories.

– *Potential constraints*: these constraints relate to the start dates of tasks. If t_i represents the start date of task i of duration d_i, then:

$$t_i \geq d_i,$$

assuming 0 is the universal starting point (date). In addition, if task j is to be performed after task i, which has a duration of d_i, then:

$$t_j \geq t_i + d_i.$$

This type of constraint, which enforces the order of task execution (between tasks), is referred to as *succession constraint*.

– *Disjunctive (or non-overlapping) constraints*: these constraints concern the execution periods of two tasks that must not overlap. For instance, this applies when a machine can only handle one task at a time. If task i occupies the time interval $I_i = [t_i, t_i + d_i]$, and task j occupies the interval $I_j = [t_j, t_j + d_j]$, the disjunctive constraint requires that:

$$I_i \cap I_j = \emptyset ,$$

which translates into two mutually exclusive inequalities:

– $t_j \geq t_i + d_i$ (task j starts after task i) or

– $t_i \geq t_j + d_j$ (task i starts after task j).

This situation can be expressed more formally using the following relationships:

$$(W + d_i)y_{ij} + t_i - t_j \geq d_j$$

$$(W + d_j)(1 - y_{ij}) + t_j - t_i \geq d_i$$

where $y_{ij} = 1$ if i precedes j, and $y_{ij} = 0$ if j precedes i. W is an arbitrarily large number.

Indeed, if task i precedes task j, then $y_{ij} = 1$, and the second relationship becomes:

$$t_j \geq t_i + d_i ,$$

expressing that task j starts after task i. In this case, the first relationship is also verified:

$$W + d_i + t_i \geq t_j + d_j \geq t_i + d_i + d_j,$$

which simplifies $W \geq d_j$. This inequality is always valid for a sufficiently large W.

Conversely, if task j precedes task i, then $y_{ij} = 0$, and the first relationship becomes:

$$t_i \geq t_j + d_j,$$

indicating that task i starts after task j . The second relationship is verified as well:

$$W + d_j + t_j \geq t_i + d_i \geq t_j + d_j + d_i,$$

which simplifies to $W \geq d_i$, a condition that is also valid for a sufficiently large W.

– *Cumulative constraints*: these constraints relate the use of limited resources such as human, material or financial resources. They are particularly complex to model and account for, as they require simultaneous management of overall resource capacities and task durations.

8.1.2. *Earliest and latest date method*

The following parameters are used to determine the critical path in a project:

– Earliest possible dates: *start* (D_{+early}) and *finish* (F_{+early}).

– Latest possible dates: *start* (D_{+late}) and *end* (F_{+late}).

– Margin (slack): (D_{+late}) - (D_{+early}) = (F_{+late}) - (F_{+early}).

Basic assumption: It is assumed that all task dependencies are of the end⟶ start type. Under this assumption, the *critical path* is the longest path through the task graph, representing the minimum possible duration of the entire project.

Cases studied

First case (task T_i at the start of the project): Let T_i have a duration of d_i and be the first task in the project (see Figure 8.4):

– *Earliest start:* $D_{+early}(T_i) = t_0$

– *Latest start:* $F{+}early(Ti) = t_0 + d_i$

Second case (task T_i at the end of the project): Let task T_i have a duration of d_i and be the last task in the project (see Figure 8.5):

– *Latest finish:* $F_{+late}(T_i) = t_f$

– *Latest start:* $D_{+late}(T_i) = t_f - d_i$

Third case (task T_i inside the project): Let task T_i have a duration d_i and be located between other tasks within the project (see Figure 8.6):

– *Earliest start:* $D_{+early}(Ti) = \sup\{F_{+early}(predecessors)\}$

– *Earliest scheduled finish:* $F_{+early}(T_i) = D_{+early}(T_i) + d_i$

– *Latest finish:* $F_{+late}(T_i) = \inf\{D_{+late}(successors)\}$

– *Start no later than:* $D_{+late}(T_i) = F_{+late}(T_i) - d_i$

By applying the three sets of rules corresponding to the previously described cases, the *critical path* of a project can be determined. The procedure consists of the following steps:

1) Determining earliest dates: starting from the initial tasks, the earliest start and finish dates are calculated for each task in the project.

2) Determining the latest dates: starting from the termina tasks, the latest start and finish dates are calculated for each task in the project.

3) Margin (slick) calculation: for each task, the margin is determined by subtracting the earliest date from the latest date.

4) Identifying the critical path: the critical path consists of tasks with a *zero margin*, meaning any delay in these tasks would result in a delay to the overall project.

Following this method allows for the critical path to be identified, highlighting the most time-sensitive tasks. These tasks require particular attention to ensure the project stays on schedule.

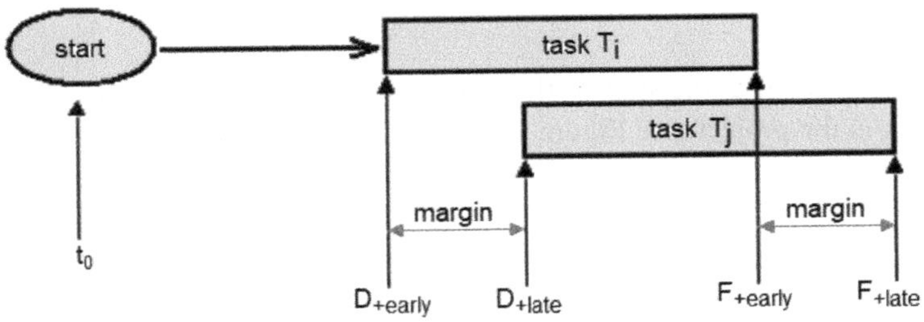

Figure 8.4. *Task at the start of the project. For a color version of this figure, see www.iste.co.uk/cochard/mathematics3.zip*

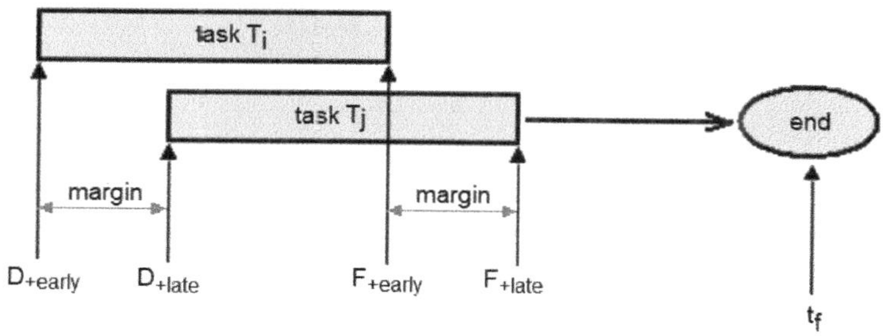

Figure 8.5. *Task at the end of the project. For a color version of this figure, see www.iste.co.uk/cochard/mathematics3.zip*

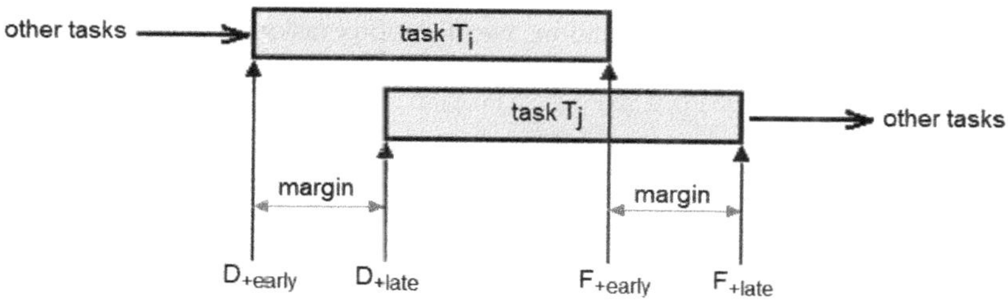

Figure 8.6. *Internal task. For a color version of this figure, see www.iste.co.uk/cochard/mathematics3.zip*

EXAMPLE 8.1.– Consider a project composed of the tasks presented in the table in Figure 8.7. This table details on the various tasks, their respective durations and the dependencies between them.

The MPM graph representing this project is shown in Figure 8.8.

task	duration	predecessors	successors
A	4		C
B	7		C, D
C	2	A, B	E, F
D	12	B	F
E	3	C	
F	6	C,D	G
G	2	F	

Figure 8.7. *Task list and timeline*

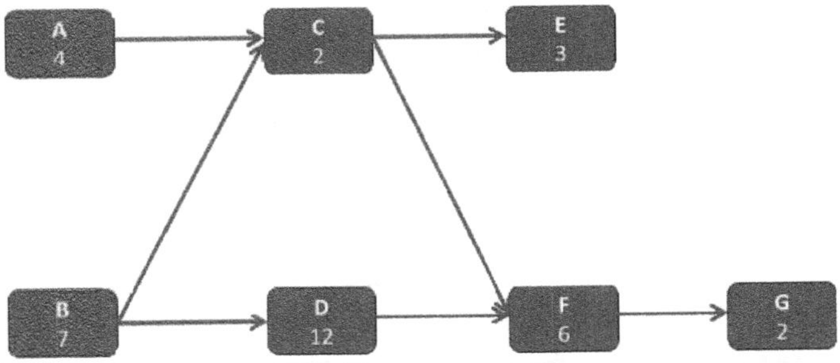

Figure 8.8. *MPM graph. For a color version of this figure, see www.iste.co.uk/cochard/mathematics3.zip*

To complete the project representation, two fictitious tasks are added: a *start task* and an *end task*, both with a duration of 0 (see Figure 8.9).

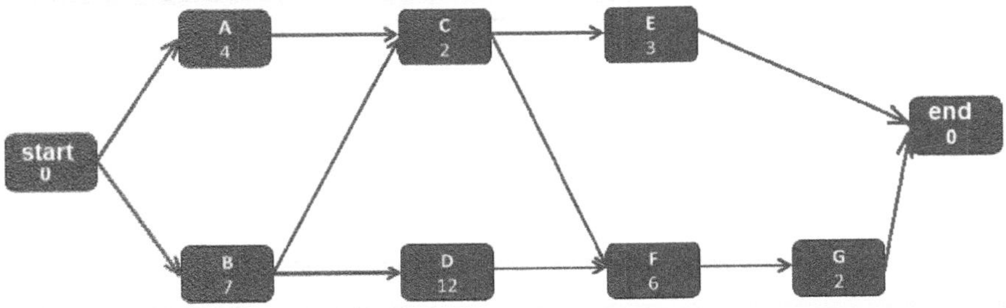

Figure 8.9. *Adding start and end tasks. For a color version of this figure, see www.iste.co.uk/cochard/mathematics3.zip*

The *earliest date method* is now applied to the project, as shown in Figure 8.10.

Note that when a task has multiple predecessors, its *earlier start date* is determined by the *largest finish date* of its predecessors' end dates.

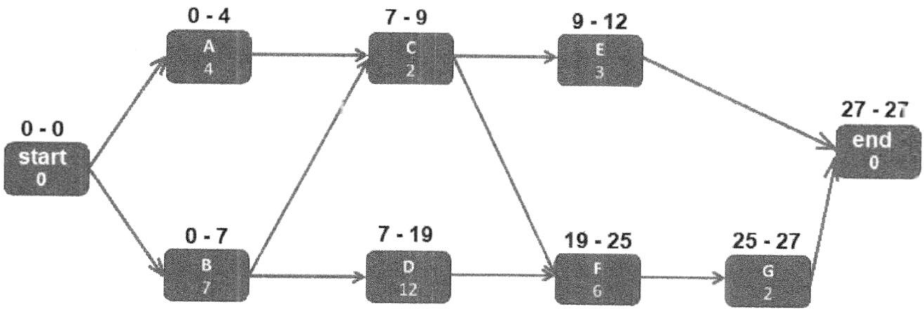

Figure 8.10. *Earliest dates. For a color version of this figure, see www.iste.co.uk/cochard/mathematics3.zip*

Let us move on to the application of the latest date method, by traversing the graph in the opposite direction from the end task (see Figure 8.11).

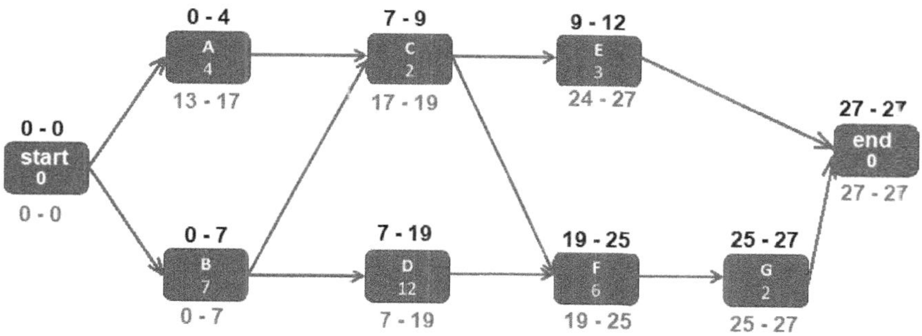

Figure 8.11. *Latest dates. For a color version of this figure, see www.iste co.uk/cochard/mathematics3.zip*

Note that when a task has multiple successors, its latest finish date is determined by the earliest (smallest) start date among its successors. Once the earliest and latest dates have been calculated for each task, the margins can be determined by calculating the difference between the latest and earliest dates for each task (see Figure 8.12).

The critical path of the project is defined as the set of tasks that have a zero margin. The critical path is highlighted in Figure 8.13, showing the sequence of tasks that must be completed on time to ensure the project is finished by its scheduled deadline.

By analyzing the *critical path* (the tasks in red) and considering the durations of the various tasks, it can be concluded that the total duration of the project will be 27 days, assuming that the necessary resources are available and the tasks are executed as scheduled without any delays.

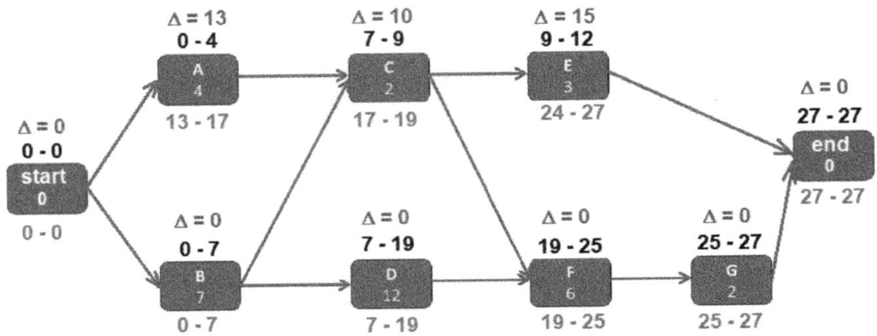

Figure 8.12. *Margin calculation. For a color version of this figure, see www.iste.co.uk/cochard/mathematics3.zip*

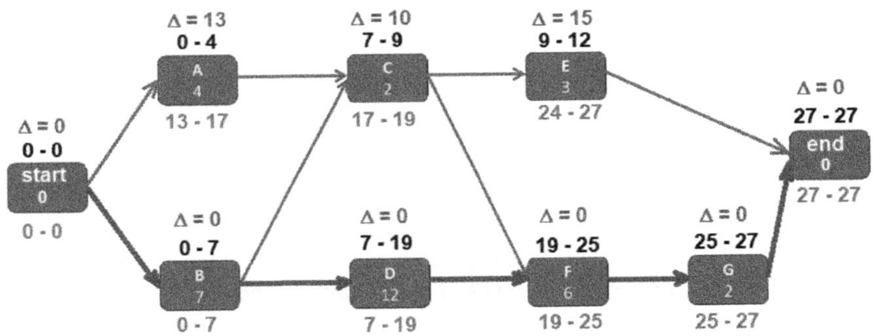

Figure 8.13. *Critical path. For a color version of this figure, see www.iste.co.uk/cochard/mathematics3.zip*

The critical path represents the backbone of the project, while the non-critical tasks provide flexibility for adjusting the schedule. This sequence of tasks determines the minimum time required to complete the project. Any subsequent changes to the project schedule should focus primarily on tasks that are not part of the critical path.

8.1.3. *Gantt chart*

From the task graph, a *Gantt chart* can be constructed to represent the project's schedule of operations. In Example 8.1, assume two interchangeable resources, R1 and R2, capable of performing the various project tasks. Figure 8.14 shows a proposed schedule, with the critical path highlighted in red.

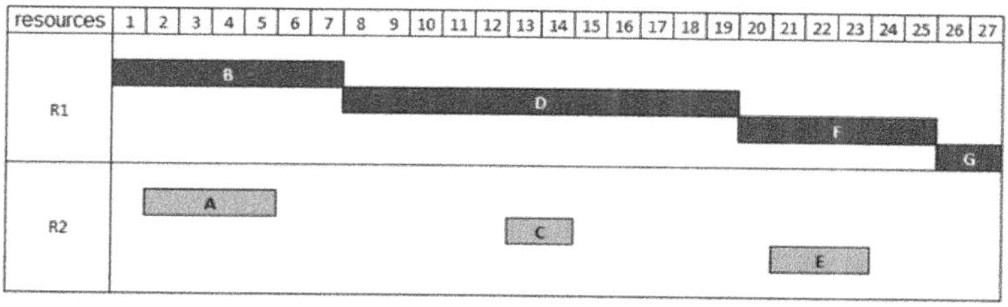

Figure 8.14. *Gantt chart. For a color version of this figure, see www.iste.co.uk/cochard/mathematics3.zip*

In the schedule proposed in Figure 8.14, resource R1 is assigned to critical path tasks, while resource R2 is allocated to non-critical tasks. This allocation ensures that critical tasks are given priority and completed within the set deadlines. It should be noted that the use of two resources is sufficient, as there are at most only two tasks running in parallel at any given time, as long as the critical path is respected.

Figure 8.15 shows a schedule based on "earliest possible" dates, where each task is started as soon as all its predecessor tasks have been completed.

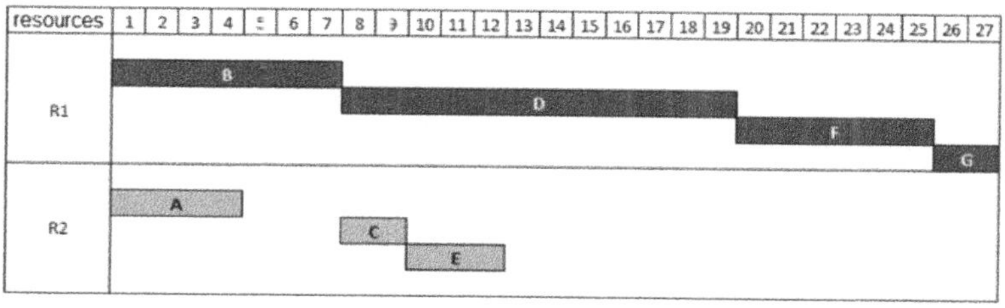

Figure 8.15. *Early planning. For a color version of this figure, see www.iste.co.uk/cochard/mathematics3.zip*

Figure 8.16 shows "at the latest" planning, where each task is scheduled as late as possible without delaying the overall project.

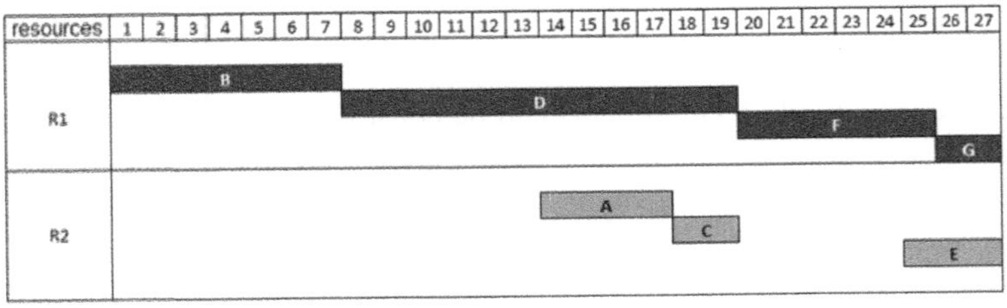

Figure 8.16. *Latest planning. For a color version of this figure, see www.iste.co.uk/cochard/mathematics3.zip*

If only one resource is available, the total duration of the project will increase. This is because a single resource cannot perform multiple tasks simultaneously. Figure 8.17 presents an example of scheduling based on the use of a single resource. The Gantt chart in this figure shows the sequence of task execution, considering both dependency constraints and the limited availability of the single resource.

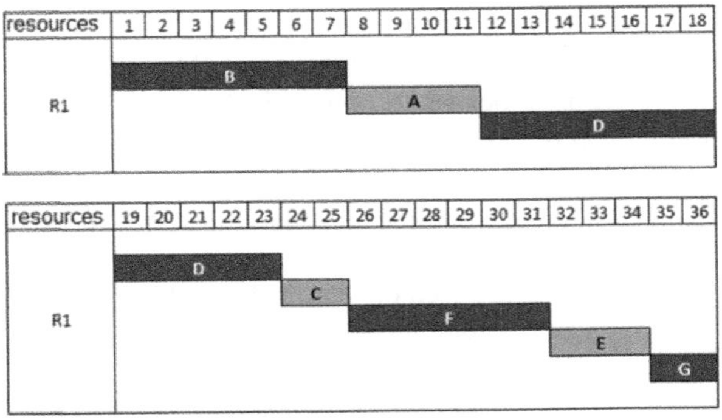

Figure 8.17. *Case of a single resource. For a color version of this figure, see www.iste.co.uk/cochard/mathematics3.zip*

Two techniques commonly used to optimize the Gantt chart are resource leveling and workload smoothing:

– Resource leveling aims to limit the number of resources used in the project, which can sometimes result in an increase in the overall project duration. This approach is often used when resources are limited or when reducing costs is a priority (see Figure 8.17).

– Workload smoothing focuses on balancing the workload across resources to avoid peaks in activity or overloading a specific resource. This results in a smoother workload and better utilization of available resources. For example, if resource R2 works half-time and resource R1 works full-time, workload smoothing can distribute tasks more evenly between the two. This results in a smoother workload and better utilization of available resources. Figure 8.18 presents a Gantt chart, showing this balanced workload distribution.

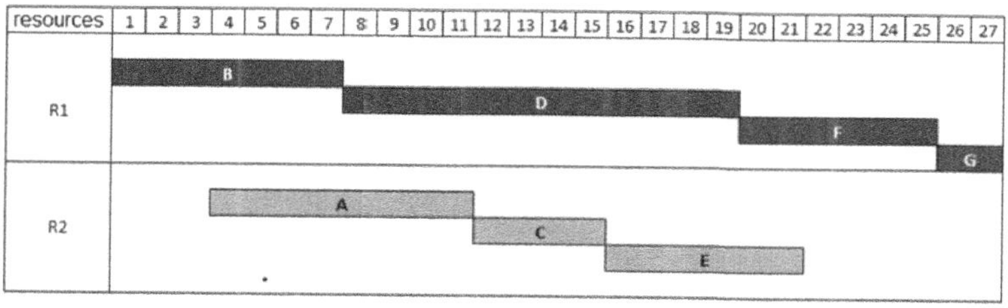

Figure 8.18. *Workload smoothing. For a color version of this figure, see www.iste.co.uk/cochard/mathematics3.zip*

8.2. Flow-shop problem

In this and the following sections, the focus is on the scheduling of a workshop equipped with machines used to manufacture products or objects. Generally, several types of objects are produced, denoted as n different objects. Each object requires machines in a specific sequence, and not all objects necessarily pass through every machine. The use of a machine for processing an object represents the execution of a task.

Flow-shop is a production system where the sequence of machines used for each object is predefined. That is, if an object requires p tasks (involving p machines), these tasks must be executed in a fixed order. The primary objective in the flow-shop setting is to determine the optimal sequence for processing the objects, typically with the goal of minimizing the total production time.

Consider the case involving two machines, M_1 and M_2, used to manufacture n objects. This situation represents the production of n objects requiring successive processing on machines M_1 and M_2, always in the same order. The processing times for each object on both machines are predefined. The objective is to find the optimal sequence for executing tasks that minimizes the total processing time. In other words, the goal is to establish a schedule that optimizes machine utilization and reduces idle and waiting times.

EXAMPLE 8.2.– Consider the table shown in Figure 8.19, which presents the production times of six objects (P_1 to P_6) on two machines (M_1 and M_2).

In this context, each object must first be processed on machine M_1 and then on machine M_2. The order of processing on the machines follows an FIFO (first-in, first-out) principle, meaning that once an object starts processing on M_1, it must later be processed on M_2 in the same sequence. Doubling up is not allowed, meaning an object cannot return to the same machine or be processed on M_1 or M_2 more than once.

	P1	P2	P3	P4	P5	P6
M1	2	2	8	6	6	6
M2	6	6	2	2	6	3

Figure 8.19. *Time taken for each object to pass through each machine*

Consider the following order of objects: P_1, P_2, P_3, P_4, P_5 and P_6. This particular arrangement represents one out of 720 possible sequences, as there are 6! (the factorial of 6) possible permutations for the objects. Figure 8.20 shows the Gantt chart corresponding to this sequence of objects.

machines	1	2	3	4	5	6	7	8	9	10	11	12	13	14	15	16	17	18
M1	P1		P2		P3								P4					
M2			P1						P2						P3			

machines	19	20	21	22	23	24	25	26	27	28	29	30	31	32	33
M1	P5						P6								
M2	P4						P5						P6		

Figure 8.20. *Gantt chart*

Question: Is it possible to find a different permutation of objects that results in a total task execution time less than $T = 33$?

Johnson's algorithm is a specialized method for solving the two-machine flow-shop scheduling problem. It determines the optimal sequence of objects to be processed on machines M_1 and M_2, aiming to minimize the overall completion time of all tasks.

8.2.1. *Johnson's algorithm for two machines*

Johnson's algorithm for the two-machine flow-shop scheduling problem involves the following steps:

1) Create a list of all tasks, specifying the processing times for each task on the first machine (M_1) and the second machine (M_2).

2) Identify the task with the shortest processing time (t_i), considering the times spent on both M_1 and M_2.

3) If t_i corresponds to a time on M_1, place the task P_i as early as possible in the sequence.

4) If t_i corresponds to a time on M_2, place the task P_i as late as possible in the sequence.

5) Repeat steps 2 to 4 until all tasks are scheduled.

Once all tasks are arranged according to Johnson's algorithm, the resulting sequence represents the optimal sequence in which the tasks should pass through machines M_1 and M_2. This sequence minimizes the total task execution time, ensuring efficient utilization of both machines and reducing idle times.

EXAMPLE 8.3.– Returning to Example 8.2 to illustrate the application of Johnson's algorithm. Consider the task execution times presented in Figure 8.19. The goal is to identify the smallest processing time among the times spent on M_1 and M_2.

The smallest time is 2, which appears four times. Selecting P_1 first, as its processing time of 2 corresponds to M_1, P_1 is placed at the head of the queue. The queue is now:

$$(P_1, x, x, x, x, x).$$

Next, P_2 also has a processing time of 2 on M_1, so it is placed behind P_1 in the queue. The queue is now:

$$(P_1, P_2, x, x, x, x).$$

P_3 has a processing time of 2 on M_2, so it is placed at the end of the queue:

$$(P_1, P_2, x, x, x, P_3).$$

P_4 also has a processing time of 2 on M_2, so it is placed before P_3 in the queue:

$$(P_1, P_2, x, x, P_4, P_3).$$

P_6 has a processing time of 3 on M_2, so it is placed before P_4 in the queue:

$$(P_1, P_2, x, P_6, P_4, P_3).$$

Finally, P_5 is placed in the last remaining place in the queue: $(P_1, P_2, P_5, P_6, P_4, P_3)$.

The optimal sequence for objects to pass through the M_1 and M_2 machines is:

$$P_1, P_2, P_5, P_6, P_4, P_3.$$

This order corresponds to the Gantt chart in Figure 8.21, which represents task scheduling in the two-machine flow-shop problem.

However, due to the redundancy of the processing time value 2, there are three other possible permutations that yield the same total duration:

$$P_1, P_2, P_5, P_6, P_3, P_4$$

$$P_2, P_1, P_5, P_6, P_4, P_3$$

$$P_2, P_1, P_5, P_6, P_3, P_4$$

<table>
<tr><td>machines</td><td>1</td><td>2</td><td>3</td><td>4</td><td>5</td><td>6</td><td>7</td><td>8</td><td>9</td><td>10</td><td>11</td><td>12</td><td>13</td><td>14</td><td>15</td><td>16</td></tr>
<tr><td>M1</td><td colspan="2">P1</td><td colspan="2">P2</td><td colspan="6">P5</td><td colspan="6">P6</td></tr>
<tr><td>M2</td><td colspan="2"></td><td colspan="6">P1</td><td colspan="6">P2</td><td colspan="2">P5</td></tr>
</table>

<table>
<tr><td>machines</td><td>17</td><td>18</td><td>19</td><td>20</td><td>21</td><td>22</td><td>23</td><td>24</td><td>25</td><td>26</td><td>27</td><td>28</td><td>29</td><td>30</td><td>31</td><td>32</td></tr>
<tr><td>M1</td><td colspan="6">P4</td><td colspan="8">P3</td><td colspan="2"></td></tr>
<tr><td>M2</td><td colspan="4">P5</td><td colspan="3">P6</td><td colspan="2">P4</td><td colspan="5"></td><td colspan="2">P3</td></tr>
</table>

Figure 8.21. *An optimal solution*

All these permutations result in a total task execution time equal to 32.

This is because P_1 and P_2 have identical processing times (2) on M_1, allowing these two tasks to be swapped without impacting the overall duration.

The proof of Johnson's algorithm for two machines is as follows.

Returning to the example with the sequence $P_1, P_2, P_3, P_4, P_5, P_6$, a few notations are introduced: the idle times $X_1 = 2, X_2 = 0, X_3 = 2, X_4 = 4, X_5 = 0$, and $X_6 = 0$. The total execution time is the sum of the times spent on M_2 and the idle times:

$$T = \sum_{i=1}^{n} t_{2i} + \sum_{i=1}^{n} X_i$$

where the index 2 of t_{2i} indicates the time taken for the object P_i to be processed on machine M_2.

To minimize T, the second term in the expression must be minimized, i.e. the dead times X_i, given that t_{2i} are fixed. For example, for $X_2 = 0$, where generally, $X_2 = t_{11} + t_{12} - t_{21} - X_1$. Then, the following expression holds:

$$X_2 = \max(t_{11} + t_{12} - t_{21} - X_1; 0)$$

This generalizes to:

$$X_2 = \max\left(\sum_{i=1}^{2} t_{1i} - \sum_{i=1}^{1} t_{2i} - \sum_{i=1}^{1} X_i\,; 0\right)$$

Now, the sum $X_1 + X_2$ becomes:

$$X_1 + X_2 = \max\left(\sum_{i=1}^{2} t_{1i} - \sum_{i=1}^{1} t_{2i}\,; X_1\right)$$

Similarly, for $X_1 + X_2 + X_3$, the expression is:

$$X_1 + X_2 + X_3 = \max\left(\sum_{i=1}^{3} t_{1i} - \sum_{i=1}^{2} t_{2i}\,;\ \sum_{i=1}^{2} t_{1i} - t_{21}\,; X_1\right)$$

Generalizing to the sum of all X_i, for a permutation p of P_i, the total is:

$$\Sigma_n(p) \equiv \sum_{i1}^{n} X_i = \max(\sum_{i=1}^{n} t_{1i} - \sum_{i=1}^{n-1} t_{2i}\,;\ \sum_{i=1}^{n-1} t_{1i} - \sum_{i=1}^{n-1} t_{2i}\ ; \ldots;\ t_{11})$$
$$= \max_{1 \le r \le n}\left(\sum_{i=1}^{r} t_{1i} - \sum_{i=1}^{r-1} t_{2i}\right)$$

Define:

$$L_r(p) = \sum_{i=1}^{r} t_{1i} - \sum_{i=1}^{r-1} t_{2i}$$

Thus, the total becomes:

$$\Sigma_n(p) = \max_{1 \le r \le n} L_r\,(p)$$

Now, consider two permutations p and p' that differ only in the exchange of P_k and P_{k+1}:

For permutation p: $P_1, P_2, \ldots, P_k, P_{k+1}, \ldots, P_n$

For permutation p': $P_1, P_2, \ldots, P_{k+1}, P_k, \ldots, P_n$

If

$$\max(L_k(p), L_{k+1}(p)) = \max(L_k(p'), L_{k+1}(p'))$$

then

$$\sum_n (p) = \sum_n (p')$$

Otherwise, one permutation is better than the other. Specifically, if:

$$\max\big(L_k(p), L_{k+1}(p)\big) < \max\big(L_k(p'), L_{k+1}(p')\big) \quad \text{[C]}$$

then permutation p is better than permutation p'.

Next, define $\max\big(L_k(p);\ L_{k+1}(p)\big)$:

$$\max\big(L_k(p);\ L_{k+1}(p)\big) = \max\left(\sum_{i=1}^{k} t_{1i} - \sum_{i=1}^{k-1} t_{2i}\ ;\ \sum_{i=1}^{k+1} t_{1i} - \sum_{i=1}^{k} t_{2i}\right).$$

For p':

$$\max\big(L_k(p');\ L_{k+1}(p')\big) = \max$$

$$\left(\sum_{i=1}^{k-1} t_{1i} + t_{1,k+1} - \sum_{i=1}^{k-1} t_{2i}\ ;\ \sum_{i=1}^{k+1} t_{1i} - \sum_{i=1}^{k-1} t_{2i} - t_{2,k+1}\right)$$

These two expressions lead to:

$$\sum_{i=1}^{k-1} t_{2i} - \sum_{i=1}^{k+1} t_{1i} + \max\big(L_k(p);\ L_{k+1}(p)\big) = \max(-t_{1,k+1}\,;\ -t_{2k})$$
$$= -\min(t_{1,k+1};\ t_{2k})$$

Similarly,

$$\sum_{i=1}^{k-1} t_{2i} - \sum_{i=1}^{k+1} t_{1i} + \max\big(L_k(p');\ L_{k+1}(\mathrm{p}')\big) = \max(-t_{1,k}\,;\ -t_{2,k+1})$$
$$= -\min(t_{1,k};\ t_{2,k+1})$$

Condition [C] becomes:

$$\min\big(t_{1,k};\ t_{2,k+1}\big) < min(t_{1,k+1};\ t_{2,k})$$

If a permutation p'' is formed by successive swaps such that P_kP_i, the order P_kP_i does not need to change if:

$$\min\big(t_{1,k};\ t_{2,i}\big) \le \min\big(t_{1,i};\ t_{2,k}\big) \qquad [\mathrm{C}']$$

This condition [C′] holds if $t_{1,k} \le t_{2,i}, t_{1,i}\ t_{2,k}$, implying:

$$\min\big(t_{1,k};\ t_{2,k}\big) \le \min(t_{1,i};\ t_{2,i}).$$

This means that if $t_{1,k}$ is less than or equal to all the others in the processing times, the order of the sought permutation *should end with* P_i.

Condition [C′] also states that if $t_{2,i}$ is less than or equal to $t_{1,k}$, $t_{1,i}$, $t_{2,k}$, then:

$$\min\big(t_{1,i};\ t_{2,i}\big) \le \min(t_{1,k};\ t_{2k}).$$

This means that if a time $t_{2,i}$ is less than or equal to all the others is found in the processing times, the order of the sought permutation *must end with* P_k.

8.2.2. *Case of three machines*

The case of two machines is easily solved with Johnson's algorithm. Now, let us consider the case of three machines, M_1, M_2 and M_3, used in that order. It can be shown that Johnson's algorithm can still be applied in a specific case, namely when:

$$\min(t_{1,i}) \geq \max(t_{2,i}) \quad \text{or} \quad \min(t_{3,i}) \geq \max(t_{2,i}).$$

In this case, two fictitious machines M_1+M_2 and M_2+M_3, can be defined. This reduces the problem to a two machines flow-shop problem, where Johnson's algorithm can then be applied.

EXAMPLE 8.4.– Consider the table showing the processing times on the three machines M_1, M_2 and M_3 for five objects (P_1, P_2, P_3, P_4 and P_5), as presented in Figure 8.22.

	P1	P2	P3	P4	P5
M1	4	6	8	3	6
M2	2	1	3	2	4
M3	6	5	7	5	8

Figure 8.22. *Manufacturing time*

Observe that $\min(t_{1,i}) = 3$ and $\max(t_{2,i}) = 4$, so the condition $\min(t_{1,i}) \geq \max(t_{2,i})$ is not satisfied. However, $\min(t_{3,i}) = 5$, and the condition $\min(t_{3,i}) \geq \max(t_{2,i})$, is satisfied.

Machines can therefore be grouped into two fictitious machines: M_1+M_2 and M_2+M_3, as shown in Figure 8.23.

	P1	P2	P3	P4	P5
M1+M2	6	7	11	5	10
M2+M3	8	6	10	7	12

Figure 8.23. *Grouping into two fictitious machines*

Looking at the table of running times on the three machines, the smallest value is 5. Therefore, P_4 is chosen as the first task in the sequence, giving (P_4 x x x x x). Next, the smallest remaining value is 6, which appears twice, corresponding to either P_1 or P_2. This results in two possible sequences: (P_4 P_1 x x x) or (P_4 x x x P_2).

For the first sequence, the smallest remaining value is 6, corresponding to P_2, leading to (P_4 P_1 x x P_2). For the second sequence, the smallest remaining value is also 6, but this time it corresponds to P_1, resulting in (P_4 P_1 x x P_2), which is identical to the first sequence. Continuing, the next smallest value is 10, corresponding to either P_3 or P_5. This leads to two further sequences: (P_4 P_1 x P_3 P_2) and (P_4 P_1 P_5 x P_2).

Finally, placing the remaining object results in the final sequence: (P_4 P_1 P_5 P_3 P_2).

In this particular example, the solution is unique. However, in other cases, multiple sequences may result in the same total execution time. The Gantt chart corresponding to this solution is shown in Figure 8.24.

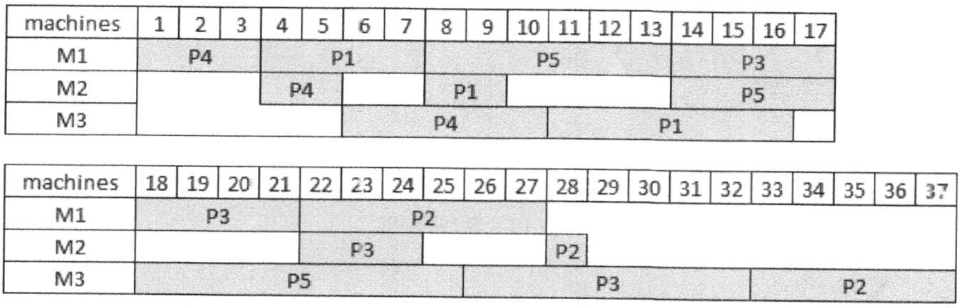

Figure 8.24. *An optimal solution*

For the three-machine case, apart from the special condition discussed earlier, Johnson's algorithm is no longer directly applicable or becomes increasingly complex to implement. In such situations, other approaches must be used to solve the flow-shop scheduling problem. These approaches include linear programming techniques or specific heuristic algorithms such as the NEH algorithm (proposed by Nawaz, Enscore and Ham) and the CDS algorithm (developed by Campbell, Dudek and Smith).

The flow-shop scheduling problem using linear programming can be formulated as follows:

Let $I = \{1, 2, \ldots, n\}$ represent the set of jobs, and $J = \{1, 2, \ldots, m\}$ represent the set of machines. Let d_{ij} represent the processing time required for job i on machine j. Between machines, a job may experience waiting time.

Jobs are scheduled in positions $k = 1$ to n according to the processing.

The decision variables are as follows:

– $x_{ik} = 1$ if job i is assigned to position k in the sequence, 0 otherwise.

– $\tau_{jk} \geq 0$: idle time of machine j between the completion of the kth and (k+1)th jobs.

– $w_{kj} \geq 0$: waiting time of the kth job before machine $j + 1$.

The objective function is to minimize the time from the start of the first job on the first machine to the completion of the last job on the last machine:

$$z = \sum_{j=1}^{m-1} \sum_{i=1}^{n} d_{ij} x_{i1} + \sum_{k=1}^{n-1} \tau_{mk}$$

The constraints are as follows:

1) Each job is assigned to exactly one position:

$$\sum_{i \in I} x_{ik} = 1 \quad \forall k \in J \quad [C1]$$

2) Each position is occupied by exactly one job:

$$\sum_{k \in J} x_{ik} = 1 \quad \forall i \in I \quad [C2]$$

3) Compatibility of waiting times, idle periods and processing times:

$$w_{kj} + \sum_{i \in I} d_{i,j+1} x_{ik} + \tau_{j+1,k} = \tau_{jk} + \sum_{i \in I} d_{ij} x_{i,k+1} + w_{k+1,j}$$

$$\forall j \in \{1, \ldots, m-1\} \;\; \forall k \in \{1, \ldots, n-1\}, \qquad [C3]$$

4) The first job starts immediately on the first machine (no idle time):

$$\tau_{1k} = 0 \quad \forall k \in J \qquad [C4]$$

5) No waiting time before the first job on each machine:

$$w_{1j} = 0 \quad \forall j \in J \quad [C5]$$

The formulation is therefore as follows:

$$\text{Minimize} \quad z = \sum_{j=1}^{m-1} \sum_{i=1}^{n} d_{ij} x_{i1} + \sum_{k=1}^{n-1} \tau_{mk}$$

Subject to [C1] to [C5].

This formulation of the flow-shop problem requires some explanation, which is best understood through an example. Consider three jobs, J1, J2 and J3, and three machines, M1, M2 and M3. The processing times of the jobs on the machines are shown in the table in Figure 8.25.

	M1	M2	M3
J1	2	4	4
J2	3	5	3
J3	4	6	2

Figure 8.25. *Runtimes*

Figure 8.26 shows an example of a schedule to support the reasoning that follows.

The objective function to be minimized is the *makespan*, representing the time interval between the start of the first job on the first machine and the completion of the last job on the last machine. For the first job, the processing steps occur consecutively without idle time, but this is not the case for the subsequent jobs. In the solution depicted in Figure 8.26, the job sequence is 231, meaning that job J2 is processed first, followed by J3 and finally J1. In this configuration, $x_{21} = x_{32} = x_{13} = 1$, with all other values of x_{ik} equal to zero, as job J2 occupies in position 1, job J3 is in position 2 and job J1 in position 3.

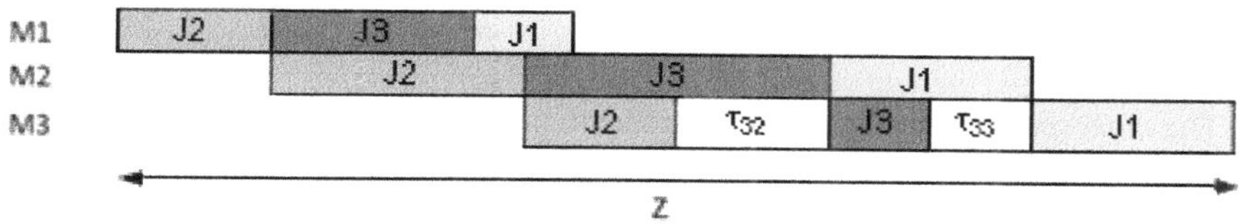

Figure 8.26. *Scheduling example*

The *makespan* z is calculated as the sum of the three components: the execution times of the first job on the first two machines, the execution times of all jobs on the last machine and the idle times on the last machine after the jobs have been processed.

For the example shown in Figure 8.26, the makespan can be expressed as:

$$z = (d_{21} + d_{22}) + (d_{23} + d_{33} + d_{13}) + (\tau_{32} + \tau_{33})$$

In this expression, the terms can be broken down as follows:

– The first term: $(d_{21} + d_{22})$ represents the execution times of the first job (J2) on machines M1 and M2. This also accounts for the idle time of machine M3 at the beginning of the scheduling process.

– The second term: $(d_{23} + d_{33} + d_{13})$ corresponds to the execution times of all jobs on machine M3.

– The last term: $(\tau_{32} + \tau_{33})$ represents the idle times of machine M3 after the first job has been completed and before the next job begins on this machine.

To generalize the expression of the makespan z, the following variable X_{kj} is introduced:

$$X_{kj} = \sum_{i \in I} d_{ij} x_{ik}$$

representing the total time the kth job has been running on machine j. This variable sums the execution times for each job i assigned to position k in the permutation, on machine j.

In the case of the solution shown in Figure 8.26, for example, the following holds:

$$X_{11} = d_{11}x_{11} + d_{21}x_{21} + d_{31}x_{31} = d_{21} \quad \text{and} \quad X_{12} = d_{22},\ X_{13} = d_{23}$$

The *makespan* z is the sum of the three components:

– Idle time before execution of the first job, T_1, on machine m (the last one).

– Execution times of all jobs on the last machine m, represented by a constant C.

– Idle time (of the last machine m) after execution of the first job on this machine, denoted as T_2.

Thus, the makespan can be written as:

$$z = z' + C$$

where $z' = T_1 + T_2$.

To minimize z, the focus is on minimizing z'. The total idle time T_1 of machine m before execution of the first job on this machine is given by:

$$T_1 = \sum_{j=1}^{m-1} X_{1j} = \sum_{j=1}^{m-1} \sum_{i=1}^{n} d_{ij} x_{i1}$$

This represents the total idle time on machine m from the start until the first job begins its execution. The total idle time T_2 after execution of the first job on machine m is:

$$T_2 = \sum_{k=1}^{n-1} \tau_{mk}$$

This term accounts for the idle time on the last machine after the first job has completed its execution.

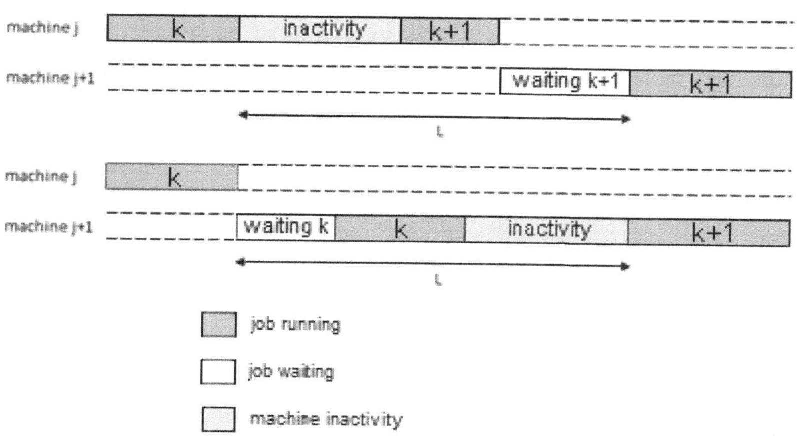

Figure 8.27. *Two ways of calculating L*

The objective function to be minimized is therefore the one proposed, since it corresponds to the sum $T_1 + T_2$. Relations [C1] and [C2] are easy to understand.

The relationship [C3] represents the time L between the end of the execution of job in rank k on machine j and the start of the execution of job in rank $(k + 1)$ on machine $(j + 1)$. There are two possible ways to compute L, as shown in Figure 8.27.

The job of rank $(k + 1)$ can be tracked. Before the job of rank $(k + 1)$ is executed on machine j, the machine has an inactivity period τ_{jk}. Then, the job of rank $(k + 1)$ is executed on machine j for $X_{k+1,j}$. This job waits for a duration $w_{k+1,j}$ before it can run on machine $(j + 1)$. This leads to the following expression for L:

$$L = \tau_{jk} + X_{k+1,j} + w_{k+1,j} = \tau_{jk} + \sum_{i\in I} d_{ij}x_{i,k+1} + w_{k+1,j}$$

Similarly, the job of rank k can be tracked. After execution on machine j, it waits for a duration $w_{k,j}$ before it can execute on machine $(j + 1)$. It then runs on this machine for $X_{k,j+1}$, followed by an idle time τ_{j+1k} on machine $(j + 1)$ before the job of rank $(k + 1)$ can be executed. The following expression for L is obtained:

$$L = w_{k,j} + X_{k,j+1} + \tau_{j+1,k} = w_{k,j} + \sum_{i\in I} d_{i,j+1}x_{ik} + \tau_{j+1,k}$$

By equalizing these two expressions for L, constraint [C3] is derived. Constraint [C4] indicates that executions on machine M_1 can be chained without waiting, and constraint [C5] indicates that the first job can pass through machines M_2 and M_3 without waiting.

EXAMPLE 8.5.– Let us take the case of the jobs in Figure 8.25 and apply the linear program defined above. The objective function to minimize is z', which is given as follows:

$$z' = d_{11}x_{11} + d_{21}x_{21} + d_{31}x_{31} + d_{12}x_{11} + d_{22}x_{21} + d_{32}x_{31} + \tau_{31} + \tau_{32}.$$

By grouping the terms associated with each job, this expression becomes:

$$z' = (d_{11} + d_{12})x_{11} + (d_{21} + d_{22})x_{21} + (d_{31} + d_{32})x_{31} + \tau_{31} + \tau_{32}.$$

The constraints of the linear program are as follows:

$$x_{11} + x_{12} + x_{13} = 1$$

$$x_{21} + x_{22} + x_{23} = 1$$

$$x_{31} + x_{32} + x_{33} = 1$$

$$x_{11} + x_{21} + x_{31} = 1$$

$$x_{12} + x_{22} + x_{32} = 1$$

$$x_{13} + x_{23} + x_{33} = 1$$

$$w_{11} + d_{12}x_{11} + d_{22}x_{21} + d_{32}x_{31} + \tau_{21}$$

$$= \tau_{11} + d_{11}x_{12} + d_{21}x_{22} + d_{31}x_{32} + w_{21}$$

$$w_{12} + d_{13}x_{11} + d_{23}x_{21} + d_{33}x_{31} + \tau_{31}$$

$$= \tau_{21} + d_{12}x_{12} + d_{22}x_{22} + d_{32}x_{32} + w_{22}$$

$$w_{21} + d_{12}x_{12} + d_{22}x_{22} + d_{32}x_{32} + \tau_{22}$$

$$= \tau_{12} + d_{11}x_{13} + d_{21}x_{23} + d_{31}x_{33} + w_{31}$$

$$w_{22} + d_{13}x_{12} + d_{23}x_{22} + d_{33}x_{32} + \tau_{32}$$

$$= \tau_{22} + d_{12}x_{13} + d_{22}x_{23} + d_{32}x_{33} + w_{32}$$

$$w_{12} = w_{13} = 0$$

$$\tau_{11} = \tau_{12} = 0$$

Solving the linear program (with either Cplex or Gurobi, for example) leads to the following solution:

z' = 10, $x_{11} = x_{22} = x_{33} = 1$, the others $x_{ik} = 0$; $w_{21} = 1$, $w_{31} = 2$, the others $w_{kj} = 0$; $\tau_{31} = 1$, $\tau_{32} = 3$, the others $\tau_{jk} = 0$.

This results in the J1-J2-J3 schedule, as shown in Figure 8.28.

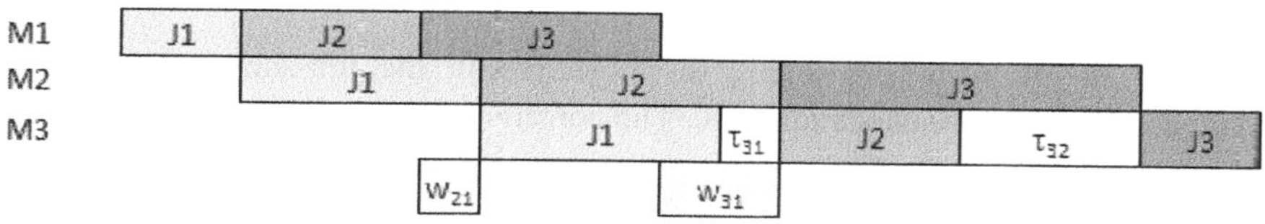

Figure 8.28. *Optimum solution*

8.3. The job-shop problem

In the flow-shop problem, each job, or manufacturing object, consists of tasks that always run in the same order. Specifically, given a set of jobs $\mathbf{P_1}, \mathbf{P_2}, \dots, \mathbf{P_m}$ and a set of machines M_1, M_2, ..., M_p, each job $\mathbf{P_1}$ must pass through the machines in this order: M_1, M_2, ..., M_p. In other words, $\mathbf{P_1}$ runs on M_1, then M_2, and so on down to M_p. Similarly, $\mathbf{P_2}$ follows the same sequence on machines M_1, M_2, ..., M_p, and this applies to all jobs $\mathbf{P_1}, \mathbf{P_2}, \dots, \mathbf{P_m}$. Thus, the sequence of machines used is identical for all jobs.

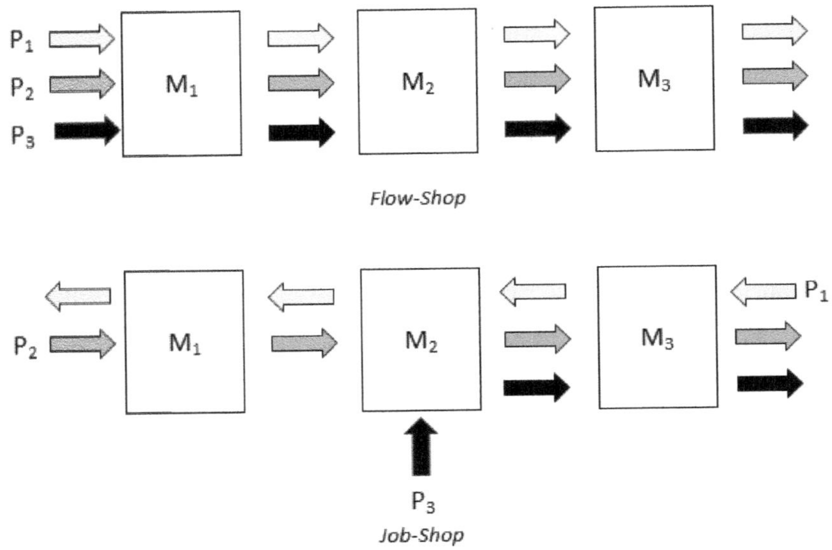

Figure 8.29. *Differences between flow-shop and job-shop*

In the job-shop problem, each job follows a particular route over a set of machines. Figure 8.29 shows the difference between flow-shop and job-shop.

As in the flow-shop problem, the objective in the job-shop problem is to minimize the total task execution time. The constraints are as follows:

– A machine can only execute one task at a time.

– A task can only run on one machine at a time.

– A task does not leave a machine until it has been fully executed.

– A machine has a job queue, which is assumed to be unlimited.

– All jobs are available from time $t = 0$.

If a job is thought of as a part to be machined on machines in a given order, the problem can be modeled as follows.

Let m be the number of jobs (or parts) and p be the number of machines. Each job consists of tasks denoted by O_{ik}, where i is the job number (from 1 to m) and k is the sequence number of the task within the job (from 1 to n_i). An O_{ik} job uses a machine M_{ik} (with a value from 1 to p) for a duration d_{ik}.

Let us define the following variables: x_{ik} and $y_{i_1k_1}^{i_2k_2}$:

– x_{ik}: The start date of task O_{ik}, assumed to be an integer (time is discrete). Thus, x_{ik} is an integer.

– $y_{i_1k_1}^{i_2k_2} = \begin{cases} 1 \text{ if } O_{i_1k_1} \text{ is a predecessor of } O_{i_2k_2} \\ 0 \text{ otherwise} \end{cases} \quad M_{i_1k_1} = M_{i_2k_2}.$

The objective function is to minimize the total execution time T of all jobs, which represents the end date of the last job, with $t = 0$ as the start date. This involves minimizing the value of T, which is represented by the end date of the last task of a job.

The constraints are as follows:

– The last task of each job must finish before or on the date:

$$x_{in_i} + d_{in_i} \leq T \quad \forall i = 1, \ldots, m \qquad [C'1]$$

– The order of tasks within each job must be respected. This means that each task O_{ik} must finish before the next task O_{ik+1} begins:

$$x_{i,k+1} \geq x_{ik} + d_{ik} \quad \forall i = 1, \ldots, m \quad \forall k = 1, \ldots, n_i \qquad [C'2]$$

– Tasks cannot overlap on the same machine. If $O_{i_1k_1}$ and $O_{i_2k_2}$ are executed on the same machine $M_{i_1k_1} = M_{i_2k_2}$, one of the following relationships must be true:

$$x_{i_1k_1} + d_{i_1k_1} \leq x_{i_2k_2} \text{ or } x_{i_2k_2} + d_{i_2k_2} \leq x_{i_1k_2}$$

which means that, in the first case, the task $O_{i_2k_2}$ can only be executed after $O_{i_1k_1}$ has been completed or vice versa. These relationships can be expressed by inequalities as follows:

$$(W + d_{i_1k_1})y_{i_1k_1}^{i_2k_2} + (x_{i_1k_1} - x_{i_2k_2}) \geq d_{i_2k_2} \quad \text{[C'3]}$$

$$(W + d_{i_2k_2})(1 - y_{i_1k_1}^{i_2k_2}) + (x_{i_2k_2} - x_{i_1k_1}) \geq d_{i_1k_1} \quad \text{[C'4]}$$

where $M_{i_1k_1} = M_{i_2k_2}$ and W is a sufficiently large constant (greater than T, which could be chosen, as the sum of all task durations).

By using linear programming with decision variables x_{ik} and $y_{i_1k_1}^{i_2k_2}$ and respecting constraints [C'1] to [C'4], an optimal solution can be obtained.

In simple cases, it is also possible to find an optimal solution using the method of earliest and latest dates, as shown in Example 8.6.

EXAMPLE 8.6.– Consider three jobs P_1, P_2 and P_3, and three machines M_1, M_2 and M_3.

– Job P_1 consists of tasks A (on M_1, duration 10-time units), B (on M_2, duration 35-time units) and C (on M_3, duration 25-time units).

– Job P_2 consists of tasks D (on M_1, duration 15-time units), E (on M_3, duration 16-time units) and F (on M_2, duration 12-time units).

– Job P_3 consists of tasks G (on M_3, duration 11-time units), H (on M_1, duration 12-time units) and I (on M_2, duration 21-time units).

The jobs must be executed in the order specified. The execution of the three jobs can be represented by a graph (see Figure 8.30).

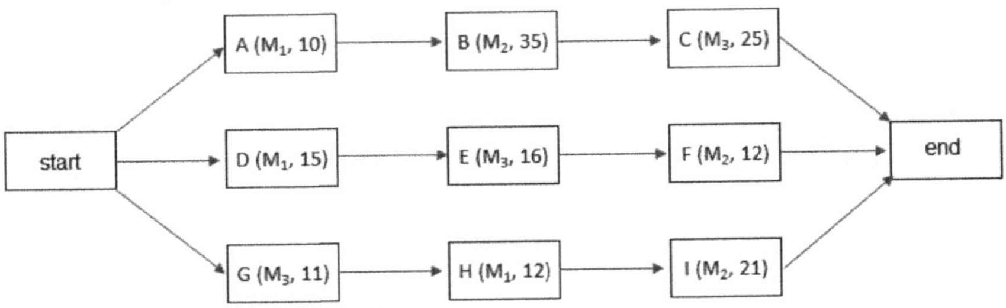

Figure 8.30. *Execution graph for the three jobs*

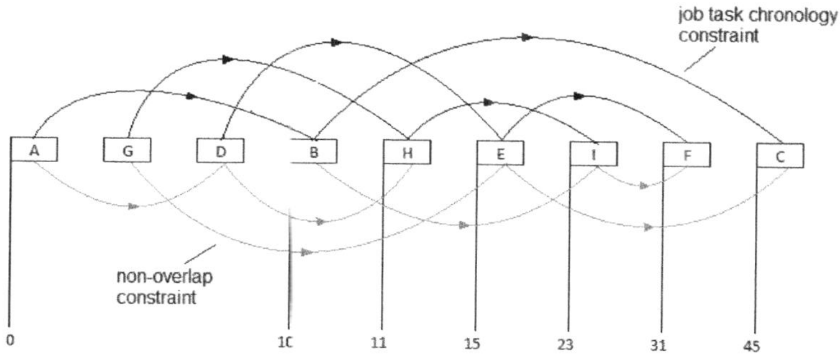

Figure 8.31. *Chronology and non-overlap constraints*

However, this graph is too simple, although it takes into account the chronology of tasks for each job, it does not consider the non-overlap constraint.

To obtain a more complete graph, the tasks are arranged in order of start of execution, assuming they could be executed without regard to the non-overlap constraint. If the start dates are identical, the tasks are then arranged in order of increasing duration. The result is the list shown in Figure 8.31, in which chronology constraints for each job and non-overlap constraints on the same machine have been added.

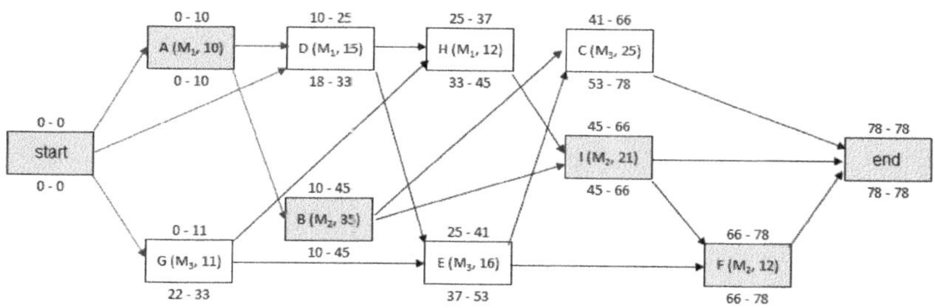

Figure 8.32. *MPM graph*

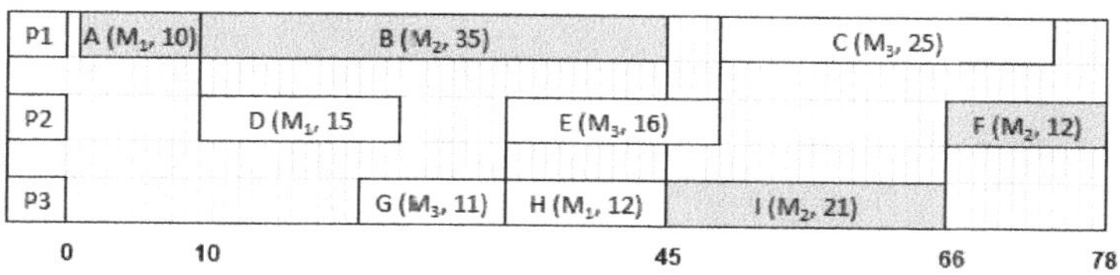

Figure 8.33. *Gantt chart*

This list, incorporating the constraints, is used to construct a more complete graph, to which the method of earliest and latest dates is applied (see Figure 8.32). This determines the critical path, which is A-B-I-F (shown in gray), with a duration of 78-time units. A corresponding Gantt chart is shown in Figure 8.33.

References

[BRO 82] BRONSON R., *Operations Research*, Schaum/McGraw Hill, New York, 1982.

[CIB 84] CIBOIS P.H., *L'analyse des données en sociologie*, PUF, Paris, 1984.

[COR 18] CORNILLON P.A. et al., *R pour la statistique des données*, Presses Universitaires de Rennes, Rennes, 2018.

[DER 16] DEROUSSI L., *Metaheuristics for Logistics*. ISTE Ltd, London, and John Wiley and Sons, New York, 2016.

[DES 76] DESBAZEILLE G., *Exercices et problèmes de recherche opérationnelle*, Dunod, Paris, 1976.

[DRO 87] DROESBEKE F., HALLIN M., LEFEVRE C.L., *Les graphes par l'exemple*, Ellipses, Paris, 1987.

[ECO 98] ECOTO F., *Initiation à la recherche opérationnelle*, Ellipses, Paris, 1998.

[ESQ 99] ESQUIROL P., LOPEZ P., *L'ordonnancement*, Economica, Paris, 1999.

[FAU 74] FAURE R., BOSS J.P., LE GARF A., "La recherche opérationnelle", *Que-sais-je*, n° 941, 1974.

[FAU 79] FAURE R., *Précis de recherche opérationnelle*, Dunod, Paris, 1979.

[FAU 14] FAURE R., LEMAIRE B., PICOULEAU C., *Précis de recherche opérationnelle, méthodes et exercices d'application*, Dunod, Paris, 2014.

[FOU 85] FOUCART T., *Analyse factorielle, programmation sur micro-ordinateurs*, Masson, Paris, 1985.

[HIL 17] HILLIER F.S., LIEBERMAN G.J., NAG B. et al. *Introduction to Operations Research*, McGraw Hill, New Delhi, 2017.

[HUS 16] HUSSON F., LE S., PAGES J., *Analyse de données avec R*, Presses Universitaires de Rennes, Rennes, 2016.

[JAC 98] JACQUET-LAGREZE E., *Programmation linéaire*, Economica, Paris, 1998.

[KAU 75] KAUFMANN A., FAURE R., *Invitation à la recherche opérationnelle*, Dunod, Paris, 1975.

[KEL 20] KELLEHER J.D., MAC NAME B., D'ARCY A., *Fundamentals of Machine Learning for Predictive Data Analysis*, MIT Press, New York, 2020.

[MOU 80] MOUKARZEL I., *Théorie des graphes*, Polycopié de l'université libanaise, Beyrouth, 1980.

[PAP 92] PAPILLON J.-C., *Éléments de recherche opérationnelle*, Dalloz-Sirey, Paris, 1992.

[PHE 75] PHELIZON J.F., *Informatique opérationnelle (tome 1)*, Economica, Paris, 1975.

[RAK 10] RAKOTOMALALA R., "Une plateforme d'expérimentation pour la fouille de données", available at: https://irma.math.unistra.fr/~fbertran/enseignement/DataMining_2010/rakotomala-32.pdf, 2010.

[SAP 11] SAPORTA G., *Probabilités, statistique et analyse de données*, Technip, Paris, 2011.

[TAN 00] TANAGRA, available at: https;//tanagra.software.informer.com/2.0/, 2000.

[TUF 12] TUFFERY S., *Data Mining et statistique décisionnelle*, Technip, Paris, 2012.

List of Authors

Gérard-Michel COCHARD
Eco-PRocédés Optimisation et Aide à la Décision (EPROAD, EA 4669)
Université de Picardie Jules Verne
Amiens
France

Mhand HIFI
Eco-PRocédés Optimisation et Aide à la Décision (EPROAD, EA 4669)
Université de Picardie Jules Verne
Amiens
France

Index

I, J

K, L

M, P

R, S

T, V, W

Printed and bound by CPI Group (UK) Ltd, Croydon, CR0 4YY

13/09/2026

14961071-0004